REACTION AND RENEWAL IN SOUTH AFRICA

Also by Paul B. Rich

* THE DYNAMICS OF CHANGE IN SOUTHERN AFRICA (*editor*)
  HOPE AND DESPAIR: English Speaking Intellectuals and Southern
  African Politics
  RACE AND EMPIRE IN BRITISH POLITICS
* STATE POWER AND BLACK POLITICS IN SOUTH AFRICA
  WHITE POWER AND THE LIBERAL CONSCIENCE

* *From the same publishers*

Reaction and Renewal in South Africa

Edited by

Paul B. Rich
Principal Lecturer in Politics
University of Luton

First published in Great Britain 1996 by
MACMILLAN PRESS LTD
Houndmills, Basingstoke, Hampshire RG21 6XS
and London
Companies and representatives
throughout the world

A catalogue record for this book is available
from the British Library.

ISBN 0–333–64251–1

 First published in the United States of America 1996 by
ST. MARTIN'S PRESS, INC.,
Scholarly and Reference Division,
175 Fifth Avenue,
New York, N.Y. 10010

ISBN 0–312–16149–2

Library of Congress Cataloging-in-Publication Data
Reaction and renewal in South Africa / edited by Paul B. Rich.
p.   cm.
"This volume stems from a conference held at the University of
Melbourne in June 1994 entitled Reconstruction in South Africa."
Includes bibliographical references and index.
ISBN 0–312–16149–2
1. South Africa—Politics and government—1994– —Congresses.
2. Democracy—South Africa—Congresses.   I. Rich, Paul B., 1950–

DT1974.R4   1996
968.06'4—dc20   96–10363
                                                                CIP

---

10   9   8   7   6   5   4   3   2   1
05   04   03   02   01   00   99   98   97   96

Printed in Great Britain by
Ipswich Book Co Ltd, Ipswich, Suffolk

To Christina and Derek Morris

Contents

Notes on the Contributors

Martin Chanock is Professor of Law and Legal Studies at La Trobe University, Melbourne. He has taught at universities in East and West Africa and the UK and USA. He is the author of *Unconsummated Union: Britain, Rhodesia and South Africa* (1977) and *Law, Custom and Social Order* (1985). He is currently working on a book on the making of South African legal culture.

Linda Chisholm is Director of the Education Policy Unit at the University of the Witwatersrand, Johannesburg. Her research interests have focused on the political economy of education policy in South Africa and the interplay of class, colour and gender in the history and politics of educational inequality in South Africa. She is currently working on the impact of policy on South African schools.

Norman Etherington is Professor of History at the University of Western Australia. He is the author of *Preachers, Peasants and Politics in Southeast Africa, Theories of Imperialism: War, Conquest and Capital* (1984), *Rider Haggard* and editor of *Peace, Politics and Violence in the New South Africa* (1992). He is a regular contributor to the *Southern African Review of Books*.

Gerhard Mare lectures in the Sociology Department and the Centre for Industrial and Labour Studies at the University of Natal, Durban. He has published widely on the politics of the Kwa Zulu Natal region (especially the Inkatha movement) and published *An Appetite for Power* (1987, co-authored with Georgina Hamilton) and *Ethnicity and Politics in South Africa* (1993).

Nicoli Nattrass teaches economics at the University of Cape Town and has written widely on issues of current economic debate in South Africa.

Jeff Peires lectured in history at Rhodes University before becoming Professor of History at the University of Transkei. In February 1994 he was one of the ANC's list elected to the new South African parliament in Cape Town. He has published *The Dead Will Arise: Nongqawuse and the Great Xhosa Cattle Killing Movement of 1856–7* (1989) and *The House of Phalo* (1982) as well as a number of scholarly articles on South African history and historiography.

Paul B. Rich has taught at the Universities of Bristol, Warwick and Melbourne and is now Principal Lecturer in the Department of Politics and Public Policy, University of Luton. He has written extensively on South African politics and has recently published *Hope and Despair: English Speaking Intellectuals and South African Politics* (1993) and *State Power and Black Politics in South Africa* (1995) as well as editing *The Dynamics of Change in Southern Africa* (1994). He is currently working on a study on *Regionalism in World Politics* as well as co-editing a collection entitled *Counter Insurgent States: State Building and Resistance to Revolutionary Change in International Politics*.

Annette Seegers is an Associate Professor in the Department of Political Studies, University of Cape Town. Her research interests have long concentrated on civil–military relations in South Africa.

Jack Spence was formerly Professor of Politics at the University of Leicester and is now Director of Research at the Royal Institute of International Affairs, Chatham House. He is the author of *Republic under Pressure – A Study of South African Foreign Policy* (1965), *Lesotho* (1968) and numerous articles on South African foreign relations.

David Tucker is a Reader and Associate Professor in the Department of Political Science at Melbourne University. He is the author of a number of books on constitutional and political theory. He recently spent six months as a Visiting Fellow at the Centre of Public Policy at Georgetown University in the United States where he completed his most recent book, *The Rehnquist Court and Civil Rights*. His other books include *An Essay on Liberalism: Looking Left and Right* (1994), *Law, Liberalism and Free Speech* (1991) and *Marxism and Individualism* (1981). Professor Tucker is an expert in applied ethics and in constitutional theory and design. He is a South African by birth and has recently visited the country.

Cherryl Walker lectures in the Department of Sociology at the University of Natal, Durban. She has written extensively on gender issues in South Africa and published *Women and Resistance in South Africa* (1982) and edited *Women and Gender in Southern Africa to 1945* (1990).

Klaas Woldring was originally born in Holland and now lectures at the Southern Cross University at Lismore, New South Wales, Australia. He has specialised in federalism in South African politics and published a number of articles on this issue.

Preface

This volume of essays stems from a conference held at the University of Melbourne in June 1994 entitled *Reconstruction in South Africa*. The conference was timed to occur three months after the April elections in South Africa and to provide analysts with an opportunity for an initial assessment of what kind of transformation has occurred in the country's political system. Since then, of course, there has been a spate of academic writing together with detailed discussion at several other academic conferences. The papers for this volume have been revised accordingly to relate to the developing scholarly debate on the political transformation in South Africa, while in addition two further chapters, Chapter 6 on the economy by Nicoli Nattrass and Chapter 8 on educational policy by Linda Chisholm, were specially commissioned for this volume.

The collection has been published for a general audience as well as the coterie of South African specialists. It is intended as a stimulus not only for debate and study on South African political developments but also for comparative study of the nature of states and societies in the developing world and the impact on them of democratisation. As a number of chapters in this volume indicate, the study of South African politics has become increasingly fluid in recent years as old paradigms become discarded and new ones are taken up. It is unlikely that a new dominant paradigm will easily or quickly emerge and in some senses it is probably undesirable for this to happen as intellectual debate is best conducted outside the tight confines of any one particular paradigm. South Africa has, moreover, lost its status as a particular and unique country as a result of the apartheid system and become 'just another country'. In this new context it is probably inevitable that the country will be seen in increasingly comparative terms.

I have inevitably a number of people to thank for help and assistance in the sometimes difficult editing of this volume. I would in particular like to thank Eddie and Kittie Brownstein of the Drakensberg Trust in Australia for providing the generous funding for the conference at the University of Melbourne. In addition, I would like to thank Jim Bird of Computer Services at Coventry University for help in converting a number of computer programmes. Finally, I would like to thank my wife Isabel for her unstinting support.

PAUL B. RICH
May 1995

List of Abbreviations

AFRA	Association for Rural Advancement
ANCWL	African National Congress Women's League
APLA	Azanian People's Liberation Army
ARMSCOR	Armaments Corporation
AVF	Afrikaner Volksfront
AWB	Afrikaner Weerstandebeweging
BAD	Bantu Affairs Department
CCSA	Cabinet Committee for Security Affairs
CLC	Cape Land Conference
CODESA	Convention for a Democratic South Africa
COIN	Counter Insurgency
CONTRALESA	Congress of Traditional Leaders of South Africa
COSAG	Concerned South African Group
COSATU	Congress of South African Trade Unions
CP	Conservative Party
DBSA	Development Bank of Southern Africa
DFA	Department of Foreign Affairs
DMI	Department of Military Intelligence
DP	Democratic Party
FAWU	Food and Agricultural Workers' Union
FP	Inkatha Freedom Party
GNU	Government of National Unity
IDASA	Institute for a Democratic South Africa
IEC	Independent Electoral Commission
IFP	Inkatha Freedom Party
IMPD	Institute for Multi Party Democracy
ISP	Industrial Strategy Project
KLA	Kwa Zulu Legislative Assembly
KZP	Kwa Zulu Police Force
KZN	Kwa Zulu Natal
LIBOR	London Interbank Offer Rate
MERG	Macroeconomic Research Group
MK	*Umkhonto we Sizwe* guerrilla army
MPNP	Multi-Party Negotiation Process
NAD	Native Affairs Department
NAM	Non Aligned Movement
NECC	National Education Crisis Committee

NEPI	National Education Policy Investigation
NETF	National Education and Training Forum
NIS	National Intelligence Service
NP	National Party
NPA	National Peace Accord
NPKP	National Peace Keeping Force
NSMS	National Security Management System
OAU	Organisation of African Unity
POPCRU	Police and Prisons Civil Rights Union
PWV	Pretoria-Witwatersrand-Vereeniging Region
RDP	*Reconstruction and Development Plan*
RWM	Rural Women's Movement
SABC	South African Broadcasting Corporation
SABRA	South African Bureau of Racial Affairs
SACM	Southern African Common Market
SACU	Southern African Customs Union
SACP	South African Communist Party
SADF	South African Defence Force
SADCC	Southern African Development Coordination Conference
SADC	Southern African Development Community
SANDF	South African National Defence Force
SANCO	South African National Civics Organisation
SANT	South African Native Trust
SAP	South African Police
SDU	Self Defence Unit
SPU	Self Protection Unit
SSC	State Security Council
SWAPO	South West Africa People's Organisation
TDF	Transkei Defence Force
TEC	Transitional Executive Committee
TRAC	Transvaal Rural Action Committee
TRACOR	Transkei Corporation
TRTC	Transkei Road Transport Corporation
TTLA	Transkei Traditional Leaders' Association
UDF	United Democratic Front
UWUSA	United Workers' Union of South Africa

Introduction
Paul B. Rich

This collection of essays surveys the question of reconstruction in South
Africa in the wake of the political transition that occurred in April 1994.
The 'one person, one vote' elections in that month marked a political
watershed in the country's history. The new government of national unity
has come into office with a huge amount of international goodwill and has
confounded the predictions of some analysts in the 1980s that the country was on the brink of revolution.[1] Nevertheless, the new government is
likely to find the task of political reconciliation a difficult one, given that
it is a rather shaky alliance of the ANC and National Party.[2]

It is in this context that debate has ensued since 1993–4 on the nature
of South African reconstruction, centred on the ANC's *Reconstruction and
Development Programme* (RDP).[3] This document has altered considerably
the whole tenor of policy debate in South Africa by injecting a language
of political participation into the generally top-down quality of South African
policy debate.[4] The RDP has laid the foundations for a new agenda that
seeks to be non-racial in political orientation as well as being oriented to a
form of social democracy. To this extent, it has shifted the focus away from
internal political debates in the 1980s anchored around ideas of ethnically-
based consociational power-sharing, as well as debates among radicals
both inside and outside the country who looked to the new government
laying the foundations for a full-scale social revolution. For the latter
group the RDP has been a particular disappointment. The Marxist ana-
lyst Martin J. Murray for instance has characterised the whole debate
on 'reconstruction' as an exercise in class accommodation by the former
forces of national liberation with the dominant white oligarchy at a time
when neither capital nor labour were powerful enough to pursue their own
interests.[5] Such 'class accommodation', though, can be seen as a highly
realistic strategy when the South African economy is viewed in global
terms. The new South African regime operates within tight parameters,
and promises in the early 1990s by Nelson Mandela, after his release from
prison, of a wide-ranging nationalisation progamme were soon abandoned.
By late 1993 Mandela had visited Europe and North America with the
Finance Minister, Derek Keys, as part of a campaign to mobilise business
interest in the South African economy.

The debate on reconstruction has therefore increasingly operated within a framework of intellectual realism. This approach is largely reflected in the chapters in this book, though the contributors do not as a group represent any one school of social and political analysis. While all are generally supportive of the efforts to reconstruct the country on non-apartheid lines, they are by no means uncritical of the new government or of its RDP. Their various contributions suggest that a new climate has begun to emerge within South African studies that has to some degree divested itself of the polarisation of past debates between 'liberals' and 'revisionists' stretching back to the 1970s.

AN END OF HISTORY?

South African political debate, though, is still likely to continue to exhibit some of the ideological divisions of the past and so it is improbable that the society will be easily defined by a variant of Francis Fukuyama's 'end of history' thesis. To some critics the thesis has always appeared highly suspect for its basic assumption that it was capitalism which was the real agent in apartheid's downfall as opposed to the popular resistance in the 1970s and 1980s combined with the pressure of international sanctions.[6] However, some things can be distilled from Fukuyama's work that are of relevance to contemporary South African political debate. Despite being widely and erroneously credited with a crude economic reductionism, Fukuyama is important for reviving eighteenth-century notions of the possibility of universal criteria for the pursuit of progress. In such a pursuit no other model is viable in the modern global order than that of liberal capitalism, though he was wise enough to separate this claim from any assertion that this was in any way imminent in all parts of the globe.[7] The point for South African radicals to face up to is that there is no ultimate alternative to liberal capitalism at the global level, though this is not necessarily going to be replicated at an early date in domestic South African politics. It is still possible indeed for alternative forms of political regime to be constructed that may well survive for a considerable period of time.

There is thus a vital middle ground in the politics of South African reconstruction centred upon the nature of the political and legal system and the form of constitution. This is one of the major concerns of this volume. If there has been a revolution in South Africa occurring over the last five or more years since the unbanning of the ANC and release of Nelson Mandela in February 1990, it has been largely a constitutional and legal one – unlike the revolutions in Eastern Europe in 1989–90. South Africa has undergone a limited experiment with mass political democratisation that may extend into other spheres of the society and economy. So far, though, it has been set on the road towards establishing what might be termed a *bourgeois liberal republic*, which, as John Dunn has cogently shown in a manner similar to Fukuyama, has effectively replaced all its rivals in the post-Cold War period as the dominant model of legitimate political authority.

The essential features of the bourgeois liberal republic is its constitutional and legal nature. The reason why it has been so successful as a political model over rivals such as Marxist-Leninist 'people's democracies', monarchies, one-party regimes and military juntas is that it secures for its citizens a fairly high degree of security along with the prospect for economic progress. '. . . it and it alone', Dunn has remarked, 'at present provides a serious political recipe for how a given human community today can hope over time to combine a fair measure of security, prosperity and opportunity to live relatively unmolested by the power of its rulers'.[8] The model, though flawed, appears to be the best on offer for limiting the powers of states and governments at the same time as providing for reasonable security for its citizens to engage in private economic activities. By the same token, its capacity to institutionalise a common national interest is limited by its relatively weak intrusion into the sphere of the domestic economy and international markets.

To this extent, the creation of a bourgeois liberal republic in South Africa will come as a considerable disappointment to those radicals who hoped it would be the first stage in a far more wide-ranging process of social and economic democratisation. The new South African state is unlikely to make wide-ranging inroads into the sphere of private capital despite the fact that, as David Tucker argues in Chapter 10, the executive has wide-ranging and quite draconian powers in the new interim constitution. The post-apartheid ANC-dominated state is more likely to be concerned for the next few years with consolidating its power. It will be particularly engaged in building up a strong local base of support rather than experimenting with radical policy proposals entailing nationalisation of assets that will almost certainly alienate foreign investment.

The project for rebuilding a new South African nation has come at a time when a radical international agenda for socialist reconstruction in the developing world has fallen into eclipse. Twenty years ago such proposals would have struck an immediate resonance in the non-aligned movement at a time when there was considerable discussion, in the wake of the 1973 OPEC oil price rises, of a New International Economic Order (NIEO). Now, however, these friends and allies no longer exist and the new regime has been forced to accommodate to the dictates of Western capitalist interests in a manner that most radical intellectuals in the ANC and South African Communist Party scarcely thought possible in the middle 1980s. It is no longer feasible to debate the reconstruction process in South Africa in isolation from global developments, and policy is increasingly being formulated with regard to a wider context of structural adjustment and the promotion of markets and private enterprise.

The theme of many of the chapters in this book is the increasingly pragmatic tone of policy debates, as the goals of the liberation movement in exile have become tempered with the realities of post-apartheid political decision-making. From a longer perspective this is not particularly surprising. The ANC and its allies did have a broadly parliamentary focus from the time of its formation in 1912 until the mid- to late 1950s. The refusal of the Nationalist governments of Malan, Strydom and Verwoerd at that time to engage in any serious political dialogue with the opposition drove the Congress Alliance in an increasingly populist political direction, best symbolised by the passage of the Freedom Charter at the Congress of the People (COP) at Kliptown, outside Johannesburg, in 1955. The COP was envisaged as a sort of alternative parliament to the racially exclusive one in Cape Town and its political demands were broadly Social Democratic in tone (despite being drafted by white radicals from the Congress of Democrats), though provision was made for the nationalisation of the mines and banks and monopoly sectors of South African industry.[9] It was only in the 1960s that the movement was driven to a revolutionary position as a result of the banning of the ANC and PAC following the declaration of a state of emergency in 1960. This revolutionary phase of ANC politics lasted some 30 years, rather less indeed than the period of constitutional politics which endured for 48 years from 1912 to 1960.

The transition back to constitutional politics has *appeared* to be far more remarkable than it in fact is because it has been linked with the life histories of a particular group of noteworthy individuals such as Nelson Mandela, Govan Mbeki, Walter Sisulu and Joe Slovo. This group has been either in exile or in gaol for as long as many analysts can remember, and has established the revolutionary credentials of the ANC to the exclusion of other more constitutionally-committed leaders such as Z.K. Matthews and Albert Luthuli, who became more or less marginalised from the pantheon of ANC heroes after the movement went intoexile in the 1960s.[10] It appeared too that the ANC from its literature and propaganda was committed to a war of national liberation in South Africa, despite the failure of its armed wing *Umkhonto we Sizwe* to emerge as a serious guerrilla organisation that looked even remotely capable of defeating the SADF.[11]

In practice the ANC was destroyed as an effective national political organisation during the exile period of 1960–90, and it has been forced to interact with other organisations and movements that emerged during this period. Lacking a major organisational base, the ANC leadership was driven into seeking a political dialogue with the ruling National Party regime of F.W. de Klerk on ground that was not entirely its own. Despite the mass upsurge of popular protest in the townships in the 1980s, the South African regime was not forced into the CODESA negotiations at the point of a gun like the Smith regime in Rhodesia in the late 1970s. The result has been a resurgence of pragmatism that has surprised some observers, who initially considered that the ANC, as an organisation, was inherently incapable of accommodating to pluralist politics given its previous commitments in exile to national liberation ideology.

Undoubtedly, one major source of this pragmatism is the figure of Nelson Mandela. It has been Mandela's capacity to develop an independent authority as a charismatic leader which has helped facilitate the transition from a movement of exile-based national liberation to a parliamentary political party. This is no mean political resource in a continent that is widely regarded as producing few leaders of world stature in the post-independence era.[12] It is clear from his memoirs that Mandela was anxious to establish some sort of a dialogue with the government from as early as 1985, despite the fact that the ANC committed itself at its Kabwe conference in that year to a strategy of mass action and armed struggle.[13] Mandela's emergence as a statesman of world stature (arguably only the second since Union, with the first being Jan Smuts) was undoubtedly a major force in containing the more quixotic demands of the ANC radicals. Under his leadership the ANC has begun to transform itself into a fairly broad political church that may entrench itself in power in South African politics for several years, though once Mandela has passed from the political stage there is a risk of the movement splitting into rival factions.

The moderating role of Mandela makes it unlikely that he will go down in South African history as a really visionary leader who manages to offer his supporters a world picture radically different from what they find around them.[14] Within a year of coming to power, for instance, he has found himself at odds with radical African students anxious for a rapid programme of Africanisaton of universities, accusing them of 'racism in reverse'.[15] Some analysts have even begun to suggest that Mandela is little more than a stop-gap figure whose chief importance is holding the political coalition of the ANC and NP together for the first few years.[16]

RECONSTRUCTION IN HISTORICAL PERSPECTIVE

The role of political leadership in orchestrating reconstruction in South Africa needs to be seen, though, in terms of a longer historical time span. This is not the first but the third time in the twentieth century that South African politics has undergone a phase of political reconstruction. The previous two occasions, of course, occurred under white minority rule and were concerned with trying to stabilise the basis of that rule and put it on a more administratively efficient basis. The first such occasion for reconstruction was after the Anglo-Boer War of 1899–1902 when the Milner Kindergarten in the Transvaal sought to rationalise the colonial state in South Africa in the interests of the labour needs of the mines, farms and nascent secondary industry. The period 1902–10 is generally recognised by historians to be a turning point in modern South African history, since it laid the foundations for the new South African state that was to take over after Union in 1910 under the dominant political ideology of racial segregation.[17]

The second 'reconstruction' in South Africa occurred in 1948 with the Nationalist Party's defeat of General Smuts's United Party government. By this time the contours of traditional 'native policy' stretching back to the period before Union had become rather obscured as a result of the rapid industrialisation during the Second World War. Moreover, the earlier appeal to a common set of standards of a white 'civilisation' had been undermined by the emergence of an educated African middle class and the progressive decline of the belief in a white imperial 'civilising mission' in Africa. This new phase of reconstruction was notable for injecting the language of ethnic nationalism into South African politics as Nationalist intellectuals sought to shift the axis of South African politics away from a common standard of 'civilisation' towards cultural and ethnic difference.[18] The discourse of ethnic difference provided the basis for the vast array of apartheid laws over the next three decades as South Africa was again reconstructed on lines that drove strong wedges between its different social groups.

'Reconstruction' therefore has had quite a mixed history in South African politics. It does not have the same sort of unambiguous political associations that Reconstruction had in the United States after the Civil War of 1861–5 when it was directed at the reincorporating of the Southern Confederate states into the Union. Until the 1990s and the ANC's RDP, 'reconstruction' in South Africa has generally meant the prosecution of policies in contradiction to those of a common society and in favour of the retrenchment of white minority rule. To this extent, the advocates of the

RDP can claim that their programme is nothing short of revolutionary in that it breaks from a deeply established pattern of South African politics, though from a wider perspective this seems rather more doubtful. If anything, it invokes memories of the model of 'reconstruction' in Europe after World War Two with assistance from the US Marshall Plan for the European Recovery Programme (ERP). This was at the start of the post-war Bretton Woods system and the Western European economies were kick-started with some US$17 billion. Nothing like this is likely to be available for the reconstruction of South Africa, whose economy in any case has not been ravaged by war. However, the RDP is based on similar premises to the ERP, that state-led economic planning of a neo-corporatist sort can lead to the upturn of the economy as well as providing the basis for wider popular democratic participation. For some economic critics this represents rather obsolete thinking given the transformation of the global economy since the late 1940s. If so, the best that can be expected from the RDP is that it will provide only a temporary programme of economic upliftment and that it would be foolhardy to expect it to lay the foundations for a programme of democratisation. This will depend upon an additional set of political considerations and choices concerning the sort of model South African democracy can realistically be expected to become.

WHAT SORT OF DEMOCRACY?

Analysts have become sharply divided on the degree to which the February 1994 elections have moved the South African political system towards democracy. Shaun Johnson has described the election as being part of an 'incrementalising normalising democracy',[19] while other analysts have been unsure what sort of democratic system is likely in the long run to emerge. Alexander Johnstone, for instance, has looked optimistically to the ANC being able to maintain its popular base of political mobilisation and perhaps eventually transform the political system from a 'managerial' to a 'mobilising' democracy.[20] On the other hand, sceptics such as Roger Southall have seen the election failing to produce anything substantially new and merely confirming a process of consolidation of a single party-dominated political system.[21]

This debate hinges to some degree on what exactly is meant by the term 'democracy'. As can be seen in the essays in this volume, 'democracy' is a contested concept which, like 'ethnicity' and 'civil society', does not easily command universal agreement. The debate on it can be considerably enriched by reference to comparable examples of semi-developed capitalist states in Africa and Latin America as well as to more mature models in metropolitan societies such as Britain and the United States. In the final analysis, though, as Jack Spence points out in Chapter 10, if South Africa is to become democratic it will be on the basis of an autochthonous model of democracy of her own that will be a home-grown hybrid with its own unique characteristics.

Nevertheless, in order to be able to have some idea of the sort of democracy South Africa is likely to develop, it will still be necessary to review the likely models on offer. In this respect, Marina Ottaway has usefully suggested three main conceptions of democracy in the South African context: a Western concept of *liberal democracy*, as reflected in the 1955 Freedom Charter, a radical concept of *people's democracy* developed during the struggles of the 1980s centred on the United Democratic Front and a third concept of *consociational democracy* upheld by the government of F.W. de Klerk in the early 1990s that was based on the preservation of minority group rights.[22]

The first concept is based on broadly based Western conceptions of representative democracy in the West and is anchored in the ideas of Joseph Schumpeter. It is elitist in many features and sees representative democracy being managed by an enlightened class of administrators who are to some degree insulated from the continuing vagaries and uncertainties of the popular will. The liberal democratic concept differs from the second concept of 'people's democracy' that is really a radical version of the more familiar concept of *participatory democracy*. It champions a model of democracy extending beyond the control of elites in order to increase popular participation and control over political decision-making. This conception is fairly strongly embedded in Western democratic thought and has wide-ranging roots in Jean Jacques Rousseau, the French Jacobin and Marxist traditions and those of the English Guild Socialists. It regained popularity with the resurgence of intellectual radicalism in the 1960s and 1970s and became known to many students through the writings of Carole Pateman.[23] To some theorists, there are a number of dangers with this concept of democracy. Liberal democratic theorists point out that it is often very difficult to mobilise a single popular will to participate in deciding major issues at the national level, and participatory democracy usually ends up increasing the avenues of popular participation at the local level. This may simply widen the numbers of organised interest groups making demands on decision-makers at the national level and add to the problem of governmental 'overload'.

The third conception of democracy based on the entrenchment of minority group rights derives from the theory of *consociational democracy* developed by Arend Lijphart.[24] This had some popularity among liberals in South Africa in the late 1970s and early 1980s as hopes rose that the promised constitutional reforms of the government of P.W. Botha would lead to a genuine shift of power. However the 1984 constitution proved to be a great disappointment as it left all effective power in the central state in white hands.[25] Consociationalism as a result received a bad press as being little more than a sophisticated version of 'neo-apartheid' and was not taken very seriously by most analysts by the time of the CODESA discussions in the early 1990s. It is only really championed at the political level now by Inkatha in Zwa Zulu Natal as part of its campaign to force the ANC to implement a federal constitution with strong powers for the provinces.

The first conception of liberal democracy is represented in this volume in Chapter 4 by David Tucker, who has criticised the interim constitution for trying to take on board too many second- and third-generation rights as well as failing to observe basic liberal democratic rules that can ensure the limitation of the powers of the executive over those of the legislature. A similar view can be found in Chapter 11 by Klaas Woldring, who sees a way of securing a check on the powers of the central executive by the classic liberal device of dispersing power between the central executive and provinces on a federal basis. By contrast, the second conception of participatory democracy is reflected in Chapter 5 by Martin Chanock on the reform of the legal system, Chapter 7 by Cherryl Walker on the extension of political and social rights to women and the issue of land reform, and Chapter 8 by Linda Chisholm on the restructuring of the education system.

The arguments of the democratic participationists need to be seen in the context of debate over the reform of the apartheid system stretching back to the late 1970s and early 1980s. During this period, there was considerable scepticism among South African liberals that a minimalist Schumpeterian approach could be easily applied in such an ethnically divided society as South Africa. They urged that refinements needed to be introduced in terms of consociational power-sharing between ethnically based groups. This undermined the Schumpeterian model of circulating elites and was criticised for conniving with a model that failed to break with the apartheid past and entrenched ethnic group divisions rather than trying to overcome them.[26] To this extent, Donald Horowitz's *A Democratic South Africa?* was a work of some significance in spelling out a strategy of constitutional engineering that attempted to transcend previous ethnic divisions rather than rely upon the goodwill of the leaders towards any consociational bargain. Horowitz's book suggested that if Schumpeterians were to avoid going down the path of consociationalism they had to investigate ways that political leaders could be encouraged to seek support outside their traditional ethnic constituencies by a system of vote pooling.[27]

In some senses, this debate has proved to be something of a way station to an alternative model of participatory democracy that came into focus after the unbanning of the ANC in 1990. A number of intellectuals have been drawn towards the vision outlined in the ANC's *Reconstruction and Development Programme* where the development of participatory democracy is closely linked to a wider integrated programme of economic growth and development and social, economic and political reconstruction.[28] For some radical analysts, the issue of South African reconstruction offers up the possibility of challenging wider international orthodoxies whereby theories of democratisation have been largely disconnected from theories of economic and societal development and, as in the case of many Latin American states, only tenuously linked to vague hopes that a democratic pact will be able to fulfil promises of economic and social reform.[29] Barry Munslow and Patrick Fitzgerald for instance have argued for a programme of 'sustainable development' that links development with democratisation in order to achieve 'in a decade or two what could otherwise take a century'.[30] This is a very ambitious goal and, even if the regime does manage to undertake a wider-ranging redistribution of resources away from defence and armaments and towards human resources development, it is unlikely to have the sufficient investment capital to transform the economy and society in such a short space of time. One of the basic objectives of the new regime must be to achieve macroeconomic balance. If its fails to do this then there will be little or no chance of any significant economic reconstruction since an unstable economy will so distort information as to frighten off potential foreign investors.[31]

It is for this reason that there must be considerable doubt over whether the objectives of the *Reconstruction and Development Programme* are really feasible in the short to medium term. While fine goals, they need to be seen as largely rhetoric that was designed to secure for the ANC a sufficient degree of support from the radical and progressive intelligentsia at the time of the election. What seems a more likely prospect over the next few years is that the new regime will seek to strengthen its political base among the emerging black political and economic elite. This will in all probability entail a considerable degree of corruption as the state is used as a vehicle for the enrichment of a new class of party *nomenklatura*, though there will be some limits on this as a result of strong imperatives to maintain credibility among potential foreign investors.

The end result could of course be – as David Tucker warns in Chapter 4 – the eventual desiccation of multi-party democracy into some form of single-party dictatorship rather than the progressive evolution of a participatory democracy. A less pessimistic analysis, on the other hand, might lead to an attenuated version of participatory democracy at the local level while enabling a new political elite, that is to some degree free in its decision-making from the demands of workplace politics, to consolidate itself at the national level. Such a model offers a legitimating base for a closer political alliance between the new black political elite and white capitalist interests that will be anxious to resist schemes for worker participation in industry. It also provides an alternative to mainstream Western liberalism based on the politics of self-interest by legitimating an appeal to a collective common interest under the guidance of an enlightened national elite that can at least claim the right to governance from the norms of popular participatory politics.

The nature and extent of 'participation' may thus become the terrain of political debate between those anxious to limit the range of popular demands on the state and those on the left of the ANC/COSATU/SACP alliance committed to a more populist style of politics. This may of course eventually lead to major divisions emerging within the alliance, though there are at present strong countervailing pressures to maintain a strong united front for external consumption. Certainly, if the government finds it cannot fulfil the grandiose objectives of the RDP – such as five million houses in the first five years followed by 300 000 per annum thereafter – then it may come under growing pressure from bodies like the World Bank for economic and financial orthodoxy. The intellectual rationale for this will be that a strong but limited democracy secures a degree of demobilisation of the political system that is preferable to either of the two main alternatives of i) a radical participatory democracy that overloads the state leading to widespread corruption and increasing government debt or ii) a complete state clamp-down on all political activity on the Nigerian model that in turn leads to internal governmental corruption as well as widespread abuse of human rights.

To this extent, even if participatory democracy in South Africa declines into a more oligarchic model it will still be able to defend the state against attack from another and potentially very dangerous quarter, namely economic libertarianism. The school of contemporary New Right libertarians have little interest in extending any sort of democratic participation outside the market place and assert indeed that it is the state itself which is the source of economic failure. If applied in South Africa, this sort of libertarian argument would threaten to terminate any sort of effective governmental control over the economy. It would also, as Kenneth Hughes has pointed out, undermine liberal arguments for state restrictions on the military, for arguably one of the main reasons for the military to remain in barracks has been the non-military functions of the state.[32]

THE OUTLINE OF THIS BOOK

It is clear from the previous discussion that South Africa's future is to some degree open-ended, with a considerable chance to institute at least a limited form of democracy in the years ahead. This cautious optimism is shared by a number of this book's contributors, though most are wary of making too many firm predictions.

In Chapter 1, Annette Seegers outlines the transition process before going on to discuss the likely role of the military under the new regime. For a long period the SADF was used as an instrument for the defence of white minority rule inside South Africa as well as a force for the destabilisation of the wider Southern African region. This role has now come to an end while even the conventional idea of the military being used to defend the state against foreign enemies has begun to be questioned by some analysts now that the Cold War is over. However, the breakdown of security in a number of African states as well as in regions like the Balkans suggests that there will still be a need for the military to protect South Africa's border as well as possibly for limited peacekeeping roles elsewhere in the African continent.

In Chapter 2 the focus shifts to Natal where Gerhard Mare examines the continuing low level civil war between followers of the ANC and Inkatha. Mare has written extensively on Gatsha Buthelezi and Inkatha and this chapter is an examination of recent developments in the early 1990s leading up to the April 1994 elections. Mare challenges the conventional view that Inkatha unambiguously represents Zulu ethnic nationhood by portraying an increasingly bitter struggle for leadership of the Zulus between King Goodwill Zwelithini and Inkatha. This struggle has continued after the election as Buthelezi has tried to reclaim from the king the focal point of Zulu loyalties by concentrating on promises made before the elections of

an international commission to investigate the question of establishing a
federal state.

The role of the state in the South African transition has been rather
neglected by scholars. In Chapter 3 I seek to address the question 'What
sort of state has developed in South Africa under segregation and apartheid and what will be its role now that it has come under the control of
a new ruling regime?' The chapter suggests that it will be quite a difficult
task to break the stranglehold of apartheid political structures. Nevertheless, the state should not be seen in a completely negative sense since –
contrary to a number of predictions in the 1980s – it was not completely
captured by a quasi-Bismarckian alliance of the military and big business.
In some respects it played a fairly creative role during the transition and
it should be possible to engineer a widespread programme of Africanisation
over the next few years that will transform it away from its former apartheid contours towards an instrument for the new ruling regime.

Whether this will lead though to the development of a participatory
democracy is another matter. In Chapter 4 David Tucker examines the new
interim constitution and casts strong doubts on its democratic credentials.
Employing a penetrating scrutiny of the text of the new constitution in a
tradition of analysis stretching back to John Plamenatz, Tucker warns that
the constitution in its present form threatens to entrench a new dominant
party in South Africa's political system with relatively few parliamentary
checks on the executive. It is possible indeed that, once Mandela retires,
a younger and more ambitious figure may well be able to turn the office
of the president into a near-dictatorship. The constitution fails to meet the
requirements of the Schumpeterian model of circulating elites and indicates rather that one former ethnic political elite of Afrikaner nationalists
has been replaced by a new one, though the ANC-led regime in its present
form is far from being ethnically exclusive in its composition.

Tucker's approach is a conventionally liberal one in terms of its rather limited expectations of the legal system and focus upon basic 'first-generation'
rights such as life, liberty and the protection of property in contrast to
second- and third-generation economic, social and environmental rights. It
contrasts quite markedly with Chapter 5 by Martin Chanock, which explores
a rather more ambitious conception of the law and the possibilities of
using the legal system in South African as part of the programme of
reconstruction and democratisation. Chanock particularly attacks conventional notions of legal formalism in South African legal discourse and
argues for a measure of deprofessionalisation of the law in a reconstructed
South Africa. There are some areas in his argument though which overlap
those of Tucker, particularly his insistence that some areas of the law such

as the new Constitutional Court can become sites of potentially major legal resistance to attempts by the state to aggregate power to itself.

The chapters by Tucker and Chanock indicate that the debate over the constitution and legal system has a certain autonomy of its own and cannot be reduced solely to economic processes. Nevertheless, much will depend upon the longer-term state of the economy. In this regard, Chapter 6 by Nicoli Nattrass on economic restructuring is a timely warning of the immense difficulties that the new regime faces. The proportion of the work force without formal jobs, for example, increased from 19 per cent to 40 per cent between 1970 and 1990, indicating that unless a major economic upturn is engineered fairly soon then the country may become ungovernable as resources fail to match popular aspirations. The economy has been characterised since the 1980s by declining growth in productivity, partly as a result of shortages of skilled labour. Nattrass argues that these weaknesses will not be tackled by mere investment or a strategy of economic redistribution since the poor are not heavy consumers of labour-intensive products. She is thus sceptical that the government can really stick with the goals outlined in the RDP and that it will be sooner or later forced to adopt a more capital-intensive growth strategy, though it may still be possible to run a parallel series of labour growth programmes in order to suck up some of the unemployment.

Nattrass's chapter makes for sombre reading, since it indicates that much of the wider debate on development and democratisation will remain on the level of fantasy if a major economic upturn ensuring an annual growth rate of 4 per cent or more is not secured. One of the first likely casualties of such an economic failure would undoubtedly be the position of women, which is the theme of Chapter 7 by Cherryl Walker. This chapter is heavily anchored in Natal and approaches the gender issue in African politics from the standpoint of wider debates over ethnic 'traditionalism'. To this extent it covers similar ground to Chapter 2 by Gerhard Mare by stressing the situational and 'invented' nature of much tradition in South Africa and its strongly patriarchal form. The chapter is critical of the RDP for failing fully to embrace gender issues and warns that the mobilisation of Zulu tradition is likely to derail the programme on issues such as land reform.

There are similar worries on education policy in Chapter 8 by Linda Chisholm. This chapter examines the policy outlined in the RDP in a wider context of international debates over education in developing societies and their relation to programmes of structural adjustment and human resource development. The debate in South Africa is complicated by competing pressures for central and provincial control. The new government faces hard policy choices between conflicting demands from, on the one hand, its own supporters who seek an element of redistribution of existing educational resources in order to create a 'non-racial' education system and, on other hand, a broad political alliance of opinion rooted in business, the white professional middle class as well as the World Bank for fiscal restraint and the introduction of cost-cutting measures involving some form of fee-based user-pays system. The way the new regime handles this particularly sensitive issue may prove to be a barometer of the way it will seek to navigate through the politically choppy waters that lie ahead of it over the next few years.

By contrast, in Chapter 9 Jeff Peires deals with the last phase of the Transkei 'homeland' before its reincorporation into South Africa. Refining categories that were initially developed in a provocative article in *African Affairs*, Peires concludes that the political elite in Transkei cannot be termed a 'middle class' since it really only consists of politicians, bureaucrats, shop keepers and teachers. There is thus no real class polarisation and the significance of its last leader General Bantu Holomisa lay in his creative role in accommodating these various classes and interests to the wider ANC. This strategy is in striking contrast to that of Gatsha Buthelezi who has consistently tried to forge an independent power base of his own that has led him from the late 1970s onwards into growing conflict with the ANC. Peires does not under-estimate the considerable problems that will accompany the imposition of new structures of provincial administration in Transkei; nevertheless, they are essentially localised problems that a pragmatically-inclined government may well be able to find manageable compared to more wide-ranging and potentially intractable political issues such as land reform and education.

This pragmatism is also likely to be replicated in the field of foreign relations, as Jack Spence indicates in Chapter 10. In a wide-ranging survey of the external issues confronting the new GNU, Spence points to the centrality of economic issues in the new regime's foreign policy as it seeks to win back overseas markets and trading and commercial links lost during the lean years of apartheid and international sanctions. This is likely to lead to a long-term policy of trade liberalisation, though there may well be some union resistance to too hasty a removal of tariff barriers. In the longer term, South Africa may seek to play a more hegemonic role in the Southern African region and re-orientate its Defence Force towards a regional peacekeeping role in such war-torn countries as Mozambique and Angola, though, as Spence points out, the new regime will be reluctant to get drawn into playing all that active a role in African conflicts. As the new regime plays itself in and develops its own reliable cadre of trained diplomats, foreign issues will tend to be subordinated to issues of domestic reconstruction. However, it can argued that the interdependent nature of the post-Cold War international order renders traditional ideas of isolated 'nation building' problematical if not obsolete, as global markets continually invade and undermine the conventional sovereignty of the traditional nation state.

The new regime will be keen to try and defend this sovereignty as much as possible in an increasingly insecure international order. It is likely therefore to be hostile to schemes for a quasi-federal dispersal of political power away from the central government to the nine provinces provided for under the interim constitution. The issue of federalism, however, is likely to remain on the political agenda over the next few years as Klaas Woldring points out in Chapter 11. Federalism as a political doctrine shares many of the doubts of classical liberalism concerning the centralisation of political power in the nation state, though this is largely a metropolitan concern. Politically, federalism has not worked well in the developing world since 1945, particularly in Africa, and it is hard to see why South Africa should be any exception. It offers, though, the potentiality of being a form of 'institutionalised bargaining' if the existing constitutional arrangement (which has only quasi-federalist features) threatens to break down. Moreover, as Woldring points out, if South Africa does end up pursuing an increasingly active regional role federalism may well come into play as a means of building closer political relationships with such weak regimes as Lesotho and Swaziland should they eventually find it in their interest to joint an enlarged South African federal political order. In this instance, federalism becomes the instrument for a regional sub-imperialism, though it would be foolish to ignore the long history of failure in this regard in Southern Africa stretching back to the ill-fated imperial schemes of Lord Carnarvon and Cecil Rhodes in the last quarter of the nineteenth century.

If there is one vision of a reconstructed South Africa eventually playing an expansionist role in the Southern African region, there is also another more dismal vision of ethnic self-destruction. Pessimists and doubters have been writing for decades on the possible eventual demise of the South African state and its fragmentation into ethnic or 'tribal' parts. The most likely first candidate for secession is usually Natal led by its 'warrior' Zulu people and in the 1980s and 1990s this image has been fed by the fragmentation of states such as Lebanon and Yugoslavia. In the final chapter, Chapter 12, Norman Etherington examines this political idea in a provocative and illuminating essay. He shows how the language used to describe ethnic conflict tends to employ a rich metaphorical imagery that has a dynamic of its own and it is very easy to transpose 'worst case' scenarios from one historical situation to another. Indeed, there is a built-in incentive to do so since such writing makes good journalistic copy.

It is the role of scholars in such situations to take such fanciful metaphorical analogies to task and this Etherington largely succeeds in doing. He points out, for instance, how different the historical trajectory of the Balkans is from that of Africa where, despite popular mythology, the state structure has held up extremely well. In the case of South Africa, moreover, the supposed ethnic fragmentation that occurred under apartheid was of a very different kind from the ethnically-based federations of the old Soviet Union and Yugoslavia, though he is perhaps a little too ready to dismiss the forced removals of whole peoples under Stalin such as the Tatars, Chechens and Georgians as being the exception rather than the rule, given the consequence this had for later nationalist revolt against Moscow. The key point to his chapter lies in his interesting discussion on the failure of apartheid to provide any serious political space for a nationalist intelligentsia, a theme that is also illuminated in Jeff Peires's discussion of the Transkei. Not only were there no real cities in the ethnic 'homelands' of South Africa, but they were surrounded by rural wastelands that were not in the remotest way comparable to the republics of Yugoslavia and the Soviet Union. To this extent, it is hard to see a vibrant Zulu nationalist intelligentsia emerging in the longer term in Kwa Zulu Natal that is going to have any serious interest in exiting from the South African state. It is far more likely indeed to be accommodated to the centralising government in Pretoria with the prospects of jobs and preferment rather than isolating itself in the hinterland of Ulundi.

It may be possible therefore to conceive South African reconstruction, entailing as it does the demise of ethnic 'homelands', as meaning the end of one route in contemporary South African history and the adoption of another, even though ethnic antagonisms are not likely to fade away in some 'non-racial' nirvana. This new course of South African history is, as was mentioned at the start, a largely open-ended process. It suggests however that the ANC is in many ways completing the process of incorporating South Africa into the West based on its political practices and conception of national difference rooted in territory rather than blood lines. This process was commenced in a fragmentary and contradictory manner by governments after Union in 1910 but then halted, and in many respects reversed, by the apartheid project from 1948–90. The ANC is now attempting to complete this modernising and Westernising project, though there is a considerable risk that it will fragment in the process as rival groups differ over its speed and scale. The essential objectives cannot be substantially in doubt, since, as the first part of this chapter has argued, the possibility of a radical alternative political model has disappeared with the end of the Cold War. The ANC may thus find its ultimate goal is really the establishment of the first genuinely Westernised democracy in the continent of Africa.

NOTES

1. See for example John S. Saul and Stephen Gelb, *The Crisis in South Africa* (London: Zed Books, 1986); Alex Callinicos, *South Africa Between Reform and Revolution* (London: Bookmarks, 1988).

2. Thus in January 1995 F.W. de Klerk was ready to resign after the ANC denied the the validity of the indemnity granted by the previous regime to 3 500 policemen and two former cabinet ministers a few days before the April 1994 elections. The rift between de Klerk and Mandela was in the event patched up but, at the time of writing, it is by no means clear that the coalition will endure for its full five year term. For details see *The Guardian*, 20 and 21 January 1995.

3. African National Congress, *The Reconstruction and Development Programme* (Johannesburg: African National Congress, 1994).

4. Robert Shrire (ed.), *Critical Choices for South Africa: an agenda for the 1990s* (Cape Town: Oxford University Press, 1990).

5. Martin J. Murray, *Revolution Deferred* (London: Verso, 1994), p. 23.

6. Francis Fukuyama discussed his ideas in relation to South Africa in 'The Next South Africa', *South Africa International*, 22 (October 1991), 71–81, emphasising how the forces of production ultimately undermined apartheid by fostering continued black urbanisation, increased education and a new black middle class. His ideas have been echoed by John Kane-Berman, *South Africa's Silent Revolution* (Johannesburg: SAIRR, 1991). For a critical discussion of this see Norman Etherington, 'Is It Too Soon to Start Devising Historical Explanations for the End of Apartheid?' in Paul B. Rich, *The Dynamics of Change in Southern Africa* (Basingstoke: The Macmillan Press, 1994), pp. 101–18.

7. Fred Halliday, *Rethinking International Relations* (Basingstoke: The Macmillan Press, 1994), pp. 228–9.

8. John Dunn, 'The Identity of the Bourgeois Liberal Republic' in Biancamara Fontana (ed.), *The Invention of the Modern Republic* (Cambridge: Cambridge University Press, 1994), pp. 207–8.

9. For a discussion see Paul B. Rich, 'Reviewing the Origins of the Freedom Charter' in Norman Etherington, *Peace, Politics and Violence in the New South Africa* (London: H. Zell, 1992), pp. 254–83.

10. Paul B. Rich, 'Z.K. Matthews and the Politics of Black Liberalism in South Africa', *International Journal of African Historical Studies* (forthcoming).

11. Howard Barrell, *MK: The ANC's Armed Struggle* (London: Penguin Books, 1990); Stephen M. Davis, *Apartheid's Rebels* (New Haven and London: Yale University Press, 1987).

12. See for example Ladipo Adamolekun, 'Political Leadership in Sub-Saharan Africa: From Giants to Dwarfs', *International Political Science Review*, 9, 2 (1988), 95–106.

13. In that year Mandela wrote to the Minister of Justice, Kobie Coetzee, for 'talks about talks' shortly after his move from Robben Island to Pollsmoor Prison in Cape Town (Nelson Mandela, *Long Walk to Freedom* (London: Little, Brown and Co, 1994), pp. 516–31). The first formal meeting of a working group that included Coetzee as well as Neil Barnard, head of National Intelligence, did not take place though until 1988.

14. Joel S. Migdal, 'Vision and Practice: the Leader, the State, and the Transformation of Society', *International Political Science Review*, 9, 1 (1988), 23–41.

15. *The Times Education Supplement*, 24 March 1995.

16. Martin Murray, for example, has accused Mandela of being a political chameleon with no clear political vision of what he wants to achieve through the new government. Murray, *op. cit.*, p. 212.

17. Andrew Ashforth, *The Politics of Official Discourse in Twentieth Century South Africa* (Oxford: Clarendon Press, 1990).

18. Saul Dubow, 'Ethnic Euphemisms and Racial Echoes', *Journal of Southern African Studies*, 20, 3 (September 1994), 356.

19. Shaun Johnson, *Strange Days Indeed* (London: Bantam Books, 1994), p. 441.

20. Alexander Johnstone, 'South Africa: The Election and the Transition Process – Five Contradictions in Search of a Resolution', *Third World Quarterly*, 15, 2 (1994), 187–201.

21. Roger Southall, 'The South African Elections of 1994: the Remaking of a Dominant-Party State', *Journal of Modern African Studies*, 32, 4 (1994), 629–55.

22. Marina Ottaway, 'Direct and Indirect Internationalization: The Case of South Africa' in Manus I. Midlarsky (ed.), *The Internationalization of Communal Strife* (London and New York: Routledge, 1992), pp. 244–7. The linkage of the Freedom Charter with Western democratic theory cannot be accepted unquestioningly. A detailed scrutiny of the Charter and its evolution through successive drafts reveals that it provides for a very strong central state with only a limited civil society. This is not altogether surprising given that it was mainly drafted by radicals from the Congress of Democrats who had close links with the underground SACP. They tended to envisage it as part of a Leninist two-stage theory of political evolution based first on 'bourgeois democracy' and then followed by a transition to communism. See Rich, 'Reviewing the Origins of the Freedom Charter', in Etherington, *op. cit.*

23. Carole Pateman, *Particpation and Democratic Theory* (Cambridge: Cambridge University Press, 1970).

24. Arnt Lijphart, *Power Sharing in South Africa* (Berkeley CA: Institute of International Studies, 1985); 'Electoral Systems, Party Systems and Conflict Management in Segmented Societies' in Shrire, *op. cit.*, pp. 2–13.

25. For details see Newell Stultz, 'Consociational Engineering in South Africa', *Journal of Contemporary African Studies*, 2, 2 (April 1983), 287–317.

26. Paul B. Rich, 'Doctrines of Political "Change"' in John D. Brewer (ed.), *Can South Africa Survive? Five Minutes to Midnight* (Basingstoke: The Macmillan Press, 1989), pp. 422–57.

27. Donald L. Horowitz, *A Democratic South Africa? Constitutional Engineering in a Divided Society* (Berkeley and Los Angeles: University of California Press, 1991); Ian Shapiro, 'Democratic Innovation: South Africa in a Comparative Context', *World Politics*, 46 (1993), 121–50.

28. *Reconstruction and Development Programme*, pp. 6–7.

29. Paul Cammack, 'Political Development Theory and the Dissemination of Democracy', *Democratization*, 1, 3 (Autumn 1994), 353–72.

30. Barry Munslow and Patrick Fitzgerald, 'South Africa: the Sustainable Challenge', *Third World Quarterly*, 15, 2 (1994), 241; Laurence Whitehead, 'The Alternatives to "Liberal Democracy": A Latin American Perspective', *Political Studies*, XL (1992), 155.

31. Jeffrey Herbst, 'Populist Demands and Government Resources in the New South Africa', *Journal of Commonwealth and Comparative Politics*, 32, 2 (July 1994), 147; Nicoli Nattrass, 'South Africa: The Economic Restructuring Agenda – A Critique of the MERG Report', *Third World Quarterly*, 15, 2 (1994), 219–25 and Chapter 6 in this volume.

32. Kenneth Hughes, 'False Antithesis: The Dispute About The Market and the State' in Merle Lipton and Charles Simkins (eds), *State and Market in Post Apartheid South Africa* (Johannesburg: Witwatersrand University Press, 1993), pp. 51–2.

Southern Africa

1 Transitional South Africa: Negotiations and the Military

Annette Seegers

The military is likely to remain a major force in South African politics. In 1993, for instance, SADF total employment amounted to 76 000; SAP employment to 115 000; and the Correctional Services to 26 000. The reconstruction of the military is as yet incomplete, though in the year since the election of the interim government a number of policy issues have emerged. This chapter will thus start by identifying the broad trends of the military's involvement in the transition process before moving, in the second part, to concentrate on emerging issues and debates about the military's military future and its place in the political system.

PART I

Negotiating about Negotiations: 2 February 1990 to the End of 1991

For roughly two years after 2 February 1990, most of the political parties had a lot of work on their hands. Exiled parties had to return home and get into shape for negotiations, while reacting to positions taken by competitors. The ANC's team for negotiations emerged in June 1991 at its first conference in South Africa in decades. Nelson Mandela became deputy president and Cyril Ramaphosa secretary-general, with Walter Sisulu remaining as president. Their initial position was that the transition should be a simple affair: a general election would produce a 'constituent assembly', which would design the new constitution.[1] The NP and IFP, fearful of what such an assembly might do to outvoted parties, wanted to design the constitution before it was known which party had won. These parties discovered notions long promoted by the DP, including constitutional and not parliamentary supremacy, an independent judiciary and a second chamber of parliament. The result was thus a lot of haggling and posturing intermingled with genuine compromises and unilateral actions.[2] The ANC and the NP marked their progress in removing obstacles with agreements and

1

'minutes' named after the venues, Groote Schuur, D F Malan Airport (February 1991) and Pretoria.

Several attempts were made to advance negotiations amidst spiralling attacks and counterattacks. Three of these are important. The first is a National Peace Accord (NPA) concluded in September 1991. The initiative to form the NPA came from many sources worried about the rising level of violence, its causes, and how to deal with the accompanying bitterness. It was not the first 'peace agreement' signed in the transition – the ANC and IFP had signed one in January 1991, for example – but the most comprehensive. It attracted a wide range of political signatories, including interest groups, churches, political parties, the security forces, and trade unions. Its principles were wide-ranging. A Code of Conduct spelled out how to promote peace and remove the causes of violence. And a network of national, regional and local peace committees was created to resolve disputes. Although the peace committees were slow to gain ground and its contribution to peace remains controversial, the NPA charted new waters. It was the first practical experience of an 'all' or multi-party conference, an objective of the NP, and it was not an outright failure.

The second effort came in October 1991 with the appointment of a Commission of Inquiry regarding the prevention of public violence and intimidation. Known as the Goldstone Commission after its chairman, Justice Richard J Goldstone, it wanted to be an independent body for gathering and co-ordinating facts related to violence and intimidation in public. The Commission proceeded to form its own committees of inquiry about specific problems, such as the violence and alleged intimidation in Thokoza, the violence and murders which took place at the President Steyn Gold Mine in Welkom, and mass action. Each inquiry submitted a report to the State President.[3]

The third effort to deal with violence was the creation of a 'patriotic front'[4] between the ANC and PAC at a conference in Durban in 1991. It resulted in the ANC dropping its demand for a constituent assembly; an 'all-party' assembly now was acceptable. The South African Government agreed, and all agreed to invite AZAPO, the CP and AWB to the conference as well. When the move towards the conference, called the Convention for a Democratic South Africa or CODESA, gathered momentum, the PAC withdrew. The ANC and NP were not quite alone again – other parties such as the DP were part of the forthcoming CODESA – but their dominance enabled them to develop a procedure which gave them a veto over proceedings. The procedure was called 'sufficient consensus' and meant that if the ANC and NP/SA Government opposed some item, it would not pass.

CODESA I and II: December 1991–June 1992

Five homeland political parties, four TBVC administrations, three political parties from the House of Delegates and Representatives, the DP, ANC, IFP, NP, Natal and Transvaal Indian Congresses, and the SA Government participated in CODESA I. A large contingent of foreign diplomats, journalists, and observers attended. Deliberations were largely conducted in public. Speeches were 'ritualistic'. The demand for breakthroughs was huge but progress came in bits and pieces.[5]

The ANC by now was in a hurry. It wanted a speedy transition, with the resulting government's hand as constitutionally free as possible. The Government pace was leisurely. The IFP was present, but seemed uninterested in, even absent from, many of the negotiations. Chief Mangosuthu Buthelezi's absence was explained as a response to the Zulu king being 'snubbed'. The CP and PAC also declined to attend CODESA I. AZAPO declared it 'unrepresentative'. The AWB made more ominous noises. Since CODESA I wanted to force people into a unitary state under majority rule and the South African Government did not heed requests for a 'Boer state', it was necessary to prepare for war. What this actually meant was unclear. But bomb blasts occurred in five Transvaal towns in the week before CODESA I convened. Other White Right organisations crept into the light.[6]

CODESA I developed a complex internal structure and the achievements of each grouping is hard to follow. For our purposes, the most important achievement was the materialisation of a Declaration of Intent, which would frame all subsequent negotiations. The Declaration attracted 'sufficient consensus' plus the support of 15 of the other 19 CODESA I participants. An overruling of any of the following would henceforth be well nigh impossible: an undivided South Africa, adult suffrage, the doctrine of a separation of powers, and a bill of rights.

CODESA II introduced a more workmanlike attitude to negotiations. Working Groups were formed to address the creation of a free political climate, constitutional principles and a constitution-making body, an interim Government, the future of the TBVC states, and the time-frames of the transition. A Gender Advisory Committee examined proposals to identify possible violations of the equality principle. And a Daily Management Committee, served by a Secretariat, managed the traffic among the GAC and the five Working Groups. From the snail's pace of CODESA I, negotiations had moved into the fast lane. But still achievements came in bits and pieces.

For the NP/SA Government, as for any of the other major parties, slow progress led to erosion of political support. The NP solved this problem by calling a referendum on 17 March 1992, which it won handsomely.[7] Much emboldened by the margin of victory, the NP/SA Government adopted a more aggressive negotiating stance. In contrast, the IFP was happy to continue the low-key approach it had adopted during CODESA I. For the ANC, the slow progress was dangerous. The populist elements of its constituency, in particular, appeared to lose patience with the process.

CODESA II ended without sufficient consensus on the dealings of Working Group I. The principles of the Declaration of Intent could as yet not be translated into practice. On 16 June, a campaign of mass action was initiated by the ANC and its allies. Its goals were to renew links between the levels of the ANC's constituency (that is, strengthen the ties between the negotiators and grassroots and other forces) and to force a speedier move towards majority rule. The mass action campaign thus was not a suspension of negotiations but designed to move them forward.

Two violent episodes, however, led to the ANC's suspension of negotiations. Residents of Boipatong in the Vaal Triangle were massacred in a raid from a nearby hostel on 17 June. A week later the ANC withdrew from negotiations and issued a list of demands to be met before their return to the CODESA II table. Accusations and memos filled the air but without flexibility from any side. Whereas the events at Boipatong were unanticipated, the next episode, at Bisho, was not. Here some members of the ANC alliance thought it possible to pressure the homeland administrations into acceding to some of Working Group I's demands for free political activity. In full view of the media, the march on Bisho on 7 September did not proceed as planned and Ciskei soldiers opened fire on the marchers, killing 28 people.

From the viewpoint of political consolidation, the ANC negotiators' participation in mass action was a necessary act. But the general reaction to Bisho flung a plague on every house. The NP/SA Government's tardiness, the ANC's hurry, the march's leadership, the Ciskei soldiers, the Ciskei Administration and indeed the entire political leadership of the country stood indicted. Henceforth, mass action was not an option; it was back to the negotiating table. The planners of the Bisho march were correct in assessing various homeland leaders' political bases as brittle. For the moment, however, they were still creatures of the NP/SA Government, and only their masters could make them fall. A populist challenge would be resisted.

From the Record of Understanding to the MPNP: September 1992–May 1993

Soon after Bisho, on 26 September 1992, the ANC and NP/SA Government signed a 'Record of Understanding' containing most of the public agreements thus far reached. On the surface, it met ANC demands about the release of prisoners, carrying of dangerous weapons, and the hostels. The Record of Understanding went further and recorded consensus between the ANC and NP/SA Government about the future. A single constitution-making body was agreed upon. The next round of CODESA would identify the constitutional principles which would bind this constitution-making body. Time frames were set. Before the constitution-making body met, an interim Government of National Unity would rule under an interim constitution and a bill of rights, also worked out by the next CODESA. The NPA guidelines would count for everybody. The ANC again pledged to follow the NPA's Code of Conduct, while the SA Government would consent to peaceful mass action. The ground had been cleared for the final rounds of negotiations.[8]

The Record of Understanding infuriated the IFP leadership. The Understanding was based on an ANC–NP/SA Government meeting – a 'bilateral' in transitionspeak – and this was regarded as presumptuous. How could two parties think they alone could determine the future? In terms of protocol, Chief Buthelezi was not even invited to the signing before a high-powered foreign audience. The IFP rejected the Understanding and withdrew from negotiations.[9]

It is a nonsense to pretend all parties were equal in negotiations; their histories, legitimacy, resources, leadership, and support base were different and unequal. In these terms, the ANC and NP/SA Government were the major parties. The sky could be darkened with agreements but, if these two parties were excluded or opposed it, it was just paper. 'Sufficient consensus' was a concession to realism. But it went over the top. In strict logical terms, it probably was a 'necessary consensus' rather than a sufficient one.[10] To label it 'sufficient' and, further, to say that it meant what the main parties wanted it to mean, gave a self-aggrandising tone to the main parties. The smaller parties to negotiations were perhaps not so deeply aggrieved by the presumption but to the IFP, who claimed to be the third major party in the process, the Record of Understanding and the protocol surrounding gave offence.

Chief Buthelezi probably also was shocked by the gratitude[11] of both the ANC and the NP/SA Government. Over the long years of separate development, Chief Buthelezi was often regarded as the main internal opponent of the NP/SA Government. He did frequently and in serious terms criticise the NP/SA Government and had substantial contact with the ANC. One of the first counter-insurgency committees in South Africa was indeed based in Durban. At one time led by (later General) Koos Lloyd, the local SADF Command formed a *TIK* (for *Teeninsurgensie Komitee*) who spent most of their time trying to undermine Chief Buthelezi.[12] In more recent years, the South African Government had found it quite useful to negotiate with the ANC while simultaneously saying that the ANC could not claim general support in the country. Chief Buthelezi aside, the existence of the IFP and poll results served to substantiate this claim. The protocol issue, in other words, only added insult to injury.

The IFP's withdrawal from negotiations was accompanied by demands about cultural weapons and the disbanding of MK. Although these issue were specific to the IFP, it found common ground with a variety of other parties through the demand for local autonomy, fear that the ANC had gained too many concessions, and issues related to violence and crime. These parties – the IFP, CP, Ciskei and Bophutatswana Administrations – formed a negotiating alliance known as COSAG (the Concerned South African Group). In addition, the PAC and White Right parties (the Afrikaner Volksfront included) decided to join in negotiations for the first time.

The MPNP to the TEC: May 1993–September 1993

In March 1993, 26 parties decided to reconvene CODESA, now under the name of the Multi-Party Negotiation Process (MPNP). By comparison with the two CODESAs, the MPNP had a complex structure. In formal terms it consisted of a plenary meeting, Negotiating Forum, and a Negotiating Council. A series of technical committees developed and scrutinised the proposals of these bodies and drafted legislation for discussion. A planning committee managed the traffic among these bodies, assisted by staff of the Administration. Around and in between, bilateral discussions took place, the material of which could be inserted, for example, via the Negotiating Council or technical committees.

What was the main aim of the MPNP? On 7th May, a 'Declaration of Intent' was signed containing an agreement on an election Some technical committees had to prepare the legislation while others set up councils and commissions related to it. The transition clearly had become focused on an event which would legitimate a changed (and changing) political order. To arrive at such an event, the approval of many parties was necessary. 'Sufficient consensus' was by no means abandoned, but it was now expanded to mean that the support of the ANC, NP/SA Government *and* the IFP was necessary to move ahead. Many issues had to be resolved before an election, but the process now moved fairly quickly because the ANC and NP/SA Government had already, in the Record of Understanding, developed a consensus among themselves. The main problem was the main parties' view of the violence in the country. The Declaration of Intent had stressed the existence of 'conditions to be created to eliminate violence'; an election date, in other words, could not be selected if the violence were not appropriately addressed.

The Technical Committee on Violence at first approached the issue generally but it soon transpired that the dispute was simple. The ANC and NP/SA Government thought the violence, although deplorable, should not be allowed to delay the election or any negotiations. To say that the violence ought to be eliminated before any election, in practice gave a veto power to any violent group. The IFP held that it could not prepare for an election or negotiate while a war against its members was in effect. The phrase 'conditions to be created to eliminate violence' thus could not be taken literally or interpreted as a humanitarian would. It was transitionspeak for meeting the IFP's demands on violence.[13]

The increasing violence was a curious horror of the transition. During the 1980s, violence had peaked during 1985. By mid-1986 and at tragic cost, some reduction in the level of violence had been effected. But in the post-2 February 1990 era it returned with a vengeance. The NPA process was a response to it and became one of the girders of the transition. The MPNP's Technical Committee on Violence or any other forum of the MPNP could do little about the general causes of violence, which stretched back into the past. It was best equipped to deal with flaws in the NPA process and with current political demands related to the violence and an election. This was not to wash one's hands of the human dimension of violence; it was merely to recognise that a substantial portion of it had to do with political rivalry. The Goldstone Commission came to the same conclusion.

Ironically, the violence could even be taken as a measure of the transition's authenticity. The reforms of the early 1980s had been seen as 'modernising apartheid', that is, excluding any real change. The current negotiations were characterised by two additional dimensions. Firstly, the White Right used all their powers to try to prevent the adoption of equality as a constitutional principle. Secondly, the weaker parties in the negotiations tried to use violent methods to augment their power. The IFP, for example, used them, as did the ANC, PAC and other parties when they felt outmanoeuvred. The negotiations could not therefore by their very nature exclude violent means.[14]

On 2 June 1993, the Technical Committee on Violence submitted its Fourth Report to the Negotiating Council recommending a phased plan to deal with armed formations. During the MPNP, various parties would audit their armed formations; after the MPNP (that is, when the TEC (Transitional Executive Committee) was in effect and until the election), military and police matters were to be handled on a separate basis; and, after the election, the installed government would rationalise and dispose of all security-related matters. A Peacekeeping Force was envisaged for use during the election itself.[15] The Negotiating Council adopted the Fourth Report, with the IFP speaking first among the sufficient consensus parties. Almost within minutes of the adoption of the Report, the date of an election was raised. Technical difficulties delayed the issue but soon 27 April 1994 was announced as the date of an election. The legitimacy of the event and its date had been accepted by the ANC, NP/SA Government and the IFP. The latter's demands about 'conditions to be created to eliminate violence' had boiled down to a guarantee that the Kwazulu Police, as a statutory armed formation, would not be required to integrate with MK. The Kwazulu Administration and its Minister of Police[16] would keep control over its police until the election.

The TEC to the Election: December 1993–April 1994

The TEC Act was passed by parliament in September 1993. The MPNP's working groups transferred their duties to the TEC on the next day, but the TEC itself met only in December 1993. Until the election of April 1994, power-sharing had arrived. But since the Record of Understanding in September 1992 and especially the setting of the election date in June 1993, the overriding concern of the civilian politicians had become the achievement of a 'free and fair' election on 27 April 1994.

The list of dangers to an election was a long one, and included entry into partisan politics by former SADF generals, like Constand Viljoen and Tienie Groenewald.[17] They were part of an *Eenheidskomitee* (Committee of Unity), formed in order to impose coherence on a collection of White Right organisations. Other generals were on the loose in the homelands, too, and their brittle positions had been revealed during the last days of the ANC's mass action campaign in 1992. Generals Holomisa and Gqozo, along with Kwazulu Police Minister Buthelezi and President Lucas Mangope, had to agree to an election and allow it to proceed on a free and fair basis.

Despite the enormous respect for Constand Viljoen among soldiers, his appearance on the political scene did not result in declarations of support by groups within or sections of the SADF. Despite even General Groenewald's long tenure in the organisation, DMI was entrusted with the politically-sensitive task of developing contingency plans on what to do should events in homelands threaten the election. The SADF's lack of challenge to the negotiating politicians was in fact the proverbial dog that did not bark. When the White Right invaded the World Trade Centre, site of MPNP negotiations, General Viljoen seemed unable to control the crowd. Later he was to lament the inability of the White Right to behave as soldiers. The strong bonds between the SADF and the White Right, so frequently suggested, had yet to be confirmed.

In their reluctance to join the TEC and participate fully in the election, the Administrations of Bophutatswana and the Ciskei chose an awkward moment to assert political independence. The central state's financial power was overwhelming but, by declining to participate in the election process, the Administrations put the salaries, pensions, and other income of their public servants at risk. The Ciskei was the first to succumb to the pressure and join the TEC. Bophutatswanan civil servants entered into a strike, riots occurred, and the central state added pressure by not intervening. With President Mangope not saved by the SADF, as he had been once in the past, the White Right arrived. After deplorable behaviour on both sides, they were escorted out by the SADF. When all seemed to break down, the TEC and the SA Government deployed the SADF and effect-ively nullified Bophutatswana's independence. In the operation, DMI's special forces, which had faithfully developed the contingency plans, were bypassed in favour of conventional SADF troops.

When the election process was finalised at the MPNP, it was politic-ally impossible to concede publicly that there was no alternative to the SADF and SAP. The National Peacekeeping Force (NPKF) thus came into being. It was supposed to be a force of about 10 000 for deployment prim-arily in Natal. The SADF ideally was going to be confined to barracks. At the time, several observers pointed out that the NPKF could not be ready for the election, and various troubles in the main training camp near Bloemfontein soon attracted attention. The TEC decided to deploy the NPKF troops, however, in Thokoza, one of the hottest spots on the East Rand. Not surprisingly, the NPKF failed and its troops were returned to barracks. Voters in the April election had to make do with the SADF and SAP.

The public conduct of most SADF and SAP personnel during the three (and more, in some areas) days of the election was exemplary. Citizens were allowed access to voting stations. Public order was maintained despite some volatile situations created by long queues and administrative problems. The electoral result was respected. In a public and symbolic sense, among others by raising the new flag outside police stations and by its presence during the inauguration of President Mandela, the SADF, now the South African National Defence Force (SANDF), and the SAP, now the South African Police Service (SAPS), confirmed the transfer of power.

PART II

Breaking with the Past: State Power and Decision Making

The restructuring of the South African military can be traced back before the political breakthrough in February 1990 to the replacement of P W Botha by F W De Klerk as State President. Within weeks of De Klerk presiding over his first cabinet meeting in late 1989, it was announced that the NSMS was to be replaced by a National Co-ordinating Mechanism (NCM). The former purpose of the NSMS, co-ordination of state actions, would henceforth be the responsibility of newly-created co-ordination committees. Co-ordination further centred on socio-economic development rather than security. At the central state level, the SSC as statutory body remained (with the new stipulation that its members be elected and accountable political figures) but a Cabinet Committee for Security Affairs (CCSA) came into being. The CCSA had its own secretariat.[18]

This re-arrangement affected decision making by the SSC and, by implication, the military. Formerly, the SSC was not supposed to make decisions – it was supposed to stick to advice – but the chairing of the SSC by P W Botha and the habit of meeting before Cabinet meetings led to an 'inner cabinet' predominantly composed of military bureaucrats. The new SSC was divested of this decision-making momentum: President De Klerk did not chair the SSC (indeed, he had never been a member of the SSC), and the SSC could formulate proposals but they had to be presented to the full Cabinet for approval. In addition, the SSC had to contend with the advice of the CCSA.[19]

The SSC secretariat also was divested of much of its administrative strength. Only two branches of the old NSMS were retained to provide support services, namely the strategy and strategic communication branches. Remaining sections of the old NSMS were abolished, principally the training and administration branch and the branch management services/systems development. The training and administration branch was an exceptionally active branch, giving lectures and courses to bureaucrats on the 'threat to

South Africa' and what should be done about it.[20] Viewed overall, 50 per cent of the NSMS posts were first frozen and then phased out by the end of 1990.[21]

President De Klerk's shifting of the SSC into the background was accompanied by three other telling signs of reduced military influence: (i) The SADF was not in the foreground in any of the negotiations. As shown earlier, the first serious entry of the SADF into negotiations came in April 1993. (ii) The length of conscription was halved. (iii) Probably most important, the first military budget presented under De Klerk's tenure (1990–1) showed a reduction of 16 per cent, a cut that was repeated in 1991–2.[22]

Because the composition of Cabinet remained unchanged, President De Klerk's position as incoming head of government was at times described as an exception to the rule that an incoming head of government consolidates power at the centre of the state. Removing the SSC and its apparatus from the centre, however, was the first step in consolidating civilian rule. The security agencies and especially the military had just about every wish indulged over the previous ten years. Yet, by not changing Cabinet, President De Klerk inhibited his attempts at consolidating civilian rule: soldiers could be protected by civilian politicians. Consolidation had to go beyond the central state too. 3 February 1990 brought new roles and rules for the security institutions from top to bottom.

The civil–military balance within the state during the 1970s and early 1980s had long turned on perceptions of efficiency among institutions. In the late 1980s, civilian institutions were perceived in a better light than the earlier indictments of failure had previously suggested. But facts could still be tortured to show security agencies had 'built the foundations' of the transition. Order, as defined by the security agencies, was indeed the root of political life. A politician errs in thinking politics does not have a hard hand. Politicians need soldiers.[23]

The SADF's own claims of its worth made a point of referring to its mastery of semi- or conventional warfare, as well as counter-insurgency, one of the notoriously difficult areas of conflict. Tactical ingenuity in semi- and conventional warfare, it is argued, was sustained under difficult circumstances when outside political support was absent and when military support from outsiders was at first erratic and later more consistent but still limited. Other problems emanated from the very nature of the SADF, which contained a large proportion of non-professionals (Citizen Force members and national servicemen) who had to be integrated in every major operation. Under these conditions, the South African military was led, at senior but especially junior command levels, by men who were themselves highly motivated and could motivate men (of diverse origin) under their command, and who were tactical innovators. The ingenuity of operations in the western side of Southern Africa is said to be underscored elsewhere in the region in, for example, reconnaissance, covert and destabilising operations. Further evidence of ingenuity is found in the South African arms industry and its ability to adapt designs to local purpose and to export successfully to overseas markets.[24]

Civilian politicians, so the claims read, had inhibited soldiers in the operational areas from doing their job properly. In Angola, for example, politicians had repeatedly qualified and inhibited military operations from achieving their full potential. This was the case from the start of Operation Savannah, when forces within sight of Luanda had to turn south on political orders. If it were not for the SADF's considerable tactical ingenuity in subsequent actions, the outcome could have been disastrous. Although the national security doctrine, with its instruction for soldiers and civilians to co-ordinate actions, continues to be used, the actual interpretation favours the military. Civilian politicians do not make a useful contribution to national security.

The blunting of the challenge of the African National Congress (ANC) and the South West African People's Organisation (SWAPO) is the root of the second perception, that the SADF regards itself to be a potent counter-insurgency force.[25] Originally COIN operations were viewed as a police responsibility but, in 1974, the SADF took over this responsibility from the SAP in Namibia. As early as the mid-1960s, the SADF had indeed already turned to the study of counter-insurgency and were set to apply the 'lessons' learnt from a variety of authors. The claim now is that the 'lessons' of such counter-insurgency theorists as Robert Thompson and John McCuen were essentially correct and that they were heeded and applied with effective consideration to local conditions and nuances.

There are many grounds on which to challenge SADF perceptions about its prowess. First, national servicemen in the area south of the border with Angola often were hard to motivate and slow to innovate. One reason was that the work, patrolling squares of 20^2 km and monitoring water holes, was not particularly exciting. The idea after all was to saturate the area or to maintain a presence in bulk. Innovation was not required. Another reason may have been lack of a sense of ideological grievance or a cause that could motivate. Participants in these operations noted that many operational practices in northern Namibia went strictly by the book.[26]

Second, was the war in Angola/Namibia not a case of applying the lessons of frontier warfare rather than counter-insurgency? Much has been made of the 'winning hearts and minds' and 'COIN is 80 per cent political and 20 per cent military' elements of operations and, as will be shown shortly, these notions have been influential. But the cross-border character, the increasingly conventional nature of operations, the use of political 'tribes' against each other, and the low political visibility of the operations rests uneasily in the category of counter-guerrilla success. Such success is, in any case, determined by political – not military – effects, and here the ANC and SWAPO emerged from the conflict politically more empowered than before.

Some soldiers, bureaucrats and civilian politicians are alert to the negative consequences of military confidence. These concern military influence in policy-making institutions at central state level. Here the resistance feeds on longstanding traditions about the apolitical nature of South Africa's bureaucracy, holding that policy should be set by politically-elected people. The SSC, for example, drew bureaucrats (including military bureaucrats) into an uncomfortable relationship with those who set policy and thus, as shown above, the SSC was largely purged of bureaucrats' influence.[27] Resistance further comes from some soldiers within the military who argued for the 'purification of military function', meaning that the military should, primarily, do military things. Thus military institutions should not function as a support service for poorly-run civilian departments.[28]

An answer to the question 'What did the soldiers feel and think?' thus does not deliver a simple answer. They think the state needs soldiers and the SADF has an excellent supply of them. Although the notion of national security has become entrenched, its local interpretation contains considerable contempt for civilian politicians' past role in its implementation. But the correct military thing to do, again based on recent experience, is to be very cautious about invitations to governance. Too much 'politics' could well erode the military excellence or professionalism acquired under difficult circumstances. Perhaps not quite chastened, soldiers were not nearly as keen on political power as some earlier had been.

Breaking with the Past: Security Forces' Actions

By 1990 security agencies and their actions were, in institutional terms, both centralised and decentralised. Statutory legislation had created many armies, linked at select points only and exercising discretion in their daily functions. Homeland armies functioned largely as police forces, while some police forces often acted as light infantry. The central state could of course issue a command, but its proper execution could not be monitored.

Between 1990 and 1992, civilian politicians did try to drive the message of 2 February 1990 home to the security agencies. Speeches were made and new instructions issued. The problem was that few significant changes were made in personnel, either by transfer or 'retirement'. Ministers Malan and Vlok stayed on, as did the senior personnel of the military. Most of the latter's careers and ideological stances were based on counter-insurgency in various operational areas. Among the local security agencies, 'intellectual' officers were usually shuffled off to institutional byways. It was the fighting man – veterans of Angola and Security Branch, for example – who rose to the top. The only area showing signs of personnel shifts was the police, in accordance with the reorganisation plan (following the De Witt Commission). The SADF's personnel was almost frozen in relief.

The only option for creating institutional support for the New South Africa was to stop ongoing Total or Revolutionary Onslaught projects. In April of 1991, the ANC sent an open letter to the Government, threatening to suspend negotiations if the problems around the security forces were not resolved. July saw the Government acknowledge its secret funding of the IFP, which led to the removal of Ministers Vlok and Malan from their portfolios (albeit staying on in cabinet). President De Klerk also revealed that 41 secret projects had been terminated, with those remaining scrutinised by an advisory committee.[29] Significantly, the NPA's later Code of Conduct applied to the security agencies.

Soldiers and policemen could still pull in their own political direction. Violence after 2 February 1990 obviously had more than one cause and form, but one ingredient consistently stood apart from all others: the appearance of aggressive groups, armed with automatic weapons, who cut a path of destruction on trains, in rural areas as much as townships, and even in inner cities, and then seemed to vanish into thin air. The pattern was not all that different to state-supported violence of the 1980s, like the 'Witdoeke' of Crossroads, the Ama-Afrika group in the Eastern Cape, and warlordism in northern Natal.[30] The emerging pattern was nevertheless sufficiently distinct from the 1980s and led many observers to speak of a 'Third Force'.

The meaning of the word 'Third Force' varied. It could consist of DMI operatives (current or former), old NSMS allies, policemen, or intelligence operatives of other service branches. The word usually implied state-supported violence even if the actual perpetrators of the violence were a collection of small and politically disparate groups. They were drawn into the same ring by either active or more passive state support. The former would come in a supply of arms, for example, while the latter would include such bureaucratic devices as failing to investigate incidents vigorously. Homeland administrations practised their own brand of Third Force actions with its separate political goals, the central state's involvement attracted most attention because it meant an anti-ANC or pro-IFP bias. If a Third Force existed in the central state labyrinth, President De Klerk was either hypocritical or not in control of the state.

The fact that so few prosecutions of Third Force-type activities occurred meant that the Departments of Justice and Law and Order, the latter including the SAP, were compromised. In appointing the Goldstone Commission in October 1991, the Government in effect conceded that its denials of state involvement in violence lacked credibility. The Commission became a part of the Department of Justice but reported to the State President and was linked with a non-government process, namely the NPA and its structures.

But who was to know and tell? President De Klerk was served by the security agencies themselves. They could tell him what they wanted him to hear. The Goldstone Commission investigated the possibility but concluded that there was no evidence of a state-supported Third Force. The Commission improved its investigative capacities over time but it was better able to explore areas of conflict in society (taxi wars, for example) than state agencies. The press, particularly the *Vrye Weekblad* and *The Weekly Mail*, pressed the issue repeatedly, but a crack in the dam wall did not appear. Best suited to engineer a crack, of course, were the security agencies themselves. By natural inclination, security agencies spy on each other as much as on anybody else. One of them had to tell.

The burden fell on the National Intelligence Service (NIS), which was now headed by Mike Louw, as Dr Neil Barnard and his key advisers had moved to the Department of Constitutional Services. Dr Barnard and his team serviced the CODESA and MPNP processes. NIS fell under the portfolio of the Minister of Justice, Kobie Coetzee, who became Minister of Defence upon the removal of Magnus Malan. Of all the security agencies, NIS was least involved in the domestic battles of the past 20 years[31] although, just in case, it was instructed to destroy incriminating files. The network attempting to control errant security agencies' behaviour became President De Klerk, the Cabinet, NIS, and the Goldstone Commission.

Cabinet was the weakest link. For political reasons, President De Klerk resisted a reshuffle for a long time. The referendum did strengthen the civilian hand in general terms but Cabinet was still filled with politicians who had power bases or other talents the President apparently could not afford to lose. That they would not support the effort to control all security agencies' action was clear after the first public skirmish with the military.

In late 1992, the Goldstone Commission raided the offices of the Department of Military Intelligence in Pretoria. It was in search of five files only. The presence of international members of the Commission lent legitimacy to the raid. The raid was a tactical success – after all, they had received very good information – but a strategic failure. Cabinet failed to press home the advantage. The various military officers named disputed their indictment and eventually returned to their duties. Their transgressions thus were never fully revealed. It took the Goldstone Commission more than a year to mount another assault on a security agency. The next time it was the SAP.

Barely a month before the election and apparently more confident of Cabinet support, President De Klerk and the Goldstone Commission announced they possessed *prima facie* evidence of misconduct by senior police officers. Albeit reluctantly, the officers consented to voluntary leave. Their misconduct has yet to be investigated in court. Traffic in illegal arms and ammunition, the cherished hobby of more than one security agency and officer, is probably the main charge.[32] The timing of the announcement and nature of the indictment were clearly related to the IFP and Kwazulu Government's refusal to participate fully in the election. Third Force actions thus existed but, for the time being, applied mainly to the events in Natal.

The Military's Purpose

The election and emergence of a new Government has prompted debate on the nature of the South African military's purpose in the post Cold War international order. Some critics have argued that the country's enemies – even if they exist – are too distant to bother preparing for a fight. The political timing for smallish countries to develop military power is in any case poor. This is particularly due to the growing importance of international financial institutions such as the International Monetary Fund and the World Bank itself. From the IMF, states can neither run nor hide. Borrowing and lending, managing exchange rates, coping with inflation and its permutations, and financial dependence and interdependence are currently the issues that increasingly concentrate states' minds. The immediate spectre thus is not military conquest but managing economic stability. Since the state is the biggest economic actor in the South African economy, it indeed has been forced to heed IMF specifications for spending on the military, in particular the percentage of its budget devoted to the military.

Fortunately, the transition in South Africa was not threatened by heightening military tensions from outside. In some neighbouring countries, the security situation did worsen and South Africa reaped the benefits of its past involvement in those conflicts. The availability of cheap automatic weapons in Natal is one example of negative return on previous Mozambican investment. Yet no military challenge from other countries was registered. No continental ballistic missiles have been introduced to the region. No potentially hostile naval task forces sailed around the Cape. In fact, the appearance of friendly naval vessels and other military contact meant that relations started to resemble normality for the first time in decades. For the foreseeable future, South Africa is safe from military attack. A degree of consensus about the future has surfaced in acceptance that the new defence force will have domestic duties relating to public order. For this reason, the backup system between military and police has been preserved in law. The outstanding question for negotiators is whether this role should be extended.

Some argue that the military's domestic deployment takes place within a narrow range. Only when the delivery of essential services by civilian agencies is made impossible should the military come to the aid of those agencies. Others argue that, given the urgency of the task of reconstruction and development, the military's assets could be used to great effect across a wider range. At times reasoning takes the form of a progressive interpretation of the national security doctrine. Security deals with armed challenges but is equally concerned about economic development, environmentalism, protecting rights, and welfare. This 'all-encompassing' notion of security is defined as enabling people 'to live in peace and harmony, enjoy equal access to resources and participate fully in the process of governance.'[33]

Both narrow and broader interpretations of the military's domestic deployment contain weaknesses. The narrow argument appears blind to the central fact of life in the post-Cold War era. Most militaries most of the time do not perceive enemies as either foreign or particularly military in kind. If domestic and non-military needs are paramount, why not address the military's contribution to those problems? Why waste time and money on fictitious armies supposedly advancing on our borders? In any case, one needs to break with such a narrow state orientation. It is not the state or military that ought to identify enemies – foreign or otherwise – but the citizens of the country. If the citizens do not want the military to have an external military orientation, that should be the end of the argument, at least for democrats. The state, including the military, exists to serve the people.

For the broader interpretation, the problems appear in three areas. First, foreign military challenges may appear. If the military's attentions have been turned elsewhere, they may be caught short. Second, if the military is assigned a developmental role, could it not delay the need to civilianise? Because of its corporate strength, the military may muscle in on civilians' ground, particularly since the soldiers – because of the past – are well acquainted with the territory. Finally, in a broad developmental notion of security, actions are justified on the basis of human need. This could mean that the military's societal intervention rests on practical justifiability and not principled demarcation of the military's place in state and society.

For both broad and narrow interpretations, the military's domestic deployment is most likely to concentrate on the area of public order. Here the interpreters land in very muddy waters. One unchallengeable line of argumentation is that the police should be demilitarised and be used to protect the community. Yet, given the past and current criminal actions – violent crime in particular – many have conceded that the police cannot cope. Hence the deployment of the military as support – and the delay of police reform.

Interestingly, some prominent strategists[34] have made the case for developing light (and not so light) infantry and special forces for domestic use in cases of domestic destabilisation. For the time being, the term 'domestic destabilisers' has referred mainly to the Inkatha Freedom Party/Kwazulu Government, the White Right, and 'Third Force' activity. Skills of this kind could also recommend South Africa as a regional peacekeeper to neighbours embroiled in internal disputes.[35] South Africa's emergence as a legitimate regional peacekeeper cannot be discounted. Besides the opportunity to cultivate a new regional reputation, the attraction could well be authorising international or regional organisations' practice of paying peacekeepers per individual soldier.

In adjusting existing military organisation, policy makers have drawn on two influential models. The first is the model for a professional military originally designed by the Prussian state in the nineteenth century. It established a distinction between line and staff units. The second is the post-1945 national security model, first developed in the USA through its National Security Act. National security focuses both on the cooperation necessary between various service arms of the military and the incorporation into a cooperative system of security-related entities. The many have to act as one and ensure that security is not only a military enterprise. Who the enemies are and how to fight them will thus determine not only the shooting side of the military, but also the chain of command, the balance between line and staff, and the connections with non-military entities.

The Military's Place in Political Life

Finding an appropriate place for the military in a political system is one of political history's oldest problems. Thucydides's account of Athens and Sparta's problems and the place of the spirited in Plato's *Republic* are indications of just how old and fundamental the issue is. For our purposes, two traditional fears about the military are relevant: that the military may challenge (civilian) political rule and that the military is too subservient to political rulers. In other words, too much and too little obedience comes from the military.

Both problems arise not in the local military's errors, for example the SADF's participation in 'conspiratorial subversive politics',[36] although this is not helpful at all. The threat emanates from the very nature of the military. It requires hierarchy to facilitate command. Even in the days when most soldiers were paid to fight and, as hired armies, could choose their political leaders, commanders long have practised strict discipline. Forms of egalitarianism have recently emerged in military history and institutions. If a military is to redeem the money invested in it, there are limits to egalitarianism. Militaries stand a greater chance of success (with the least number of casualties) by successful and justifiable implementation of the principle of inequality within their own ranks.[37] If both are true to themselves, military and democracy thus are supposed to exist in tension.[38]

With regard to the potential challenge of the military to the civilian politicians as such, many procedures are available for subordinating the military part of the state to the civilian part. Major items in this regard are: (i) The base of civilian power, in democracies inevitably the legislature, controls the money available to the military and affirms its allocation within the military. No legislature would fund its own demise. (ii) The legislature develops expertise in military affairs by means of standing committees, so that even military choices are not made solely by the military. (iii) Lest the military march on the legislature, power to declare war is given to the legislature. (iv) To avoid legislators developing in it, the military is prohibited from allowing partisan political activity in its own ranks. (v) The legislature controls, by ratification, the senior appointments and promotions in the military.[39] These items are formal or procedural in nature and may be augmented by more informal means. But most of the battle is within government itself, restricting military influence over the rest of the state to the degree necessary.

Because of our immediate past, much of current writing efforts has been concentrated on the issue of civilian supremacy at the highest level of state. Deon Fourie's survey of constitutional formulae for the control of armed forces is very useful in identifying an array of constitutional mechanisms. It includes constitutional criteria, direct and indirect parliamentary control, as well as enhancing civilian control in the American and Swiss way, reduction of security agencies' powers, and the self-restraint of military forces through discipline, loyalty and professionalism. Fourie uses Samuel Huntington's objective and subjective dimensions[40] to remind us that the battle for civilian control is wide and multi-dimensional. Virtually no area of society is exempt from it.

The second democratic fear is of situations wherein political rulers and the military make common cause against the people in society. Recent history is filled with politicians, even elected ones, who, when faced with the slightest challenge, reach for the gun. One potential ally for citizen resistance to this actually lives in the state: the judiciary. Citizens need indeed to develop a constitution giving the judiciary ammunition against politicians who want to act against the people. This ammunition is often couched in terms of procedure yet contains, as its centrepiece, the requirement that politicians respect the rights of individuals. Even if the majority of the legislators want to damage rights, the courts can pronounce their actions unconstitutional. South Africa's Interim Constitution follows this route. Of course it remains to be seen whether the ideal of a constitutional democracy can be realised. South Africa's highest court, the Appellate Division, is notoriously literal and statutory in its reading of state actions. Whatever the legislature has willed, the courts have approved. If judicial review is to become real, the Appellate Division and Constitutional Court will have to break with the tradition of timidity. It also remains to be seen whether legislators are altogether comfortable with the new role of the courts.

Besides the constitutional option, the democratic idea is for all militaries to be 'people's' or popular militaries because then the military would not hurt itself. Popular control over the military is, in the first instance, enhanced by the measures taken to circumscribe military influence in the state and the legislature's control over the military. The people shape the legislature and, in turn, it shapes the military. But two additional procedures are essential if the military is not to turn on its own people.

First, a democratic military encourages popular participation, including national (military) service, part-time military service, and judicious recruitment. Participation is as inclusive as possible, with no citizen in principle exempt from military duty. The military's composition has to take account of demographic contours, however, to ensure the institution is not perceived as alienated from the main sectors of society. Quotas and crude forms of 'affirmative action' spoil the integrity of command but substantial attention must be paid to the demographic character of the institution's personnel. If not, a warrior caste/class might develop or some sectors of society be used as cannon fodder.

Secondly, according to the Interim Constitution, the military must be accountable to more than one authority. The legislature is the supplier of money and demands to know how it in fact has been spent. The executive draws up the plans for war. Judges rule whether the constitution and/or

domestic laws have or have not been undermined by war. Thus executive, legislature and judiciary all claim some authority over the military. The
democratic requirement of civilian supremacy has not simply been understood as the supremacy of the legislature. Vital powers, especially in allocating state revenue, are given to the legislature. But the negotiators, perhaps
in memory of nationalist and opposition legislators' courage in the face of
imperial presidents, thought it best to empower other state institutions so
they could challenge legislators.

To say that South Africa's efforts now should be aimed primarily at
re-establishing parliamentary control of the armed forces, as Jakkie Cilliers
and Paul Bolko-Mertz of the Institute for Defence Policy have suggested,
begs the question of the quality of the legislators.[41] The chamber may for
instance be dominated by political demagogues. Even if parliamentary control over the military is enhanced by mechanisms such as elected politicians'
control over defence spending, a bipartisan defence standing committee,
an ombudsman, parliamentary questions and answers and the right to lodge
a petition, legislators may still be imprudent about the military and its
actions. Hence the role of the courts and a military belonging to the people.[42]

CONCLUSION

After 2 February 1990, the military in South Africa was on the receiving
end of negotiations. Yet negotiators, too, could be on the receiving end of
what security agencies did or failed to do. The military is now not keen
on acquiring formal powers at the central state level; indeed the constitution
and executive arrangements suggest that the military will be subordinate
to the constitution and secondarily to parliament and its subcommittees.
As far as debate on the future role of the military is concerned, one of the
most interesting developments is a set of problems under the heading of
'labour relations'. This is likely to have a direct impact on professionalism,
rationalisation, and the political passivity of the military.

NOTES

1. For details see Chapter 4.
2. In October 1990, for example, the government released thousands of prisoners

serving longterm sentences from jail. Why this was done has never been fully explained.

3. Statement read by Justice R J Goldstone on the presentation of the *First Report of the Commission of Inquiry Regarding the Prevention of Public Violence and Intimidation*, 24 January 1992, pp. 2–6.

4. As previously had been effected in Zimbabwe.

5. Steven Friedman, *The Long Journey* (Johannesburg: Ravan Press, 1992), pp. 21–33.

6. The *Boere Republikeinse Leer* claimed responsibility for some of the bomb blasts. SAIRR, *Race Relations Survey 1991/92* (Johannesburg: SA Institute of Race Relations, 1992), pp. il–li.

7. 68.7 per cent of the white voters approved of continued negotiations.

8. SAIRR, *Race Relations Survey 1992/93* (Johannesburg: SA Institute of Race Relations, 1993), pp. 35–6.

9. *Ibid.*, p. 36.

10. Necessary conditions usually refer to those without which a phenomenon cannot occur. Sufficient conditions are those which are enough to make a phenomenon occur.

11. After the Spanish Civil War, General Franco was asked what his government would do with liberals who had supported the fascist cause. His reply was: 'We will shock them with our gratitude'.

12. Interview with a former member of the *TIK* based in Durban, Piet Gerber, then of the Department of Information and now employed by the Department of Foreign Affairs.

13. See the discussion in the Negotiating Council (of 28 May) on a report of the Technical Committee on Violence.

14. Remarks from the floor by Professor Bernard Crick at a conference in London.

15. Fourth Report of the Technical Committee on Violence (of the MPNP), 2 June 1993, pp. 4–6. The location of the National Peacekeeping Force in this report suggested it was a political necessity (rather than a security necessity) in getting an election date declared. Many a strategist nevertheless lamented another set of 'kitskonstables' appearing on the scene.

16. Chief Buthelezi.

17. Other imporant figures were Generals Klopper and Visser.

18. The Secretary of Cabinet, *Handleiding: Nasionale Koordineringsmeganisme* (NKM), 22 March 1990, 1–3 and further.

19. Information supplied by Mr A P Stemmet, administrative head of the NSMS, on 5 March 1990.

20. An NSMS source (Mr A P Stemmet, administrative head of the NSMS, on 5 March 1990) estimated the number of bureaucrats thus trained at several thousand (''n paar duisend'). Branch management/systems development was mainly a research operation and was much less active.

21. Information supplied by Mr A P Stemmet on 5 March 1990.

22. For more detail, see Laurie Nathan and Mark Phillips, 'Crosscurrents: Security Developments under F W De Klerk' in Glenn Moss and Ingrid Obery (eds), *South African Review 6* (Johannesburg: Ravan Press, 1992).

23. See the parliamentary debate of May 1990 on the SADF's interpretations.

24. See Simon Baynham's interview with General Meiring, 'South Africa, Namibia and Angola', *Southern African Record*, 40 (October 1985); Jan

Breytenbach, *Forged in Battle* (Cape Town: Saayman and Weber, 1986); Fred Bridgland, *Jonas Savimbi: A Key to Africa* (Sevenoaks, Kent: Hodder and Stoughton, 1986); Jakkie Cilliers, *The Role and Development of the SADF*, unpublished paper; Roland De Vries, *Mobiele Oorlogvoering* (Pretoria: F J N Hartman Uitgewers, 1987); N L Dodd, 'South African Operations and Deployments in South West Africa/Namibia', *Army Quarterly* (July 1980); Sophia Du Preez, *Avontuur in Angola: Die Verhaal van Suid-Afrika se Soldate in Angola 1975–1976* (Pretoria: J L Van Schaik, 1989); Robin Hallett, 'The South African Intervention in Angola', *African Affairs* (July 1978); Robert Jaster, *South Africa in Namibia: The Botha Strategy* (Lanham: University Press of America, 1985); David Martin and Phyllis Johnson (eds), *Destructive Engagement* (Harare: The Zimbabwe Publishing House, 1986); and Paul Moorcraft, *Africa's Superpower* (Johannesburg: Sygma Collins, 1981).

25.   See Simon Baynham, 'South Africa, Namibia and Angola'; Jakkie Cilliers, *The Role and Development of the SADF*; W Gutteridge, *South Africa: Strategy for Survival* (London: Conflict Studies No. 131); T H Henrikson, 'Namibia: A Comparison with Anti-Portuguese Insurgency' *Round Table* (April 1980); and Francis Toase, 'The South African Army: The Campaign in South West Africa/Namibia since 1966' in Ian F. Beckett and John Pimlott (eds), *Armed Forces and Modern Counter-Insurgency* (London: Croom Helm, 1985).

26.   This was suggested to me by University of Cape Town students in 1986. All had done service in the Operational Zone.

27.   Information supplied by Mr A P Stemmet on 11 November 1989 and 5 March 1990.

28.   Information supplied by Mr Peet Du Preez of MILISTAN, a private firm specialising in military contracts, on 20 December 1989.

29.   SAIRR, *Race Relations Survey 1991/92* (Johannesburg: SA Institute of Race Relations, 1992), pp. 68–9.

30.   Documented by human rights groups, journalists and scholars. See Chapter 10.

31.   Its international record is controversial.

32.   Arms supplies were a critical component of the logistical aid to UNITA and RENAMO. Reconnaissance and special operations also required the right weapons, for example AK 47s, not controlled by the Quartermaster-General but by '*Spesmagte*' themselves. Trade in arms and ammunition is immensely lucrative. Those without ideological motivation picked up in the counter-insurgency years are often attracted by the money. The thieves probably outnumber the ideologues.

33.   Laurie Nathan, 'Beyond Arms and Armed Forces: A New Approach to Security', *South African Defence Review*, 4 (1992), 15–16.

34.   Chris Hani at the Lusaka Conference arranged by IDASA in Helmoed-Romer Heitman, 'Creating a Special Operations Capability', *South African Defence Review*, 4 (1992), 31–8.

35.   Helmoed-Romer Heitman, *op. cit.*, p. 31.

36.   Deon F S Fourie, 'Control of the Armed Forces in South Africa: Constitutional Formulae', *South African Defence Review*, 5 (1992), 18.

37.   The military is not the only organisation or social creature justified in its practise of inequality. Parents and educational institutions, for example, also find it good and necessary to do the same.

38. Although this discussion approaches the issue from a democratic perspective, the problem is not peculiar to democracies. Marxist practice, too, devotes considerable effort to subordinating the military to its centre of political power, the Communist party.

39. The American Congress, for example, has to confirm US Army appointments above colonel level.

40. Found in Samuel P Huntington, *The Soldier and the State* (New York: Random House, 1957).

41. *The Role and Composition of the Armed Forces*, Submission to CODESA Working Group 1, 2 March 1992, and J K Cilliers, 'Security Policy for a Democratic South Africa', Paper delivered at the 1992 conference of the Professors' World Peace Academy on *Foreign Policy Issues in a Democratic South Africa*, 20 and 21 March 1992.

42. *The Role and Composition of the Armed Forces*, Submission to CODESA Working Group 1, 2 March 1992, pp. 19–29.

2 Civil War Regions and Ethnic Mobilisation: Inkatha and Zulu Nationalism in the Transition to South African Democracy

Gerhard Mare

INTRODUCTION

During the period 1985–9 approximately 5 400 people were killed in politically-related violence in South Africa (in 1989 alone, the highest figure during this period, 1 400 people died). From 1990 until the end of March 1994 a further 14 211 died (2101 in 1990; 2 582 in 1991; 3 499 in 1992; 4 398 in 1993; and 1 631 during the first three months of 1994). The majority of these people died in Natal and KwaZulu.[1]

While this chapter concentrates on the political processes leading up to the elections at the end of April 1994, it must be read against the pervasive presence of the extreme violence, indicated by the figures above, that characterised both political oppression and political competition in South Africa. This violence was not merely the background, but also an essential element in the politics of Natal (the province) and KwaZulu (the bantustan or 'homeland'). These are now amalgamated into one of the nine provinces within post-apartheid South Africa, and rather cumbersomely known as KwaZulu Natal – KZN in this chapter.

There was a certain tragic inevitability to the violence, born as it was out of the casting of Inkatha as part of the 'system'. It was inevitable because of the movement's structural location within an essential element of the apartheid policy; through the deliberate choice by Buthelezi and the Inkatha movement of an approach to 'change the system from within'; and, hence, because of its enforcement of, and collaboration with, many aspects of the apartheid state's political agenda. Furthermore, Inkatha leadership and the

Zulu king drew rigid boundaries around the ethnic social identity that was to serve to mobilise a regional population during the 1980s. Ethnic mobilisation was to be a central part, along with attempts to mesh the provincial and bantustan structures, of regional consolidation. However, the violence has also to be located in the extremes of the policy of 'ungovernability' acted out by members of ANC-supporting organisations, especially during the second half of the 1980s. Some of these issues are investigated in the next two parts of this chapter.

The manner in which Inkatha and Buthelezi's strategy during the lead-up to the elections built on the past (both as achievements and as ideological construct) forms the subject matter of the next part; the final part deals with the post-election period.

REGIONS AND NATIONS: NATIONAL PARTY AND INKATHA APPROACHES

The editor of the Afrikaans-language Sunday paper *Rapport* (27 February 1994) argued that while most federal systems came about through drawing in fairly autonomous units, the opposite was happening in South Africa under the new constitution. He was partly correct, in that provincial powers had been systematically devalued since the creation of the Union of South Africa in 1910 and became increasingly centralised in Pretoria. However, it does not hold for the bantustans. In their case they were given extensive powers (exactly those powers of control and administration that Buthelezi attempted to have extended to the region during the 1980s).[2] In all instances except in the new Eastern Cape and KwaZulu Natal provinces, the bantustans form extremely fragmented and small portions of the new regional spaces of post-apartheid South Africa.

The bantustans owed their specific origin to the idea that apartheid South Africa, and the National Party government, could solve their legitimacy problem by devolving power and 'nationhood' to nine (later ten) 'homelands'. On one level the policy, legislatively constructed through measures such as the Bantu Authorities Act (1951) and the Promotion of Bantu Self-Government Act (1959) was visionary in linking ethnic nationalisms to territory. The powers that were delegated to the bantustans were extensive – even to the extent of nominal 'independence' in the four cases of Transkei, Ciskei, Venda and Bophuthaswana. They remained nevertheless economically and militarily totally dependent on the central state, a dependence that the NP government was quite willing to use over the years. Such historical devolution of power is of cardinal importance in the case of KZN where the previous bantustan leadership and ruling (and sole) political movement, Inkatha, won the 1994 election.

In Natal and Zululand there was little doubt in the minds and words of the participants that a 'nation' existed at the time when the Zululand Territorial Authority was formed in 1970. The debates in the KwaZulu Legislative Assembly (the KLA) were filled with references to the 'Zulu nation'. It might not have been satisfactory, in terms of size and the degree of consolidation, to serve as a state, but KwaZulu was seen as the land of the Zulus. The only occasions during the 1970s when there was mention of the possibility of accepting 'independence' were when calls were made for the consolidation and addition of territory to the patchwork that was the bantustan. It was widely recognised that 'independence' would sever people as well as political power from the rest of South Africa and such an ultimate status was consistently rejected.

The bantustan assemblies were patriarchal and hierarchical institutions. Until its dissolution with the election of a first democratic government, the KLA remained dominated by chiefs numerically, as well as in most of the issues that were discussed and the policies that were implemented. The chiefs in the KLA were all male, and the vast majority of elected (most frequently unopposed) members were also men. It is these structures that Buthelezi wanted to carry into the future to secure a base beyond the threat of democracy. Tensions did exist between these institutions and the modernising role that was demanded for the KLA by the economic policies aimed at fostering a trading class. In many cases these tensions were overcome by chiefs entering the field of trading (especially in liquor). One of the most visible signs of the tension came at the formation of Inkatha, the National Cultural Liberation Movement. The constitution that was proposed for Inkatha at its formation in 1975 would have relegated the chief-dominated KLA to a role subsidiary to the political movement. The chiefs baulked at this and the constitution was rewritten.

Buthelezi and Inkatha struggled during the 1970s for control of the region, mostly against intrigues fomented by state departments (who were concerned with undermining Buthelezi who had indicated that he was not going to take independence), around the young Zulu king (who wanted extended powers), certain chiefs (royalists and arch-traditionalists), and certain disgruntled trading interests (because of Buthelezi's economic policy of partnership with white-owned capital). This was a battle that Buthelezi won. By the end of the decade KwaZulu had been granted extended powers by the central government in terms of 'chapter two' of the Bantu Homelands Constitution Act and had taken these with alacrity in the fields of policing and education. It now had the status of a 'self-governing territory'.[3]

The areas within which Inkatha was assuming power were precisely the most concentrated foci of the township revolts of the post-1976 period. Conflict around such issues as schooling, rents, policing, local government, transport and labour became inevitable. The first indication came in 1980 with an educational boycott in KwaMashu.

The Inkatha central committee decided at the beginning of 1980 that the next step, forced upon the movement by the break with the ANC and the new politics of urban revolt, was to be 'regional consolidation'. The reasons for the break with the ANC in 1979/80 were largely to do with elements within the ANC who were less willing to compromise, and Inkatha's need to state its own internal claims.[4] However, the implications were that Inkatha lost a major source of legitimacy, its ambiguous relationship to the legacy of the ANC.

WORKING THE SYSTEM OR BEING WORKED BY THE SYSTEM?

When the central committee decided to embark on steps that would extend the influence, if not the power, of Inkatha over the whole region they were finally squashing any notion the apartheid government might have had that 'independence' might still be accepted by this largest ethnic unit in its grand scheme. Inkatha was set, during the 1980s, to create a larger unit, a first federal state in a post-apartheid South Africa. There were several aspects to regional consolidation. These included moving into a 'paramilitary' phase. Langner noted in a 1983 study that 'The decision (to embark on a para-military strategy) was taken by the Central Committee on 19 July 1980 after noting "the increasing crescendo of attacks by the top hierarchy of the (ANC) in exile, the South African Communist Party and the so-called Radio Freedom"'. Langner continued:

> So as not to create the impression that Inkatha was a 'tribal development' and had diminished its strength, the Central Committee explained that 'Social, economic, historical and strategic factors made it necessary for the President [of Inkatha] to use Natal as a springboard to national problems'.[5]

Buthelezi himself expressed the decision as follows:

> I think it is time for Inkatha to establish training camps where branches and regions are schooled in the employment of anger in an orderly fashion. We need to be able to control riots. We need to be able to conduct meetings in the midst of chaos which other people try to create. We

need to tone up our muscles so that the dove of peace sits easily on the spear. I think we need to create well-disciplined and regimented impis in every Inkatha region which can be called out for the protection of that which is so sacred to Inkatha and black South Africa.[6]

The KwaZulu Police Force (KZP) (formed in 1980) was stated to be in the vanguard of the struggle against the ANC and its 'surrogates' in the townships. Thirteen years later Inkatha would be involved, as it had several times in its history, in training additional 'soldiers' in its 'Self-Protection Units' (SPUs) to fight the ANC's 'Self-Defence Units' (SDUs), this time at the Mlaba camp in Zululand. During the 1980s the training was partly formal, part of Inkatha stated policy, such as at the Emandleni-Matleng camp and within the KZP; some of it was secret and part of the central government's plan to fight the ANC-supporting organisations, using surrogates, such as the Inkatha members trained in northern Namibia in the period 1986–9;[7] while some of the para-military activity was localised and controlled by warlords, such as the notorious Mandla Shabalala.

Regional consolidation was not only military but covered several other areas as well. Initially Inkatha and its allies, drawn especially from the regional business community, moved too fast for the National Party (NP) government. The Buthelezi Commission report (1982) was rejected on the grounds that it exceeded the bounds of competence of the bantustan in its investigation of the political, social and economic interdependence of the province and the bantustan. These findings were to provide the ammunition to argue for a post-bantustan/province region.

By the mid-1980s, the National Party had its own 'observers' at the Natal/KwaZulu Indaba, a multi-party negotiating forum that was to draw up a constitution for the region. The resulting constitution, released at the end of 1986, was rejected by the National Party, though this had more to do with the election that was soon to take place than with an in-principle rejection of the notion of a dispensation 'beyond apartheid'.[8] As government, the relevant ministers were careful not to close doors on the Inkatha initiative. When the Joint Executive Authority (JEA) was created in 1986 to rationalise planning in the region it received central government blessing. In the same year elected provincial government was abolished – provincial councillors were subsequently to be appointed from Pretoria.

By now apartheid was acknowledged to be in crisis, and the search continued to find participants in schemes that would restore order without altering the face of South Africa too dramatically. The tri-cameral parliament was established in 1984, but suggestions of a fourth parliament for black South Africans was rejected (the year was described as one in which

SA 'experienced the most widespread black civil unrest since the Soweto disturbances in 1976').[9] In 1986 influx control restrictions were abolished with extensive implications not just for the movement of people but also for the political arguments that had served as justification for the exclusion of black people from central government. It was to take only a few more years before apartheid was finally laid to rest. By 1989 the government had entered into negotiations with Inkatha based on the Indaba constitution.

One major question to emerge from this decade is how the strategy employed by Inkatha of working within the system brought the movement into direct and violent confrontation with other anti-apartheid groups. Such confrontation increased in intensity from 1985. During the Indaba negotiations Inkatha made it clear that it was not interested in having the diluted powers of the province written into a regional constitution. The extensive powers of the bantustan were extended to the regional government envisaged by the drafters of that constitution.

Frequent explanations in the media, sometimes presented as sufficient in themselves, are that people have been killing each other because of primordial ethnic sentiments (NP member of parliament Danie Schutte, later a cabinet minister, for example, told the BBC some years ago that Inkatha represented 'the Zulus', while the ANC was a 'Xhosa' organisation); or else that the violence is due to the legacy of socio-economic impoverishment and dislocation of the apartheid system, that there is a direct material base that explains people's actions.

While it is accepted that both ethnic conflict and material conditions play an important part in explaining the violence, neither offers much in their crude versions. Social deprivation has created the desperate conditions within which people act *in extremis* to ensure the basics of survival (land, housing, employment) in competition with others, but the same could be said for many other parts of South Africa that have not known violence at all or where it has taken a very different form. Ethnicity has been an essential element in the mobilisation of political constituencies, but then in a much more complex fashion than the adherents of the inter-ethnic (as primordial sentiment) conflict school would have it. What Buthelezi did, with extensive help from the king, was to argue for a 'true' version of Zuluness, from which political opponents were cast as 'traitors'.

'Working within the system' was a debated and accepted alternative to armed struggle for Inkatha. As Buthelezi told a meeting in Washington, 'We must not destroy the foundations of the post-apartheid society we long for'.[10] A year before, he had told another overseas audience, this time in Canada, that, ironically, it would be the instruments of apartheid that would be used to revive 'voices within South Africa'.[11] This position was presented in different ways, reflecting in part the complexity of politics under an extremely repressive regime: sometimes as being forced upon a reluctant participant, at other times as a chosen strategy, and at yet other moments as reflecting the destiny that Buthelezi so often sees in his life.

In 1981 Buthelezi made one of the clearest statements about this strategy, at a time when Inkatha was launched on the path of regional consolidation and after the break with the ANC, placing itself outside of the new politics of mass revolt that would sweep across the country in the 1980s. It is worth quoting at some length:

> Inkatha leaders believe that the institutional structure of South African society has to start changing soon. Underlying the institutional structure are structures of power and control. In order to understand these structures and influence them Inkatha cannot afford to be a marginal protest movement. Our policy is to become institutionalized ourselves so that we gain experience of power and that we become linked into the major structures in our society.
>
> We have shares in business, we participate on the Board of the KwaZulu Development Corporation and we are the cabinet of KwaZulu. This means that we are not so vulnerable as we might otherwise have been. We also have an ongoing interface with the Government. We are in control of whether or not Government policy succeeds or fails, at least for the group that the Government regards as KwaZulu citizens.[12]

While Inkatha did remain integrated into 'major structures of society', during the 1980s those same structures of power were crumbling. Inkatha was also becoming peripheralised from the protest movement that owed its existence to the mass politics launched by the 1973 strikes in Natal and the 1976 Soweto scholars' revolt in Soweto. Mass protest politics was soon to take organisational form in the United Democratic Front (UDF), formed in 1983, and the Congress of South African Trade Unions (COSATU), formed in 1985. It is the manner in which Inkatha became associated, often unfairly, but as often accurately, with the apartheid state that accounts for the vicious war that broke out during the 1980s. Apartheid did not have to be analysed in detail for political mobilisation against the system since it was usually painted in unproblematic extremes. International rejection quite correctly placed apartheid – the policy and its practitioners – beyond the community of nations and the values that (at least in expressed principle) informed its behaviour. At the same time the African National Congress became the international and national arbiter of who was for and who was against the regime. That Inkatha itself received approval from the ANC during the 1970s in an attempt to rectify its failure to penetrate rural areas did not matter much once the battle-lines were drawn in the 1980s. In 1985 at the Kabwe national consultative conference, ANC president Oliver Tambo admitted that the organisation had to accept a measure of reponsibility, if not in the creation, then in the direction of the Inkatha movement:

> Unfortunately we failed to mobilise our own people on the task of resurrecting Inkatha as the kind of organisation that we wanted, owing to the understandable antipathy of many of our comrades towards what they considered as working within the Bantustan system. The task of reconstituting Inkatha therefore fell on Gatsha Buthelezi himself, who then built Inkatha as a personal power base far removed from the kind of organisation we had visualized, as an instrument for the mobilisation of our people in the countryside into an active and conscious force for revolutionary change.[13]

An additional factor was the influx of new recruits into the ANC after the 1976 revolt and during the repression that followed those events. These were young people, disgruntled with the slow pace of change, and people who had experienced the bantustan leaders and their complicity in apartheid control for several years already.

There was, however, another side to the coin of working within the system. The violence that formed an essential element within ANC thinking on how change would be achieved in the country was perceived, from the Inkatha side, as aimed at 'destroying the basis of a post-apartheid society' along with the National Party government and its structures. Inkatha resented being cast in the role of 'puppet' of the apartheid regime, as just another bantustan government, along with figures such as Patrick Mphephu of Venda and the pro-apartheid Kaiser Matanzima of the Transkei. 'Ungovernability' and the creation of parallel structures rooted in 'the people' or 'the community' informed much of the anti-apartheid struggles of the second half of the 1980s. Such a strategy can be seen in the clearing of opponents from the social space controlled by any other party – housing, transport routes, schools, clinics, hospitals, and even employment, claimed for exclusive use by supporters of one political position.

'People's courts' were established to mete out justice in conditions where the policing and justice agencies of the state operating in the region had so clearly failed or acted in an extremely partisan fashion. One of the most notorious incidents of collaboration with Inkatha was the Trust Feed massacre in December 1988, where police, acting with the local Inkatha leadership, had been involved in killing 11 people at a vigil for a deceased child. The general operation of the KwaZulu Police Force, with Buthelezi as minister of police, has been similarly one-sided with many cases of biased or non-existent action reported over the years.

These 'people's courts', while often respected and directed at rehabilitation of offenders and filling in for organs of justice such as in Imbali outside Pietermaritzburg,[14] became organs advancing ANC 'organisational needs'.[15] In a number of instances, they have also become the vehicles of local terror against political opponents or those who attempted neutrality. Informal justice of this kind is most extensive in areas such as informal housing settlements which are administered by hierarchical and conservative leaders. They have often been aided though by the effective collapse of the state's policing and judicial structures.

The role of the youth, both in the excesses and generally in rejecting the conservatism of their parents, took a particularly conflictual form in Natal and KwaZulu. After Soweto 1976, and the frequent privileging of the political category of 'youth', a generation gap characterised much of the political language and action in South Africa. In Natal, however, there was a political (and cultural) home for the older generation – Inkatha. The movement stressed the respect that many felt should characterise the relationship between youth and their parents. Two early examples are the manner in which a schools boycott in KwaMashu township, north of Durban, in 1980 was crushed by 'parents' mobilised by Inkatha and the KwaZulu government.[16] The content of the 'Inkatha syllabus' for KwaZulu schools stressed the notion of respect, which in this case included allegiance to the political position of Inkatha.[17] Later the inter-generational political conflict led to the horrifying killings in mid-1993 in the Natal midlands of young people by older people. At least 18 young people were killed in incidents directly related to the issue of 'respect'. Some of the youths were accused of having insulted a local regiment by using a derogatory name for Inkatha supporters. In another case a local businessman, whose son was killed, said that his family supported the Inkatha Freedom Party (IFP) 'but my son was seen toyi-toying somewhere and people said he had become ANC.'[18] Tensions continued in the area, with warnings that parents had to bring their children to meetings called by the local chief. At a meeting in August one woman said that 'mothers whose children are traitors and support the ANC should report them to councillors'. 'Traitors' were also identified as having come from the Transkei.[19] Eighty per cent of callers to a phone-in programme on Radio Zulu at the time said that peace could only be achieved if black children returned 'to learning and go back to the African cultural tradition of *ukuhlonipha* (respect) . . .'.[20]

The political strategy followed by Inkatha during the 1980s of 'working within the system', and the policy of 'ungovernability' followed by

ANC-supporting organisations and grassroots structures, contributed to a large extent to the violence of political competition within the region. Along with material conditions and the particular form of conflictual ethnic mobilisation, this aspect serves to sketch the background to 'the killing fields of Natal'. Politically-linked violence led directly to the deaths of many people in the region:

1986 – 171
1987 – 644
1988 – 725
1989 – 728
1990 – 1784
1991 – 1190
1992 – 1735
1993 – 2145
1994 – 1105 (to May)

The figures for 1994 are broken down as follows: January, 172; February, 180; March, 311; April, 338.[21] Tens of thousands more people became refugees within the region while the destruction of property has not been possible to quantify.

POLITICS OF THE 1990S

The figures above indicate a horrifying increase in the number of deaths related to political conflict since the early outbreaks in the mid-1980s. In 1990 deaths more than doubled, and by 1993 the death toll stood at three times the number of people killed four years earlier. In February 1990 president F.W. de Klerk announced the unbanning of political organisations and the release of political prisoners. At the end of April 1994 all South Africans had their first opportunity to cast votes for the same government. After a chaotic few days the process had been completed to the satisfaction of the Independent Electoral Commission (IEC), and was declared 'substantially free and fair'. In Natal and KwaZulu, however, doubt was immediately cast over this rather loose stamp of approval. In Natal more than 300 people were killed in the election month.

The IFP's participation in the elections came at the last moment, after a tense and costly process that stretched throughout the 1990s. One of its major themes was the extensive use of the notion of 'the Zulu kingdom' in formulating political demands, and consolidating political power outside of the negotiations process. There are several essential elements to the notion of the 'Zulu kingdom': first, the Zulu king, Goodwill Zwelithini, defeated by Buthelezi after a long and intense struggle during the 1970s, but playing a central ideological role during the 1980s to give legitimacy to Buthelezi's version of Zulu ethnic identity and to Buthelezi himself; second, Buthelezi as chief, and as 'traditional prime minister of the kingdom of KwaZulu'; third, a territory ('the Zulu kingdom'), the boundaries of which were never clearly stipulated in the secessionist calls but including most, if not all, of the present KZN province; fourth, a government of the Zulu people, which ironically came to be equated with the apartheid-created KwaZulu Legislative Assembly; and, fifth, the chiefs and their subordinate officials.

When the first talks got under way as the Convention for a Democratic SA (CODESA) in December 1991, Buthelezi was absent and the IFP (Inkatha Freedom Party) became a party as opposed to being simply a movement in December 1990, under the leadership of Dr Frank Mdlalose. Buthelezi played on the distinction between the IFP, which he claimed was a national non-racial body, and the 'Zulu nation', when he refused to attend. He said that his king, monarch of the largest 'nation' in South Africa, had been 'snubbed' in not being invited. Buthelezi subsequently never attended the formal negotiations, even though he was central to a parallel process of political gamesmanship. The IFP delegation immediately gave notice of a related strategy when it refused to endorse the first CODESA declaration in that its commitment to 'an undivided South Africa, with one nation, would undermine federal options'.[22] Buthelezi warned that if significant sectors of the population were ignored 'the activities of RENAMO [in Mozambique] and UNITA [in Angola] would look like child's play'.[23] Such threats of further violence by Buthelezi became a common occurrence during the 1990s.[24]

In 1992 CODESA 2 met to continue the process towards a new constitution. CODESA 2 came to a halt in June after the Boipatong massacre on 17 June when the ANC said that it would return to mass action. In 1994 IFP-supporting hostel dwellers were found guilty of the massacre but the police were exonerated. In December 1992 the KwaZulu Legislative Assembly adopted yet another proposed constitution for the region and threatened to take it to a regional referendum, as had been suggested with the 1986 Indaba constitution.[25] This constitution disappeared, except for a few references by Buthelezi.

The process resumed in March 1993, but some parties, including the IFP and the KwaZulu administration (which had joined in 1993), walked out after the date for the elections was agreed upon under the principle of 'sufficient consensus' despite the fact that several participants had not supported the date. The IFP took the issue of 'sufficient consensus' to the supreme court but lost the case in September 1993. The walk-out led to the formation of the Freedom Alliance (an odd mix of bantustan parties and governments, and the white right). The most important principles that held them together were that there should be recognition of the right of 'peoples' of South Africa to self-determination, and that the first elections should take place after a new constitution had been negotiated. In December 1993 the transitional constitution, along with a list of 'principles' that would bind the constituent assembly, and a bill of rights, was agreed upon by the remaining 21 negotiating parties.[26]

In early 1994 the direction of the Inkatha strategy was confirmed by the clear indication that king Goodwill was not to be wooed away from Buthelezi before the election. On 14 February some 40 000 Zulus gathered in a sports stadium and then marched into Durban city centre to support their king in a meeting with De Klerk. Buthelezi was also there, confirming the demand from king Goodwill that autonomy (*secession* was the word used for the first time) be granted to the province of Natal (restoration of the Zulu kingdom as it was in 1834 was demanded). The day before, at an Inkatha Youth Brigade gathering, Buthelezi had called for ethnic groups to stand together in South Africa; he had called specifically on Tswanas and Afrikaners, referring to two of his staunchest allies in the Freedom Alliance.

In April there was another attempt to gain the participation of the IFP. In the Transvaal bushveld, at a game camp at Skukuza, the ANC the government and the IFP met, along with king Goodwill. The ANC offered the king considerable symbolic relevance in the region (and even in South Africa). In seven main clauses and many sub-clauses, following on a preamble that acknowledged the 'historic role played by the King, the Royal House of kwaZulu and their forebears in the struggle against colonialism and apartheid and in the promotion of the national objective of an independent, unfragmented, democratic, non-racial and non-sexist South Africa', the ANC spelt out its position.[27] This remarkable statement could be questioned on several levels, not least the implicit acceptance of the patriarchal order that the king stood for, and the fragmentation that had underpinned his interventions in politics. The ANC had shown over the months that they were willing to compromise several other principles in their attempt to separate the king from Buthelezi. Even SA Communist Party executive members in the region filled their appeals with calls to 'the Zulu people' and 'His Majesty' whose 'office' was being 'dragged . . . into party political battles'.[28]

What the ANC document at Skukukza did was to define in specific detail what the King would be able to do, and what not. For example, it intended largely 'ceremonial and traditional powers and prerogatives' for the monarch. Importantly it also specified that the elected 'Premier of the Province of kwaZulu/Natal', rather than the 'traditional prime minister' (the role Buthelezi claimed), should serve on the advisory 'Royal Council'.[29] The document unambiguously supported the continuation of a role for 'all traditional leaders and authorities' in the province. Whereupon the king reminded the ANC, in a document submitted to the meeting of the royal regiments (the *amabutho*),[30] that the ANC document offered him a 'Royal Constabulary', intended to be part of the 'kwaZulu/Natal policing authority'. This level of detail Buthelezi and the IFP could not permit.

What they did formally accept 11 days later, as sufficient conditions for entering the elections, was a recognition of the 'Zulu kingdom' in the constitutional principles and a return to the mediation process, now to give content to the much vaguer notion of 'the kingdom'. The purpose of this second round of mediation was to differ somewhat from what had been agreed to at a meeting between the ANC and the IFP in Durban in March 1994,[31] and failed in April when the election date was excluded from the process. The commitment to the first mediation process by the ANC had been, I would argue, a tactical mistake as it made them partners in the obvious delaying tactics intended by Inkatha through the mediation process. When it came to the process itself, with mediators such as Henry Kissinger and Lord Carrington already present, the exclusion of the election date (argued by the IFP to have been a breach of faith by the ANC) brought the attempt to an abrupt halt.

Whether it was then 'an act of God'; the equally mysterious involvement of 'the African mind' as expressed by the curious Professor Washington Okumu (one of the mediators); a range of pressures including the threat of total ostracism from the new South Africa; a realisation by Inkatha leaders that there was another way in which a 'traditional' power centre could be confirmed (but at a later date); or, as some commentators have speculated, that the IFP had in any case had a plan of staying out as long as possible; or a combination of reasons, is still not entirely clear. However, the IFP agreed (on 19 April 1994) to participate in the elections. Along with 'the kingdom' it gained an acceptance of the principle of 'assymetry' (as Buthelezi called it), namely the right of regions to write different constitutions.[32] Through mediation after the election Buthelezi could not get less than what was offered at Skukuza and, if he gained considerable electoral support, he could get much more. However, his future was now even more firmly linked to the king.

It is the king who bestows legitimacy on the various elements within the 'traditionalist' platform that Buthelezi had built up during the 1980s, but especially during the 1990s. The ANC acknowledged, and accepted, the power of the monarch in their 'Skukuza document' when they proposed that the king install chiefs, and accepted his position over 'the Zulu people' – a rather problematic notion that holds very wide and uncritical sway in the most unexpected quarters, ranging from *Time Magazine* to the SACP. The ANC promised that Goodwill Zwelithini and the royal house 'shall have and enjoy a place suitable for persons in their regal position'.[33]

The acceptance by all major political parties of the king's ceremonial and ideological legitimacy has enormous implications on levels that are not being addressed at present. The Congress of Traditional Leaders of South Africa (Contralesa), for example, welcomed the decision to accept the Zulu king and called for the further acknowledgement of six other monarchies in other regions of South Africa. In regions such as the Eastern Cape, where there were six 'monarchs', they could rotate the office they suggested.[34] Contralesa, while 'officially non-aligned', was formed in 1990 with the specific intention of providing an organisational home for 'traditional authority' members who wished to separate themselves from apartheid.[35] The body, as expected, has been in conflict with Buthelezi and the KLA since its inception as chiefs have played such a central role in Inkatha organisational strategy and are at the core of 'the Zulu kingdom'. Chief Mhlabunzima Maphumulo, a prominent member of Contralesa in Natal, was murdered in February 1991. The same chief had also played a role in the state-supported resistance to Buthelezi in the 1970s, giving some credibility to Buthelezi's recent claim that some of the same people who had been involved then were now aligning themselves with the ANC.

The issue of the land grant is another case in point – the KLA quietly signed over all communal land in KwaZulu to the trusteeship of the king a few days before the elections, a move that also received the necessary central government approval through a signature by president F.W. de Klerk. While the ANC followed newspaper opinion in condemning the action, officials were not confident in their rejection. Recently it was accepted by a committee appointed by the new government that the move was proper and that only the details had to be defined in new legislation. Said Land Affairs minister Derek Hanekom, 'The intention [of the legislation] was to create a mechanism to preserve tribal interests in the land, within the present framework of traditional authority structures'.[36] Journalist Donna Hornby caught the essence of the deal, but the aspect that was not addressed by the ANC statement, in an article entitled 'Impact of the KwaZulu Land Issue'.[37]

The KwaZulu land deal has created a twin power system in KwaZulu/ Natal. The one is hereditary and feudal and rests on patronage. The other is modern, democratic and rests on regular elections. One of the main characteristics of the tribal system of authority is communal land tenure. Land control ultimately resides with the king but is delegated to the king's representatives: the chiefs, indunas and councillors.

It is little wonder then that both the IFP and the ANC should be involved in accusations and counter-accusations of 'improperly' using the king. It seems that, as in the conflict in the 1970s, Buthelezi is again in a struggle with the central government over who should define 'traditional authority'. ANC southern Natal media officer Dumisani Makhaye referred rather ironically, if we keep in mind the ANC government's action, to the 1970s conflict that had, in his words, not been forgotten by 'proud Zulus'.[38] What he neglected to mention was that the king was then being manipulated by the apartheid state.

THE RESULTS

Before the election several opinion polls were conducted. Beyond the usual difficulties with such research in South Africa (such as the high levels of illiteracy, extreme political divisions, fear, inaccessibility of rural people, and a state of emergency in Natal and KwaZulu), pollsters also had to contend with the facts that these were the first democratic elections for most of the population and that nobody really had an accurate idea of the demography of the country – how many people there were, how old they were, and where they lived. However, the polls make for interesting retrospective reading. In March an SABC-commissioned survey found that in Natal/KwaZulu the king was the most popular person to run the province, with Nelson Mandela coming second, Buthelezi third and De Klerk fourth. The ANC candidate for regional premiership, Jacob Zuma, achieved a negative rating from nearly half the sample.[39]

As for party support, this was obviously confused by the boycott stance of the IFP during the run-up. A Markinor poll found that by March 1994 support for the ANC in the region had fallen from 40.9 per cent in November 1993, to 32.3 per cent. Voters said that they would support the NP if the IFP did not participate, giving that party 29.9 per cent of the vote (up from 21 per cent in November), while the Democratic Party (DP) was up from 3.5 per cent to 6.4 per cent. The same research predicted that if the IFP had agreed to participate at that stage it would have enjoyed equal support with the ANC.[40] A report on a survey for the Institute for Multi-Party Democracy (IMPD), released on the same day, gave the IFP 24.8 per cent of support against the ANC's 50.3 per cent.[41]

An important finding, with implications for both the boycott as well as a subsequent participation position by the IFP, came from an earlier IMPD survey. Here it was found that a disturbing 49 per cent of black respondents said they lived in areas where only one party was dominant.[42] This, read along with other findings that indicated a high level of intolerance of opposing views and the non-acceptance of the right of opposing parties to hold meetings, as well as a rejection by four out of ten ANC supporters of a result that did not favour their party, seemed to indicate possible increased levels of violence during the elections.[43] A characteristic of the violence in Natal and KwaZulu has been the 'cleansing' of areas and institutions (especially schools) of supporters of opposing parties.[44] If the IFP had continued with its non-participation, any person voting in certain areas would have been visibly breaking the boycott. Similarly, people who might have decided not to vote, or had stayed away for any other reason, would potentially have been cast as IFP supporters on election day. At least this element was removed from the days of voting and they passed relatively peacefully, with elation and perseverance under the chaotic conditions the most frequent feelings reported.

The results gave an absolute majority to the IFP. The vote was immediately contested by the ANC's Harry Gwala and Dumisani Makhaye (leaders of the midlands and southern Natal regions respectively). Makhaye claimed that the elections in the province had been fraudulent and the results would rest on the consciences of IEC leaders. 'All the evidence' he claimed 'is of massive rigging in terms of millions [sic] . . . even the IFP knows it didn't win Natal'.[45] By the weekend following the release of the results the ANC regional leaders were reported to have met in 'crisis session' and said they rejected the outcome of the regional election and had handed the matter over to their lawyers as part of a concerted campaign to have the election restaged.[46] After apparent pressure from ANC national leadership, the region decided to abandon the court action.

Interestingly, Buthelezi also cast doubt on the results, claiming 'malpractices . . . which robbed us of many votes'.[47] Since the results were announced there have been repeated delays in setting in place the provincial government and conflict continued between the members elected from the IFP and the ANC lists, around issues such as the location of departments (Ulundi or Pietermaritzburg); the future capital (the same centres); the portfolios allocated to the ANC in the provincial government of unity; the role of the king; and the role, in the province, of Buthelezi who was placed on the national list in the proportional vote system and is now minister of home affairs in the national cabinet.

Of the votes cast, after an extremely chaotic process that was extended for a fourth day, and counted after an equally long and disputed process where contested ballots were not considered, the IFP won 50.3 per cent, or 1 844 070 votes (41 of the 81 seats in the provincial parliament); the ANC 32.2 per cent (26 seats); the NP 11.2 per cent (nine seats); the DP 2.2 per cent (two seats); while one seat went to each of the Minority Front, the Pan Africanist Congress and the African Christian Democratic Party.

At the national level the IFP was only able to win 2 058 000 votes. Ninety per cent of the votes came from the region in which it had ensconced itself during the nearly 20 years of its existence. At provincial level, outside of KZN, the IFP managed to win seats only in the PWV province (three). Its 10.5 per cent of the national vote did give it 43 seats in the national assembly. The most extensive claims and evidence of irregularities came from Natal and KwaZulu. However, with the exclusion of many (if not most) of the contested votes it is difficult to see how the ANC could claim to have won in the region. What is probably correctly in dispute is the absolute majority that the IFP enjoys. To understand the ANC defeat would need an investigation of the distribution of votes cast for the parties; of the domination that Inkatha achieved over rural areas; of the regionally-specific strategies followed by ANC supporters; and of the politics of the UDF and of COSATU (and before that of the Federation of South African Trade Unions) during the 1980s. Accusations of intimidation and voting irregularities do not provide the full picture.

CONCLUSION

The new Province of KwaZulu Natal is not simply the old apartheid order in new guise. What Buthelezi and his backers attempted to establish during the 1980s – the wider notion of region – has now in part been ensured through the new form, the province of KwaZulu Natal. There are many similarities, but there are also some important differences. With the bantustan finally goes the ethnic curtain behind which certain members of the Zulu trading class, as well as civil servants, had been protected. The new ruling party in KZN will be subject to a much wider range of pressures and will also have greater resources at its disposal.

What does an Inkatha victory mean? There are some new problems that are already visible and others that remain from the old order. Many of these will affect the next elections set for 1999. First, it is difficult to see, considering the history of conflict in the region, how any result, except an overwhelming ANC victory, could have resolved tensions in the short-term. The results will probably continue to be undermined provincially, despite acceptance at national level after the IEC imprimatur. Therefore, as long as the democratic process remains open to question, the tendency that became practice in the past, to resort to violence, will remain in some communities. The question of legitimacy will hang over issues that are far removed from the specific party in power. KZN transport minister in KZN, the ANC's S'bu Ndebele may not have intended it that way, but said that, 'if we were not able to reach an agreement [on the issue of where the capital should be] it would have meant that Natal was descending to anarchy. The problems, if they had worsened, would have started violence and this province would have become ungovernable'.[48] Second, the province will no doubt continue with the same civil servants, as is the case elsewhere, where efforts are being made to allay the fears of such personnel. What it does mean in KZN is that the conflict between teachers, nurses and other professionals and the 'new' government will continue. The ANC had drawn considerable support from this class, especially in the urban areas where its strength lay. The ANC may well try to use these supporters to ensure a measure of power beyond that given by the seats won in the provincial parliament. Strikes in the health care sector during the past few months give warning of what may continue.

Third, the economic policy to be followed in the KZN may well conflict with the redistributive intent of the *Reconstruction and Development Plan* (RDP). It is not all that clear whether all the grand plans and promises made during the election lead-up can be executed. It may, therefore, be tempting for the central government to blame recalcitrant provincial governments, such as Western Province (NP), and KZN (IFP), for the failure or delays in implementation. There is another dimension, one that I have alluded to, namely that the IFP government will continue to follow an anti-union policy or a policy that discriminates against unions it does not control. The intention may be to offer 'disciplined' cheap labour to enable rapid employment creation and economic growth, as measured by investment.

Now, with its extended powers, the IFP has brought other racialised categories from the old order into class politics directed at the new regional political centre. Inkatha had enjoyed the support of a large number of black traders and influential large-scale business in Natal and KwaZulu. Within the first few weeks after the elections, even before powers had been devolved formally to the province, certain business sectors moved to establish new lines of communication and favour. To take one example, a body called the Pakistan Family Welfare Association (PFWA) protested at the deportation of two 'illegal Muslim immigrants from India' who had been employed in a Durban textile firm. The workers involved said they had entered South Africa through the Transkei and had been working in Durban for two years. The businessmen employed foreign cheap labour, especially immigrants who guaranteed they would not join trade unions or complain at their treatment by officials. These employers and Dr Hoosen of the PFWA 'confirmed a meeting with Home Affairs Minister Dr Mangosuthu Buthelezi to request the relaxation of immigration laws with a view to securing cheap foreign labour'.[49] The same day it was reported that the Islamic Business Development Corporation Ltd had invited king Goodwill to a private dinner, which was 'crucial as businessmen were poised to discuss the possibility of lowering import/export tariffs, relaxing immigration laws with a view to securing cheap foreign labour and addressing the issue of unemployment'. They had also invited Buthelezi and provincial premier Mdlalose.[50]

Fourth, on the political level the issue of the separation of powers between the province and the central government is the most immediate point of contention. The extreme version of that relationship was the threat of secession made by the king. Buthelezi has always argued for a strongly federal system, going back to the early 1970s. The role of the king, and the package that accompanies the notion of the Zulu kingdom, is still unresolved. Some form of mediation still remains a possibility on this issue, especially as Buthelezi has stressed that if the Constitutional Assembly got started without such mediation 'it would be impossible to then have international mediation. We most definitely still want that mediation'.[51]

If the mediation process continues then another point of conflict will have been resurrected. Buthelezi now heads the printed versions of his speeches with the titles 'President of the IFP, Minister of Home Affairs and Traditional Prime Minister of the Kingdom of KwaZulu'. Previously he had been 'Chief Minister of KwaZulu' rather than the last-mentioned appellation. He has certainly not relinquished this alternative power base and has claimed the 'traditional' role on the grounds that he was not relinquishing his 'traditional role and function of traditional Prime Minister to His Majesty the King and the Kingdom of KwaZulu which has always been a distinct position and separate from that of the Chief Minister (of KwaZulu)'.[52]

A wild card could have been introduced into this presentation of Buthelezi as 'traditional prime minister' in that the ANC government, much like the NP government in the 1970s, is desperately wooing the king away from the IFP president. The rumours of splits, of deals, of divisions is a reminder of the centrality given to the version of 'tradition' which pivoted on the role of the king two decades ago. The king could, or has already (according to the ANC), decided to divorce his fortune (literally) from the largesse of Buthelezi. If he did so it would remove the foundations of part of the edifice of the Zulu kingdom, most importantly of the legitimisation of Buthelezi as 'traditional prime minister'. Such a move could either escalate the intensity of specifically-Zulu politics with further opportunities for violence, or it could leave the IFP simply with their command over the elected bodies of the province of KZN. The latter situation is unlikely. It is more in keeping with Buthelezi's political style to 'remove' the king's threat in some way, as he had done once before, constitutionally and politically, during the 1970s. He is much more intertwined in Zulu politics and intrigue than the ANC leadership is, and may well have points of leverage that they do not have.

Fifth, and related to the previous point, there is little doubt that the IFP and Buthelezi will continue to mobilise on the basis of ethnicity – possibly through a new body that has been mentioned, which appears to bear some resemblance to Inkatha as it was intended in 1975. The message from the election was unambiguous: the IFP remains an ethnically and regionally bound party. There is absolutely no chance that the IFP will feature any more strongly on the national level in 1999. The province will, therefore, see another period of regional consolidation.

Finally, the region may simply be paralysed during the period to 1999 through a range of struggles, some of which are referred to above. In conflict over the devolution of power ANC followers and provincial structures may well decide to continue with a policy of 'ungovernability' where a number of arenas are chosen to confront the provincial government. These could range from the location of the capital or departments, to the role of the police, to economic policy, to continuing ground-level violence. An increasingly repressive IFP could well counter such a strategy and itself build or strengthen the structures, particularly those around the notion of the kingdom, to ensure electoral victory in 1999 as it had in 1994. Both parties have gained through the elections. The IFP has gained acceptance for the notion of the Zulu kingdom, is now the legitimately chosen government in a process that carried the stamp of 'substantially free and fair', and has gained control over the region it had tried to establish during the 1980s. The provincial ANC, on the other hand, might have lost the elections and been forced into accepting a process that it claims, with considerable justification, was anything but free and fair, but it has gained the support of a sympathetic government in Pretoria.

NOTES

1. These figures were supplied on request by the SA Institute of Race Relations, May 1994.
2. Paul Forsyth and Gerhard Mare, 'Natal in the New South Africa' in Glenn Mos and Ingrid Obery (eds), *South African Review 6: from 'Red Friday' to CODESA* (Johannesburg: Ravan Press, 1992).
3. SAIRR, *Race Relations Survey, 1978*, pp. 353–4.
4. Gerhard Mare and Georgina Hamilton, *An Appetite for Power: Buthelezi's Inkatha and South Africa* (Bloomington and Indianapolis: Indiana University Press, and Johannesburg: Ravan Press, 1987), pp. 136–49.
5. E.J. Langner, 'The Founding and development of Inkatha Yenkululeko Yesiziwe', M.A. Diss., University of South Africa, 1983, p. 198.
6. Typescript of Buthelezi Speech, 20 June 1980.
7. G. Mare, 'Inkathagate Revisited', *Southern African Report*, 7, 2 (1991).
8. See Hugh Murray (ed.), *Indaba* (a publication of the journal *Leadership*: 1987); Karin Roberts and Grahame Howe (eds), *New Frontiers: the KwaZulu/ Natal debates* (Johannesburg: SAIRR, 1987).
9. South African Institute of Race Relations, *Race Relations Survey 1984* (Johannesburg: SAIRR, 1984), p. xvii.
10. *The Star*, 9 November 1976.
11. *The Star*, 6 November 1975.
12. *The Sowetan*, 11 August 1981.
13. Quoted in Mzala, *Gatsha Buthelezi: Chief With a Double Agenda* (London: Zed Press, 1988), p. 124.
14. Daniel Nina, 'Popular Justice and Civil Society in Transition: a Report from the "Front Line" – Natal', *Transformation*, 21 (1993), 59–60.
15. *Ibid.*, p. 61.
16. Mare and Hamilton, *op. cit.*, pp. 186–7.
17. Praisley Mdluli (Blake Nzimande), Ubuntu-Botho: 'Inkatha's "people's education"', *Transformation*, 5, 1987; Gerhard Mare, 'Education in a liberated zone: Inkatha and education in Kwazulu', *Critical Arts*, 4, 4–5 (1988/9).
18. *Natal Witness*, 10 June 1993.
19. *Natal Witness*, 9 August 1993.
20. *Natal Witness*, 12 August 1993; also see Catherine Campbell, Gerhard Mare and Cherryl Walker, 'Evidence for an Ethnic Identity in the Life Histories of Zulu Speaking Durban Township Residents', paper presented to African Studies Seminar, University of Natal, Durban, 1993, p. 20.
21. Figures supplied on request by the Conflict Trends In Natal Project, University of Natal, Durban; also Human Rights Commission of SA, 'Natal's Total Onslaught', mimeo, 1994.
22. SAIRR, *Race Relations Survey*, 1991/2, il.
23. *Ibid.*, liii.
24. See, for example, *Natal Witness Echo*, 2 December 1993.
25. SAIRR, 1992/3: 39–40.
26. J.C. Bekker and G. Carpenter, *Butterworths Selection of Statutes Constitutional Law* (Durban: Butterworths, 1994).

27.   African National Congress, *Agreement between the African National Congress and the Royal House of Kwazulu* ('Skukuza document'), 8 April 1994, p. 1.
28.   Blade Nzimande in *Natal Witness*, 21 December 1993.
29.   'Skukuza document', p. 3.
30.   King Goodwill, 'Presentation by His Majesty King Zwelithini Goodwill ka Bhekuzulu ... to Mr Nelson Mandela', 8 April 1994, p. 5.
31.   *Natal Witness*, 23 March 1994.
32.   Buthelezi Statement, 19 April 1994.
33.   'Skukuza document', p. 4.
34.   *Natal Witness*, 14 April 1994.
35.   Anton Harber and Barbara Ludman (eds), *A-Z of South African Politics: the essential handbook* (Harmondsworth: Penguin Books, 1994), p. 182.
36.   *Daily News*, 16 June 1994.
37.   *Natal Witness*, 24 May 1994.
38.   *Natal Witness*, 13 April 1994.
39.   *Daily News*, 4 March 1994.
40.   *Sunday Times* (Johannesburg), 3 April 1994.
41.   *Sunday Tribune*, 3 April 1994.
42.   *Daily News*, 24 March 1994.
43.   *Sunday Tribune*, 8 August 1993.
44.   For an early indication of this strategy, see William Kentridge, *An Unofficial War: Inside the Conflict in Pietermaritzburg* (Cape Town: David Philip, 1990).
45.   *Natal on Saturday*, 7 May 1994.
46.   *Sunday Tribune*, 8 May 1994.
47.   *Daily News*, 22 June 1994.
48.   *Daily News*, 22 June 1994.
49.   *Sunday Tribune Herald*, 29 May 1994.
50.   *Ibid.*
51.   *Daily News*, 22 June 1994. [Since Dr Mare wrote this, Gatsha Buthelezi withdrew his IFP members from the South African parliament in February 1995 in protest at the failure of the government to agree to international mediation on the issue –Editor.]
52.   Buthelezi Speech, 20 May 1994.

3 Apartheid, the State and the Reconstruction of the Political System
Paul B. Rich

THE PROBLEM OF THE STATE

Analysts of South African politics and society have been reluctant to focus upon the role of the state despite the fact that the April election was largely about who was to take control of it. It is true that the political transition that has been occurring since 1990 represents a wide ranging process of political mobilisation that, after decades of conflict and repression, pushed the white state in February 1990 into a path of political negotiation. However, the new interim constitution that was negotiated between the NP and ANC was also a device for the transfer of power from a white settler state to a new ruling group made up of a coalition of different parties. This transfer was not a colonial one whereby a European metropole handed over power to a new nationalist regime, for it occurred within the existing sovereign state structure of South Africa that had been created in 1910. If a revolution has been occurring in South Africa, it is largely one within juridical and constitutional means and has avoided the breakdown of state structures that has happened in some other African societies such as Mozambique and Angola. It seems particularly relevant therefore to ask what sort of state system has facilitated this political transition and what will be its role and influence on the programme of reconstruction of the new South African government.

What first of all *is* the state? It is clearly a contested concept that does not easily produce agreement. At the heart of any theory of the state lies the notion of power, though analysts have disputed the degree to which this can be brought under check through the operation of law and ethics. For Weberians the state has been traditionally conceived in terms of the monopoly of the legitimate use of force, anchoring it in a tradition of political thought which emphasises how the state is bound by some form of contract with those over whom power is exercised.

Some scholars, however, such as Charles Tilly, have suggested that the state needs to be seen, along with war making, as simply another form of organised crime rendering the idea of a social contract between rulers and ruled nothing less than a fiction.[1] Such an apparently harsh conception of state power has never been easily accepted by political scientists reared in the Anglo-Saxon tradition where there is no tradition of the state in the legal system. Some have questioned whether the 'state' as such really exists and have argued that it is largely the creation of philosophers. What really exists for this group of sceptics is human organisation binding together individuals in a complex system of relationships.[2]

The cynics and the sceptics are unlikely to agree on the nature of the state. The state concept still has considerable use for political analysts, though, since ideas about the state organise the perceptions not only of political decision-makers but of opposition movements as well. In so far as political activists *think* of themselves as participating in activities centred upon the state, the idea of the state acquires a material force. The state needs to be distinguished from ruling regimes. Both 'regime' on the one hand and 'state' on the other are abstract notions which provide focus to political activity. Regimes change while state stuctures, short of revolutionary transformation, continue; regimes can make some impact on the nature of the state, but states in turn extert subtle influences on ruling regimes.

This chapter will explore the nature of the state in South African politics as well as how it has been understood by political analysts. It is divided into four main sections. The first section examines the way that the state has been analysed in South African academic research before the focus moves, in the second section, to the transformation of the state under the regimes of P.W. Botha and F.W. de Klerk (1978–94). The third section outlines the sort of political strategies open to the new regime as it seeks to consolidate its power over the state while the final section looks at four possible models for the South African state to evolve towards in the medium to longer term.

The State in South African Research

Debates between liberals and Marxists in the 1970s and 1980s were orientated to the operation of class and ethnic dynamics within South African society. With a few notable exceptions, they generally ignored the role of the state in favour of sub-state agents and societal forces. The often heated academic debate on South African political economy tended to marginalise the role of the state in South African politics and history despite considerable comparative evidence to suggest that it has played a major role in peripheral or 'backward' societies initiating a process of industrialisation.[3]

Liberals, until at least the late 1960s, tended to conceive of the state in terms of a frontier thesis developed by such scholars as C.W. de Kiewiet, I.D. MacCrone and Eric Walker. According to this view the South African state was captured from the time of Union in 1910 by an Afrikaner nationalist political oligarchy whose mind-set had been already fixed by generations of 'frontier wars' with African tribes stretching back to the pre-industrial past. Many liberals continued to see the state standing against the forces of industrialisation, though they hoped that in time it would be forced by the exigencies of economic change to abandon its ideology of racial segregation for one favouring the creation of a common multi-racial society.[4]

By contrast, Marxists of the revisionist school that emerged in the 1970s saw the South African state as the instrument of a capitalist class. The cheap labour thesis of Wolpe, Legassick, Johnston and Trapido saw the state developing the apartheid system as a means for the super-exploitation of African labour through the subsistence economies of the reserves and Homelands. In its original form, the revisionists saw apartheid ideology as largely reflecting the interests of capital, particularly mining capital, though some scholars such as Dan O'Meara began refining this by pointing out that the Nationalist party regime that captured control of the state in 1948 was an alliance of the white working class, the white petty bourgeoisie and Afrikaner farmers.[5] This conception ascribed little importance either to the class of state bureaucrats on the Nationalist party or to the development of subsequent state policy.

For all its weaknesses, the Marxist school did encourage a debate on the nature of the South African state, reflecting a general resurgence of academic interest in the late 1970s and early 1980s for 'bringing the state back in' to social and political research.[6] One notable landmark in this respect was Stanley B. Greenberg's comparative study *Race and State in Capitalist Development* (1980) which examines the political trajectory of the American South, South Africa, Israel and Northern Ireland under the impact of capitalist industrialisation. Greenberg argued that the South African state intensified racial cleavages during the initial phase of industrialisation lasting from approximately 1890 to 1960. After this time the state came under growing capitalist pressure to liberalise its policies as these appeared increasingly to conflict with market imperatives as well as rising black political demands. State officials found themselves as a result confronting a 'crisis of hegemony' in which they were forced to move to adopt policies that would progressively deracialise the society.[7]

Greenberg's work has widened the intellectual context in which South African state power can be examined, though it tends to overlook the pressure exerted from opposition movements and sees race rather than the state as the ultimate defining variable of South African politics and economy. The state, he wrote, 'reflected the racial and political climate necessary to class formation but, in turn, began representing and managing the increasing formalisation of racial lines'.[8] Greenberg concluded that the South African state developed a 'Bonapartist' political autonomy as a 'racial state', making it qualitatively different to the state models derived from the Western European experience.[9] The thesis relies heavily on the assumption that the South African state intensified racial cleavages in the countryside as part of a 'Prussian Path' of capitalist industrialisation and labour-repressive agriculture, though critics have pointed to the ambiguous historical evidence to support this.[10] Tim Keegan has suggested that state action in South Africa was not directed towards a coherent strategy of reconstructing rural social relations in the longer-term interests of industrialisation and was frequently eclipsed by non-state processes of investment by private entrepreneurs.[11]

Greenberg's initial conceptualisation of the state in South Africa was rather economistic and overlooked the bureaucratic struggles within the state, though he sought to rectify this in later work. Saul Dubow, by contrast, has shown the importance of the rivalry in the inter-war years between the Justice and Native Affairs Departments (NAD) in shaping policies of segregation. The passage of the 1927 Native Administration Act, making the Governor General the Supreme Chief of all Africans in what was then the Union of South Africa, signified the steady emergence of the NAD as the premier organ of the state dealing with the management and control of the African population. In the years up to 1948 the NAD implemented a segregationist programme that led to differential sovereignty inside South Africa, though never an actual fissuring of the state machinery itself. South African policy was a variant of indirect rule that was common elsewhere at this time in colonial Africa and the real drive to devolve power on chiefs and tribal authorities only took place in earnest after the advent of the Nationalist government in 1948.[12]

The South African state's role in the implementation of apartheid from the early 1950s to the late 1970s has also led to some contention among historians and political analysts. Some liberal scholars have moved beyond the frontier thesis into a broader interpretation of apartheid as an example of a modern ideological design that was considerably shaped by its grand master, H.F. Verwoerd. Henry Kenny, for instance, has argued that Verwoerd was a major figure in driving the state bureaucracy into fulfilling the vision of Afrikaner ethnic domination rather than the needs of the economy. This interpretation stresses the autonomy of apartheid ideology and its ability to determine policy over and above the rationality of the market place.[13]

This ideological interpretation of apartheid has come in for some important recent criticism from radical analysts. Saul Dubow has pointed out that Afrikaner racial ideology was by no means so rigid as has often been supposed and Afrikaner intellectuals rationalised racial separation on a series of scientific, cultural and language grounds that proved to be quite fluid.[14] Likewise, Roberta Balstad Miller has seen Verwoerd as less an ideological zealot than an ambitious politician prepared to trim with the prevailing wind. After an early academic career when he had little to say about racial segregation, Verwoerd got increasingly involved in Afrikaner nationalist politics after he became editor of *Die Transvaler* in 1937 and his ideological vision of apartheid was largely imbibed from wider debates in the Broederbond.[15]

Neither the liberal nor the revisionist school has looked in detail at the actual working of the state bureaucracy during the period of apartheid construction, which appears to fit neither historical interpretation exactly. Deborah Posel has shown, though, in her important study *The Making of Apartheid, 1948–1961*, that the apartheid state was divided between pragmatists and hardliners, or what she terms 'visionaries', linked to bodies like the South African Bureau of Racial Affairs (SABRA). The former wanted to compromise with the demands of industrialists and accept the permanency for the time being of urban blacks while the latter wanted to implement rigid urban segregation that excluded all blacks from urban areas except as units of labour. During the 1950s and 1960s the Native Affairs Department (renamed the Bantu Affairs Department in 1958) became a premier arm of the state in the implementation of the apartheid doctrine. The party ideologists failed to turn it into a Leninist instrument to fulfil party dogma; Afrikaner industrialists and agriculturalists proved strong enough to resist many of the visionaries' plans despite the fact that they did not have a hegemonic position at this stage within either the NP or the NAD.[16] The NP in the early 1950s did not yet have a dominating control of parliament or a fully trained class of Afrikaner bureaucrats to implement the policy. It was sensitive to political pressure to proceed slowly and proved reluctant to accede to the request by the SABRA-dominated Tomlinson Commission in 1955 to spend £30 million over ten years to create 50 000 new jobs in the African reserves.

In the wake of Sharpeville in 1960 ideological and security issues came increasingly to the fore and the state went into a second phase of apartheid social engineering based on development of the Homelands. The BAD became more responsive to the demands from the SABRA visionaries and increasingly rigid in its implementation of influx control, despite opposition from industrialists and urban municipalities. This process was accompanied

by a restructuring of the state as it centralised control through new structures such as labour bureaux and urban administration boards. This did not
occur without political divisions and Posel has concluded that 'if the construction of Apartheid depended centrally on the restructuring of the state,
it was also profoundly shaped by the cleavages and struggles within the
state spawned by this restructuring'.[17]

Posel's study is a good example of what occurs when the state is
brought back in as an actor into the study of South African politics. Though
her study finishes in 1961, her approach can be used to explain some later
developments in policy, though any interpretations of these must be provisional until the state archives are opened. After John Vorster succeeded
Verwoerd in 1966 there was a steady if rather uneven *verligte* (enlightened)
permeation of state policy. In some areas of the Bantu Affairs bureaucracy
policy remained quite rigid until the 1970s: in 1971, for example, the Bantu
Homelands Citizenship Act was passed, beginning the process of dispos-
sessing blacks of South African citizenship. In the wake of the 1973 Durban
strikes, however, the bureaucracy started to come under more concerted
pressure from *verligte* Afrikaners anxious for a rethink on some of the
basic trajectories of apartheid policy.

A *verkrampte* (hard-line) faction of bureaucrats led by Andries Treurnicht
mounted a rearguard action by insisting on compulsory Afrikaans in the
African school curriculum as part of a strategy to ensure the survival of
Afrikaner culture. Despite opposition from *verligtes* who wanted to see an
increase in the technical training of urban blacks, the *verkramptes* secured
the support of the prime minister, John Vorster, who was preoccupied with
pushing through a more pragmatic economic agenda and did not consider
the issue to be of major political importance. There was a tighter enforcement of the 50–50 Afrikaans–English language rule in African secondary
schools and this in turn culminated in the June 1976 Soweto school children's revolt.[18] The crisis that ensued can be seen as contributing to the
end of the 'second phase' of apartheid that began in the early 1960s and
to the final phase of 'neo-apartheid' in the 1980s that made one last desperate
attempt to remodel the state in alliance with the military to secure the
continuation of white rule. One important feature of the crisis was that it
was partially initiated by internal struggles within the state itself in the
early 1970s.

The Remodelling of the Apartheid State

The upsurge of unrest that began with the Durban strikes in 1973 and the
Soweto students' 'revolt' of 1976 initiated a major new challenge to the

South African government that grew over the following decade into a nation-wide revolt that seemed to some analysts to threaten, unless checked, a full-scale revolution.[19] This crisis forced the state to start trying to re-formulate once again its basic policy of control given the upsurge of mass protest in the townships. The Afrikaner political elite began to consider the conditions that would be necessary for longer-term white survival in a post-apartheid South Africa as some intellectuals defected from its ranks in the wake of the Muldergate scandal in 1978 which led to P.W. Botha replacing John Vorster as prime minister.[20]

Militarily the South African state proved capable of containing the threat of guerrilla insurgency from the ANC's *Umkhonto we Sizwe*, whose quix-otic leadership appears to have had a poor understanding of the sort of state they were up against. On the domestic front, though, it found itself under growing pressure to end the exclusion of the black trade union movement. In 1979, following the publication of the Wiehahn Report, the state finally acceded to the full recognition of African trade unions with the Industrial Conciliation Amendment Act. This opened the way for the rapid growth of black trade unions in the course of the 1980s, in many cases closely linked to more general township movements.

By attempting to reform the apartheid system the state placed itself in a major political dilemma. Its central aim was the liberalising of structures of control by introducing market mechanisms. Following the Riekert Commission report there was an attempt to reform the pass laws, though strong resistance was mounted to this from the bureaucracy in the Urban Administration Boards. The laws were only finally scrapped in 1986 after they became effectively unworkable due to mass unrest.[21] At the same time the state had widened the gulf between economic rights, particularly for those organised into trade unions, and political rights of citizenship.[22] It attempted to bridge this gulf with the 1983 constitution that provided for a new tricameral parliament of separate ethnic chambers for whites, Coloureds and Indians. This failed to meet the most minimal demands of black leaders, who were still expected to look for political representation through the Homelands. Some analysts began to suggest that state officials were moving towards a technocratic 'revolution from above' in an attempt to pre-empt more popular mass protest.[23]

The state lacked the independent moral authority necessary to initiate such a revolutionary transformation of its own. Though the NP regime removed most major apartheid legislation in the decade after 1984, what is interesting is the way that it clung on to some features of the apartheid system right up to the end of its hold on state power. In November 1991, for instance, the government announced the transfer of land still held by

the South African Development Trust (the successor to the SANT established in 1936) to the homeland of Bophuthaswana, despite the fact that the
1913 and 1936 Land Acts had already been abrogated in June the same year
by the Abolition of Racially Based Land Measures Act. The motive behind
this action was less the consolidation of the homelands, which were now
manifestly doomed as serious political entities, than the pre-emption of land
reform by the new ANC-led administration.[24] A similar motive appears to
have been behind de Klerk's decision right before the April 1994 election
to hand over 3 million hectares of land to King Zwelithini under the Kwa
Zulu Ingonyama Trust Act government, though an added consideration
here was the need to ensure the IFP's participation in the election.[25]

The feasibility of technocratic revolution from above was continually
undermined by the South African state's lack of any real autonomy over
civil society. Its power increasingly rested in the 1980s upon the security
establishment centred upon the police and SADF. It lacked a class of state
officials with any real degree of independent authority to initiate major
revolutionary transformation of the society's institutional structures such
as occurred in Japan under the Meiji and Turkey under Kamal Ataturk in
order to pre-empt revolutionary demands from below. The state's legitimacy was inextricably linked to the widely despised and hated apartheid
doctrine and this severely limited its capacity to engage in activities that
could command even partial consent from the majority of the population
at the local level.[26]

The state compounded this dilemma by militarising the administrative
apparatus during the 1980s as it became involved in wars in Namibia,
Angola and Mozambique. This phase of militarisation saw the establishment of parallel structures of administration through the National Security Management System (NSMS) under the control of the State Security
Council (SCC). This was designed to neutralise guerrilla insurgency and
short-circuit much of the Bantu Affairs bureaucracy by subordinating
decision-making to a new set of goals termed Total Strategy. The NSMS
linked reform with counter-revolutionary repression and produced a quite
deep-rooted bureaucratic network based on Joint Management Centres at
the local level headed by a police or military officer.[27] It acted in a similar
manner to some modern Latin American military regimes in transforming
some of the surviving colonial features in the administrative structure,
though like these regimes it did not completely remove the older structures
of civilian administration but worked in alliance with them.[28]

The South African military moved some way in the course of the 1980s
towards establishing a bureaucratic–authoritarian state in order to contain
political demands at the local level. Its control did not come as the result

of a single 'Brumairean moment' in the form of a seizure of power in a coup or putsch but through a gradual permeation of the state from the early 1970s.[29] This permeation amounted to a form of political praetorianism in which it took a leading role on a narrow range of policy issues pertaining to defence and security on the State Security Council. Civil society in South Africa remained too strong for the military to achieve anything like a full 'garrison state' in which it could demand more or less as much decision-making as it required. Different factions within the SADF and intelligence were also too disunited for it to establish a 'guardian state' in which it could perform a strong steering role in place of civil institutions. The militarisation of the state increasingly ended up fitting into the praetorian model 'in which military organisations lose their unity and purpose as particular military factions pursue power and influence in coalition with particular civilian factions'.[30]

Some of the defence intellectuals in the SADF hoped to use the influence they had on the state to develop a more thorough-going counter-insurgency focus within the overall framework of Total Strategy. The models to which they were drawn derived from post-war Western counter-insurgency campaigns, particularly the French experiences in Indo-China and Algeria and the United States involvement in South East Asia. From Andre Beaufre they learned of the need for the mobilisation of political will to counter the appeals of revolutionary nationalism, while from John McCuen they imbibed the idea of counter-revolutionary organisation of the society to meet the insurgent threat at its own level whether this be mobile warfare, guerrilla insurgency, terrorism or political organisation These ideas stressed the need for closer inter-penetration between the military and civil society in order to mobilise political, economic and psychological resources in the 'total strategy' needed to counter revolutionary subversion.[31]

Military leaders tend to have a relatively poor understanding of public policy issues, though, and the SADF was not really in a position – Michael Evans and Mark Philip suggest – to displace civilian authority through a version of the Nazis' 'Gauleiter option' of the 1930s.[32] As Philip Frankel has noted, the leaders of military institutions 'are frequently weak in linking the demands of rulership with social plans and ideological conceptions of society' and tend as a result to be better at organising short-term strategies of social control rather than longer-term ones involving wide-scale social engineering.[33] Military regimes also depend upon some form of pact with the middle class for their continued existence, since the middle class in the post-World War Two era have usually only acceded to authoritarian rule by the military if they are convinced that it will be in their long-term interests. In an extreme case such as Chile the middle class was prepared to put up with a military regime for some 20 years after the 1973 coup even though it affected its economic interests as it undertook a radical free market restructuring of the economy. This reflected the degree to which political ideology had become an autonomous variable and the intense fear felt by the Chilean upper class of a possible return to a radical government such as that of Salvador Allende from 1970–3. Usually, bourgeois compliance with modern authoritarian rule – in the period since 1945 at least – is rather shorter lived, indicating that right wing military rule does not simply reflect the interests of capitalism, but is directed first and foremost towards securing and maintaining 'national security' and internal political stability.[34]

Similar features can be observed in the South African setting, in which the military faced increasing hostility from the business sector in the course of the 1980s as the economy was hit by divestment as well as sanctions. By 1985 feeling was such that Gavin Relly, chairman of Anglo American, led a party of businessmen to meet the exiled ANC in Zambia.[35] The haemorrhaging of business support increasingly undermined the legitimacy of the P.W. Botha regime and helped to drive Total Strategy off course.[36] What started out as an attempt at remodelling the apartheid state at the national level increasingly lost focus and ended up being deflected into sporadic and uncoordinated efforts by different sections of the military in terrorism and destabilisation in the townships, squatter camps and Homelands. The upsurge of mass unrest at the local level between 1984 and 1986 also undermined political consensus within the state as the military increasingly resorted to repression in order to enforce the reform programme. Such methods could do little more than contain the black population in the townships as the military did its best to try and shore up the existing structures of civil authority such as township councils.[37] Total Strategy failed to represent a national political solution and lost credibility after the military's defeat in Angola.

Some of the major reasons for the *abertura* in South Africa in 1990, therefore, need to be located in terms of a crisis in civil–military relations within the South African state in the late 1980s. Analysts have been rather reluctant to search for explanations at this level and have tended to focus upon external economic and political forces operating on the South African state. Robert Price, for example, has seen the de Klerk government's volteface as a result of the failure by the end of 1988 of the strategy of 'inward industrialisation' that had been developed in the face of the Western sanctions package of 1985–6.[38] Likewise, Hermann Giliomee has looked for a wider ideological explanation for the decision to negotiate, in terms of the end of the Cold War in 1989 which deprived the Total Strategy of any real intellectual credibility as the external communist threat to white power was removed.[39]

These factors undoubtedly played some role in government decision-making, though they fail to examine it in the context of continuing power struggles within the state. The official ideology of Total Strategy came severely unstuck during 1988 even before the collapse of the Berlin Wall and was replaced by the more general counter-insurgency doctrine of Revolutionary Onslaught. It failed to prevent rivalry continuing among first-tier state departments and Annette Seegers has observed at this time a preoccupation with the outwardly strong which only thinly disguised a cynicism among many state bureaucrats about the overall direction of state policy.[40] The loss of momentum in the military's strategy needs also to be seen as a result of the shift within the ANC away from 'armed struggle' in the course of 1989 towards a diplomatic offensive in a number of Western capitals. The ANC appeared to be willing to negotiate a new constitutional dispensation for South Africa and the military influence on the South African state seemed to be increasingly a hindrance to this process. A classic stalemate situation had been reached which theorists of negotiation such as William Zartman have seen as the key precipitant for a breakthrough to negotiation.[41]

Neither Price's nor Giliomee's explanation for the South African state's *abertura* centrally confronts the issue in terms of a crisis of state authority in South Africa following military defeat or least severe loss of face. This is a major reason for states to exit from authoritarian modes of political rule – the Greek military regime for example returned to barracks in 1974 following the war with Turkey over Cyprus as did the Argentinian junta in 1992 after the Falklands war. When seen in these terms, the decision of the South African military to do the same is not so peculiar, though it did not in fact lead to an automatic end to the destabilisation strategy, which moved out to the Homelands. Hit squads formed originally by the SADF in Homelands such as Kwa Zulu, Bophuthatswana and Transkei continued to operate after 1990, though on nothing like on the scale of those in Central and South America.[42]

These fragmented attempts at destabilisation proved increasingly incapable of reversing the momentum of the constitutional negotiations. A degree of interdependence between the government and the ANC became evident as early as the Groote Schuur Minute of 2–3 May 1990, since both sides in a sense needed each other if they were going to be able to deal with violence and instability.[43] This factor was a major reason for the changing assessments by senior officers in the SADF. By the time of the final agreement on the interim constitution at the end of 1993 this strategy had

become more or less abandoned at the national level. While some officers
had links with extreme right wing groups, it was becoming clear to the far
white right that the SADF was no longer interested in a coherent plan of
destabilisation. A military coup was guaranteed to fail since it would lead
to massive unrest in the townships, fail to gain any international support
and lead in fact to the restoration of sanctions. Many officers by 1993–4
had come to realise that it was in their interests to support the new ANC-
led regime that would be put in place by the April 1994 elections. This
would be the best means of securing their pensions as well as securing a
strong economy in the longer term.[44] A leading figure in this political
volte face was General Constand Viljoen, head of the SADF from 1980–
5. Viljoen initially tried to unite the various opposition groups on the far
right but gave up and ended up supporting the 1994 elections after Eugene
Terreblanche's Afrikaner Veerstandsbeweging entered the Bophuthaswana
homeland in order to try and maintain Lucas Mangope in power after a
popular uprising against his rule.

   Attempts at destabilisation were thus rather sporadic and half hearted.
The Afrikaner Volksfront (AVF) and the Freedom Alliance tried to hijack
the SADF's Rapid Deployment Force and use former SADF special force
members to paralyse communications. Their efforts merely indicated just
how weak the far right's links now were with the military establishment.[45]
This loss of military influence was also seen in the intelligence sphere
as Military Intelligence was down-graded in the early 1990s while the
National Intelligence Service consolidated itself as the premier arm of the
state's intelligence-gathering apparatus under a new triumvirate, Mo Sheik,
the second in command of the ANC's intelligence, his chief Joe Nhlanhla
and the current NIS head Mike Louw – a group popularly known as the
'Mo, Joe and Louw show'. The new line-up ensures that NIS will have
direct access to the ruling party and can re-orient its functions towards
gathering intelligence for the new regime, though there are doubts over
how effective it will be in the initial stages.[46]

   The loss of military influence at the centre of the South African state in
Pretoria was reflected in an increasingly selective attitude towards challenges to the authority of the leaderships in the Homelands. In 1988 the
SADF came to the rescue of Lucas Mangope in Bophuthatswana when
he was threatened with overthrow in a coup, while it refused to intervene
to prevent another coup against Bantu Holomisa in Transkei. However,
some of the Homelands by this time had begun to outgrow their origins as
statelets dominated by militarised bureaucracies.[47] As Jeff Peires has shown
in the case of the Transkei, a new black middle class had begun to emerge
which increasingly aligned itself with the ANC. This disaffection from the

ruling regime of Kaiser Matanzima in turn enabled the successor regime of Bantu Holomisa to weaken its links with Pretoria.[48] This black petty bourgeois pressure from the Homelands compounded the loss of support at the centre from the business sector and increased the military's isolation after the defeat at Cuito Canavale.

The State and the ANC's Reconstruction Programme

The emergence of the new ANC government in April 1994 marks the final phase in the decolonisation of the South African state that was tentatively begun in the late 1970s. In the short to medium term it ensures the stabilisation of the state's power and authority in South African politics, since it will lead to a structure that is likely to be resistant to popular revolutionary overthrow. As Goodwin and Skocpol have pointed out, those states that have been most prone to revolutionary breakdown in the years since 1945 have tended to be those which not only had poverty, repression and a class of revolutionary intellectuals but also are politically exclusionary and have armies that engage in random repression. These are examples either of direct colonialism – such as French colonial rule in Algeria – or exclusive Sultanistic rule such as Iran under the Shah before 1979.[49] Neither really matches up to the South African model in the short to medium term as the remaining quasi-colonial structures based on the Homelands are reincorporated into a new South African political system and many of the former revolutionary intellectuals become incorporated into the administration.[50]

South Africa may therefore be undergoing a revolution of a peculiar and idiosyncratic kind. Its 'revolution' may end up as a hybrid model combining some features of the older style revolutions of national liberation with some features of more contemporary post-Marxist revolution against authoritarian state forms and in favour of some degree of political decentralisation. The main theme within the new state's political agenda, though, is likely to be a fairly conventional package of economic reforms to ensure the freeing up of the economy and the provision of jobs and public services.

The military, for instance, is likely to undergo considerable restructuring over the next five to ten years as it is offered the carrot of new equipment and a boost in the exports of the defence industry. While the existing defence budget of R9 885 billion will almost certainly be considerably cut, the end of international sanctions will mean the up-grading of some obsolete hardware. New planes such as the Swiss Pilatius aircraft may be bought for the air force to replace the ageing Harvard trainers. The government is likely to demand they be partially assembled in South Africa to provide employment since it is almost certain to continue the previous regime's opposition to counter-trade and bartering (which is seen as signifying third world status). The navy too may well acquire four new corvettes to add to its fleet for coastal protection against drug trafficking and smuggling.[51] This new equipment will confirm the state's support for the defence industry, which will be a major player in the government's bid to return to world markets.

This economic strategy will not in itself assist the ANC to consolidate its hold over the centre ground of South African politics except in the minimal sense that it will help to boost, in the medium to long term, economic growth and employment. The ANC's political standing will depend largely on its capacity to develop as an effective party machine that can leverage the support of major constituencies to the policies of the state. This may prove to be a hard task, as the movement found it difficult to raise overseas funds for the April election despite the fact that this was the first time it had ever gone to the polls. It failed to reach its target of US$17 million in international contributions and is unlikely to raise anything like as much in the future if international interest in domestic South African politics declines.[52] The signs are therefore that it may take it some while to establish a well-organised and reliable party apparatus.

The ANC's performance in the April election was clearly helped by the fact that it was as yet untested and had as its leader the dominating figurehead of Nelson Mandela. It was also helped by the opposition PAC which proved to be weakly led, financially hamstrung, with poor control over its APLA guerrilla force and apparently willing to make use even of the discredited Homelands as political platforms.[53] The ANC's victory in the election disguised the fact that a large number of voters had the PAC as their second preference and were only willing to support the ANC providing it could deliver on at least some of its promises. At the local level the PAC still commands considerable emotional support, as was evidenced at the time of the collapse of the Bophuthatswana Homeland in March. The ANC had been reluctant to intervene in the Homeland and it was a strike by civil servants which was the immediate precipitant of the breakdown of authority. PAC and AZAPO banners declaring 'one settler, one bullet' were much in evidence when Mandela entered the capital Mmabatho in triumph after Mangope had fled, and the civil servants were far from unanimous over whether to accept his reassurances on pensions and job security.[54]

The ANC has a major task in binding major groupings in black politics to itself and avoiding internal divisions. This might prove to be extremely difficult given the external pressures on the new state to conform to financial orthodoxy and enhance the economy's competitiveness.[55]

A number of ANC leaders including Nelson Mandela have tried to deflate high expectations from their supporters over what the new government can feasibly do, stating that it will take at least five years to attend to major 'social problems'.[56] This is probably the length of time that the new regime feels that it has to contain radical demands for more interventionist policies on issues like wealth redistribution, land reform and major schemes for up-grading housing and education. It is helped in this by the new constitution which prevents its members in parliament from voting against it on pain of expulsion. In the long run, it may well find that the radical opposition becomes irresistible if nothing tangible appears to be done.

The pragmatic wing of the ANC has been aided by the absence of any particularly charismatic leader who can galvanise the opposition ranks. The emergence of Winnie Mandela is a sign that at the local level there is the potential for mounting dissatisfaction with an overly cautious leadership. Winnie Mandela re-surfaced at the end of 1993 as a figure with considerable grassroots support when she defeated Albertina Sisulu for the presidency of the ANC Women's League by 392 votes to 168. She gained a widespread following among the squatters in places such as the East Rand, ANC branches in the Eastern Cape, Transkei, Border and Natal Midlands regions, the ANC Youth League and many of the former cadres of *Umkhonto we Sizwe*. In addition to the presidency of the Women's League she is the deputy president of the South African National Asso-ciation of Civics (SANCO) and controls the head office of the ANC. A secret ANC survey reportedly found her to be one of the most popular leaders among the rank and file, and, after a short-lived spell in govern-ment as a junior minister, she may be able to galvanise these groups into a significant opposition movement.[57]

Winnie Mandela's main power base has been largely outside the organ-ised trade union movement and her emergence led to a weakening of the position of Cyril Ramaphosa in the ANC leadership. She forged quite close links with Thabo Mbeki, though her volatile character ensured that she could not become any sort of credible substitute for Chris Hani as a figure who defines the acceptable limits of radical discourse inside the ANC. In her rhetoric, though, she has been fond of emphasising the need for working outside parliamentary structures. 'Grassroots politics is the only struggle I understand,' she said in one interview. 'I don't believe in the politics of driving a black Merc and abandoning the masses'.[58] For all her populism, Winnie Mandela remains a key figure within the new black political establishment even though she has now been removed from the government after failing to obey an order not to travel to a conference in West Africa. It is still possible that after the retirement of her estranged husband she may try once again to act as a power broker with leaders and communities at the local level.

The interesting question to ask about political figures like Winnie Mandela is whether ultimately they will accommodate towards the clientelist politics that the ANC government is developing as it seeks to consolidate its position inside the South African state. The power base of the regime will rest on compliant political factions who will support the ANC political machine in return for access to funds and resources. Such patronage, however, is likely to reinforce existing wealth disparities rather than radically challenge them since it will reinforce ties of dependency upon the regime at the centre of decision-making rather than encourage more horizontal forms of political mobilisation.

This can be seen particularly clearly in the case of the issue of squatting. The lack of housing in urban areas in South Africa has led to a huge increase of squatting and shack settlements in the last 10 to 15 years. Alan Mabin has suggested that in the Transvaal planned and informal non-rural settlements may well now count for half the housing in the province.[59] Squatting communities have been a cause of violent conflict with surrounding African townships, though this so-called 'black on black' violence linked to struggles between rival taxi gangs has frequently been manipulated by external agencies such as the police and the IFP. It will not be an easy task to incorporate the squatting communities into the new apparatus of decision-making at the centre and studies in other societies such as Peru and Argentina indicate that regimes that have to cope with a massive and rapid influx of new settlers into shanty towns and *favelas* on the perimeters of metropolitan areas opt for a paternalistic relationship with the poor in order to weaken links between the squatting communities and class-based parties and unions. At its most dramatic this paternalism is sometimes personified by a charismatic female leader embodying hopes of motherhood and family life such as Eva Peron or, on a lesser scale in Peru, Maria Delgado de Odria.[60]

It might seem absurd at one level to see Winnie Mandela as a sort of South African Eva Peron! However, she has already a widespread following in many communities and undoubtedly embodies many of their hopes and aspirations. This is occurring at a time when the state is under growing political pressure from both the business sector and external NGOs like the World Bank to opt for a market solution to housing issues making considerable use of the banks. This will lead to an up-grading of the dwellings of the organised working class in the townships and threatens to exclude for the most part the squatting communities.[61]

In the rural areas, squatter communities organised through rural civics are likely to seek a solution based on land reform rather than market-based housing schemes. If this does occur, there is still a danger that a lot of people, particularly women, could be worse rather than better off. Only 10–15 per cent of rural incomes comes from subsistence farming while the rest accrues from remittances and seasonal jobs, many of which are performed by women. If large amounts of white-owned land are taken out of commercial agricultural use and turned towards subsistence farming, this could reduce the incomes of many rural women at the same time as consolidating the position of men. Those with money in the rural areas who can pay bribes are men such as taxi operators and it is these who may be the winners out of a poorly implemented land reform programme.[62] The marginal and the dispossessed are not usually the most revolutionary of social groups in any case and the South African state may well decide that maintaining a policy of excluding such groups is a price worth paying in the short to medium term if the new regime opts for a state model that can promote capitalist development.

WHAT SORT OF STATE?

If the political interregnum in South Africa is at last resolved, the question of the form of the new state is to some degree open-ended. The new regime can move towards a number of possible new state models as it seeks to break with the previous apartheid and neo-apartheid state forms, though it will need to move fairly speedily as time is not really on its side. The African continent faces the grim prospect of being increasingly marginalised in the post-Cold War era unless decisive action is taken in the next decade.[63] What sort of model, therefore, is it likely to try and develop? How feasible can this be in the context of contemporary international political economy? In this concluding section, we will outline the possible alternative roads that the new regime might go down as it seeks to restructure the state.

There are, it will be suggested, four main state models that the new regime could try to move towards, though only two of these look at all plausible. The four are 1) a Marxist Leninist regime run by a vanguard party seeking to use the state to advance South African society towards a socialist order; 2) a capitalist state that seeks to use its power to withdraw from the economy, engage in wide-scale privatisation and trust busting in order to initiate a free market economy; 3) a social democratic state geared to the promotion of a mixed economy and a welfare state on lines similar to the post-war British Labour Party and West European social democratic parties; and 4) a capitalist developmental state (CDS) on lines similar to the Asian Tigers such as South Korea and Taiwan that maintains strong state intervention in the capitalist economy and engages in promotional politics to advance key sectors in pursuit of export-led industrialisation.

The first two of these are extremely unlikely in the short to medium term. As far as the first Marxist Leninist model is concerned, the ANC has arrived in power 20 years too late, since it was the 1970s that was the decade of experimentation with such models in Africa. All came disastrously unstuck, due both to internal problems of soft state forms and to external destabilisation in countries such as Angola and Mozambique. Even if the end of the Cold War fails to lead to an 'end of history', the collapse of the Soviet Union and East Germany, the retreat of Cuba from Africa and the shift in China towards a capitalist market economy make this form of government virtually impossible to sustain in the current global economy even if there was the will within the ANC to do so. The new regime does not conform to anything like a party vanguard and the SACP has begun to move some way from its former commitment to orthodox Marxism Leninism, despite the resistance of the surviving Stalinists in the party such as Harry Gwala. Younger party leaders such as Raymond Suttner have moved it towards becoming a democratic political party, though it has not gone as far as many European communist parties in the 1980s in the form of Eurocommunism and a radical social democracy. It is under some pressure from a large class of comrades and youth in the townships who have swelled its ranks in the last four years (giving it a membership of 60 000 and rendering it the only growing Communist party in the world) and this is likely to ensure it maintains some commitment to socialist principles. However, it is unclear how this will translate into policies now that some of its leading figures have entered the government. Unless tight discipline is exerted at the local level this support may ultimately drift behind a more diffuse radical populism under a charismatic leader such as Winnie Mandela. This may in turn lead to its energy being diverted away from direct pressure on the state, though here much will depend on the internal power struggles within the ANC leadership.

The second model is also very unlikely since it lacks any real political constituency in contemporary South African politics. The Reagan/Thatcher era of the 1980s has drawn to a close and many economic theorists have begun to move back towards a neo-Keynesianism. If the ANC moved towards this model it would alienate not only its traditional supporters in the black trade union movement but also large sections of South African business, particularly Anglo American, who would face being broken up into smaller and more competitive concerns. The new state may want to implement some trust busting, but it is more likely to seek to do so cautiously and over a longish period of time. Comparative evidence suggests that for developing states to adopt this model they need to have draconian powers like the Pinochet regime in Chile after 1973 and these the new regime in South Africa does not as yet have. It is a model though that NGOs like the World Bank and IMF would like to see the new South African government move at least some way towards. If it does so, it will have to maintain a large part of the existing security and defence apparatus inherited from the previous regime in order to be able to contain political opposition by repressive means.

The third model is a rather more plausible one. Leaders such as Nelson Mandela have traditionally had strong sympathies for the British Labour party and would have as their first preference some sort of Attlee-type socialism. The South African economy, though, could not sustain a welfare state on West European lines, certainly not a full-scale national health service. This model might simply cash out as one that includes the urban insiders in the townships who are organised through the civics and trade union movement, and excludes most squatting communities and marginal groups left behind in the former Homelands and rural areas. To be implemented according to notions of social justice it would need a large and coherent state bureaucracy, and planning apparatus that is reliable and trustworthy. This might take two to three decades to establish in South Africa. It is more likely therefore that a truncated version of this will be implemented to appease well-organised groups and on a scale that does not produce too much alienation from the business sector.

The welfare state model says relatively little about economic growth: social democracy was largely a product of the era of post-war economic growth and political consensus in Western societies, and social democratic theorists such as Anthony Crosland tended to presume a reasonably high level of economic prosperity on a par with Sweden in order to be able to implement ideals of equality within a mixed capitalist economy. South Africa is not Sweden; it has a high population growth and needs to look to high rates of economic growth just to maintain its existing employment levels. The fourth capitalist development state model therefore has some attraction since it seeks to emulate states that have maintained over the last 20 years the highest rates of economic growth in the world (over 10 per cent per annum) whilst at the same time maintaining a high degree of state intervention.

The capitalist developmental state model was one derived from a specific set of circumstances and it is not easy to see how it can be transplanted neat to the South African setting. Societies such as Taiwan and South Korea have a high degree of ethnic homogeneity and were buttressed with large amounts of American aid during the Cold War. The existence of a common external enemy in the form of the Chinese People's Republic or North Korea helped bind these societies together according to a Confucian code of values, and economic growth was pursued as part of a wider goal of national security. They are interesting as economic models, though, since they succeeded not according to the criteria of market allocation but on the basis of promotional politics pursued by a strong and authoritarian state which crushed political opposition. Indeed, some analysts have seen a close resemblance between the state form of capitalist development states and the Chinese and Korean model state directed by a Marxist Leninist vanguard party.[64]

In essence the CDS, according to Chalmers Johnson, is marked by four main features: i) a political–bureaucratic elite that is strong enough to resist popular demands, ii) cooperation betweeen public and private sectors under the guidance of a planning agency, iii) massive and protracted investment in mass education and iv) a govenment that understands how to intervene in the economy without abandoning the price mechanism.[65] The new South African state may be able to employ at least some of the features though it is unlikely to fulfill all the criteria of the model. It may for example develop a new political–bureaucratic elite that can for a period at least resist poplar demands for high public expenditure on welfare measures. However, it is doubtful if such an elite will be able to acquire the same sort of homogeneous ethos as those of the 'Confucian' regimes of South East Asia. Likewise, it will be able to build on existing cooperation between state and private sector built up by the previous apartheid regime, though this is unlikely to be guided by a single planning agency. The nearest thing to this is likely to be the Development Bank of Southern Africa. It is also of course committed to expanding and universal education, though as Linda Chisholm points out in Chapter 8 this may well be subordinated in the end to a more limited set of goals to train a small elite to work in the capital intensive sector. Finally, the government already intervenes in the economy without abandoning the price mechanism, though to emulate the CDS it would need to develop much more wide ranging and draconian methods that have not as yet been seriously debated.

The South African state may try to develop its own rather more limited model of capitalist-based development that would avoid a draconian crushing of the political opposition, particularly the trade union movement. It may find severe obstacles to this project, though, as it comes under growing pressures to meet the demands of its supporters for increased state spending on welfare projects as well as for economic redistribution.

This could also lead, as Martin Murray has suggested, to a sort of 'feud-alisation' of the state as it is taken over by a variety of different interests, each creating their own separate mini-bureaucratic fiefdoms. The result would obviously be a paralysed administration and inability to develop any long range strategic policy goals.[66]

It might look to some parastatals such as ESCOM for instance as key sectors to promote not only South African but regional economic growth through a common power grid, though it is likely that its priorities will be initially based on internal economic development. Similarly the arms indus-try and its parastatal ARMSCOR, as has already been pointed out, may prove to be a key sector in promoting South African return to international markets. The state will initially try and promote the development of such key sectors in alliance with the trade union movement, though whether it will be possible to maintain such an alliance in the medium to long term is rather more doubtful. As the state develops a more coherent bureau-cratic class of its own, it is likely to develop a specific interest which may well drive it apart from its allies in COSATU. It may thus try to use wel-fare state policies to offset its capitalist development objectives that are likely to run into union opposition.

In short, therefore, the South African state may move to a rather uneasy combination of models three and four over the next two decades. As it entrenches itself in power it is likely increasingly to develop a technocratic interest in capitalist economic development that will favour the emergence of a black business class. In the initial phase of this it should be able to bind the trade unions and civics behind this programme under a banner of nationalism and black economic and political empowerment. In the longer term, it is possible to see new political divisions emerging from this, particularly if South Africa continues to fall further behind internationally in terms of economic competitiveness. The degree to which it can implement the capitalist development model will depend upon a series of bargains it will have to make both with internal opposition movements such as COSATU and with external agencies such as the World Bank, which will be more concerned with seeing the freeing up of the economy than with a state-directed model of capitalist development.[67]

The new state may not be able to resolve these competing political pres-sures and simply send out confused and contradictory signals. A clear and unambiguous state model may thus take some years to become estab-lished; this is a pattern that has been seen before in South Africa as the apartheid state took some decades to emerge out of the earlier segregation-ist one that was forged in the years after 1910. Much will depend upon the nature of political leadership and the degree to which a clear policy agenda can be crafted out of contradictory pressures. It is clear though that the next two to three decades will be another period of state building in twentieth century South African political history.

NOTES

1. Charles Tilly, 'War Making and State Making as Organised Crime' in Peter B. Evans, Dietrich Rueschemeyer and Theda Skocpol (eds), *Bringing the State Back In* (Cambridge: Cambridge University Press, 1985), pp. 169–86; Charles Tilly, *Coercion, Capital and European States* (Cambridge and Oxford: Blackwell, 1990).
2. A.R. Radcliffe Brown, 'Preface' in M. Fortes and E.E. Evans Pritchard (eds), *African Political Systems* (London: Oxford University Press for the International African Institute, 1970) (1st ed. 1940), p. xxiii. See also Philip Abrams, 'Notes on the Difficulty of Studying the State', *Journal of Historical Sociology*, 1, 1 (March 1988), 63; Sabino Cassese, 'The Rise and Decline of the Notion of the State', *International Political Science Review*, 7, 2 (April 1986), 120–30; and more generally Kenneth H.F. Dyson, *The State Tradition in Western Europe* (Oxford: Martin Robertson, 1980). A version of this criticism has recently appeared in the field of International Relations. See Yale H. Ferguson and Rochard W. Mansbach, *The State, Conceptual Chaos and the Future of International Relations Theory* (Boulder and London: Lynne Rienner, 1989).
3. Alexander Gerschenkron, *Economic Backwardness in Historical Perspective* (Cambridge MA: The Belknap Press, 1966), esp. pp. 5–30.
4. For a review of this historiography see Christopher Saunders, *The Making of the South African Past: Major Historians on Race and Class* (Cape Town and Johannesburg: David Philip, 1988). For the intellectual climate that led to this view among South African liberals see Paul B. Rich, *Hope and Despair: English Speaking Intellectuals and South African Politics, 1896–1976* (London: British Academic Press, 1993).
5. Dan O'Meara, *Volkskapitalisme* (Johannesburg: Ravan Press, 1983).
6. Peter B. Evans et al, *Bringing the State Back In* (Cambridge: Cambridge University Press, 1985).
7. Stanley B. Greenberg, *Race and State in Capitalist Development* (New Haven and London: Yale Univesity Press, 1980), esp. pp. 385–410.
8. *Ibid.*, p. 388.
9. *Ibid.*, pp. 389–90. This is a point particularly noted by Belinda Bozzoli, 'Challenging Local Orthodoxies', *Social Dynamics*, 6, 2 (1981), 58.
10. M.L. Morris, 'The Development of Capitalism in South African Agriculture: Class Struggle in the Countryside', *Economy and Society*, 5, 3 (1976), 292–343; Mike Morris, 'Apartheid, Agriculture and the State: The Farm Labour Question', paper presented to the SALDRU Farm Labour Conference, University of Cape Town, September 1976. See also Stanley Trapido,

'South Africa in a Comparative Study of Industrialisation', *Journal of Development Studies*, 7, 3 (1971), 309–20; Martin Legassick, 'South Africa: Capital Accumulation and Violence', *Economy and Society*, 3, 3 (1974), 253–329. Greenberg accepts the substance of Morris's thesis, though argues that if anything it incorporates too little of the 'Prussian Path' model. He considers that Morris 'neglects the struggle of landowners, steeped in traditions of unfree labor and racial domination, who sought to expand production and respond to markets for food, even create labor forms, while repeatedly seeking to circumvent the market in labor. It fails to outline a process, similar in some respects to the German one, that led landowners and farmers to hold on to their "feudal baggage" in a modern world, with important consequences for the nature of the state and the place of unfree labour', Greenberg, *Race and State*, p. 73.

11. Tim Keegan, 'The Dynamics of Rural Accumulation in South Africa: Comparative and Historical Perspectives', *Comparative Studies in Society and History*, 28, 4 (1986), 628–50. See the Marxist critique of this by Martin Murray, who argues that Keegan's social history perspective has meant that he has failed to break through the more conventional liberal perspective that sees segregation on the land as a result of a drive for white racial supremacy, 'The Origins of Agrarian Capitalism in South Africa: a Critique of the "Social History" Perspective', *Journal of Southern African Studies*, 15, 3 (October 1989), 645–65; Tim Keegan, 'The Origins of Agrarian Capitalism: A reply', *Journal of Southern African Studies*, 15, 3 (October 1989), 666–84. Martin J. Murray, 'The Triumph of Marxist Approaches in South African Social and Labour History', *Journal of Asian and African Studies*, XXXIII, 1–2 (1988), 79–101; and for similar doubts on the 'anti-theoretical stance' of the social historians Helen Bradford, 'Highways, Byways and Cul-de-Sacs: the Transition to Agrarian Capitalism in Revisionist South African History', *Radical History Review*, 46/7 (1990), 59–88.

12. Saul Dubow, *Racial Segregation and the Origins of Apartheid* (Basingstoke: The Macmillan Press, 1989); ' "Holding a Just Balance Between White and Black": the Native Affairs Department in South Africa, c. 1920–1933', *Journal of Southern African Studies*, 12, 2 (April 1986), 217–39; Ivan Evans, 'The Native Affairs Department and the Reserves in the 1940s and 1950s' in Robin Cohen et al. (eds), *Repression and Resistance: Insider Accounts of Apartheid* (London: Hans Zell, 1990), pp. 17–51; Paul B. Rich, *State Power and Black Politics in South Africa* (Basingstoke: The Macmillan Press, 1995).

13. Henry Kenny, *Architect of Apartheid: H.F. Verwoerd – An Appraisal* (Johannesburg: Jonathan Ball, 1980). Some radical analysts such as Robin Cohen took a similar view. See Robin Cohen, *Endgame in South Africa* (London: James Currey, 1986), esp. pp. 1–14.

14. Saul Dubow, 'Afrikaner Nationalism, Apartheid and the Concept of Race', *Journal of African History*, 33, 2 (1992), 209–37.

15. Roberta Balstad Miller, 'Science and Society in the Early Career of H.F. Verwoerd', *Journal of Southern African Studies*, 19, 4 (1993), 634–61.

16. Deborah Posel, *The Making of Apartheid, 1948–1961* (Oxford: Clarendon Press, 1991), p. 70.

17. *Ibid.*, p. 271.

18. Jonathan Hyslop, 'State Educational Policy and the Social Reproduction

of the Urban Working Class; the Case of the Southern Transvaal', *Journal of Southern African Studies*, 14, 3 (April 1988), 468–75.

19. Calvin A. Woodward, 'Reform or Revolution in South Africa', *Round Table*, 202 (April 1981), 101–15.

20. Heribert Adam, 'Survival Politics: Afrikanerdom in Search of a New Ideology', *Journal of Modern African Studies*, 16, 4 (1978), 657–69; Andre Du Toit, 'Facing up to the future: Some Personal Reflections on the Predicament of Afrikaner Intellectuals in the Legitimation Crisis of Afrikaner Nationalism and the Apartheid State', *Social Dynamics*, 7, 2 (1981), 1–27.

21. Andrew Ashforth, *The Politics of Official Discourse in Twentieth Century South Africa* (Oxford: Clarendon Press, 1990), p. 217. See also Stanley B. Greenberg, 'Ideological Struggles Within the South African State' in S. Marks and S. Trapido (eds), *The Politics of Race, Class and Nationalism in Twentieth Century South Africa* (London and New York: Longman, 1987), pp. 389–418.

22. Ashforth, *op. cit.*, p. 230.

23. Kogila A. Moodley, 'The Legitimation Crisis of the South African State', *Journal of Modern African Studies*, 24, 2 (1986), 187–201.

24. Marina Ottaway, *South Africa: The Struggle for a New Order* (Washington DC: The Brookings Institution, 1993), p. 170.

25. *Weekly Mail*, 20–26 May 1994.

26. See Ellen Kay Trimberger, *Revolution from Above* (Brunswick NJ: Transaction Books, 1978).

27. Robert M. Price, *The Apartheid State in Crisis: Political Transformation in South Africa, 1975–1990* (New York and Oxford: Oxford University Press, 1991), pp. 252–7; Kenneth W. Grundy, *The Rise of the South African Security Establishment* (Johannesburg: South African Institute of International Affairs, 1983); Thomas Young, 'Restructuring the State in South Africa: New Strategies of Incorporation and Control', *Political Studies*, XXXVII (1989), 62–80; Annette Seegers, 'South Africa's National Security Management System, 1972–1990', *Journal of Modern African Studies*, 29, 2 (1991), 253–73.

28. Michael Lowy and Eder Sader, 'The Militarisation of the State in Latin America', *Latin American Perspectives*, vol. 12, no. 4, issue 47 (Fall 1985), 7–40; Susanne Jonas, 'Contradictions of Guatemala's "Political Opening"', *Latin American Perspectives*, 58, 3 (Summer 1988), 26–46.

29. Seegers, *op. cit.*, 256.

30. Robert Pinkney, *Right Wing Military Government* (Boston: Twayne Publishing, 1990), p. 29.

31. Andre Beaufre, *An Introduction to Strategy* (London: Faber and Faber, 1963); John J. McCuen, *The Art of Counter Revolutionary Warfare* (London: Faber and Faber, 1966). See also Philip Frankel, *Pretoria's Praetorians: civil-military relations in South Africa* (Cambridge: Cambridge University Press, 1984), pp. 46–50; Gavin Cawthra, *Policing South Africa* (London and New Jersey: Zed Books, 1994), pp. 30–4.

32. Michael Evans and Mark Philip, 'Intensifying Civil War: The Role of the South African Defence Force' in Philip Frankel, Noam Pines and Mark Swilling (eds), *State, Resistance and Change in South Africa* (London: Croom Helm, 1988), p. 139.

33. Frankel, *op. cit.*, p. 174; Paul Cammack and Philip O'Brien, 'Conclusion' in Philip O'Brien and Paul Cammack (eds), *Generals in Retreat: The Crisis of Military Rule in Latin America* (Manchester: Manchester University Press, 1985), p. 195.

34. Alfred Stepan, 'State Power and the Strength of Civil Society in the Southern Cone of Latin America' in Evans *et al.*, *Bringing the State Back In*, pp. 317–40; Philip O'Brien, 'Authoritarianism and the New Economic Orthodoxy: the political economy of the Chilean regime' in O'Brien and Cammack, *op. cit.*, pp. 144–80. The notion of 'national security', though, can itself be a contested concept within the military. This has been especially so in the case of the Peruvian military's campaign against the Sendero Luminoso guerrilla movement. See Philip Mauceri, 'Military Politics and Counter-Insurgency in Peru', *Journal of Inter American Studies*, 33, 4 (Winter 1991), 83–105.

35. R. Price, *The Apartheid State in Crisis* (New York and Oxford: Oxford University Press, 1991), pp. 265–6.

36. To this extent it is difficult to accept the argument of some analysts that there was a full-scale class alliance forged between the government of P.W. Botha and big business in the early 1980s. See, for example, Gregor Houston, 'Capital Accumulation, Influx Control and the State in South Africa, 1970–1982', *Journal of Contemporary African Studies*, 7, 1/2 (April/October 1988), 111–31.

37. Andrew Boraine, 'The Militarisation of Urban Controls: the Security Management System in Mamelodi, 1986–1988' in Jacklyn Cock and Laurie Nathan (eds), *War and Society: the Militarisation of South Africa* (Cape Town and Johannesburg: David Philip, 1989), pp. 159–73.

38. Price, *op. cit.*, pp. 273–5.

39. Hermann Giliomee, '*Broedertwis*: Intra Afrikaner Conflicts in the Transition from Apartheid', *African Affairs*, 91 (1992), 339–64.

40. Seegers, *op. cit.*, 268–9.

41. I. William Zartman, 'Negotiations in South Africa', *The Washington Quarterly* (Autumn 1988), 141–58. See also 'South Africa: the Diplomatic Offensive', *Africa Confidential*, 23 June 1989.

42. One hit squad of five Kwa Zulu policemen, for instance, was alleged by the Goldstone Commission to have killed nine people in 1992–3 including ANC leaders; see the *Weekly Mail*, 5–11 November 1993, 11–17 February and 25 February–3 March 1994.

43. Susan Booysen, 'Transition, the State and Relations of Political Power in South Africa', *Politikon*, 17, 2 (December 1990), 53.

44. Herbert M. Howe, 'The South African Defence Force and Political Reform', *The Journal of Modern African Studies*, 32, 1 (1994), 45–7.

45. *Weekly Mail*, 4–10 March 1994.

46. *Weekly Mail*, 20–26 May 1994.

47. See for example Carole Cooper, 'The Militarisation of the Bantustans: Control and Contradiction' in Cock and Nathan, *op. cit.*, pp. 174–87.

48. J.B. Peires, 'The Implosion of Transkei and Ciskei', *African Affairs*, 91 (1992), 365–87. In some other Homelands, though, such as Qwa Qwa, the tribal establishment maintained tight political control and marginalised the class of petty bourgeois traders. This meant that there were no buffers to

insulate it from more popular resistance and after the re-legalisation of the ANC in 1990 it was overthrown by mass action. Leslie Bank, 'Between Traders and Tribalists: Implosion and the Politics of Disjuncture in a South African Homeland', *African Affairs*, 93 (1994), 75–98.

49. Jeff Goodwin and Theda Skocpol, 'Explaining Revolutions in the Contemporary Third World', *Politics and Society*, 17, 4 (1989), 489–509.

50. It may, in any case, be necessary to rethink the whole concept of revolutionary change in the light of the popular upsurge in Eastern Europe in the late 1980s. The spontaneity and relative non-violence of these revolutions and their successful overthrow of totalitarian regimes suggests that older classifications of 'Eastern' and 'Western' revolutions is now rather redundant. Robert H. Dix, 'Eastern Europe's Implications for Revolutionary Theory', *Polity*, XXIV, 2 (Winter 1991), 227–42.

51. *Weekly Mail*, 20–26 May 1994.

52. *Weekly Mail*, 18–24 February 1994.

53. In Ciskei apparently some cabinet members held dual ADM and PAC membership; *Weekly Mail*, 4–10 February 1994.

54. *Southern African Report*, 18 March 1994; *Weekly Mail*, 4–10 February 1994.

55. The World Competitiveness Report ranked South Africa 30 out of 36 in 1992 and 32 out of 37 in 1993. Even when put in a league of 'newly emerging industrial nations' it only ranked 11 out of 15 and was outclassed by Singapore, Hong Kong and Taiwan. *The Star International Weekly*, 18–24 November 1993.

56. *Southern African Report*, 4 February 1994.

57. *Weekly Mail*, 10–16 December and 17–22 December 1993.

58. *Star International Weekly*, 9–15 December 1993.

59. Alan Mabin, 'Struggle for the City: Urbanisation and Political Strategies of the South African State', *Social Dynamics*, 15, 1 (1989), 10. See also Hilary Sapire, 'Politics and Protest in Shack Settlements of the Pretoria-Witwatersrand-Vereeniging', *Journal of Southern African Studies*, 18, 3 (September 1992), 670–97.

60. David Collier, *Squatters and Oligarchs: Authoritarian Rule and Policy Change in Peru* (Baltimore and London: Johns Hopkins University Press, 1976), p. 60.

61. *Weekly Mail*, 5–11 November 1993.

62. *Weekly Mail*, 29 April–5 May 1994.

63. Paul Kennedy, *Preparing for the Twenty First Century* (New York: Vintage Books, 1993), pp. 217–18.

64. See in particular Gordon White (ed.), *Developmental States in East Asia* (Basingstoke: The Macmillan Press, 1988).

65. Chalmers Johnson, 'Political Institutions and Economic Performance: the Government–Business Relationship in Japan, South Korea and Taiwan' in Frederick C. Deyo (ed.), *The Political Economy of the New Asian Industrialisation* (Ithaca and London: Cornell University Press, 1983), p. 145.

66. Martin J. Murray, *Revolution Deferred* (London: Verso, 1994), p. 215.

67. Michael H. Allen, 'Bargaining Environments of a Post Apartheid State: Market, Class and Ethnic Dimensions' in Paul B. Rich (ed.), *The Dynamics of Change in Southern Africa* (Basingstoke: The Macmillan Press, 1994), pp. 71–97.

4 Some Reflections on the Interim Constitutional Arrangements

David Tucker

South Africa has experienced its first free election and now operates under an interim Constitution that embodies many democratic features. The society is also committed to evolve further towards a more permanent and comprehensive democratic system once the five year period of the government of national unity is over in 1999.

Against this background, I shall try to stimulate a discussion about the more pressing constitutional issues. Some of the questions that I address are: what key constitutional issues have already been resolved? Are the choices that have been made sensible? What further tasks must the newly elected Constituent Assembly now proceed to accomplish? In the course of the discussion I will be critical of the present arrangements which, as I show, have not been well thought out. The interim Constitution is the unfortunate result of a political compromise between parties who are more interested in power than accountability. It is the result of a deal between Afrikaner Nationalists, whose contempt for liberal democracy had already been clearly demonstrated throughout the years of apartheid, and members of the African National Congress intelligentsia who are very significantly influenced by the anti-liberal rhetoric of Marxism. Neither of these two protagonists has ever exhibited any respect for the concerns of liberal democrats, yet in the past few years they managed to reach an accommodation that has been widely acclaimed. This praise is justified, for the accomplishment of peaceful change in South Africa is by any reckoning a substantial achievement, and the ending of apartheid deserves to be celebrated. But this success should not be confused with the achievement of a liberal democracy. For this we need institutions that offer a regular alternation of government or a genuine dispersal of power and whether the current arrangements will allow for this is extremely doubtful.

The Constituent Assembly must now advance the potential for a democratic future that has already been achieved, building on the goodwill that seems to have emerged by finding the arrangements that have the best chance of securing viable accountable and limited government. The great danger is that the politicians who are responsible for this important task will be more concerned with implementing the agendas of the various political parties or with seeking ways to consolidate their power. To combat this tendency, I offer my chapter as a cautionary reminder – the achievement of democracy should not be taken for granted. By focusing on what I take to be serious weakness in the interim design, I hope to urge the Assembly members to nurture norms and values (such as individualism, and respect for the rule of law) that have allowed liberal systems to flourish in other parts of the world. South Africans should plan for the future and they must not think that their problems are so unusual that they cannot learn from the experiences of those countries in Europe and America that have sustained democratic institutions over many years.

THE COMPETING CONSTITUTIONAL THEORIES

The interim Constitution of South Africa is animated by a fundamental commitment to the pursuit of equality. This goal is stated in the Preamble where the future South Africa is defined as a society in which 'there is equality between men and women and people of all races so that all citizens shall be able to enjoy and exercise their fundamental rights and freedoms'; it is reaffirmed in Chapter 2 which outlines a Charter of Rights (where we are told that the Constitutional Court must interpret the Constitution so as to 'promote the values which underlie an open and democratic society based on freedom and equality') and, again, in Schedule 4, where the commitment is expressed in the following way:

> The legal system shall ensure the equality of all before the law and an equitable legal process. Equality before the law includes laws, programs or activities that have as their object the amelioration of the conditions of the disadvantaged, including those disadvantaged on the grounds of race, colour or gender.

We see here that the interim South African Constitution is built on a founding commitment to depart from the apartheid practice of racial discrimination. The inclusion of the phrase 'the amelioration of the conditions of the disadvantaged' shows that it is also concerned to facilitate changes designed to address the legacy of deprivation and poverty that apartheid has left in its wake.

These clear purposes provide a common source of reference for all participants in the on-going national dialogue. But the agreement is not very extensive, for when we probe the competing conceptions of 'equality' that inform the various political ideologies of the parties, we find that they are incompatible. Consider for example the orientations of the two most important parties.

THE ANC'S COMMITMENT TO EQUALITY

The African National Congress (ANC) takes its orientation from the Freedom Charter of 1955 which envisages a non-racial democratic order for South Africa. According to the ANC, the purpose of their political struggle is to bring about a social order in which all individuals will be treated as equals and in which fundamental liberties, such as those of speech and of association, are protected. Like liberal individualists, then, the ANC rejects any proposals for recognising group rights as a matter of principle, refusing to concede that race or ethnicity will remain important in a fully democratic South Africa, and committing itself to pursue unity through the articulation of a common national identity for all South Africans.[1]

In adopting this orientation, the leading intellectuals of the ANC (African National Congress) are heavily influenced by Marxist ideas. While they accept that ethnic conflicts are important they see the present focus on ethnicity as a residual product of apartheid; as they see it, ethnicity will be replaced by class differences as the most salient source of conflict so long as capitalism is retained as the mode of production. What the ANC sees itself as representing in effect is a coalition of the disadvantaged in South Africa, composed of individuals from all the various ethnic groups who are willing to work together. The ANC's negotiators are untroubled by the claims of those who argue that ethnic and racial divisions will destroy any constitutional structure that fails to recognise group rights. As far as they are concerned, the common interest in confronting apartheid that most ethnic groups in South Africa have recently shared will now secure a new alliance working to eliminate poverty by ending the huge disparities of wealth between classes. On this account, class solidarity will be sufficiently strong to unite most South Africans and their coalition to advance egalitarian ideals will be an enduring one.

These assumptions about the salience of class, race and ethnicity explain why ANC intellectuals are so comfortable with the principle of majority rule. A majority-rule democracy seems fair to them because, in the light of the universalistic perspective they have acquired from Marxism, no discrete insular minorities will be systematically excluded from a share of political power so long as the majority coalition (represented by the ANC) controls the state.[2] According to them, there are no cultural and social interests that are so important that they need to be specially privileged. Thus, no group in South Africa should be entitled to claim special privileges to sustain its distinct identity. Rather, each citizen should have an equal chance to signal, through the ballot, the direction of policy. Moreover, racial and ethnic privileges ought to be relegated to history as the nation moves forward towards a democratic future and those who insist on campaigning to secure ethnic loyalties should not be encouraged or advantaged in any way.

It is important to stress that although the ANC articulates these Enlightenment ideas, its intellectuals reject the liberal individualism with which this kind of position is usually associated. As a government the ANC plans to address the issue of compensation for past harms and to govern without too many inhibitions. No frustrating checks and balances are thought to be necessary so long as the government enjoys genuine majority support. No devolution of power is necessary, except to facilitate good administration. No special constitutional devices to ensure 'separate institutions, sharing powers' need to be set in place (for, according to the ANC's way of thinking, constitutional checks on the majority are usually designed to protect the privileges of minorities). Most ANC intellectuals also believe that liberals are much too enamoured of negative liberties and are inclined to ignore the fact that poor people are often unable to make use of abstract rights. Nor are they deeply concerned about the coercive instrumentality of the state. Far from it. They want to see an active state, enjoying substantial powers, securing the economic and social well-being of people and sustaining effective rather than merely formal liberties (for example, regulating the media so that the voices of the poor can be heard as often as the voices of the rich).

All this means that liberal liberties and commitments are qualified by the Marxist-inspired intellectuals within the ANC with phrases that allow the present government to pursue 'second generation' social and political rights – even 'third generation' environmental rights. (For example, the right not to be discriminated against on the basis of criteria such as race or gender is qualified to allow the state 'to pursue racial and gender equality and national unity'; the right to freedom of speech and expression is qualified to allow media to be 'regulated in a manner which ensures impartiality and the expression of a diversity of opinion').[3] When talking about rights, ANC theorists place almost all their emphasis on substantive entitlements – to health, education, housing – and do not seem preoccupied, as liberals are, with the processes by means of which governments may go about securing these desirable objectives. In short, they do not share the liberals' fear of regulators – for example, they have difficulty understanding why anyone of goodwill will be cautious about agreeing that the media should be regulated to impose fairness standards and diversity or to protect every person's right to dignity.[4]

The ANC has also rejected the notion that South Africa should be a federation, calling for a non-racial democracy in a unitary state.[5] Although it recognises the benefits of securing strong regional governments, it has opposed most devices designed to allow ethnic self-determination. In its manifesto for a future South Africa and in choosing the composition of its party list, the ANC recommends its ideal of a non-racial and non-ethnically divided South Africa. It also campaigned throughout the country, trying to gain the support of all ethnic groups. Indeed, its leaders went out of their way to reassure white South Africans that their interests would be fully recognised by an ANC-dominated government. The ANC also campaigned vigorously in Natal and in the Cape, claiming that the Zulu people and the Coloureds would be better off supporting a non-ethnic coalition than remaining locked into the apartheid legacy of ethnic chauvinism that leaders like Chief Gatsha Buthelezi and President F.W. de Klerk espoused.

ETHNIC APPROACHES: INKATHA AND THE NATIONAL PARTY

Opposed to the ANC were those for whom ethnicity and race are of vital and abiding importance. The governing National Party that had for years sustained apartheid in order to secure the cultural survival and economic well-being of Afrikaners was until the early 1990s the most prominent advocate of group rights. The Zulu Inkatha Freedom Party however has become even more strident in its claims for the recognition of ethnicity as an organising political principle.[6] Within the National Party, Afrikaner intellectuals are worried about the future of the Afrikaans language and about retaining their identity as European-Africans. They want to entrench various protections in the Constitution in order to secure what they take to be the distinct interests of various minorities.[7] Of course, the Afrikaners are supported by other whites who are less concerned about ethnicity but see advantages to themselves, as a minority, if group rights are acknowledged. This is because they fear uninhibited majority rule in the South African context. The Afrikaners are also supported by those Asian-Africans and Coloureds who fear African nationalism more than Afrikaner nationalism.

Gatsha Buthelezi, the leader of the Inkatha Freedom Party, demands recognition of the historically grounded claims of Zulus to ethnic self-determination. Speaking in a voice that echoes around the world, he demands recognition of the fact that Zulus were forced into the Union of South Africa without consultation. He holds that the whole of Natal was traditionally Zulu territory and that, with the dismantling of apartheid, this territorial claim should be recognised. Although he does not demand that all the land be transferred back to the indigenous owners, he argues that the whites and Indians who now live there should be required to negotiate with the Zulus so that arrangements can be found that respect the their status as the original owners of all the land.[8]

Buthelezi and de Klerk have few political allies internationally. But they enjoy intellectual support from an influential school of constitutional theorists because they each make use of ideas that have come to be known as 'consociationalism'.[9] Briefly stated, this approach holds that 'power-sharing' and the recognition of group rights represent the best way forward in deeply divided plural societies. This view is fashionable today because liberal individualism is under attack. Many people reject the ideal of equality under law that liberals embrace because they see this kind of universalism as a threat to their sense of communal identity. Because more and more ethnic communities who had previously enjoyed no voice in politics now assert themselves, individualism as a constitutional ideal has found itself in retreat. Theorists like Lijphart would like to see an open recognition of the claim that democracies work best when the elites within the various subcultures are willing to accept as legitimate the divergent cultural interests and demands made by elites representing the other communities – even those made on behalf of minority groups. According to this view, South Africans who indulge ethnicity and celebrate difference, demanding the recognition of group rights (like de Klerk and Buthelezi), must be supported; they certainly have allies today that were unavailable 20 years ago.

In reviewing the different theoretical assumptions of the more important parties in the on-going South African constitutional debates, it is interesting to note the absence of a liberal voice. Although all sides make formal commitments to liberal ideals, on closer inspection we find that they are uncommitted to the realisation of a liberal democracy in South Africa, as this term is generally understood. From the point of view of a political theorist the circumstances in South Africa reflect a particular irony in that two of the groups who are amongst the most hostile critics of liberal ideals, Marxists and communitarians, have been forced to reach an accommodation on terrain that is distinctively liberal. Let us now consider the result of this rather unlikely contract.

THE INTERIM CONSTITUTION

If we look at the interim Constitution we find that it contain some con-sociational guarantees for minorities. (And verbal assurances that minority interests will not be ignored have also been given by Nelson Mandela.) The specific accommodations are (1) the choice of a list proportional representation voting system with a departure from the principle of equality to allow for regional representation in the Senate, (2) the power-sharing arrangements that have been agreed to for the composition of the executive, (3) the incorporation of a Charter of Rights and the promise of an independent constitutional court, (4) some of the commitments for the future contained in the 32 governing principles listed at the end of the Constitution, and (5) the devolution of power to nine provincial parliaments and to local government authorities. Let me consider each of these arrangements briefly.

1.   The Choice of List-PR as the Electoral System

The election in April was conducted under list-system proportional representation. This was designed to ensure that minority parties would be represented (in contrast to the results that could have been expected from a constituency-based plurality system).[10] In terms of the list-PR arrangements, every elector in the April election was required to cast two votes – one for a national list and one for a provincial list. They were not voting for candidates but for the competing parties. Thus, South Africans did not have an opportunity of supporting particular candidates in April in 1994. They had to accept everyone on the list of their choice (for example, citizens who favoured the ANC because they trusted Mandela but disliked Marxists were not free to eliminate communist party members from the ANC list, nor could they eliminate specific candidates they thought unworthy of political office). The votes for the party lists were counted in different ways. The first vote established the composition of the 400-member National Assembly. The second vote determined the representation in the nine provinces and in the second chamber of the national parliament, the 90-member Senate. The National Assembly seats were allocated in the light of the proportion of votes each party achieved nationally. In contrast, the composition of the Senate reflects geographical units rather than the number of votes achieved by each party overall. Ten Senate seats were allocated to each province regardless of its size, and a fair proportion of these was allocated to each party depending on the votes it succeeded in securing for its provincial lists.[11]

An electoral system based on a party list gives the leaders of the various parties a good deal of control over their members. This is because seats are allocated to the parties, not to the candidates. If a party member disagrees with his or her leader, the punishment can be very severe. It will also be difficult for parties to poach members, enticing them from their opponents. Party members will be extremely jealous about their positions on the various lists. Those members on any given list who have not achieved a seat in a parliament will be impatiently waiting to move ahead in the queue so that they can finally achieve this goal. They will deeply resent it if someone from another party is suddenly advanced ahead of them. Nor will there be much incentive for party leaders to try and secure support from members from rival parties. The numbers are fixed – a member who crosses the floor forfeits his or her seat. Even a party with a single seat advantage, such as Inkatha in Natal, can govern comfortably in the period between elections knowing that their marginal advantage is secure.

Given these circumstances and incentives, the ability of the various parliaments to constrain governments is weak, regardless of the allocation of formal powers. Control over the party lists strengthens the capacity of executives to secure their authority – this may however be a good thing in a country that is as difficult to govern as South Africa. Because of list-PR, the party leaders will also have a capacity to ignore some preferences within the electorate if they choose. For example, it was feasible for the ANC to include individuals on its party list who would have had difficulty gaining the approval of voters if they had been required to stand as individual candidates, even as candidates using a popular party label. Many of the individuals on the ANC's list had no proven record as politicians. Their qualification to be included on the party list had been secured by a willingness to join in the struggle against apartheid when this was a dangerous thing to do. Far from representing their communities, many of these individuals were amongst their most alienated members. Similarly, it was possible for the National Party to run with candidates whose record during the years when the party supported racial segregation was difficult to justify to an electorate that was now responding to the post-apartheid rhetoric.[12]

Let us now look at some of the problems that list-system PR presents for an ethnically divided country like South Africa. Consider:

(a)   corruption
List-PR makes it more difficult to avoid corruption. The fact that executives are able to lead without facing effective opposition does not necessarily result in corruption or abuse (as the honourable Swedish Democrats illustrate); but continuity in office, immunity from parliamentary review and

the freedom of politicians from close personal scrutiny in contests in which they must personally secure election does sometimes result in corruption (as the cases of Italy and Japan make only too clear). A list-system also makes it more difficult to correct any abuse of power that is detected, a point reflected in the fact that Winnie Mandela was retained on the ANC list despite her personal record.

(b)   secure incumbency

Another problem with list-PR is that many members in the national and provincial parliaments will enjoy safe seats, making a cosy relationship with powerful lobbyists very likely. Once the profile of a particular parliament (in terms of the proportion of seats allocated to the competing parties) has settled, the lucky party members who are well placed on the lists can expect to be secure in power for a very long time. Indeed, there will be a large number of members in every parliament who enjoy a relatively secure tenure; and these are the very politicians most likely to be in the position of power (for example, as floor leaders and committee chairs). Even when their own party does badly, these politicians can expect to be returned. In seven of the provinces of South Africa (that is, all except Natal and the Western Cape which are held by the Inkatha and the NP respectively) there is one-party dominance and this is also the case in the National Assembly and Senate. For most politicians, the risk of losing office will be dependent on a massive swing against the ANC at the next election or on an internal party division within the party resulting in a split or a substantial reshuffling of the names on the party's list. So long as list-PR is retained as the electoral system, almost all of South Africa's parliaments are likely to be dominated by the ANC whose members will not anticipate losing control.

This kind of permanency is not unusual in democracies where list-system PR is used. It occurs even when one-party dominance of the kind that is now manifest in South Africa has not resulted. This is because deals made between parties of the centre (Italy) or on the left (Sweden) can ensure that the same officials remain in office even when the leadership of a ruling coalition shifts from one party to another. Continuity of this kind is not unique to list-systems as the case of the United States Congress demonstrates.

(c)   excessive executive power

I will explore the considerable powers that have been allocated in the interim Constitution to the President shortly. Because of list-PR, President

Mandela is able to govern without much regard for South Africa's National Assembly, the Senate or the provinces (apart from Natal and Western Cape where the ANC is not in power). This is because he can demand complete loyalty from all ANC members in exchange for a position on the relevant party list. Every politician, whether provincial or national, knows that he or she depends on his or her party for election. Because of the important patronage afforded by the ANC's party list, anyone who crosses the leader risks political oblivion.

(d)　enhanced ethnic conflict

Perhaps the most damaging potential consequence that the list-PR electoral system is likely to have is that it can sometimes provide dysfunctional incentives for politicians in circumstances where ethnic divisions are likely to present serious difficulties. This is because political leaders will be tempted to appeal to specific ethnic groups, devising lists that reflect racial and ethnic sentiments. So long as leaders on an ethnic party's list are reliably returned to office, they will have little incentive to move beyond their own group by embracing moderate positions that appeal to non-members, and they will have every incentive to whip up ethnic conflicts to ensure that the voters who feel strongly about ethnicity are not too apathetic. The problem here is that so long as ethnic chauvinism offers a safe route to office, politicians will follow it; and the more they do this, the more likely it will be that this is indeed the safest route to take. The problem with list-systems is that they facilitate this process.

These considerations all suggest that the Constituent Assembly should reconsider the electoral system. Democracy succeeds or fails because of the signals that are sent to politicians at elections. It is important that politicians are encouraged to respond to those sections of the electorate whose demands are the most constructive. As we have seen, list-PR is unlikely to perform this function because it threatens to encourage the least functional ethnic incentives. If a list-system is used, this should be combined with some further arrangements that will give politicians incentives to reach beyond their own communities towards an accommodation with others. What South Africa needs is a system that will reward those politicians who seek the second preferences of its ethnically orientated voters. Whether a practical system of this kind is likely to be agreed to by those who have already benefited from the list-system now in place is, however, extremely doubtful. Nevertheless, some good suggestions for reform have been recommended by well-meaning observers.[13]

2. 'Power-sharing' and Executive Power

The presidential system we find in South Africa differs significantly from the familiar variant that is exemplified in the United States. In the American system, restraints on the executive arise because of shared constitutional powers, a division between state and federal authorities, and staggered elections. The President must work with the States, Congress and an independent Supreme Court. Nor is the composition of these co-equal branches of government in his hands; indeed, it is usually shaped by electoral moods very different from those that enabled him to secure his own period in office. Moreover, these co-equal branches of government enjoy considerable powers in their own right. This kind of separation of powers was not possible in South Africa because nobody wanted to complicate the first elections by holding independent presidential elections. Thus, Presidents Mandela, de Klerk and Mbeki were elected by the National Assembly at its first sitting and this means that executive and legislative powers are necessarily closely interrelated. Paradoxically, the fact that the Presidency is a product of the National Assembly means that President Mandela is now effectively able to take the powers of the legislature into his own hands.

President Mandela also enjoys significant powers in his own right (unlike the Deputy Presidents whose constitutional prerogatives are very few). In this respect, the South African executive differs from the familiar position of prime minister in parliamentary systems who enjoys power only if the members of their parliamentary parties agree. Prime ministers are not well constrained in normal times because they are able to discipline their party followers, controlling the parliaments that secure them in office; but they do occasionally face rebellions and this possibility is a constraint upon them. In contrast, Presidents are usually less constrained by the fear of losing parliamentary support and this is also the case in South Africa where the new President enjoys special and extensive powers that flow from his office.[14] Here, we see the overlap with the United States system except that there is no separate presidential election; also, because the National Assembly in South Africa is so well controlled by the ruling ANC, President Mandela is unlikely to face any potentially embarrassing enquiries of the kind that made life so difficult for President Nixon in the 1970s or President Clinton over the Whitewater enquiry. Like Nixon and Clinton he enjoys his position until the fixed term allowed for is over and an election is constitutionally required. But, unlike any US President, Mandela is very unlikely to lose office or power even if there is a massive swing against the ANC. He is able to act on his own authority in most circumstances and, though he is constitutionally required to consult his Cabinet as well as the Deputy Presidents on major matters, it is not clear what 'consultation' actually means. It certainly does not mean that Mandela will have to defer to the wishes of these officials. In any event President Mandela now: (1) controls foreign policy as the person designated to negotiate and sign international agreements and to receive and appoint Ambassadors and other diplomats (the US President must obtain the support of the Senate and cannot make high-level appointments or sign treaties or declare war without consultation); (2) serves as Commander-in-Chief of the National Defence Force (anyone who has followed discussions about the American Presidency will know how significant this power is); (3) enjoys a presidential veto that allows him full control over the legislative process (for he must also sign and promulgate all the Bills duly passed by the Parliament).[15] Nor does the National Assembly enjoy the power to overrule the President's veto (as is the case in the United States if Congress can secure a 2/3 override when a President refuses to sign a Bill). Another control that President Mandela now exercises concerns money bills. In the United States Congress controls the flow of money to the executive. This is how the Congress exercises influence. In South Africa, by contrast, the National Assembly and Senate may not consider any Bill appropriating revenue unless such a Bill has been initiated by the Minister responsible for national financial matters.[16]

Like American Presidents, Mandela also enjoys enormous patronage – making critical appointments or sharing the power of appointments in a number of areas (for example, he shares the appointment power to the Constitutional Court with the Judicial Service Commission; he will also appoint all Ambassadors, the Chief of the National Defence Force as well as the National Commissioner of Police.)[17]

Although the President can be removed from office by a vote of no-confidence that would force an election or by a vote of impeachment for violating the Constitution or failing to execute his or her duties effectively (by two-thirds majority of both chambers in joint sitting),[18] these provisions are unlikely to weaken President Mandela's authority. For one thing, his personal stature gives him a role something like that which George Washington enjoyed in the United States as the first President. Also, as many on the ANC party list will be threatened by an election in these circumstances, they are unlikely to call for the President's removal or force the President's hand by moving a motion of impeachment. It is also significant that there are no limitations on the length of time that President Mandela may serve. In his own case, of course, he will be limited by his age; but it is surely dangerous to allow a situation in which his successor can expect to serve indefinitely so long as the ANC can control a majority in the Assembly.

The dangers inherent in all forms of presidentialism are too well-known to need outlining here.[19] Even those who wish to see a strong executive in South Africa should find the powers afforded to Mandela in the interim Constitution far too extensive. The temptation to abuse this authority will be enormous and history teaches that we cannot always rely on recruiting individuals with integrity and good sense to the office. Sometimes abuse will occur because subordinates are too diligent in pursuing what they take to be the wishes of a leader. Sometimes a leader will rationalise an abuse by supposing that he or she is indispensable. Either way, incumbents will inevitably push constitutional authority to its outer limits. Unfortunately, in South Africa, there are no adequate limits. This is why the arrangements urgently need to be changed.

The emphasis placed on executive authority in South Africa is deliberate. It is a result of a compromise the parties agreed to in order to secure the ending of apartheid. Thus, Mandela's Cabinet is not formed by the dominant party allocating all the positions, with the party's leader deciding the portfolios. Rather, President Mandela accepted that he is bound by the 'power-sharing' plan specified in the Constitution. Under # 88 (2) both the National Party and the Inkatha Freedom Party qualified for seats in the Cabinet because they obtained more than 20 seats in the National Assembly (5 per cent of the national vote in the election). (The portfolios were to be allocated by the President after consultations with the two Executive Deputy Presidents and the leaders of the participating parties, as required under # 88 (4).)[20] There is also provision in the constitution for a sharing of power through the office of Executive Deputy President.[21] This is because any party with 20 per cent of the votes (or if there are none, except for the winning party, this party and the second largest party) is entitled to nominate an Executive Deputy President.

We can only speculate at this stage about what motivated the various negotiators to agree to these 'power-sharing' arrangements. One possibility is that those who felt vulnerable when they perceived the ANC as a mass movement mobilising the people for revolutionary changes were reassured when they actually came to negotiate with the likes of Nelson Mandela, Cyril Ramaphosa and Thabo Mbeki. As for Mandela and the other ANC negotiators, they may have believed that a non-ANC presence in the Cabinet would serve as a reassurance to the world, particularly to bankers. And the minority parties may have speculated that they could enjoy power even within an ANC-dominated Cabinet because a threatened resignation of National Party and Inkatha members would send signals to international investors that Presidents Mandela and Mbeki would find very undesirable.

Whatever the reasons for its adoption, the unusual 'power-sharing' arrangement envisaged in the Interim Constitution is fraught with difficulties for it is unlikely that National Party and the Inkatha Freedom Party members allocated Cabinet seats will be co-operative. It is not as though this unlikely coalition has been the product of a recognition of mutual interest. Far from it. It is the product of mutual suspicion. In any event, the 'honeymoon' period between de Klerk and Mandela is unlikely to last for very long – and there has been no honeymoon at all with Buthelezi. In practice, what is likely to happen is that President Mandela will operate within Cabinet sub-committees that are unlikely to include de Klerk or Buthelezi, or he may govern outside of the formal Cabinet arrangements, so that power will be shared with minority party leaders only when this is thought to be expedient by the ANC leadership.

Will these power-sharing arrangements be sufficient to blunt the edge of potential ethnic conflict? This is very unlikely.

3.   The Charter of Rights

In Chapter 2, the Interim Constitution includes a list of rights that are to be protected. However it also includes a provision for suspending rights under a State of Emergency declared prospectively by an ordinary Act of the National Assembly.[22] Such an emergency declaration allows for a period of 21 days in which rights are suspended; after that, it requires a resolution of the National Assembly adopted by a majority of at least two-thirds. This allows for three months at a time of emergency government, though it is significant that the Senate is excluded from sharing review of an emergency declaration.

The list of protected rights is very ambitious – including 33 sections with many additional clauses. But it is also unclear just how the Constitutional Court is supposed to execute its responsibility as the guardian of these rights. This is because the listed rights include more than the purely negative liberties that characterise, say, the Bill of Rights attached to the United States Constitution. The South African Constitutional Court is also responsible for securing welfare programmes as well as for providing services (thus: # 30 lists the rights of children to adequate nutrition, basic health, and parental care; and # 32 sets out a right to basic education and equal access to educational institutions). Many of the listed rights are inspirational. They set forth goals that the community should aspire to see realised, even if it fails as it undoubtedly will. It is difficult to see how the judicial branch of government can serve in a useful way as guardian of these aspirations. What can it do when a parent abandons a child? What can it do if schools are inadequate? Yet when we list rights in a constitution, we are surely intending to allocate some responsibilities to the judiciary. Judges are severely constrained in the instruments that they have available for achieving policy goals, however desirable they may be. They have no capacity to raise money or to administer and they are unable to use incentives such as offers of tax relief to ensure that other agents will co-operate. Nor are judges well advised by bureaucrats who are experts in housing, education or health. They must also function from case to case and cannot easily monitor the consequences of what they have done or make directives to help those charged with carrying out their programmes. For all these reasons and more that could be listed, judges are not the appropriate authority for making the difficult decisions all communities must make in allocating resources between competing uses.[23] It may be that in providing schools there will be less police or fewer houses. Why should judges have to decide which of the many competing priorities is the more pressing?

Because second generation rights have been included in the Bill of Rights for South Africa, there is a danger the judiciary will assume roles for which it is not suited, using the aspirational goals that have been listed as a basis for this claim to authority. Another problem is that they may be forced to ignore rights claims that are justified by reference to the plain meaning of the text and this may encourage them to play fast and loose with the words that attempt to bind them. No good consequences are likely to follow from a poorly drafted list of rights.

Consider the issue of equality. Understandably, in the light of South Africa's experience with racial discrimination, the Constitution contains provisions that forbid the use of racial categories. Thus # 8 (1) states that 'Every person shall have the right to equality before the law and to the equal protection of the law', and # 8 (2) lists the suspect categories: 'race, gender, sex, ethnic or social origin, colour, sexual orientation, age, disability, religion, conscience, belief, culture, or language'. This list is incredibly ambitious and is in advance of most other countries, for example, in protecting gays and lesbians. One must seriously doubt whether there is a national consensus in South Africa amongst the general population to secure such extensive protections.

One of the most contentious issues for the future will be the issue of affirmative action – including the practice of race being considered as part of general ability testing together with other measures that might be introduced to ensure the advancement of Africans. Despite its concern with race as an illicit category in law, the Constitution encourages affirmative action to remedy the past effects of apartheid. Thus, it insulates from challenge 'measures aimed at the adequate protection and advancement of persons disadvantaged by discrimination in order to enable their full and equal enjoyment of all rights and freedoms'. This is a clear signal that affirmative action plans will be part of instruments available to future governments to advance groups – some groups will be advanced simply because of their race. The problem the Constitutional Court will face is to determine whether these programs are advanced in a rational way – rationally related to the legitimate goal of advancing the previously disadvantaged – or are simply new forms of racial discrimination by those who have succeeded to political power. But how is the Constitutional Court to decide whether it is reasonable to require one of South Africa's leading Universities to ensure that at least 60 per cent of its students be African? This was a demand made by students. Administrators and managers of all major institutions within the new South Africa will be faced by the demand that they make use of racial quotas in hiring, promoting and firing. In some cases, organisations that fail to meet racial quotas will be faced by penalties (such as the loss of government contracts or funding). The Constitutional Court will have to rule as to when the demand for quotas is unreasonable and whether companies that have failed were making 'good faith' efforts to meet them. But there is no rational way to do this.

For example, # 8 (4) makes it clear that proof of discrimination may be established statistically – establishing a *prima facie* case that the person charged with discrimination must answer. This is the problem that the American courts brought upon themselves in the landmark *Griggs v. Duke Power Co.* ruling.[24] Unfortunately, as a matter of fact – as opposed to law – statistical disparity (that is a showing that a disproportionate number of a particular group are advanced) does not constitute sufficient evidence to establish discrimination so that *prima facie* claims based on statistical evidence will often be fanciful. This is because the individuals that make up various groups are differently motivated and enjoy different skills. Can we expect 80 per cent of South Africa's managers to be Africans? Yet South African companies will now face legal claims if they cannot show why disparities in their workforce have arisen. I can only see enormous problems for the future South Africa, relating to the constitutionally mandated misuse of statistical evidence. It will be a constant cause of ethnic friction and the Constitution does little to prevent this from happening. It will also ensure that South African companies are less efficient and competitive than they could be and this is likely to make all the various communities in the country worse off.

The framers of the interim arrangements seem to overlook the fact that the African community that has been excluded under the years of apartheid is now able to dominate the Assembly. Its leaders are able to advance their interest using public money to pay for housing, education and health. They can also forbid discrimination, as they have. So there is little reason for them to impose quotas. This is very different from the circumstance in the United States. In that country, only 15 per cent of the workforce might be eligible for advancement as 'minorities'. The problem in that country has been to ensure a fair allocation of opportunities to those groups in the community who are not in a good position to use the political process to protect themselves. Even so, the use of affirmative action strategies has not been very successful. There are no good reasons for thinking that experiences with this kind of strategy in South Africa will prove more successful.

One area where the future government is constrained in pursuing equality concerns the issue of compensation for the loss of traditional land. The Constitution states that anyone dispossessed of land because of past discrimination is entitled to claim restitution.[25] This is fair enough. But having a right to claim is not the same as actually receiving just compensation. The problem here is that very many people in South Africa are eligible to make claims for land, so it is obvious that a future government will be unable to meet the costs of securing justice. Significantly, the claims of whites to the property they now hold is also guaranteed. Under #s 121, 122, 123 the Constitution sets out conditions for the restitution of land rights, establishing a Commission to investigate the merits of any claims. However, where the Commission orders the expropriation of property it must pay compensation to the present owners.[26]

Now consider some free speech problems. In # 15 (1) there is a protection of 'free speech' which we are told includes 'freedom of the press and other media, and the freedom of artistic creativity and scientific research'. But the very next clause, # 15 (2), undermines this commitment because it allows governments to regulate 'all media financed by or under the control of the state'. In effect this means that there will be state regulation of the broadcasting system which is currently state-owned or operates under licence. The government is free to impose standards that ensure 'impartiality and the expression of a diversity of opinions'.[27] These phrases are vague and it is crucial to decide the level at which the provisions apply – whether every journalist and editor has an obligation to observe both 'diversity' and 'impartiality' or whether the obligation is applicable only to the licensee. Presumably these matters will be settled by the government regulators. What if the regulators decide that fairness and diversity require that the voice of the ANC, representing 60 per cent of the people, be heard 60 per cent of the time? Suppose that they withdraw the licences of all stations that do not meet this standard. However it is packaged, the regulation of the speech content of major media means national censorship.

Another serious problem will arise if the government proceeds to enact a hate speech code, as the ANC has promised it will. Are those who are 'racist' according to the state definition going to be protected by the Constitutional Court? Will people who are racist be vulnerable to prison sentences simply because of the written materials they disseminate? If so, what does 'freedom of speech' and the right 'of conscience, belief [and] culture' mean in practice?

One last problem with the Charter of Rights is worth noting. The framers have included clauses that have proved very controversial and unhelpful in other jurisdictions. Thus, # 9 states 'every person shall have the right to life', # 11 (2) includes the phrase 'nor shall any person be subject to cruel, inhuman or degrading treatment or punishment' and # 33 (3) includes phrases that could have been taken from the notoriously impractical Ninth Amendment to the United States Constitution. To include these vague and essentially meaningless phrases is simply to invite judicial activism, yet this may not be helpful in the early years of a democracy. Do South Africans really want anti-abortion activists to pursue their concerns about abortion through the courts? What if the Constitutional Court finds that the listed right to life extends to protect the life of a foetus? Even if the Constitutional Court does not read this phrase to forbid abortions, religious fundamentalists will claim that they should do this (because this is the plain meaning) and this will add an edge to their rhetoric. Nor is it desirable to make capital punishment a judicial issue in a country where it is a widely accepted practice to leave courts as the guardians of what forms of punishment are acceptable. The prison system in South Africa is in an appalling state and the criminal justice process is also in disarray. These problems will not be fixed by judicial fiat and little progress will come from a Court challenge to the prevailing practices, even if it proves successful. Large sums of money will have to be spent on something other than legal fees before even minimum standards of humane treatment are met. Judicial orders to prison officials when these are obtained after a constitutional challenge will simply be ignored in present circumstances because the prisons will have no capacity to implement them successfully. As for capital punishment – if the people of South Africa wish to continue with this barbaric practice no court will be able to prevent them. Do we really want the judges selected against a 'litmus test' of their willingness to read the Constitution in a way that allows the imposition of death sentences?

Finally, it is interesting to observe that the Constitutional Court is not the only authority mentioned that has been charged with responsibility for securing rights, There is to be a Human Rights Commission, a Commission on Gender Equality, and a Commission on the Restitution of Land Rights. Each of these agencies will receive funding to establish a small bureaucracy that will investigate claims, mediate disputes, draw up reports, and generally promote the observance of, respect for, and the protection of rights. These commissions will also support individuals who seek redress through the courts, acting as a legal aid service for those who are pursuing constitutional claims. It would seem that, in many important constitutional cases, it will usually be one of the Commissioners vs. the relevant Solicitor General. A further important role for the commissions is that they are required to scrutinise proposed legislation and issue reports to the relevant parliament when they believe Bills are in conflict with the national commitment to secure human rights.

It would seem, then, that South Africa has taken a massive step towards the very unimpressive American tradition by means of which every major social issue has to be contested in both the courts and the parliaments. Not only is this going to prove costly and extremely divisive but it is likely to bring the nation to the brink of crisis whenever the Constitutional Court is out of step with the wider community (as is highly probable, given its likely composition); or if one or other of the provinces insists on defying the Court.

4. The Constitutional Court

The Constitutional Court will consist of the President of the Court, appointed by the state President in consultation with Cabinet and the Chief Justice of the Supreme Court, and ten other judges – all holding tenure for a non-renewable period of seven years.

Given the important role allocated to the judges who are responsible for interpreting the Constitution – a role that includes responsibility for ensuring that the 33 binding principles that have been listed are incorporated in the future constitution – it matters a good deal how these judges will be selected. This is a matter that South Africans have considered carefully and elaborate arrangements have been set in place. Responsibility for selecting the judges is shared by the President (who must consult the Cabinet) and a Judicial Service Commission that is heavily representative of the legal profession (it includes the Chief Justice, President of the Constitutional Court when she or he is appointed, one Judge President, the Minister responsible for the administration of justice, two practising advocates nominated by the profession, two practising attorneys nominated by the profession, one professor of law designated by the deans, four senators, four attorneys or advocates nominated by the President). The Commission must endeavour to ensure that the future Constitutional Court is representative in respect of race and gender but competent and independent. It must construct a short-list of ten names, all experienced individuals who are qualified in law, and present these to the President. The President is responsible for selecting six candidates from the list for appointment to the Court and he must also select four further members from the members of the current Supreme Court (the Chief Justice must be consulted about this). If the President does not like the list presented by the Judicial Service Commission, he must state his reasons for rejecting the initial selection and the Commission is obliged to provide another list.

These arrangement seem sensible. However, the country cannot proceed for long with the rule that the members of the Constitutional Court are appointed for non-renewable periods of seven years. Such a rule will destroy the independence of any court because the ideological composition of its members will be changed whenever there is a conflict with leading politicians. This is probably a good thing for the present in South Africa because the country cannot afford a constitutional crisis in its early years; thus, it will help if the judiciary is extremely deferential. But the seven-year-term rule should not be carried over into the new Constitution.

5.   The Devolution of Power

Buthelezi has demanded that 'federalism' be placed on the agenda for discussion by the Constituent Assembly.[28] Before the election he had been holding out for federal arrangements to be negotiated because he knew that it was unrealistic for Zulus to expect to be well represented in the National Assembly.[29] He seems to have been persuaded to allow Inkatha to participate in the elections, accepting the interim constitutional arrangements, only when a substantial grant of land was made to the Zulu King by (then) President de Klerk. There is no doubt that the Inkatha Freedom Party will continue to press for a more far-reaching devolution of power and to have land directly under their control.

But the Zulus are not alone in suggesting federal schemes. One pressure for this will be the calls to include neighbouring states in a confederation to encourage economic development within the region. If any moves are made to incorporate Swaziland, Lesotho, Namibia, Mozambique and Botswana into a greater South African free trade area, the Zulus will certainly demand the same status in Natal-KwaZulu as that enjoyed by the Swazi and the Basuto people. Another area that may well seek greater autonomy is the Western Cape.

The present devolution of power to the provincial parliaments in no way meets the demand for regional autonomy because the provincial legislatures enjoy only concurrent competence with the National Assembly.[30] Besides its constitutional power to overrule the provinces by passing controlling legislation, the central government also controls national revenues. This enables it to secure compliance with its wishes by offering grants of money for very specific purposes and only when the provinces agree to various conditions. Although provinces are competent to impose taxes they may do so only when these are recommended by the Financial and Fiscal Commission which is an instrument of the national executive. A final instrument for ensuring national compliance with standards set at the centre will be the Constitutional Court for it can rule on any issue because of the broad-ranging discretion it has been afforded by the vague commitments made in the interim Constitution. Given these arrangements, it is clear that the provinces may be dictated to by the national government.

It was foolish to ignore the call for a federal structure by the Zulus in drafting the interim Constitution and it will be foolish to continue to ignore it. A society as divided as South Africa has a great deal to gain through federal arrangements because it allows all the people to feel more confident that their vital interests will not be overlooked. Also it is useful that people learn to deal with one another in a variety of different political arenas and it is desirable that groups such as the Coloureds in the Cape and Zulus in Natal KwaZulu will feel that they are in control of some important aspects of their own destinies. Of course, consociational arrangements of this kind do have the adverse consequence that ethnic divisions may come to be entrenched. But ethnic divisions do not disappear simply because constitutions ignore them and it is far better to encourage co-operation, giving people a reason for joining a union, than to risk an on-going disaffection that may eventually lead to calls for secession.

Unless people are made to feel secure within the new nation, they will not be ready to acquire a new sense of loyalty. And there are enough economic incentives in South Africa to hold the two ethnically distinct provinces in the union, even if they were to become separate states. Nor is it necessary to see federal arrangements solely as a mechanism to allow ethnic self-determination. A dispersal of power will also have the advantage of preventing the accumulation of too much power at the centre. This should not be threatening to the new ANC-dominated government. It will still have to manage the national economy and, in the circumstances of contemporary South Africa, this will provide it with enough means to persuade future states to co-operate on matters of importance. Thus, there is no need for the provincial authorities to remain as subordinate as they are at present, and there are good reasons for thinking that South Africans would be better off if separate states were established under a federal arrangement.

CONCLUSIONS

The interim Constitution in South Africa is the result of negotiations between parties who are not very sensitive to the concerns of the liberal political theorists. The ANC is eager to address the many major problems the nation faces and its leaders have not been in power long enough to become distrusted. People turn to Nelson Mandela (and to many of the other leaders who opposed apartheid) for moral inspiration and nobody within the ANC has thought it necessary to bridle executive authority. In contrast, the National Party and the Inkatha Freedom Party are fearful of unbridled majority rule and advocate the recognition of group rights. But they are ethnically orientated movements and also reject liberal values.

As we have seen, the interim Constitution does not offer an adequate constitutional framework for the future. If the present arrangements are not changed, South Africa is likely to emerge as a dominant one-party system with a very powerful executive. This is not a recipe that is likely to produce an enduring democracy. There are also phrases included in the Constitution which are likely to precipitate a constitutional crisis. If these are resolved in favour of the national government, South Africa will move towards a one-party dictatorship. This is why South Africans need to nurture a respect for the rule of law but this is unlikely to happen if its courts and commissions are encouraged to play a blatantly political role. These flaws in the present system are easily remedied if the political will could be found to think seriously about the long-term future. I have recommended a reconsideration of some of the interim Constitution's more ill-considered features, such as the commitment to list-PR, the reliance on the Constitutional Court for policy making, the enormous powers allocated to the President, and the failure to take into account the demand by Zulus and others for a genuine devolution of power.

NOTES

1. On the ANC see Marina Ottaway, 'Liberation Movement and Tradition to Democracy: The Case of the ANC', *Journal of Modern African Studies*, 29 (1991), 61–82 and *South Africa: The Struggle for a New Order* (Washington DC: The Brookings Institute, 1993), pp. 43–55, 99–101; Tom Lodge, 'State of Exile: The African National Congress of South Africa, 1976–86' in Philip Frankel, Noam Pines and Mark Swilling (eds), *State, Resistance and Change in South Africa* (Johannesburg: Southern Book Publishers, 1988).
2. See Albie Sachs, 'Post-Apartheid South Africa: A Constitutional Framework', *World Policy Journal*, vol. 6, no. 3 (1989), 503–29; also *Protecting Human Rights in a New South Africa* (Cape Town: Oxford University Press, 1990).
3. See interim Constitution, Chapter 3, para. xxxx.
4. These values are reflected in what is said about free speech in the interim Constitution (para. xx) and by the inclusion of welfare rights (para. xx). See Sachs, *Protecting Human Rights*, pp. xxxff.
5. See African National Congress Constitutional Committee, 'A Discussion Document on Structures and Principles of a Constitution for a Democratic South Africa' (Belville: Centre for Development Studies, April 1991).
6. See Ottaway, *South Africa*, pp. 95–103.
7. *Ibid.*, pp. 90–9.
8. For details see Chapter 2.
9. Arend Lijphart, *Power-Sharing in South Africa* (Berkeley CA: University of California Press, 1985) proposes a consociational solution for South Africa. This is based on his earlier work *The Politics of Accommodation: Pluralism and Democracy in the Netherlands* (Berkeley CA: University of California Press, 1968). His recommendations have been taken up by others and some have even been embodied in the interim Constitution (for example the provision for a government of national unity, requiring the representation of minority parties in the Cabinet). On the application of consociational theory to South Africa see Hermann Giliomee and Lawrence Schlemmer (eds), *Negotiating South Africa's Future* (New York: St. Martin's Press, 1979); Frederik van Zyl Slabbert and David Welsh, *South Africa's Options: Strategies for Sharing Power* (New York: St. Martin's Press, 1979). The idea of a consociational democracy has been critically evaluated by Brian Barry in two long essays, included in B. Barry, *Democracy and Political Power* (Oxford: Oxford University Press, 1989), pp. 100–55. The application of consociational plans to an ethnically divided society such as South Africa has been questioned by Donald L. Horowitz, *A Democratic South Africa? Constitutional Engineering in a Divided Society* (Berkeley CA: University of California, 1991), pp. 137–48.
10. In which the dominant party is massively over-represented and can win control of government even when it does not secure majority support within the electorate. Thus, the move towards a PR system has meant that minorities will be represented if they choose to assert themselves politically. This seems eminently fair. However, as Donald Horowitz notes, experience shows minorities do not necessarily assert themselves politically and may not vote

for ethnically distinct parties. In other words, an election under list-PR may not define a society in the manner envisaged by Arend Lijphart (Horowitz, *A Democratic South Africa? Constitutional Engineering in a Divided Society*, pp. 167–70). Indeed, because the ANC achieved over 60 per cent of the vote in April 1994, South Africans must now face the reality that their country's political life will be dominated by one major party that is able to secure the support of all the various African groups, apart from the Zulus, for the foreseeable future. This means that other ethnic communities left out of the coalition, such as Indians, Zulus, Coloureds, Afrikaners and English are now vulnerable as 'discrete insular minorities'.

11. It has to be said that this regional advantage is undermined by the fact that the Senate seems to enjoy very little power to reverse or delay initiatives presented by the National Assembly.

12. Richard Johnson claims that many of the negotiators at CODESA (Council for a Democratic South Africa) shared a perception that they might face personal difficulties as politicians in a democratic South Africa. Supposing this were so, he suggests that they could not have selected an electoral system that was more likely than list-PR to ensure that people very much like themselves (unrepresentative lawyers, intellectuals and tainted Afrikaner nationalists) could come to be elected.

13. Horowitz, *op. cit.*, pp. 168–73.

14. This is why I disagree with David Welsh who tells us that the new South African President enjoys 'normal' powers. He writes: 'The incumbent, apart from duties as Head of State, will not have powers that exceed those of a prime minister in a British-type system (or of the Chancellor in the German system).' (David Welsh, 'South Africa's Prospects for Constitutional Democracy', *Occasional Paper No. 13*, Australian Institute of International Affairs, Dyason House, 124 Jolimont Road, East Melbourne, Victoria 3 002, Australia, 1994.)

15. I cannot work out how to reconcile # 64 (1) which states that 'A Bill duly passed by Parliament . . . shall be assented to by the President' with # 82 (1c) which says that the President may refer a Bill passed by parliament back for further consideration 'in the event of a procedural shortcoming in the legislative process'. Does this mean that the President cannot veto unless there has been some relevant 'procedural shortcoming'? But what if there is a dispute about what constitutes a shortcoming or whether there has been one or not? The most likely way these phrases will be read is that President Mandela comes close to enjoying what Americans refer to a 'line-item veto' for he can warn that he will not sign a Bill unless it is amended in a particular way, and he can send a Bill back claiming that certain clauses have not been considered carefully enough, attaching his objections. This falls short of the capacity to sign a Bill after striking out various clauses he dislikes but it is a potent weapon that leaves Mandela in a much stronger position *vis-à-vis* the Assembly than President Clinton is *vis-à-vis* Congress (in that the latter must confront the threat of a potential congressional override, whereas the former's veto cannot be overruled).

16. See interim Constitution, para. 60 (3).

17. *Ibid.*, # 216 (2)a and para. 225.

18. *Ibid.*, # 87 and para. 93.

19. See Juan J. Linz, 'The Perils of Presidentialism', *Journal of Democracy*, vol. 1 (1990), pp. 51–69; and Fred W. Riggs, 'The Survival of Presidentialism in America: Paraconstitutional Practices', *International Political Science Review*, vol. 9 (1988), pp. 247–78.

20. Power-sharing is required under # 84; the portfolios are allocated by the President after consultations with the two Executive Deputy Presidents and the leaders of the participating parties, as required under # 88 (4).

21. Under # 84 (1).

22. Interim Constitution para. 34.

23. On these points see Donald Horowitz, *The Courts and Social Policy* (Washington DC: The Brookings Institute, 1977); also Gerald Rosenberg, *The Hollow Hope: Can Courts Bring about Social Change?* (Chicago: University of Chicago Press, 1991).

24. 401 US 424 (1971). The problems with the ruling in this case are discussed by numerous commentators including Charles Fried who served as President Reagan's Solicitor General. See C. Fried, *Order & Law: Arguing the Reagan Revolution* (New York: Simon & Schuster, 1991), p. xxx. The 'Griggs test' has recently been abandoned, first through judicial interpretation and in 1991 by an amendment to the Civil Rights Act.

25. Interim Constitution, # 8 (c).

26. As specified under # 28 (3) of the interim Constitution that requires the Commission to act 'taking into account all relevant factors, including, . . . the use to which the property is being put, the history of its acquisition, its market value, the value of the investments in it by those affected and the interests of those affected.'

27. Interim Constitution, # 15 (2).

28. For more details on this see Chapter 11.

29. Buthelezi's views and his role in early negotiations are described by Ottaway, *South Africa*, pp. 95–9, 102–4.

30. The areas of competence allocated to the provincial governments are enumerated in Schedule 6 of the interim Constitution. However, sweeping powers allowing the federal government to override the provinces in various circumstances are listed in # 126 (3).

5 Reconstructing South African Law: Legal Formalism and Legal Culture in a New State
Martin Chanock

... (J)udges characteristically do not create law, but kill it. Theirs is the jurispathic office. Confronting the luxurious growth of a hundred legal traditions, they assert that *this one* is the law and destroy or try to destroy the rest.[1]

This chapter considers the future of legal formalism in South Africa. By formalism I mean the broad ideology of Western law which separates the 'legal' from the 'political' both institutionally and in terms of justification for decision making. Legal formalism amounts in fact to a paradigm in which legal decisions are made according to legal rules and doctrines. Rights and entitlements made according to these rules are seen in turn as different from substantive decisions in which political and other considerations govern.

This chapter will be concerned first of all with attempting to generate an idea of legal culture. It will then turn to consider what the elements of South African legal culture have been, and discuss the relationship, in the period of the white state, between the formalism of the superior courts, and other legal discourses and practices. It records a failure to situate formal legal discourses and actions within the broader spectrum of legality, as well as the close association between official legal culture and white rule. In considering reconstruction the chapter argues that only if the formal aspects of the legal culture are understood to be part of a wider setting of practice and discourse will formalism have a future.

It is a peculiarity of much of transition rhetoric in South Africa, at least among the political classes, that it proclaims that the political processes will be subject to and regulated by a new legality. The protracted constitution-making processes which produced the interim constitution have been full of discussion, disagreements, and compromises about the nature of powers to be granted to different bodies, the content and nature of rights to be

98

protected, and new adjudicating bodies. Negotiations have been accompanied by a grisly counterpoint outside in the streets and fields as guns fire and people die. Paradoxically it is this violence that has led to the exaggeration of the security that will be provided by law. What are we to expect about the relationship between these two processes? Which will rule which?

A new legal order for South Africa will struggle to develop within a context of turbulent political instability. And if we are to think about the legal future we must imagine that this instability will not go away after a brief 'teething' period, and will not be unquestioningly mediated by proclamations about rights. Once a new political order has been established there will still be local instances of resistance, disorder, violence and breakdown with which courts will have eventually to deal. The weakening of the administrative organs of the state by political turbulence and an unprecedented 'transition' may render problematic the carrying out of court decisions. With this realisation we need to consider not just the 'content' of a new legal order, the ultimate 'whats' and 'wheres' of revolutionary change, but the processes in the short term. How will legal institutions work?

The South African state has never been stable. Its political legitimacy has been under challenge since the first process of formation, and we have much to mull over in considering the roles and responses of law and legal institutions to these challenges. The Union of South Africa, the white-ruled state which came into being in 1910, was not born peacefully from the womb of the parliament at Westminster but was the result of a major imperial war. The process of forming the new state began in 1902, especially in relation to law, as many of the legal building blocks were put into place in this period. The period from 1910 to 1922, when the new dominion became self-governing, was marked by even more political violence, and the decades of Nationalist rule after 1948 by yet more.

LEGAL CULTURE

In this chapter I consider the responses of law to these earlier challenges, partly for the purposes of comparison, but more importantly because I want to generate a notion of the development of a South African legal culture. This distances analysis from a number of paths. It attempts no sort of overall functional explanation of the interrelationships of law, society and economy, and none of the 'role' of law in politics and society. It also does not proceed from the assumption that legal discourses are a facade to be thrust aside in order to reveal the real world of actions and effects. A legal culture consists of a set of assumptions, a way of doing things, a repertoire of language, of legal forms and institutional practices. As with all aspects of a culture, it changes in response to new situations, but it also reproduces itself; its responses fit into existing forms. This sort of continuity is important to all aspects of culture, but perhaps especially to lawyers who depend on the 'authority' of old texts, precedents and established meanings and constitutional forms. A legal culture, like other aspects of culture, embodies a narrative, encompassing both past and future, which gives meaning to thought and actions. Such an approach to understanding a legal system will focus on process and style, as much as on rules (the lawyers' paradigm), and on discourses within and about law, rather than on outcomes (the 'law in action/realist' paradigm). What I am here calling a legal culture is made up of an interrelated set of discourses about law: some professional, some administrative, some political, some popular. They understand and represent law, and therefore inform action in relation to it, in different ways. While they differ, they do not exist in isolation from each other, and they draw upon each other, sometimes critically, sometimes affirmatively. And they are all set within the broader political and social discourses of the state and society.

An excursion into history is needed to see what can be said about the development of a South African legal culture from particular circumstances as well as considering how it has influenced the relationship between 'law' and 'politics'. If we think about the basic characteristics of South Africa's legal discourse and practices we might be able to think more clearly about what 'newness' could mean. Legal discourses do not exist (in spite of their self-image) apart form other social discourses. The legal construction of race, for example, could hardly be understood apart from the wider discourses, scientific, political and popular, about race. Similarly the legal construction of rights is attached to a broader cultural and political discourse. And, most importantly, a legal culture cannot be understood by reference only to judges, or even more broadly to lawyers. It is carried on in other fora. Politics is the most obvious, but perhaps the most important is bureaucratic. In any highly bureaucratised state the main generators and users of law are the bureaucracy, and they are a major influence on the growth of a legal culture.[2] I shall deliberately spread my consideration thinly over a wide range of issues in an attempt to encompass the underpinnings of a legal culture which the new state will have to work with, or against.

There is the further consideration that the concept of legal culture may be peculiarly appropriate to the analysis of radical transition when in the glaring light of revolution more of the legal landscape becomes plainly visible. As long as the hold of the political centre is longstanding and unchallenged, the claims of formalism, restricting 'law' to rule formation, application and the professional discourses connected to these, are very powerful. The common responses to the dominance of formalism – both materialist and political/realist analyses – have been forms of 'unmasking', of trying to pierce the formalist veil to reveal the parts of 'law' that it conceals. But when the centre's grip has drastically weakened and all features of the legal system are in contention, the claims of formalism have been weakened and the unmasking has already been done. The complexity and interrelationships of the component parts are more easily seen.

LAW AND POLITICS

After 1902 the main task of government was to absorb the newly conquered republics into the British imperial system. The focus was the Transvaal, with its mining industry and growing economy. It is a workable exaggeration to see the legal institutions created in the Transvaal in this period providing the basic foundation for the institutions and practices for the Union which followed. The new government was suspicious of the loyalty of the conquered Afrikaners. Law and order was secured by the creation of a para-military police force which was to combine the roles of policing and internal occupation. A magistracy, which also combined the political roles of district administration and surveillance with adjudication, was put in place. Over these institutions, both of which blurred the boundaries between administration and law, was placed a judiciary with an overstated and self-styled separation from the world of the political. Thus while most of the legal business of the state was carried out by institutions and personnel which were part of the coercive bureaucratic apparatus, the top of the system embodied a symbolic separation between 'law' and other aspects of state power. Between 1902 and 1910 the new regime in the Transvaal faced several challenges to 'law and order' of a basic nature. Most important were the violent conflicts with white labour, and the 'non-violent' confrontation with Indian South African passive resisters led by Gandhi. Two basic features of the state's response can be noted. One was the determination of the government to crush its opponents without compromise or concession, and the enactment of what it hoped were the necessary statutes. The second was the limitation by a literalist style of interpretation of the actions of officials by the Transvaal Supreme Court. These responses did not sit easily together, though more than simple judicial literalism was at work. We must remember other things: the faith put in formalism in relation to the external reputation of the country and its mining industry; the sensitivity of the judges to political criticism (the targets of the anti-labour action were white); and, in relation both to Indians and trade unions, the fact that the country was not yet independent and that there were persistent voices on their behalf at Westminster.

The constitutional issues which were canvassed during the making of the new Union were of major importance. On the whole the judges did not yearn for the pivotal position of power which a federal constitution and a consequent 'testing right' in relation to the constitutional validity of legislation would have given them. For many the lesson of the dismissal of Chief Justice Kotze, who had claimed this right in the South African Republic, was that judges should keep their heads down. There were even doubts at the highest level about the desirability of establishing an Appellate Division for the Union, in case it got involved in political and racial cases. The judges' timidity was matched by the unpopularity among the politicians of the idea of giving the judiciary an overtly political role. Most important was the consideration that such a role could pit the judiciary against the executive government in matters affecting the governing of non-whites, and thereby endanger stability and white prestige. On the other hand there was allegiance to the idea of the 'rule of law' which the unresolved balance between white political groups made for all a necessary shield. The idea did have roots in the white self-narrative of civiliser ruling over barbarian; and it could still be flourished, with weakening effect, at the articulate elites of the subject races. Appeal to the Privy Council remained as a form of guarantee of commercial and property rights. The outcome for law of the constitution-making process was a model of judges divorced from 'politics', yet attached to 'law'. This could only mean an entrenchment of the literal style of formalism.

Yet the Bench was highly political, and it had to operate in an intensely politically charged environment. Most of the senior judges had had political careers of note.[3] They were plunged immediately into a series of crises. The government's confrontations with the white labour movement in 1913 required the intervention of imperial troops to restore order. In 1914 the new South African Defence Force was in action against white strikers. After the outbreak of war in 1914, a segment of the Army, led by senior officers, and with widespread support in the Orange Free State, went into rebellion to restore republican independence. These events, involving as they did numerous politically-related prosecutions in the courts, had important ramifications for legality in the new state, establishing at an early stage the role of the courts as a political arena. On the one hand they began what was to become a familiar dialogue between government and the courts.

The courts were not generous to the executive in their interpretations either of the common law relating to sedition and treason or of the statute law. They forced the government into either detailed legislative changes designed to tighten up controls over political activities or 'legalised' ways of by-passing the ordinary courts altogether. The new Riotous Assembly laws were one way; the proclamation of martial law followed by Acts of Indemnity, or simply illegal executive action so excused, another. The pattern continued. Special courts were created to hear the charges arising out of the rebellions in 1914/15 and 1922. New legislation to control strikes and speech was passed in the 1920s. When the latter was strictly interpreted by the courts it was put beyond their reach for much of the population via the mechanisms of the Native Administration Act. By the time the Nationalist government came into power in 1948 the rules of the game seemed well established. Over the next 40 years the government dealt with setbacks in the courts by the constant production of more detailed restrictive rules, and by the increasing of measures to exclude jurisdiction by the extension of the creation of emergency powers and the quarantining of ministerial discretions.[4]

In retrospect there are questions to be asked about this process. What did the Courts achieve, and why did they act as they did? What effect did this (serious) play have on the nature of legality? In one sense both sides won: the judges re-affirmed a major tenet of their view of law, while the government eventually achieved its aim within the law and could be confident of doing so once it had arrived at the right verbal formula. Individual litigants often won also, which is an important consideration. The government merely lost a little prestige. But the effect was to keep the possibility open for individual litigants to use the courts against the government's attempts to use law to control their political opposition. This had a number of consequences in that it simultaneously strengthened the notions over the long term that a 'rule of law' prevailed; that the essence of its defence was a formalist judicial style; and that the law courts were useable arenas of political struggle, but within the confines of form, not by challenging substance. One outcome of the decades of bitter struggles for rights in the courts was the embedding of a formalist approach to rights and interpretation within the legal culture.

Two other themes from the early political confrontations were to be of continuing importance. One arose from executive efforts to exclude the jurisdiction of the courts from politically sensitive areas. This early battle, which was won by the executive, was fought over the Immigration Act, which sought to end Asian immigration. The second concerned the role of the courts when state security was threatened. In this instance it was the cases arising out of the Afrikaner rebellion in 1914 which drew from the courts the affirmation of the doctrine *salus republicae suprema lex est*. In both cases the course taken by the South African courts was hugely influenced by developments in similar contests between courts and executive in Britain. The British judges, caught in the intense struggle over the beginnings of the welfare state, tried to define themselves out of the line of fire. Under the impact of two world wars they subordinated themselves entirely to the demands of the executive in security areas. South Africa's judges did the same. Neither set of judges had much option in the substantive directions taken, but they could affect detail and degree.

The main point here is that, while the choices were forced upon South African judges by specific local conflicts, their solutions drew almost entirely on external discourses and examples. A notion of South African legal culture must therefore involve an evaluation of the changing relationship between the external and the local elements of legal developments. In the period of state formation the influence of English legal practices was enormous, not simply in terms of doctrine and precedent, but in relation to more basic forms. The organisation of the courts and their procedures, the self-conception of the judiciary and the profession, the language and linguistic forms of statute and judgement, all mimicked those of England and other parts of the empire. After nearly a century in which there have been important efforts to diminish this endowment, this remains the case. In Britain itself the elaborate facade of formalism has been to some extent tempered by juries and a large lay magistracy. But in its colonial version in Africa and Asia where it has usually persisted beyond the end of empire, the formalist facade has tended to operate in isolation from other social forces. Typically it has produced in Africa and in Asia, either acknowledged or unacknowledged, binary systems which relegate the greater part of the population to subordinate systems which have provided little guarantee of legal rights. This dualism, extreme formalism in some areas, almost none in others, has been an important feature of South Africa's law.

THE COMMON LAW

The dominance of British law has sometimes been underestimated in accounts of South Africa's legal system because of the crafted image of a unique Roman-Dutch law. The development of a South African common law under this name has been in many respects an admirable achievement, yet it is one which must be understood in its historical context if we are to begin to think about its place in future developments. Considered historically rather than mythologically, South Africa's Roman-Dutch law was created during the opening decades of this century. Given the over-whelming influence of English legal forms at this time, the success of the venture was neither assured nor unquestioningly accepted by the profession. While Australia, for example, sought deliberately to align its common law as closely as possible to England's to reap the advantages of uniformity and experience, an alternative white nationalism in South Africa made this course infeasible. Roman-Dutch law was created in opposition to English law (and African law) as part of the writing of a national self-narrative. (It also protected the South African Bar from English barristers).[5] Voices which called for a codified civil law system for South Africa were weak and ignored, and neither a European-style code, nor even American-style re-statements, were embarked on. Instead the local common law was developed by the judges, case by case, by a mixture of doctrinal scholar-ship and establishment of and adherence to precedent, in rambling discursive judgements, for which discontented litigants often had to wait for long periods. To put it at its barest, this gave the judiciary something to do. Excluded increasingly from the political realm by frequent bruising public criticism and executive determination, their prestige and their independence were developed in the field of common law, in which they were granted a wide degree of latitude. This was an integral part of the development of white cultural nationalism, taken up with renewed vigour when nationalist-minded judges finally took command of the Appellate Courts in the 1950s and 1960s. This process also contributed to the entrenchment and projection of formalism in the legal culture.

This is even clearer once we consider the contemporaneous elaboration of African customary law. The legal rules and concepts which came to be enforced in South Africa's courts under this name were the product of this period, in which South African jurists produced not one new system of common law but two. Rules and concepts, in areas like land law, marriage, and contractual capacity, were developed in conscious opposition. Different sets of rules were seen as appropriate for the bearers of a two-thousand-year-old legal tradition, and for barbarians who were still infants in evolu-tionary development. Increasingly these latter rules began to lose their applicability to the real life of Africans as they had access to land dras-tically reduced, were driven into the cash economy as labourers and were caught up in the process of urbanisation. One South African tradition had assumed that this would ultimately lead to legal integration. But, just as these economic and social developments intensified, the white state under-lined the importance which it placed on legal differentiation by passing the

1927 Native Administration Act, which institutionalised, nationwide, separate courts applying separate law. Migrant labour and the gender imbalances in urbanisation, pressure on land, and the political and cultural defence of traditionalism, gave to many Africans an interest in the symbolism, if not always the substance, of this customary law. But African input into the development and exposition of the customary law administered by the state's courts remained small. Segregated from the 'real' law reports and from the syllabuses of professional legal studies in the universities, a mystical 'expert' field to most lawyers and judges, it was embellished in the cheaply produced and rarely consulted reports of the Native Appeal Courts, and in handbooks of rules for administrators. Yet, if we are to generate an idea of South African legal culture it is important to grasp that it was not just a matter of there being two systems of common law, but that they were interrelated, and that they are not historically comprehensible without each other. The Roman-Dutch law grew in an intimate relationship with English common law, and also in another with customary law. Conversely customary law cannot be understood without its white 'other'. Neither of these systems created bodies of common law or had much purchase on either of the populations to which they respectively applied. Few identified them, even rhetorically, as the source of their inherent rights. The ideological posture of the English common law, that it was the source of the rights of 'free-born Englishmen' was absent in South Africa where the racialised state was the identifiable source of rights or oppression.

It is with this way of formulating the historical formation of the culture of South Africa's common laws that we can begin to approach the issues around transition. We must grasp the legal *creativity* of the period of transition to white statehood in 1910. The evolution of the different system of common laws embodied national, cultural, and political narratives specific to circumstance, rather than a mystical ancient unfolding. Moreover, the continued dominance of English legal style inhibited consistent purposive intervention by the legislature in the areas claimed by common law. Development of the common law was therefore confined to the judiciary and the bar, and this, because of the incremental nature of their methods, limited the ways in which it could be developed.

In the current period of transition some of the subordinated narratives can be resurrected. Forms of codification may be one. The sources of common law, no longer tied by a nationalist and racist search for non-English, non-African roots, may be another. Legal creativity could create a single common law out of the racialised dual system. Much will clearly depend here on the nature of the new state's adherence to international conventions and the attitude taken by the courts to the effect of these on local law. Together with this, the effect on the common law of the adopting of a constitution with a bill of rights opens up the prospect of new avenues of development. Experience elsewhere suggests, though, that a bill of rights will only have any real meaning if a culture of rights is closely connected to rights in the common law rather than being confined to a political/public law sphere. Furthermore both the common law and the bill of rights need to be responsive to wider elements in the legal culture.

JUDGES

This excursion into the story of the development of South African common law helps us understand the place of the judiciary and bar in South African legal culture. The judges were the targets of public criticism throughout the life of the white state. They were criticised by sections of the public for persecuting the rebels of 1915 and 1922, and (while four rebels were hung after 1922) most of those convicted of political violence in the two rebellions were amnestied soon after the events involved – as were the pro-Nazis convicted for rebellion during the Second World War. Judges were castigated by government ministers for protecting the rights of labour in the early strikes, and those of communist, ICU and other opponents of the state in the 1920s. Indeed, one of the enduring features of South African legal culture has been the intensity of public criticism of the courts from all sides of politics.[6] There is no doubt that part of the context of this criticism was the adherence by judges to a weak version of civil liberties. If we wonder why such a stance should have developed, the answer lies chiefly in the divisions among the ruling white elite. Nearly all the beneficiaries were white opponents of the government. Indeed it is to the existence of white trade unions, and the white Labour Party, and to the continuing activity of Afrikaner republicans, all strong forms of white opposition that *had* to be accepted as legitimate, that South Africa owes its 'rule of law' tradition.[7] African opposition did not receive the same respect from law.

It was in the period after 1948 that the issue of the proper judicial role in constitutional and public life became perennially controversial. The constitutional confrontation of the 'old' appellate judges and the new Nationalist government over the removal of coloured voters from the common voters' roll had an enduring impact on South African legal life. The judges' political intentions were honourable, their ambition to thwart the government impossible, and their contrived legal reasoning in part responsible

for the accelerated politicisation of the court.[8] After their defeat what role
was possible, in relation to public law, for a judiciary which was broadly
supportive of government, yet which operated self-consciously within the
confines of legal formalism? With the broader moral/legal avenues closed,
all that opposition could wring from the law depended on the interpretation of statutes. A literalist approach by a judiciary is usually a way of
delaying and perhaps frustrating an executive bent upon change, while a
strategy of interpretation more sensitive to giving effect to the purpose and
policy of legislation is one which facilitates executive ambitions. During the twentieth century, the British courts, protective of the status quo
against legislative changes arising out the labour and welfare agendas, had
developed, and passed on to South Africa's judges, the tactics of obstructive
literalism. The voice of legal progressives in the United Kingdom had
long urged an approach to interpretation based on the intention of the
legislature. In the 1950s the South African judges began to free themselves from the grip of literalism, with progressive generosity towards the
intentions of the legislation of apartheid. The vast scope of apartheid's
agenda, which involved detailed interference in every aspect of the country's
life and economy, spawned a legislative style heavily dependent on delegated legislation and regulations, and on ministerial and official discretions.
Sometimes the administrative ambitions were so far reaching (or impossible
of performance) that, even with generosity, they could not, within the
formalist paradigm, possibly be held to come within the compass of legislation. Sometimes too the exercise of official discretions was baulked at,
but for two decades after the crisis of the mid-1950s the courts on the
whole lived comfortably with the government.

As opposition to apartheid intensified, this accommodation increasingly
caused discomfort. The strength of black political opposition meant that
the growing numbers of cases involved the use of ever more widely-drawn
repressive political statutes being funnelled into the courts. No longer
were they able to bask in a mantle of legal impartiality, which had been
bestowed in part by the acquittal of those charged with treason in 1956.
More and more they became instruments of punishment, their reputation
among whites for legal correctness being exploited by the government,
and consequently dwindling swiftly in the eyes of the majority of the
population. Parts of the legal profession were filled with an anxiety which
became an important ingredient in legal discourses. One strand of this was
expressed in concern for the legitimacy of 'law' as an abstract entity in the
eyes of black South Africa. In its worst form, the nightmare (or the threat)
was that 'they' would just cease to believe in it altogether and that a ter-
rible harvest would consequently be reaped.[9] Another strand was the debate

which developed over the moral position of judges. Calls were made for them to resign on the grounds that the 'true' function of a judiciary could no longer be carried out.[10] Among those lawyers who did not support the regime, another powerful line of argument was mounted. This claimed that the judges could do different things *without departing from the formalist paradigm* because there were different paths inherent within South African common law itself.[11]

Perhaps one of the effects of these struggles within the law was the almost exclusive focus on the judiciary as vectors of law.[12] But it is important to set the judges not just within the framework of the political system of the country, as has usually been done, but within the larger legal culture of which they were a part. For the judges remained plausible, if flawed, actors, to those within that culture. As I have suggested above, the internal discourses and practices of the courts and legal professions do not constitute the whole of a legal culture.

The most important of the other legal discourses in South African legal culture existed within the bureaucracy, or within the dialogue between bureaucrats and politicians, both of which are distinct from the discourse among lawyers, or that between lawyers and the public or politicians and public on legal matters. South African law in this century has essentially been the atmosphere in which the bureaucracy breathed. The state was a (large and sophisticated) colonial state in the sense that it was throughout self-consciously involved in the process of using power to create a society and an economy. We can usefully think of two periods of such construction, the one following 1902 in which the basic endowments of twentieth-century British-type institutions were put in place, and a second great endeavour from the 1950s to create apartheid. The creation and working of a vast statist enterprise of this kind used law for effective centralised management of officials, and achievement of policy goals. In the culture which created and used the larger part of the legal universe, law was policy-oriented command.

From this standpoint the controversies about the role of judges must be re-ranked in importance. For a more complete picture of legal culture we must ask ourselves about administration. Writers about law do of course frequently consider administration, but they tend to adopt the perspective of administrative law, a perspective which assumes that the rules which limit the ways in which officials exercise power is the main game, and that the judiciary is responsible for making these rules. But if we adopt the perspective of policy goals, efficient management and effective achievement of ends, the place of the judges and their rules looks different. To comprehend South Africa's legal culture we must be sensitive to this perspective as the state is poised to embark on an even larger venture of (re)construction. The impatience of the administrative state with legal formalism is not just a South African theme but an important strand in the history of twentieth-century law. Each legal culture develops its own ways of accommodating the ideal worlds of lawyer and administrator, and the differing concepts of legal process and rights involved depending on whether the subject is conceived of as *citoyen* or *administré*.

What of South Africa's accommodation? Africans were not citizens in this respect but were the objects of state action and received scant protection from administrative law. Legislation largely affecting Africans gave greater and wider discretion to officials, and at lower levels, than that affecting others. In particular, from the 1920s onwards the Urban Areas Act and the Native Administration Act gave to officials far-reaching powers over personal liberty, by-passing the formalities of criminal and administrative law, and these were endorsed by the courts. The limited protections of the courts (which were used, for example, by Asians faced with economic discrimination by officials) were not extended to major predicaments of African life. Courts would not review the exercise of powers of banishment and detention by officials under the Urban Areas Act, or the use of similar powers by officials of the Native Affairs Department acting under the delegated authority of the head of state as 'Supreme Chief'.

There is also a broader public set of discourses about the role of law in society. In South Africa this was dominated for much of the existence of the white state by an affirmation of a liberal idea of a neutral law on one level, with a pragmatic acceptance of, indeed insistence on, the use of law to secure racial advantage. One response of African elites was to try to hold 'law' to its empty promises. But in the closing period of white rule the response which alarmed white lawyers was the envisioning, and the beginnings of the practising, of a completely different kind of law. In the last decade, as the white state began to lose control of African areas, informal courts under the control of local militants began (sporadically) to operate.[13] They are part of the legacy of legal practices with which the country will enter the new era. Ideological attachment to so-called 'popular justice' will be a part of the environment of reform. Various forms of popular justice have not been successful in Western countries where, whatever the obvious failings of state institutions, the state's courts and police have maintained a central relevance to people's conceptions of law and justice. In those situations the development of alternatives in the area of dispute resolution have more to do with perceptions of cost and convenience than rejection of the state's law. But in South Africa where the state's legal processes have been at best irrelevant to the needs of most of the population as mechanisms for disputing, alternative courts might hold an appeal even once the fuel of revolutionary rhetoric has run out. At least one could expect that admiring eyes will be cast on the neighbouring African experiments in staffing state courts with various kinds of alternative judges, from chiefs to party cadres.[14]

Another part of the breaking of the unity of the old set of practices has been the development of new forms of legal practice. The growth of, for example, the Legal Resources Centre, involving not an impatient discarding of legal forms, but an effort to realise the promises of law on an entirely new scale, might create a far broader consciousness of the possibilities of 'legal rights'. This may not always be compatible with 'popular justice'.[15]

In the South African revolution neither Bastille nor Winter Palace has been stormed and the image projected in the absence of these dramatic symbolisings has been one of a managed and consensual transition. This has had effects on the ways in which the legal future has been imagined. But of course the real meaning of the political transition has yet to unfold and may well prove to be more far-reaching than envisaged. How far can the existing practices and meanings stretch? Even if we do not think of these as constraints, but as resources to be drawn upon (as is implied, for instance, in the strategy of grounding rights thinking in the existing common law which has already been discussed), how far can they continue to be useable as a part of a fundamental rejection of the order of which they were a part? Asking this question implies that there is or will be something else to use, something new. And even now much of the reformist (not a critical word) thinking, activity and scholarship about the legal future has been occupied with scouring the legal resources of the world for models with which to proceed. Much of South Africa's legal revolution may be made, like the legal system of the original Union, by bringing in answers from outside.[16]

Two connected questions emerge here. One is how large the legal repertoire available and suitable to a late twentieth-century industrial state really is? Is it not a purpose of the reconstruction to make South Africa's legal system look like those of other 'normal' countries? The second concerns the nature of the new state's relationship with the emerging globalisation of law. What place is there, as a widening range of uniformities are developing in the world's law, for specific local transformations? Increasingly caught in a tightening web of international agreements, conventions and expectations, how relevant can the specific cultural features of local meanings and practices, narratives and purposes, be for any legal system?

The states created in Asia and Africa by the European empires, of which South Africa is one, all used legal pluralism. At the end of empire the anticipation was that, as foreign and racial rule receded, the plural legal systems would be both modernised and indigenised into single, culturally appropriate, national legal systems. But it is not easy to fit postwar developments anywhere in the former empires into this narrative. In both Asia and Africa the gap continues to persist between an externally-oriented sector of law with global content and working within a formalist paradigm, and local law for the local population and local transactions, less formal and more culturally specific. There may be nothing 'wrong' with this at all; it is just that it was not expected by lawyers who have always had centralising ambitions and illusions. It does give us some insight into the possible development of South African legal culture. Current debates about the remaking of South African law have tended to assume that somehow a new accommodation will have to be made with African law and that courts will have to reflect a greater degree of public accessibility and participation, but that these developments will take place within a single 'system'. But perhaps the paradigm will fragment, leaving formalism confined to an economic sector using a global legal culture, while the keeping of order and the settlement of local disputes is abandoned to the realms of ministerial discretion and executive action (with the attendant dangers of political corruption) or to varying forms of popular court and customary law.[17]

If we are to avoid the pitfalls involved in a cult of courts and judges[18] we must consider that part of a legal culture which has been given least serious consideration in formal legal literature – the discourses about law in the culture at large, and in particular the conversations between lawyers and public about legal institutions, practices and values. A formalist approach to writing about law has been most likely to separate this area of legal discourse from consideration of law itself as being largely irrelevant to the professionalised internal methods of the legal world. Indeed there is much sense in separating internal professional legal discourses from discourses about law as their categories and ways of reasoning can be, and have often been in the South African case, vastly different. But one needs to do this without forgetting, and when necessary exhuming, the relationship between the discourses internal to law, and those about law. An exaggerated formalism is in many circumstances developed as a response to demands from the public for 'substance', while public and political demands made of the law's processes are often a response to the perceived failures of an unrealistic formalism.

The formalist style of South African law owes much to its complex relationship with these external or popular discourses about law. Inasmuch as formalism represents a claim not just to authority over decision making in a particular area, but to the values according to which the decisions will be made, it involves both a denial of and a response to alternative claims and pressures. These have been constantly present in the history of a polity where the drive to establish and maintain the advantages of racial rule drove public discourses about the law. The courts conducted the dialogue very largely with whites not blacks. Black criticisms of the discriminatory enforcement of law (especially criminal law, the labour and pass laws, and land law) was constant and vocal, and was, until the last years of the 1980s, rarely even denied, but simply ignored. The conversational partner of the courts was white 'opinion' of varying kinds. There were many areas of substantial overlap between discourses internal to law, and those about law, but the dialogue which helped to shape the formal law excluded most of the population.

RACE

It is primarily within this area of dialogue, and of overlap, that we can place the issue of race in South African legal culture. If we confine our consideration to discourses internal to law it is not difficult to catalogue the frequent occasions on which non-racial principles were declared, and to place the 'responsibility' for racism on statutory commands made to the courts. But if we consider the dialogue we cannot escape the sense that South Africa's legal culture has been permeated with a sense of struggle against the country's non-white population. The most basic self-conception of the legal enterprise was that it was inherent to white government and white civilisation and from this most other things flowed. In spite of the series of white revolts the most dangerous enemies of law and order in the political sense were not white. The criminal law was informed by a criminology underpinned by racism, evolutionism and eugenics, which focussed increasingly on the inherent differences and dangerousness of Africans.[19] Even if we were to leave aside the huge enterprise of coercion which used the apparatus (institutions, personnel and language) of the criminal law to enforce economic and political discipline on Africans through a range of racially discriminatory statutes, the administration of the common law relating to crime was inseparable from racial rule. The axiom of white political discourses was that whites and Africans had different capacities, and this provided the justification for their exclusion from political rights. It is hardly surprising that these themes overlapped with the legal discourses which were founded on such differences. In the separate legal regimes which whites defined as belonging to Africans, they were seen to be not simply different, but deficient. Africans, in the white view, conceived of holding land in common because they had not yet reached the stage of understanding that it ought to be held individually. Africans were polygamous because of moral backwardness, not simply cultural distinctiveness. There were similar reasons attributed to Africans' inability to understand contract. The elaboration of, and continued working with, plural systems of common law were a part of a regime of subordination, not equality. Roman-Dutch law which developed as part of the bifurcation was anything but racially innocent, its identity being celebrated in its European origins.[20]

Those elements of racial discrimination which were added by statute produced some complex problems. But most of the formal doctrinal difficulties for the courts were caused when discrimination was enacted against Asians, in immigration, in rights to property, in residence and licensing. It is on this frontier that the courts were boldest in requiring specifically discriminatory instructions from statutes.[21] This underlines the point made about the inherence of the narratives of difference in the common law. Asian legal rights could not so easily be isolated into a separated legal realm as those of Africans.[22] In any case this judicial sensitivity waned markedly during the 1950s when judges became readier to intuit implied powers to discriminate.[23]

No account of the place of race within South Africa's legal culture can ignore the questions of racial classification by law, and the issues of interracial sex and marital relations. The definitions of excluded groups tended to vary from law to law, depending on its purposes, but their most common feature is that they were originally based on a social definition of racial identity, not a genealogical or a biological one. South African legal definitions, not for want of knowledge of the examples, steered away from the inheritance-based definitions which prevailed in some American state legislation (particularly, though by no means exclusively, in the South).[24] Clearly also there was no development of the German example of health courts and 'scientific' determination. South African tests and processes, though cruel, were pragmatic. Courts and administrators applied tests of appearance, circumstances and habits of life, and social acceptance, as determinants of racial status. Policing the racial borderlines became an increasingly complex legal and administrative operation because of the differential rights available to members of different groups in the areas of civil rights, property rights, places to live, jobs which could be done. But in all of this it remained conceptually possible, particularly if one wanted to move down scale legally, to be classified as a member of a racial group on social grounds alone. Despite the flourishing discourses of biological racism in the broader culture, they remain strangely absent from the discourses internal to law.

Racism in South African legal culture was always opposed in the name of legal liberalism for which discrimination between those who ought to be equal rights bearers in all aspects of law and life is anathema. In emphasising a history of pervasive and dominant racism, it is by no means my aim to exclude from the story the constant opposing of the alternative path of non-discrimination projected and maintained by some at all levels. Liberal legalism was a powerful rhetorical weapon in the struggle to de-legitimise apartheid since it was perhaps the only non-racially based doctrine with significant purchase among all parts of the white elite. Even so the constant display of the limited repertoire of legal dicta from cases past should not be allowed to distort the picture of the racial foundations and purposes of South Africa's law. This lesser tradition of non-racism in law appeared to be about to have its historic moment as the apartheid state collapsed. Legal aspects of racial discrimination were dismantled, those relevant to racial identity itself in personal law being among the first to go. What could seem more obvious than to conclude that liberalism had been triumphant in law, and that the legal culture would henceforth be constructed along lines in which racial identity was irrelevant? Where law had seen little but race, race would now become legally invisible. But a society of acutely self-conscious racial identities remains. Can one imagine a legal culture reconstructing itself which could or should not see them?

Two things were at once obvious. One was that a law based upon a complete and formal ignoring of race as a factor in constituting rights would contribute to entrenching the economic status quo unless and until the 'market' put it right. A second, and also politically charged, problem was that of the accommodation of cultural difference within a framework of legal uniformity. Apartheid was born at the beginning of the end of the era of European colonialism. After 1948 South African legal culture had swung more determinedly towards a racially based law in the period when legal systems elsewhere in the world were moving towards a formal non-racism. Similar ironies are presented now. As multi-national states begin to fragment elsewhere South Africa seeks to create a new one. This does not, of course, necessarily cast doubt on the enterprise. It serves only as background to the point that the apparent historical moment of a non-racial legalism is fraught with difficulties. A liberal rights discourse which emphasises rights as the basis of entitlement to equal treatment, and which

had long been part of the conceptual basis of the aspirations and objectives of liberals in South African law, now competes with other concepts of
rights which are gaining strength in those external discourses on which the
debate about reconstruction in South Africa relies so heavily.[25]

A liberal rights discourse in South Africa faces two obvious struggles.
One is with the remnants of Marxist jurisprudence. While the informing historical trajectory has lost credibility, and the former vocabulary has forfeited
its persuasive capacities, the obvious power of its emphasis on substantive
economic rights as a necessary constituting part of a rights order remains.
One of the oddities of the 1980s was the opposition of some lawyers on
the left to a bill of rights.[26] The nature of the current transition, and its conceivable outcomes, are markedly different from those envisaged by many
in the liberation movements. But historical trajectories formerly envisaged
are unlikely to be suddenly erased from consciousness. The way in which
they interact with unfolding circumstances will provide the context for the
influence of substantive concepts of economic rights. Those discourses
which emphasised substantive rights did not dominate in the bill of rights
which became a part of the interim constitution. The more substantive
versions may exert considerable pressure when the 'final' constitution comes
to be drawn.

The second struggle is with the growing influence of the post-liberal
discourse of rights which insists that recognition of difference rather than
a fictional sameness be the basis for the assertion and recognition of rights.
These conceptualisations, developed primarily in the evolution of a new
rights culture in the USA which demands the acknowledgment and effective recognition of the gender and race of rights bearers, have instant purchase in South African debates. The search for ways in which the need for
affirmative action in relation to jobs and property rights can be fitted into
an equal rights paradigm draws its essential intellectual support from these
new rights. And in South Africa now there are other more complex cross
currents. The assertions of gender equality and of cultural rights may not
fit easily together. It is very probable that gender discrimination in customary law will give way to the new culture of rights. Furthermore, in the
context of South African history, there must be political misgivings about
the extent and effects of the assertion of rights based on 'cultural' difference.
Expecting South Africa's jurists, living and working in a new state which
will be struggling to maintain order and hold the centre, to solve the
problems of a fragmented and sophisticated post-modern jurisprudence
of rights would be droll. But these are the issues with which an emerging
legal culture is already having to grapple and they are harder than those
envisaged in the former liberal agenda.

Finally in relation to race one can return to the question of the future of formalism, for issues relating to race are one of the most testing frontiers of the contest between form and substance. They involve (as do issues relating to gender) the basic question of how the legal subject is perceived. I have suggested above that in the first decades of the Union, South Africa's legal culture grappled with, and essentially rejected, the constitution of Africans as rights bearers in law. The rejection of the 'Cape' policy is often discussed in terms of political rights only. This also involved the rejection of the assumption that the legal regimes for whites and Africans would eventually be assimilated into one (the European). There turned out to be an essential connection (which some judges had tried to avoid) between political and common law rights. Once Africans were not members of the community constituting the state, and as it became plain that they would never be so considered, so legal assimilation was abandoned and Africans relegated to a separate legal regime. The reconstitution of Africans as full legal actors and bearers of rights in a new state will strengthen liberal legalism, providing for the first time a political base for the recognition of equal rights in law.

The end of the white state has produced for South Africa's legal culture a powerful challenge to the brand of legal formalism discredited by its association with apartheid. But it may be that South Africa's lawyers will have to learn again, in a turbulent political environment, that the problems of balancing form and substance will not go away. People with all their eggs in the new rights-based formalist basket will be bitterly disappointed. Neither law nor rights will trump politics particularly as both may depend on an administrative capacity that the state may not have. And conversely those who celebrate the discarding of form in the dash for change will soon discover their exposure and vulnerability.

To consider this we can conclude by returning to the importance of generating a concept of legal culture because it is more than simply a tool of analysis. By emphasising that 'law' is not confined to the law talk of limited professional sites, that there is no easily-made separation between law and talk about law, or between popular and professional concepts, and by widening and emphasising the essential unity of the broader field thus constituted, the concept of legal culture could have an inherently democratising effect. It tends to weaken the claim of professionals (and also of bureaucrats) to have the only valid way of speaking law. This claim is of course fundamental to the formalist paradigm, which among other things was a claim to situate authority in institutions which forswore all considerations other than their own particular mode of framing and deciding issues.[27]

Can there be a formalism without this claim? Is it possible to maintain the integrity of the processes and judgements of the courts, while at the same time denying the claim of judges and courts to constitute and control the discourses of the legal culture? While all legal systems need to consider this question it is especially important in a system in a revolutionary transition. There will be obvious fears for a 'rule of law' if the narrow claim to control the definition of law is abandoned, and the danger of the possible rejection of law if it is maintained. Pragmatists who treat 'reconstruction' as technical exercises in 'what is to be done' may be irritated by such questions. So much of the internal culture of law is instrumental pragmatism, a set of meticulous answers to 'how to' questions. But this kind of instrumentalism does not work where order is fundamentally contested. The tensions which exist, and which must be accommodated in any legal system, between painstaking care and the rhetoric of justice, are much stronger in these circumstances. Overwhelming force is one answer, and it may not be available here. A new rhetoric of rights, as it will not be accompanied by commensurate economic changes, could increase cynicism about and rejection of law.

One of the most important features, in some eyes the saving grace, of legalism in South Africa in the closing decades of the white state was the way in which the courts became the arena in which vital political positions were manifested and battles were fought. Even though there will now be other places in which these causes can be heard, it is likely that, given the new rights jurisprudence and the need to give it meaning in practice, the courts – particularly the new Constitutional Court – will continue to be a focus for 'political' cases. The experience in other 'new' states after the end of colonialism has been that the legal repertoire of actions and choices is limited, and that any high court will have to be determined in order that the new order will work. Politically this limits its freedom in proclaiming rights. Given that this is so, it is important that such a court does not become the only focus for new legal discourses or practices. The sensitivity of judges to broader fields of discourse has been clearly apparent in South Africa in the past decade. While the period opened with a judiciary alive to the Government's belief in 'total onslaught', it has changed dramatically in apartheid's closing years along with government policy, reversing previous doctrines and practices. The already demonstrated sensitivity to political prevailing winds will now have a new institutional setting in the Constitutional Court. Politicians and lawyers have positively welcomed the involvement of a new court which is in an exposed and political position. Obviously not all sides want the same things from such a court. For the whites who are relinquishing power it represents a possible shield, and a symbolic guarantee of a state governed by law. For the new rulers it will be the means by which policies receive the ultimate stamp of legitimacy. Defenders of the old order will expect too much; governors of the new order too little. Like any court of last resort, but in an especially acute way, it will be caught between the paradigms of form and substance. An uncompromising formalism has never been appropriate to the settlement of constitutional disputes, and is in any case hard to adhere to in the interpretation of a rights instrument which is one of the major avenues by which the broader legal culture finds its way into the decisions of courts.

The activities of the Constitutional Court will have enormous implications for the evolution of South Africa's legal culture. The way in which it deals with its difficult and fascinating task will absorb the attention of lawyers and commentators. Because South Africa has been a common law culture in the sense that judges are the focus of legal attention, a new cult of the court seems likely to develop, in which broader forms of discourse about law and rights will be subsumed in and subordinated to a 'new formalism'. The complexity of the new constitution, and the invitation to draw on international law, could further entrench the role of legal 'experts' and the rule of external discourses. The peculiar habits of common law cultures, which use superior court judgements as the primary resource of legal argument which is built on passages ripped from the contexts which created them, creates a discourse which limits the possibilities of what can validly be said about law and how to say it. It may not be the best time to argue for a less controlled and wider sourcing of law in a situation where the centre will have to struggle to establish its authority. And there is the prospect, too, that progressive lawyers, having at last found a court in South Africa that is mostly on their side, will gladly identify it as the only valid source of legal wisdom. The inherent tensions in the power of judicial review will strengthen legal formalism, for it is formalism which is the judiciary's only real weapon against democratically elected politicians, as it is the only basis on which judges can legitimately substitute their opinions for those of a parliament.

In the white state many South African lawyers struggled to maintain a legal liberalism implied by the forms they had inherited. They did not entirely succeed. While there were occasions on which the judiciary were able to uphold a 'rule of law', the common law was in important respects bifurcated, and the courts continued to administer the laws of the racial state. It is important to acknowledge both parts of the story: that they tried and the effort was rarely successful. In the new state where there are urgent political necessities, unresolved historical antagonisms, many wants and much anger, can an attempt to maintain formal 'liberal' law of the type envisaged in the new constitutional arrangements be successful? In the white state the courts were not wholly successful in the endeavour to have the formalist representations of law controlling the state's action, and nor did this law gain substantial acceptability in the wider society. Given the highly authoritarian and patriarchal nature of South African society, both white and African, this failure of 'law' was remarkable. There are many obvious things to be thought about if a version of formal liberal law is this time to be more successful: a lower court system not entirely staffed by public officials; perhaps a return of the jury; a less remote bar; a less exalted judiciary more widely chosen; a more comprehensible and accessible common law; different forms of legal practice. All of which are a part of situating the existing narrow notion of law in a wider legal universe of practices, and part of a rescuing of the law from both politicians and judges.

These are answers, of course, to the question as to how 'legal formalism' might survive, not whether it should. Proponents of various forms of 'popular justice' will find them without value. And there are other basic issues. From the point of view of the experience of most South Africans 'law' has meant, primarily, 'police'. In re-creating a legal culture a new policing will mean more on the ground than a new constitutional discourse. But abandoning a highly centralised para-military force (with its concomitant police culture) will be difficult for any future government. Though there are extensive plans for police reform the transition has been accompanied by a perceived experience among all communities of a collapse of effective policing and a rising tide of crime and violence. The perception of anarchy poses the greatest threat to the emergence of a more responsive legal order, and it is more far-reaching than a question of a response to crime, chaos and disorder. Law depends on administrative efficiency, rights upon a strong state, not a weak one. The current bureaucracy in transition is not an effective instrument. Many court orders are unenforceable, tax collection and payments for services by no means regular. In a situation of 'structural corruption' where the rewards of belonging to the highly paid political class and bureaucracy are very large in terms of the normal living standard, the struggle to have a share in the resources of the state machine may take precedence over ensuring its effectiveness.[28] A declining effectiveness of the state's administrative machinery at a time in which new rights are being proclaimed will weaken any new legal order. Against this could be set the immense advantages of, for the first time in South Africa, a developing democratic political culture. This too is having to struggle with the muting effects of a government of national unity, and with an eerie absence of confidence. The acceptance that the Constitutional Court, rather than the national parliament, should be the appropriate body to make the decision on the abolition of the death penalty emphasises the curiously exaggerated place that 'law' has in the current polity. Administrative effectiveness and a more confident democracy could be better guarantees for a new legal order.

NOTES

1. R. Cover, *Justice Accused: Anti Slavery and the Judicial Process* (New Haven: Yale University Press, 1975).
2. Studies of legal culture have, on the whole, tended to emphasise popular legal consciousness, rather than bureaucracy. These issues may be pursued in S. Merry, *Getting Justice and Getting Even, Legal Consciousness among Working Class Americans* (Chicago: University of Chicago Press, 1990), B. Yngvesson, 'Inventing Law in Local Settings: Re-Thinking Popular Legal Culture', *Yale Law Journal*, vol. 98 (1989), 1689–1709; M. Horwitz, *The Transformation of American Law* (New York: Oxford University Press, 1992), Chapter 8. In drawing attention to the breadth and variety of discourses that constitute a legal culture it is not my intention to indicate that the professional, 'internal' legal discourses are less 'real' than, or should be subordinated to, a more popular consciousness of law. Indeed, I incline towards a view that would stress the importance of professional formalism. My argument is rather that this formalism must be clearly acknowledged to be a part of a wider spectrum, and not mistaken for all of 'law', if it is to have a viable future in the regulation of social relations in South Africa. I am also not writing about the falsity of a distinction between 'law' and 'politics', nor suggesting that a 'pretence' that law is apolitical be overcome. The suggestion here is that even when broadly constituted, legal discourses are distinguishable (if not distinct) from political ones.
3. H. Corder, *Judges at Work* (Johannesburg: Juta, 1984), Chapter 1.
4. C. Forsyth, *In Danger for Their Talents* (Johannesburg: Juta, 1985); J. Dugard, *Human Rights and the South African Legal Order* (Princeton: Princeton University Press, 1978); D. Davis, 'Post Apartheid South Africa: What Future for the Legal System', *Acta Juridica* (Cape Town: Juta, 1987).
5. M. Chanock, 'Race and Nation in South African Common Law' in P. Fitzpatrick (ed.), *Nationalism, Racism and the Rule of Law* (New York: Dartmonth, 1994), pp. 265–88. See also Forsyth, *op. cit.*, chapter 5; Cover, *op. cit.*
6. It is worth noting that in spite of the continuing public disapproval, the judiciary was virtually beyond criticism inside the profession and in its

journals, where a deferential and congratulatory sense, protected by the judges' use of contempt laws, reigned virtually without interruption. Judicial prestige was also protected during the apartheid years because it offered to opponents of the regime a slender hope of justice, while to its supporters judges were an embodiment of the state's propriety.

7.   The debates in Parliament and Select Committee about the wording of the Riotous Assemblies Act are instructive. From 1929 control of African political expression was for a long period left largely to the separate machinery of the Native Administration Act.

8.   Liberals and the 'Left', if there is such a position in legal scholarship, have praised the decisions, writing a story of defeat with honour. (Though none of the defeated judges resigned over this, or other issues related to apartheid.) It is not my view that the decisions were 'wrong' because I do not think there are right or wrong decisions in this sense in law. But the judges certainly tested the limits of expected behaviour and reasoning which exist in any legal system. It might be worth considering what the reaction would be if a court in the future were to rule similarly against a major political initiative by the government. A summary of the cases can be found in Forsyth, *op. cit.*, Chapter 2.

9.   Davis, *op. cit.*

10.   R. Wacks, 'Judges and Injustice', *South African Law Journal*, 266 (1984), 266–85.

11.   Dugard, *op. cit.* While I acknowledge both the strategic attractiveness of this argument, and the fact that there was (and is) nothing to prevent judges needing an historical myth from acting as if the Roman-Dutch law were inherently liberal, it will be evident from my remarks above that I do not think that this reflects the historical origins or trajectory of the Roman-Dutch law.

12.   Both of the important and substantial historical reviews of South Africa's legal system produced in this period, Corder *op. cit.* and Forsyth *op. cit.*, focussed on the judges of the Appellate Division. See also A. van Blerk, *Judge and Be Judged* (Cape Town: Juta, 1988).

13.   S. Burman and W. Scharf, 'Creating People's Justice: Street Committees and Peoples Courts in a South African City', *Law and Society Review*, 24, 3 (1990), 693–744.

14.   M. Chanock, '"Law, State and Culture": Thinking about Customary Law', *Acta Juridica* (1991).

15.   Legal Resources Centre, *Annual Reports*; L. White, 'To Learn and to Teach: Lawyering and Power in South Africa, 1981–85', *Wisconsin Law Review*, 699 (1988), 699–769. In this context one might also think of the growth of, and successes of, labour law during the 1980s. While the jurisprudence evolved in this area departed in many respects from the traditional forms and sources of South African law, nonetheless labour struggle and trade union activity was funnelled into and mediated by legal institutions. While this may suggest a strengthening of 'law' in what was an unlikely area for success, the willingness of labour to use this arena may have arisen because it was the only effective and available means of pursuing goals available then, and was open on good terms. Now that the labour leadership is a part of the ruling elite, and the labour movement a vital part of the governing

constituency, it could well pursue its goals in the political rather than the legal arena. Conflicts between labour and government, as the latter embraces the employers' agenda of increased productivity, are unlikely to be resolved in the courts.

16. There is encouragement to do this in the new constitution. There may well be an eagerness among lawyers to take this road, rather than to look to the development of local discourses, if only because these ideas have already been validated as 'law' elsewhere, by courts, or in conventions.

17. There are two important 'frontiers' between the two parts to be considered. One is property in land, which is essentially local yet hard to separate from the 'rights' in property protected by the externally oriented sector. The other is the area of constitutional and human rights, again essentially local, yet increasingly subject to international scrutiny. Changes to land law are of particular importance in the current transition. Restitution of land seized by the white state (going back to 1913) will not in itself resolve the tensions between land as symbol of community and security and land as economic asset. What kind of 'title' anyone, white or black, will have poses a real challenge for legal thinking and will be a complex matter to link with a global economic order. Similarly the urgent demands of 'law and order' will create limitations on the emergence of a 'rights culture'.

18. The phrasing is derived from John Brigham, *The Cult of the Court* (Philadelphia: Temple University Press, 1987).

19. M. Chanock, 'The Ecology of Coercion: Criminal Law and Criminology in a New State', unpublished paper. We should remember that one of the largest legal/racist enterprises, the attempt to impose prohibition of alcohol on Africans, was founded on these fears.

20. Chanock, 'Race and Nation in South African Common Law'.

21. The most significant exception which would have affected African workers, soon remedied by statute, was the ruling of the Transvaal Provincial Division in *R v Hildick Smith* in 1923 that regulations made under the Mines and Works Act of 1913 could not contain a colour bar. See M. Doxey, *The Industrial Colour Bar in South Africa* (Cape Town: Oxford University Press, 1961).

22. They could be in relation to marriage, where the possibility of polygamy in Hindu and Muslim religious law provided a sufficiently different cultural narrative in which to situate a common law discrimination against Asian marriages. See *Seedat's Executors v The Master (Natal) 1917 AD 302*.

23. Forsyth, *op. cit.*, p. 95 *et seq.*

24. One could fill pages with examples of these definitions, but here I will note just one, the definition of a coloured in the Population Registration Act of 1950. Precisely where, in cases of race mixture, other jurisdictions had searched for certainty, the Act could come up with nothing more precise than that coloureds were 'persons who are, or who are *generally accepted as*, members of a race *or class* known as Cape Coloured' (Section 5, my italics). It is significant that a prohibition on marriage between whites and other races was not enacted until 1949. In the context of the processes of the creation of the new urban and industrial society, it reflected the ruling elite's anxiety that there was insufficient racial consciousness among whites.

25. For the difference between the liberal discourses related to the 'rule of law', and those related to 'rights' see M. Chanock, 'The South African Bill

of Rights' in P. Alston (ed.), *Human Rights in the World* (Oxford: Clarendon Press, 1994).

26. See Davis, *op. cit.*
27. It is as yet too early to deal usefully with the question of language, which is central to any legal culture. Languages other than English and Afrikaans will find their way into court through lawyers and judges and new and different meanings will become possible.
28. Much can be understood about the history of Afrikaners and their absurd mismanagement of the South African state in these terms.

6 Economic Reconstruction and Development in South Africa

Nicoli Nattrass

INTRODUCTION

A new political age has dawned in South Africa, yet the country remains plagued by inequality, weak growth and chronic unemployment. Nelson Mandela's Government of National Unity now faces the delicate task of furthering redistribution whilst promoting industrial restructuring and sustained growth. The *Reconstruction and Development Programme* (RDP) spearheads the attempt.

This chapter outlines South Africa's main economic challenges and then moves on to discuss recent trends in government economic philosophy. As explained below, a central notion is that social and economic infrastructural development will benefit both disadvantaged communities and further economic growth. An outline of the RDP is provided, along with a critical overview of some of the more fashionable ideas concerning industrial restructuring. It is argued that without substantial injections of foreign and domestic investment, reconstruction and development in South Africa will fail miserably.

SOUTH AFRICA'S ECONOMIC CONTEXT

Under the new dispensation, South Africa has been divided up into nine provinces. As can be seen from Tables 6.1 and 6.2, these regions differ quite radically in terms of development indicators and economic output. In recognition of such fundamental differences in living standards, the constitution provides for the transfer of government revenues from rich to poor regions. The PWV (i.e. the Pretoria-Witwatersrand-Vereeniging triangle, now called Gauteng), which covers the smallest area, is by far the richest region in per capita income terms. This is not surprising given that most of South Africa's industrial and mining output comes from that province. It also has the highest life expectancy and the greatest number of hospital

125

Table 6.1 Socio-Economic Indicators

	GGP per rate	Fertility rate	Inf. mort. rate	Literacy	Pupil/ teacher ratio	Life expec. index	Human dev. index	Hosp beds	Health points
		%	(per 000 live births)	%				(per 000 pop.)	
PWV	9 841	3.0	35.2	69.0	27	65.6	0.71	6.5	0.2
W Cape	6 635	2.7	26.8	71.9	23	64.8	0.76	5.6	0.2
E Tvl	5 362	4.3	41.2	59.1	36	63.5	0.61	2.4	0.1
N Cape	5 297	2.9	31.5	67.6	25	64.0	0.73	5.5	0.4
Free State	4 604	3.7	45.4	62.1	34	63.6	0.66	4.1	0.2
North West	3 611	4.5	43.3	62.0	24	64.1	0.57	4.5	0.1
Kwa-Natal	3 136	4.3	44.7	65.1	37	62.6	0.58	5.8	0.1
E Cape	2 045	4.6	58.2	67.7	39	59.6	0.48	4.6	0.1
N Tvl	1 113	5.8	57.0	61.1	35	62.7	0.40	4.7	0.2
Total SA	4 479	3.3	41.8*	61.4	32	63.4	0.69	5.1	0.1

Source: Development Bank of Southern Africa (DBSA), South Africa's Nine Provinces (Halfway House: DBSA, 1994).
Notes: GGP = Gross Geographic Product (Rands per capita). The most recent figures provided for South Africa's regions were for 1988.
Health points include hospitals, clinics and health centres.
Human Development Index: Index taking into account income, life expectancy and literacy.
Infant mortality: per thousand live births
* According to Rojas et al., infant mortality in South Africa is 54 per 1 000 live births, with that for Africans being over five times the rate for whites.[1]

Table 6.2 Other Key Statistics

	Area	Population	Urbanland	Employment	Unemployment	Dependency ratio
	(000km²)	(millions)	%	(% of workforce)	%	
PWV	18.8	0.2	99.6	54.4	16.6	0.9
W Cape	129.4	0.2	95.1	56.9	13.3	1.2
E Tvl	81.8	0.1	43.2	51.8	16.3	2.1
N Cape	363.4	0.4	78.2	52.9	16.7	1.6
Free State	129.4	0.2	73.7	55.3	15.3	1.4
North West	118.7	0.1	43.9	48.0	22.3	1.6
Kwa-Natal	91.5	0.1	77.9	44.8	25.2	2.3
E Cape	170.6	0.1	55.4	44.8	23.6	3.7
N Tvl	119.6	0.2	12.1	40.3	24.8	4.8
Total SA	1 223.2	0.1	65.5	50.0	19.4	1.9

Source: DBSA, 1994.
Notes: Dependency ratio: the number of people supported by a single member of the labour force (employed or unemployed).

beds per 1 000 people. The other rich area of note is the Western Cape which has the highest literacy figures, the lowest infant mortality and unemployment rates, the lowest pupil/teacher ratio, and the highest human development index.

The poorer regions such as the North-West Province, KwaZulu-Natal, the Eastern Cape and the Northern Transvaal tend to be more rural, have higher fertility rates, higher unemployment, higher dependency rates and a greater reliance on male migrant workers for household survival. Given that their per capita income figures are below the average for South Africa, these provinces will have a claim on the richer five regions for resource transfers. However, for such transfers to have a significant and sustained impact on poverty alleviation, they must be channeled in such a way as to promote economic growth and job creation.

It is no accident that the poorest regions are uniformly those regions with the lowest percentage of the labour force in formal employment. The single greatest determinant of poverty is lack of access to formal employment opportunities. Boosting economic growth and job creation is thus essential if meaningful redistribution is to occur.

Unfortunately South Africa's investment and output growth performance has been depressingly weak over the past two decades. Between 1980 and 1993, economic growth averaged only just over 1 per cent per annum. Given that the South African economy needs to grow by at least 4 per cent a year simply to absorb new entrants into the labour market, this has resulted in rising unemployment and declining per capita incomes. Between 1970 and 1990, the proportion of the labour force without formal jobs rose from 19 to 40 per cent.[2] Even though the economy has recovered somewhat to grow at 1.2 per cent in 1993 and at an estimated 2.5 per cent in 1994, this has not been sufficient to dent the rise in unemployment.

Although slow growth in the global economy during the 1980s, the debt crisis, and political unrest contributed to the poor economic performance, the roots of South Africa's economic crisis extend back in history. In particular, policies of import substitution and inadequate levels of investment in black education and training have contributed significantly to the structural problems faced by the South African economy today.

Reduced investment is one part of the story of chronic economic decline in South Africa, but it does not fully explain South Africa's growth performance. As can be seen in Table 6.3, investment growth remained relatively strong until the 1980s, and for many years economic decline was accompanied by a high and rising ratio of investment to GDP. The problem was one of faltering productivity growth as South Africa invested a substantial share of its income, but received progressively less from it in terms of output.

Table 6.3 South Africa's Long Run Economic Growth Performance

	Average annual growth rates %					
	1961–5	1966–70	1971–5	1976–80	1981–5	1986–92
Real gross domestic product	5.9	5.2	3.5	3.1	1.4	1.0
Real gross domestic investment	4.6	5.8	6.4	4.0	0.0	0.3
Employment	3.2	2.5	2.4	1.4	0.1	−0.2

Source: P. Fallon and L.P. de Silva, 'South Africa: Economic Performance and Policies', *World Bank Discussion Paper No. 7* (Washington DC: The World Bank, 1994), p. 32.

Table 6.4 Productivity in South Africa

Growth in productivity	Manufacturing			Total private sector		
	1971–9	1980–9	1990–2	1971–9	1980–9	1990–2
			%			
Labour	2.0	0.5	−0.8	0.8	1.3	0.3
Capital	−2.3	−1.5	−5.5	−2.8	−1.0	−2.0
Multifactor	0.7	−0.1	−3.0	−0.5	0.2	−0.8

Source: J. Du Toit and H. Falkena, *The Structure of the South African Economy* (Johannesburg: Absa Bank, 1994), p. 24.
Note: Multifactor productivity is a combined measure of labour and capital productivity.

Table 6.4 shows that productivity growth in South Africa has been poor, especially since 1980. This applies particularly to capital productivity. Factors which have contributed to South Africa's dismal productivity performance include shortages of high-level manpower and management skills, a lack of cheap money policies (particularly in the 1970s), and investment incentives as well as industrial unrest. The challenge facing South Africa is thus to increase not only the rate of investment, but also its efficiency and labour intensity. This will not be easy.

However, there is an up-side to the picture too. Most encouragingly, the macroeconomy is stable and firmly under control. As can be seen in Table 6.5, inflation and interest rates have come down substantially in the past

Table 6.5 Recent Economic Indicators for South Africa

	Real GDP	Real exports	Real imports	Real GDFI	R billion capital account	$–R exchange rate	Prime interest rate	Rate of inflation
				(% growth rates)				
1988	4.2	9.8	21.9	8.9	–6.8	2.3	18.0	12.9
1989	2.3	4.6	–0.2	5.1	–4.7	2.6	21.0	14.7
1990	–0.3	1.9	–5.8	–2.0	–2.4	2.6	21.0	14.4
1991	–1.0	0.3	2.1	–8.4	–4.8	2.8	20.3	15.3
1992	–2.2	1.0	5.4	–9.9	–3.7	2.9	17.3	13.9
1993	1.2	4.9	4.3	–3.9	–16.3	3.3	15.3	9.7
1994	2.5	4.5	6.0	4.7	–6.0	3.6	16.3	8.8

Source: Estimates from Nedcor, *Guide to the Economy*: Third Quarter (1994).
Note: GDFI = Gross domestic fixed investment.

few years. The budget deficit has declined from 7.8 per cent of GDP in 1992 to 6.9 per cent in 1993 and, given the sound fiscal stance of the 1994 budget, could well fall further. As discussed below, the orthodox approach to macroeconomic management of the ruling African National Congress (ANC) is encouraging in this regard.

Other positive factors for South Africa include the continued upswing in the advanced capitalist countries (which should boost South African exports), improved access to international finance and aid, and the potential for some of South Africa's advanced industrial sectors to break into international markets such as mining machinery and chemicals.[3]

However, South Africa's binding constraints on growth are close at hand. Historically, South Africa's boom periods have been cut short by skills shortages, inflation and balance of payments problems. Rising output and investment implied rising imports relative to exports, and when these could no longer be financed by capital inflow, the monetary authorities were obliged to slam on the brakes – usually by increasing interest rates. This old pattern is in danger of raising its ugly head very soon. As shown in Table 6.5, imports have started to pick up and grow faster than exports. This is the result of both growing consumer demand and investment growth.

These structural weaknesses in the South African economy need to be addressed if growth is to continue in any stable and sustained way. In essence, South Africa has to become less reliant on gold and primary exports for foreign exchange earnings. This entails making the manufacturing sector more internationally competitive. South Africa's recently concluded GATT agreement should help on this score by bringing about a substantial improvement to the trade regime which is currently too fluid, complex and biased against exports.[4] However, the phasing out of the General Export Incentive Scheme (GEIS) – because it contravened GATT rules – could put exports under pressure in the shorter term. Other policies favoured by the new South African government to promote industrial restructuring include selective state intervention and wage policy. These are discussed in the following section, which traces key shifts in ANC economic thinking from 1990 to the 1994 RDP White Paper.

FROM 'GROWTH THROUGH REDISTRIBUTION' TO THE RDP

Growth through Redistribution

The idea that certain forms of redistribution are compatible with economic growth can be traced back to the ANC's 1990 *Discussion Document on Economic Policy*. The paper argued that instead of there being any trade-off between redistribution and growth, redistribution could further economic growth via its impact on restructuring. In addition, increased government spending could boost growth by stimulating the level of demand:

> Programs and policies that increase output – particularly of social infrastructure and basic consumer products – will increase employment and produce new incentives to growth which will benefit all sectors of our economy. We thus call for a program of Growth through Redistribution in which redistribution acts as a spur to growth and in which the fruits of growth are redistributed to satisfy basic needs.[5]

According to the document, apartheid policies had created an uncompetitive economy geared towards 'producing consumer goods for a wealthy minority'.[6] This pattern of demand was argued to be associated with capital-intensive production and hence with inadequate job creation. By restructuring demand towards the poor it was hoped that South Africa's economic structure would become more oriented towards the labour-intensive provision of basic needs. This argument assumes that if income is redistributed from rich to poor, this will increase the demand for labour-intensive basic goods, decrease pressure on the balance of payments (by reducing the demand for consumer imports) and boost employment.

Unfortunately, international experience indicates that altering the structure of demand to tilt the balance towards the poor has complex and often contradictory effects; poor groups do not always consume labour-intensive products, and cutting the income of the rich can result in a fall in the demand for labour-intensive services. In extreme cases, the pursuit of such policies has resulted in macroeconomic chaos.[7] In South Africa's case, it is doubtful whether demand from wealthy households was a significant factor in promoting either capital intensity or driving import demand. The dramatic rise in capital intensity in manufacturing from the 1970s, for example, has been related primarily to large state-aided investments in synthetic fuels, aluminium and steel.[8] These investments were undertaken for strategic reasons rather than being motivated by any desire to satisfy the consumption demands of richer consumers. Similarly, given that over 70 per cent of South Africa's imports consist of capital goods, the impact of the demand for luxury imports is likely to have been minimal.[9]

As regards altering the level of demand, the 1990 ANC document proposed a Keynesian demand-led policy by arguing that a 'massive injection of finance will be required to meet basic social needs'.[10] Although the document was also at pains to stress that 'inflationary financing through money creation should be avoided'[11] and that macroeconomic balance and financial discipline should be maintained, it was not clear how this fiscal conservatism was thought to be compatible with the proposed massive stimulation in aggregate demand. The problem is that a 'massive injection' will most likely result in inflation if substantial spare capacity does not exist; bottlenecks will soon appear and drive up prices. As imports rise to meet demand, pressure will be placed on the balance of payments. Such a scenario is highly likely in South Africa. Spare capacity is unevenly distributed in the economy and bottlenecks are likely to appear very quickly once demand is stimulated.[12] For macro balance to be maintained under such circumstances any increase in demand would have to be limited and gradual.

The ANC's 1990 discussion document sparked off intense debate and re-evaluation. During the course of 1991 and 1992, ANC economic policy statements became increasingly wary of demand-led policies and more concerned with encouraging business to invest.[13] The emphasis shifted from altering the level and pattern of demand (by boosting government spend-ing and redistributing from rich to poor) as a means of promoting growth, to one which prioritized fiscal discipline and sustainable redistribution. By the time ANC economic policy became officially adopted at the 1992 National Conference, the slogan 'Growth through Redistribution', along with promises of 'massive injections of finance', had quietly disappeared.

This change in focus was partly fed by the global collapse of communism and growing hostility on the part of international economic organizations and investors to massive state intervention in the economy. The ANC's economic thinking also began to reflect its own rapidly changing status from an essentially oppositional liberation movement to a government-in-waiting that would all too soon find itself responsible for the fiscal health of the economy.

This policy evolution is understandable given that the new government simply does not have the resources at its disposal to address all of the pent-up demand for redistribution. South Africa already spends a greater proportion of GDP on education and welfare-related spending than do other upper middle income countries.[14] Likewise, South Africa's share of personal income taxation is comparatively high by international standards.[15] Rather than raising more revenue and spending more resources, the ANC government has little choice other than to restructure the tax system and to re-orient spending within existing levels.

The key fiscal challenge is to redirecting spending within categories, such as that from curative to preventative care in the health sector.[16] In the case of education, this means that white schools are going to suffer a substantial decline in funding.[17] According to the new Minister of Education, the South African government still spends nearly three times as much on the education of white children as it does on black.[18] This will have to change dramatically. Although some shifts are possible between categories, such as from defence to housing, these are smaller than commonly thought – particularly in light of the recent difficulties experienced in incorporating ex-guerrillas into the South African National Defence Force. Distressingly few extra resources will become available to the state as a result of the abolition of apartheid structures. Although apartheid absorbed and wasted vast resources, eliminating apartheid will not bring back this money.[19] Furthermore, given the need to create regional government structures in South Africa's nine provinces, the chances of creating a 'slimmer' state are becoming ever smaller. Public sector employment in fact rose by 11 000 in the first six months of the democratic regime.

The Reconstruction and Development Programme

During the 1994 election campaign, the ANC fought on a ticket of reconstruction and development. A glossy pamphlet entitled *The Reconstruction and Development Program* was produced and distributed widely.[20] When President Nelson Mandela presided over the first meeting of his new cabinet, he made it clear that continued cabinet membership was conditional on support for the RDP. This was immediately obtained. Now politicians of all descriptions regularly pay homage to the RDP. Even astute businessmen make passing references to it when expounding on the important role the private sector has in generating jobs.

On one level, the RDP has become so widely bandied about that it is rapidly losing meaning. Is it a broad vision, a set of specific development policies or simply a fancy term for government economic policy? No one is quite sure. But judging by the way in which the term 'RDP' is sprinkled like holy water across speeches, and invoked by community organisations when demanding improved facilities and services, the term is rapidly assuming the status of a magical cure-all.

Some clarity was gained in September 1994 when the government released its White Paper on the RDP. The document, which described itself as a 'vision for the fundamental transformation of our society', focused particularly on 'people-driven development', restructuring the civil service, and creating more favourable conditions for economic growth.[21] Central to the White Paper was the social democratic notion that channeling resources into economic and social infrastructure (especially education, health and housing) will enhance both social welfare and economic growth. This is a much watered down version of the ANC's earlier policy of Growth through Redistribution.

As a statement of principles, the RDP White Paper was a reasonable first shot at a development strategy. The problem was that there were no clear guidelines as to what should be prioritized, or within what broad budget constraints. Even though Jay Naidoo (the minister in charge of the RDP) nicknamed the programme 'Operation Bootstrap' in order to stress its cash-constrained character, expectations are likely to continue running out of line with economic reality.

Essentially, the RDP is primarily an exercise in reorienting existing spending. The revenues allocated to the 'RDP fund' are drawn mainly from cuts in national government departments.[22] Other sources of funding for the RDP fund include the sale of state assets, the proceeds of a state lottery, and aid grants from foreign governments. It is interesting to note that because the sale of state assets is linked to the RDP, there has been no significant objection raised to such privatization. Considering that the debate over privatization versus nationalization was so heated during the early 1990s, this transformation in public opinion is nothing short of remarkable.

How the RDP fund will end up being allocated remains unclear – largely because so much of the process is supposed to emerge out of broad-based consultation through RDP Task Teams, the National Economic Labour and Development Council, and sectoral and other local forums. While consultation is to be welcomed, this should not be at the cost of policy coherence. There is a real danger that the RDP might simply drown in a mass of sclerotic bureaucracy as activists, parliamentarians and government officials race from one meeting, Task Team, council, commission, forum, or committee to the next.

Although some transfers are to take place from rich to poor regions, local and provincial governments are expected to fund their 'own RDPs' through local level reorientation of budgetary priorities. According to the White Paper, only those local governments which perform well in terms of efficiency, accountability and democracy are supposed to be able to get access to additional funding through the national RDP fund. A major stumbling block facing many local governments, however, is how to get people to start paying again for services. Ever since rent boycotts were instituted against the apartheid regime, local authority finances have been a disaster. The coming to power of the new legitimate democratic government has done little to improve the situation.

Given that rent boycotts extended to bond boycotts in many low-income housing areas, this had the further effect of driving private sector financial institutions out of the market for low-income housing. In order to encourage the private sector to participate in the provision of housing, the late Joe Slovo, as Minister of Housing, brokered a deal with the banks whereby the government is to act as a guarantor in case of bond boycotts. In this way, part of the funding for the RDP is being used to encourage additional funding from the private sector. However, unless the new government can convince people to start paying their service charges, this creative initiative will grind to a halt.

In October 1994, the government significantly improved the credibility of its conservative fiscal stance by announcing a set of concrete measures aimed at radically restructuring government finances.[23] These included developing an internal monitoring mechanism to ensure that money is spent efficiently, privatizing state assets (such as South African Airways) to reduce the government debt and freezing the salaries of top civil servants. The government also stated its intention to reduce (largely through the process of attrition) the number of bureaucrats by 200 000 by the turn of the century.[24] As part of an attempt to establish a 'culture of thrift' and rid the new administration of its 'gravy train' image, the salaries of the president and two deputy presidents were cut by 20 per cent, and the salaries of cabinet ministers, regional premiers and heads of the senate and national assembly were trimmed by 10 per cent. In addition, it was also announced that greater controls will be exercised on items such as first class travel, hotel expenses, car allowances etc. These are welcome developments.

INDUSTRIAL STRATEGY

Selective Intervention

Although the more conventional, restrictive economic arguments appear to have won the day as regards fiscal policy, there is still strong support within the ANC camp for an interventionist industrial strategy. This can be seen in the work of the Congress of South African Trade Unions-aligned Industrial Strategy Project (ISP), and the Macroeconomic Research Group (MERG).

Both MERG and the ISP see competition and the price mechanism as an important component of the 'incentive system', but argue that selective intervention is necessary in cases of market failure (e.g. technological development),[25] and where 'the market-determination of resource allocation may be economically and socially suboptimal'.[26] In such cases, the strategic use of the following instruments is proposed: differential taxation,[27] tariffs, subsidies, accelerated depreciation allowances and other special allowances (such as that for training). Although the ISP recommends 'targeting the broad underlying competitive fundamentals' rather than 'picking winners' as such, some 'hard targeting' of 'specific manufacturing sub-sectors' is clearly on the agenda.[28]

This raises the obvious question of how future planners intend to select such sub-sectors. The idea seems to be to pick industries that will help South Africa 'move up the value-chain' and contribute to foreign exchange earnings. But whether these will be successful remains to be seen.[29] Considering that the classic developmental states of South Korea and Japan made as many mistakes as they had successes[30] it is far from self-evident which sectors one should support. It is also worth bearing in mind that

> competitive industries in a given economy are not always associated with the pursuit of sectorally-focussed policies. Instead, they are often the fruit of individual success stories, within the general framework of adequate policies and a climate that favours innovation and enhanced productivity . . . Within the same product line, competitive advantage tends to be distributed differently in different countries.[31]

In other words, selecting potential winners can be a very fine-tuned micro-level business. Until the new South African state and its institutions develop close trusting relationships with private sector enterprises in order to facilitate constructive flows of information, targeting is likely to be crude and haphazard.[32] If the new South African state is going to be able to develop good (and non-corrupt) relations with business, pick industrial winners and discipline and support capitalism appropriately, then interventionist industrial policies will probably do more good than harm. If, however, the state ends up bloated and technically inept, then the reverse scenario is more likely.

Another problem with the idea of selecting winners concerns dealing with the losers – i.e. those firms industries and sectors which fail to meet the new criteria of competitiveness and are judged unfavourably when it comes to state support. Given that no industry, firm or labour union is going to voluntarily assist in its own demise, this imposes limits on how far industrial restructuring can be done democratically – in the sense of 'with the co-operation of all interested parties'. Businesses will of course support the call for restructuring towards a more market-based open economy if they stand to benefit from it. However, those who rely on government incentives, tariffs, etc. to keep their businesses afloat will be vocal in their opposition to any restructuring which implies the removal of such incentives. Given that workers in these industries would stand to lose their jobs as a result, they could very well opt to join forces with employers in this regard.

One way of limiting the danger of co-ordinated trade union and employer opposition to restructuring would be to guarantee retraining for workers who lose their jobs because of restructuring. This is a major thrust of the ISP proposals. Another way of diffusing opposition would be for the state to offer continued protection to industries – but to reduce it gradually and make such protection conditional on adequate performance (for example as regards training, exports, productivity improvements etc.). Such a strategy is consistent with the developmental state type intervention supported by MERG:

> confronting the necessity to restructure innovatively inevitably raises questions regarding enterprise bargaining and the argument that it is more flexible and better able to secure the productivity enhancement that is central to the restructuring project.[33]

Wage Strategy

Another important idea emanating from the work of MERG and the ISP, is that the economy can be restructured through labour market interventions (most notably through training and higher minimum wages), and through measures affecting the structure and operation of business. Both research initiatives see greater worker participation as part of the necessary restructuring. Joffe et al. argue that it is indeed a 'requirement of globally competitive production'[34] that 'management sees its workforce as an asset whose potential has had to be maximized than as a cost which has to be minimized'.[35] Quality and variety is regarded as more important than price in winning international markets: 'In these changing global circumstances competitive advantage arises less from access to reservoirs of cheap labour and natural resources, than from an endowment of widely spread skills'.[36]

Although skills are clearly vital to sustained growth and competitiveness, it is cavalier to assume away the role of lower costs (especially wage costs) in gaining markets and competitiveness. Not all markets value quality and variety above costs – particularly as regards mass-produced goods for low-income consumers.[37] But both the ISP and MERG manifest a general disenchantment with productive activities based on low-wage unskilled labour. Joffe et al. favour removing tariff protection on low-price wage goods 'not only because it would increase low wage real incomes, but also because South Africa cannot (and presumably does not) want to pay the low wages required to compete in this range of the competitive spectrum'.[38] Similarly, in supporting higher minimum wages, MERG argues that they will

> act as a spur for many enterprises throughout the economy to restructure, innovate and provide their workers with transferable skills. Unprofitable and inefficient enterprises should not receive long-term subsidies from the poor, ie, from those of their employees who are accepting very low wages.[39]

High wage policies can, theoretically, prevent an economy from being caught in a low-wage, low-tech trap.[40] Singapore's strategy of pricing itself out of the low-cost manufacturing market (by raising minimum wages) is a case in point. However, the Singaporean model rests on the notion of raising wages to facilitate structural change in an economy with a reasonably skilled labour force. South Africa, in contrast, is saddled with a predominantly unskilled labour force.[41] It is worth bearing in mind that Singapore's high wage strategy was embarked upon only after a long period of growth based on lower wages.

Allowing the parallel development of a low-wage, low-skill sector in South Africa may be necessary to reduce unemployment and to lessen the risk of total commitment to a high-wage, high-tech strategy. State planners must be very sure that an increase in minimum wages will not increase (or will have only a small short-term effect on) unemployment. If a minimum wage is to be set, it should be done so after careful economic research to ensure that unemployment does not worsen as a result of its implementation.

ENCOURAGING INVESTMENT

Although many of the strategic interventions proposed by MERG and the ISP have been used successfully in South East Asia, this does not necessarily mean that they are feasible in South Africa today. The world economy in the 1990s is a very different place from that in the heyday of development state intervention. Capital is substantially more mobile, and is faced with a much wider range of investment opportunities across the planet.[42] This inevitably reduces the scope of government policy at the national level. Disciplining and coercing capital is a great deal more difficult. Capital simply leaves (or does not enter) if the policy environment is perceived as unfriendly.

Investors are cautious animals. Even though indicators of business confidence in South Africa have improved recently,[43] a lag of a couple of years is to be expected before investment takes off on a large scale. Foreign investors are adopting a 'wait and see' approach and are keeping investments relatively small. They are apparently avoiding the manufacturing sector and most activity is taking place in the field of indirect investment (such as franchise and licensing deals).

Caution applies even more strongly in the field of labour relations. In the first six months of 1994, 1.4 million man days were lost in South Africa due to strike action, i.e. double the amount lost during the same period in 1993.[44] The inauguration of President Nelson Mandela did little to slow the impetus. In his first 80 days in office, over 100 000 workers downed tools. This, along with fears of inflation as a consequence of possible over-spending by the government on the RDP, contributed to the 'speculative' BB rating of South Africa by Standard and Poor Corporation. This meant that South Africa could expect to pay substantially over 80 basis points above the LIBOR[45] when borrowing on financial markets abroad.[46]

As Table 6.6 shows, Moody's Investor Services gave South Africa a higher investment grade rating. This was followed shortly thereafter by an

Table 6.6   South Africa's Split Investment Rating

	Moody's	Standard and Poor's
Investment Grade		
United States	Aaa	AAA
Canada	Aa1	AA+
Australia	Aa2	AA
Ireland	Aa2	AA–
Portugal	A1	AA–
Malaysia	A2	A
Hong Kong	A3	A
China	A3	BBB
Chile	Baa2	BBB+
Indonesia	Baa3	BBB–
SOUTH AFRICA	–	Baa3
Colombia	–	BBB–
Speculative Grade		
SOUTH AFRICA	–	BB
India	Ba2	BB+
Philippines	Ba3	BB–
Argentina	B1	BB–
Venezuela	Ba2	B+

Sources: *Weekend Argus*, 8–9 October 1994; *Weekly Mail*, 7–13 October 1994.

even higher investor grade rating by Nippon (the Japanese rating agency). Where foreign lenders take these grades more seriously than those of Standard and Poor (which they may well, given that Moody's ratings are usually perceived to be the tougher of the two), then lending to South Africa could be cheaper. It is unlikely to fall below 80 basis points above the LIBOR.

Hopefully, the two investment grade ratings along with the recently announced World Bank financial support for the RDP[47] will alleviate investor concerns somewhat. South African growth prospects are thus reasonably positive – at least in the medium term. However, given the power of unions to maintain real wage growth, and the government's stated policy of developing industrial skills and furthering technological development, the chances of such growth being labour-intensive are not promising. Job creation in the formal sector is thus unlikely to dent the growth of unemployment in the foreseeable future.

NOTES

1. P. Rojas, D. McMurchy, C. Moji and T. Wilson, *Health Services in Lesotho: A Study of New Possibilities for Cooperation with South Africa*, report prepared by the Lesotho Country Team of the World Health Organization (July 1994), p. 15.
2. B.A. Kahn, A. Sehadji and M. Walton, 'South Africa: Macroeconomic Issues for the Transition', Informal Discussion Paper on Aspects of the Economy of South Africa, No. 2 (Southern African Department of the World Bank, May 1992), p. 2.
3. T. Moll, 'Supply Led Development', paper prepared for the IFAA Conference on Demand/Supply-Led Growth, University of the Witwatersrand, July 1994.
4. P. Belli, M. Finger and A. Ballivan, 'South Africa: A Review of Trade Policies', *World Bank Discussion Paper No. 4* (Washington DC: World Bank, 1993).
5. *Ibid.*, p. 5.
6. *Ibid.*, p. 4.
7. R. Dornbusch and S. Edwards, 'Macroeconomic Populism', *Journal of Development Economics*, 32 (1990); T. Moll, 'Growth Through Redistribution: A Dangerous Fantasy', *South African Journal of Economics*, 59, 3 (1991).
8. P. Fallon and L.P. de Silva, 'South Africa: Economic Performance and Policies', *World Bank Discussion Paper No. 7* (Washington DC: The World Bank, 1994).
9. B. Kahn, 'The Crisis of South Africa's Balance of Payments' in S. Gelb (ed.), *South Africa's Economic Crisis* (Cape Town: David Philip, 1991).

10.   African National Congress (ANC), *Discussion Document on Economic Policy* (Johannesburg: ANC, 1990), p. 7.

11.   *Ibid.*, p. 1.

12.   T. Moll, 'Growth Through Redistribution'; Kahn et al., *op. cit.*

13.   N. Nattrass, 'Politics and Economics in ANC Economic Policy', *African Affairs*, 93 (July 1994).

14.   See N. Nattrass and A. Roux, 'Making Welfare Spending Work', in P. Moll, N. Nattrass and L. Loots (eds), *Redistribution: How Can It Work in South Africa?* (Cape Town: David Philip, 1991), p. 90, and J. Du Toit and H. Falkena, *The Structure of the South African Economy* (Johannesburg: Absa Bank, 1994), pp. 6–7.

15.   Du Toit and Falkena, *op. cit.*, p. 28.

16.   It has been estimated that South Africa's entire population could be provided with primary health care services at a current cost of one tenth of the amount presently being spent by the state on health (Nattrass and Roux, *op. cit.*, pp. 93–4).

17.   It has been shown that if the government were to spend the same amount on the education of all children as it did on whites in the late 1980s, this would absorb between 17 and 18 per cent of the GDP (S. Van der Berg, 'Redirecting Government Expenditure' in Moll, Nattrass and Loots, *op. cit.*, p. 79). Given that South Africa spends between 5 and 6 per cent of the GDP on education – a proportion which puts the country amongst the top spenders on education in the world – it is clear that a radical re-orientation of the education budget vote is more economically feasible than equalizing educational spending at white levels. This makes a decline in white educational standards inevitable.

18.   Press conference, 31 October 1994.

19.   For example, Van der Berg has shown that if defence spending had not risen above its 1972 level of 2.2 per cent of GDP, the savings in the period 1973 to 1990 would have been more than sufficient to eliminate the current housing backlog (Van der Berg, *op. cit.*, p. 81).

20.   Johannesburg: ANC, 1994.

21.   The RDP White Paper accepted that poverty can only be alleviated in the context of rapid economic growth and stressed the need to create an enabling environment for growth. This includes macroeconomic goals of low inflation, a stable exchange rate and real interest rates. Mention is also made of industrial and trade policies to promote investment and competitiveness, competition policy and support for small firms to weaken economic concentration, and the development of human resources in the context of trade union rights.

22.   Most RDP funding will come from rationalization of existing structures, improved and reformed tax systems, the financial sector and donor aid. The government will ensure that public utilities such as electrification and telecommunications are self-financing. The intention is to reduce the deficit steadily. A zero-based budgetary process will be introduced by which line departments and other institutions will have to motivate their spending each year. Tax incentives which meet RDP goals will remain. All others will be terminated.

23.   These were reported in the *Sunday Times*, 30 October 1994.

24. Because the transitional constitution guaranteed jobs for five years to state bureaucrats from the old regime, it is difficult to cut back on civil service employment in any way other than through natural attrition.

25. The ISP and MERG propose restructuring the funding of existing science councils and encouraging greater co-operation between university and private sector (A. Joffe, D. Kaplan, R. Kaplinsky and D. Lewis, 'Meeting the Global Challenge: a Framework for Industrial Revival in South Africa', paper presented at Mabula Lodge (April 1993), pp. 24–5; Macroeconomic Research Group (MERG), *Making Democracy Work* (Cape Town: Oxford University Press, 1994), pp. 231–3.

26. Joffe et al., *op. cit.*, p. 14.

27. This includes tax-breaks for higher value-added industries such as mineral beneficiation and using a multiple rate VAT structure.

28. Industrial Strategy Project (ISP), 'Industrial Strategy for South Africa: The Recommendations of the ISP', *South African Labour Bulletin*, 18 (1994), 60.

29. See MERG, *op. cit.*; Joffe et al., *op. cit.*, and ISP, *op. cit.*

30. M. Porter, *The Competitive Advantage of Nations* (New York: The Free Press, 1990).

31. E. Iglesias, *Reflections on Economic Development: towards a new Latin American Consensus* (Washington DC: The Inter-American Development Bank, 1994), p. 89.

32. For a more detailed argument, see N. Nattrass, 'Economic Restructuring in South Africa: the Debate continues', *Journal of Southern African Studies*, 20, 4 (December 1994), 517–31.

33. MERG, *op. cit.*, p. 19.

34. Joffe et al., *op. cit.*, p. 16.

35. *Ibid.*, p. 18.

36. *Ibid.*, p. 3.

37. J. Curry, 'The Flexibility Fetish: a Review Essay on Flexible Specialization', *Capital and Class*, 50 (1993), 113–14.

38. Joffe et al., *op. cit.*, p. 28.

39. MERG, *op. cit.*, p. 163.

40. D. Rodrik, 'Do Low Income Countries Have a High Wage Option?', paper presented at the Trade and Development Workshop, Yale University (November 1993).

41. As Joffe et al. themselves note, one quarter of the African working population and one eighth of the coloured population were without formal education in 1985 and 45 per cent of blacks cannot read or write (Joffe et al., *op. cit.*, p. 15).

42. M. Desai, 'The New International Economic Order: Ideology or Reality', *Journal of International Development*, 5, 2 (1993), 145–8.

43. See Old Mutual, *Economic Monitor*, Third Quarter (1994), 7.

44. *Sunday Times*, 24 July 1994.

45. The LIBOR is the London Inter-Bank Offer Rate which is the prime interest rate on world financial markets.

46. Nedcor, *Guide to the Economy*, Third Quarter (1994).

47. *Sunday Times*, 9 October 1994.

7 Reconstructing Tradition: Women and Land Reform

Cherryl Walker

This chapter addresses the tension that exists within the new government over the issue of 'the politics of traditionalism'.[1] These politics have been most evident in the deadly struggle to out-manoeuvre the Inkatha Freedom Party (IFP) in the run-up to the April 1994 elections and the post-election quest for reconciliation, nation-building and party political advantage. In this struggle the contestation around the Zulu monarchy has been the most visible – but not the only – manifestation of the resurgent traditionalism that the ANC has been attempting to diffuse and coopt.

In this chapter I argue that the 'tradition' being negotiated is fundamentally patriarchal and that the twin goals of gender equality and accommodating 'tradition' are, therefore, ultimately incompatible. Given the limitations to the way in which gender equality is perceived within the ANC, as well as the absence of a politically powerful mass women's movement on the ground, it appears likely that, in seeking to manage this incompatibility, the ANC-led government will end up compromising on its commitment to gender equality as it starts to deliver on its reconstruction programme.

One area where this scenario is of immediate concern is the land reform programme. The ANC recognises land reform as of considerable importance, politically in terms of its emotional and symbolic significance in the struggle against black and specifically African dispossession, and economically as the cornerstone of its rural reconstruction programme. Its *Reconstruction and Development Programme* (RDP) recognises that rural women are particularly disadvantaged in terms of access to land, as does the *Report from the Macroeconomic Research Group* (MERG), which informed much of the RDP. This is the area where the clash between the principle of gender equality and the continued accommodation to the aspirations of traditional leaders is most apparent – and where women are likely to continue to suffer the consequences of a patriarchal domination legitimised as 'tradition'.

This chapter develops this argument in five parts. The first part examines the degree to which patriarchal social relations structure key aspects of rural society and argues that if the democratisation of society is to include women, then what is being defended in the name of 'tradition' has to be subjected to a very serious review. The second part assesses the legal gains that have been made in the struggle to empower women, through an examination of the interim Constitution and the Constitutional Principles that are guiding the next round of constitution-making. Two issues are critical here: firstly, the clear endorsement of the principle of gender equality and secondly, the ambiguous status accorded tradition, custom and traditional authority in the Constitution, which stand in uneasy relationship to the gender equality clause. Because I am arguing that, despite important gains, the principle of gender equality is still a recent graft on ANC thinking (and that of its principal allies), the third part moves beyond the formal principles to look at the limitations implicit in the ANC's analysis of women and gender relations, with specific reference to the RDP. The significance of this becomes more apparent when placed in the context of the recent politics of traditionalism, the focus of the fourth part: troubling lacunae or inconsistencies in gender policy become potentially major breaches of principle when viewed alongside the ANC's attempts to accommodate the patriarchal world-view embodied in the 'tradition' espoused by traditional leaders and their champions. This part examines the likely consequences for gender politics as a result of the strategic and tactical choices the ANC appears to have made in this regard. Finally, the fifth part attempts to pull the discussion together, by looking at the way in which these different strands are likely to intersect in the implementation of a land reform programme, and the implications of this for women.

RURAL PATRIARCHY

In an era when the run-on phrase 'non-racialandnon-sexist' operates as a ready-made badge of political respectability, one is unlikely to encounter much opposition when one describes South Africa as a patriarchal society, at least not from the newly triumphant progressive establishment. Few in these circles would contest the additional claim that, in a generally patriarchal context, rural society is specifically patriarchal in its functioning, and that, compared to other women, rural African women are particularly disadvantaged as a result.[2]

What is less likely to be as tolerantly received is the more disruptive claim that, in order to redress these disadvantages, not only do key institutions in rural society have to be radically transformed, including the institutions of local government (the chief and tribal authorities), customary law and polygyny, but also the legitimating discourses of 'tradition', 'custom' and 'African culture' that are used to defend these politico-legal institutions.

Together these interlocking systems of authority constitute an 'official rural patriarchy', as distinct from the more amorphous, contradictory and fluid patriarchy of domestic relationships and popular culture. Here I argue that while the latter has also to be challenged and transformed, it is the former that poses the more serious institutional obstacle to the achievement of gender equality in and through a state-initiated rural reconstruction programme.

The combined mobilisation of traditional authority, customary law and 'tradition' in defence of patriarchal gender relations was clearly in evidence in the Multi-Party Negotiating Council during the protracted debate between May and November 1993 on the principle of gender equality in relation to customary or indigenous law in the interim Constitution. Initially the representatives of traditional leaders attempted to get customary law exempted from the ambit of any gender equality clause. As reported in IDASA's *Negotiation News*:

> 'We are in Africa and we remain in Africa. We are not prepared to give up and sacrifice our Africanism,' one traditional leader declared. Chief Mwelo Nonkonyana agreed, rejecting the notion of equality for women as 'foreign to us'. The whole impact of equality was having an impact on the lobola [bridewealth] custom, Nonkonyana complained. 'Who must lobola whom, if we are all equal?' he asked. 'If we say "all will be equal", then the custom of lobola is threatened.'[3]

When, as a result of fierce lobbying by women's groups, the exemption bid failed, traditional leaders attempted to get customary law itself entrenched as a fundamental constitutional right. Ultimately this attempt was defeated as well – although not as finally as many women in the ANC Women's League (ANCWL) believed. The preservation of customary law was not specifically enshrined in the chapter of the interim Constitution dealing with Fundamental Rights (Chapter 3) and the interpretation and application of both customary and common law will be subjected to the general equality clause. Nevertheless, support for the women's lobby was not wholehearted among party leaders, and traditional leaders are continuing to mobilise for a larger role in government. In this process they are invoking an emotive vocabulary of 'Africanism' and respect for indigenous culture, to 'reaffirm', in the words of the ANC-leaning Congress of Traditional Leaders of South Africa (CONTRALESA), 'the status and dignity of traditional leaders', and 'provide a unifying focus for the community'.[4]

What the traditionalists fail to acknowledge is the degree to which gender relations in the rural areas do not fit the mould in which they would fix them. Far from reflecting timeless continuities and certitudes, gender relations are more likely to be in a state of considerable flux and often painful con-testation and renegotiation.[5] A report on a recent community meeting in Natal captures some of the complex dynamics of this process and its uneven impact on local organisation. This particular meeting, at a community called Cornfields in the Natal Midlands, had been called to discuss the composition of a committee to represent the community in negotiations to acquire and administer a number of adjoining white-owned farms; the dis-cussion immediately ran into the question of whether women were eligible for election to the committee or not. A fieldworker from a non-governmental organisation involved in the negotiations urged the meeting to elect women to the committee, referring to other rural communities where this had hap-pened. The report records the subsequent discussion thus:

> A woman's voice came out of the crowd and said 'But we are not allowed to speak.' The fieldworker said that in the past it had been said that women were discriminated against twice, by the government be-cause they were black and by men because they were women. At this there was much noise. The fieldworker continued: 'Since we are busy telling whites not to discriminate against blacks, now men must not discriminate against women.' An old man said: 'It has always been said that men are better than women, but I know there are some women here who can do things better than some men.' There was much clapping of hands by the women. A man stood up and said: 'A woman will not be over me as long as I live.' There was much noise after this. Another man then got up and said: 'OK, it's alright now for women to take over, because the tough fight with the government for land is now over.' At this an older woman responded that he was being unfair since women had also fought the battle for more land.[6]

A similar process of debate could be seen at the historic Community Land Conference in February 1994, where representatives of 353 rural com-munities working with the National Land Committee formulated their demands for a Land Charter that would articulate and guide their claims for land reform. Chapter 4 of the Land Charter deals with women's land rights. While the demand put forward by women's organisations for the abolition of polygyny and the levirate (the obligation to marry a dead husband's brother) did not win a majority, the conference did endorse a number of far-reaching demands for equal rights for men and women with regard to inheritance, ownership of land and housing, and representation in local government – demands which cut right across the 'traditional order' CONTRALESA is attempting to shore up.[7] For the rural men at the conference, the challenge to their personal status within the homestead was more threatening than the rather less immediate empowerment of women at the level of property rights and local government (although the two are deeply intertwined and, in the opinion of some observers at the conference, the acceptance of the property demands 'might effectively force the demise of polygamous marriages').[8]

With regard to local government, the CLC was cautiously reformist in relation to chiefs. In one section the Land Charter calls for 'democratic, non-racial, non-sexist local government' but in another it makes a place for chiefs so long as they 'become accountable to the people – we do not want chiefs imposed on us'.[9] Significantly, this paragraph stipulates that chiefs should not have control over land allocation.

Clearly, any process of rural institutional and social transformation has to proceed carefully, mindful of the brittle nature of social networks in areas that have suffered decades of underdevelopment and abuse by a simultaneously interventionist and neglectful white state and its benefi-ciaries. At the same time, people's commitment to 'custom', 'culture' and 'tradition' has to be taken seriously and treated with respect if any pro-gramme of rural reconstruction is to succeed, and here the level of sup-port of many rural people, including women, for 'tradition' has to be acknowledged and its extent and ambiguities explored. Both 'tradition' and 'custom' need to be critically deconstructed, so that rural policy is not developed on the basis of the ahistorical, partisan and essentially self-serving use that the traditionalists make of these emotive terms. The discourse of 'tradition' is not gender-neutral. Men and women do not stand in the same relation to 'tradition' and do not necessarily agree on what is valuable or significant, or on what practices should be retained today and in what form.

A 1994 survey of attitudes to land reform among household heads in the Cornfields community referred to above illustrates this. The survey found opinion divided as to the desirability of the local chief participating in the committee that was being set up to administer the new land acquired by the community. Among both the female and male heads interviewed, more were in favour of the chief's participation than not (even though he was not resident, was not a landowner and had not been actively involved in community affairs, including the fight against population removals in the apartheid years). What is noteworthy is that those supporting the chief's participation did not form a majority. Out of the 27 women interviewed, only 12 were in favour, citing such reasons as 'his place', 'his dignity' and 'his authority', with seven against the chief's participation and eight unsure. The response of the 23 men interviewed was similar, with ten in favour, nine disagreeing and four unsure.[10]

Equally noteworthy, when it came to a question about who should decide how land should be inherited on the death of a (male) landowner, clear gender differences emerged in the sample. While the largest group of female heads interviewed (12 out of 27) argued for the widow's right to decide how to allocate her husband's property, the largest group of men (12 out of 23) favoured the deceased himself, through a will.[11] Furthermore, despite the level of support for the institution of chief amongst the women, they were, as a group, far more strongly in agreement with propositions that the law should be changed to allow women to own land and that women should be allowed to inherit: 22 out of the 27 women agreed with both statements.

Focus-group discussions on inheritance brought out even more clearly the range of attitudes and practices that coexist in this one community on what can be regarded as a cornerstone of patriarchal domestic relations. In the group discussions there were considerable differences of interpretation both of traditional practice with regard to inheritance of land and the transmission of headship within a household, and of what practices ought to be followed, as the following exchange among a group of single mothers illustrates:

FACILITATOR: Who is the head of this family?

RESPONDENT 1: Traditionally *mkhulu* [the old man/grandfather] is supposed to be the head of the family but I think it should be both *gogo* [the old woman, his wife] and *mkhulu*.

RESPONDENT 2: I think the elder son is the head of the family.

FACILITATOR: Is this applicable when the father is still alive?

RESPONDENT 3: I think *mkhulu* is the head. The mother cannot say or take a decision without *mkhulu*.

RESPONDENT 1: The *mkhulu* cannot take a decision alone; he must consult *gogo*. . . . she will influence his decision. So this proves that both *mkhulu* and *gogo* head the household.

RESPONDENT 4: But I think the father is the one who takes decisions, so I think he is the head.

RESPONDENT 1: I think the two should administer the household together. Both have equal say.

FACILITATOR: Who becomes head when the father dies?

RESPONDENT 4: *Gogo* is supposed to be in charge.

RESPONDENT 2: The eldest son in Johannesburg is in charge. He must now come back and head the household.

RESPONDENT 1: I think if *gogo* has been involved in decision-making in the household, this is not going to be a problem. She will automatically become the head of the household.[12]

This case study illustrates clearly that both 'what was' and 'what ought to be' are not firmly fixed, unquestioned reference points in rural communities. Policy-makers need to acknowledge both the dynamism and the gendered nature of the popular discourse on 'tradition' in rural society. Too often it is official, male definitions of 'culture' that are accepted uncritically as those of 'the community', a cultural hegemony that the proponents of this view readily promote. Given their subordinate position, many rural women find it difficult to challenge the dominant view of 'tradition' head-on and their views are likely to display a degree of ambivalence, even contradiction, as a result. There is often a disjuncture between what women want in concrete terms to improve their position (in this case, that they should control the property of a deceased husband) and what they say about 'tradition' in the abstract (here, supporting a distant chief's right to sit on a local land committee).

This disjuncture can provide the basis for more self-conscious attitudinal and programmatic shifts on the ground. The history of the Rural Women's Movement (RWM) in the Transvaal and Northern Cape – established in 1986 to link up women in communities suffering under apartheid's forced removals policy – illustrates very vividly a process of radicalisation in relation to established gender norms as women organised as women to confront basic needs and general community issues. In the words of one member:

> Women shouldn't have to go through members of the royal family to get access to the chief because these people do not understand women's problems. Women want to be able to send their own representatives to speak directly to the *kgotla*.[13] They must be under the tree [ie the *kgotla* tree] taking decisions with men.[14]

It is now well-established, at least in academic circles, that what is today cast as 'custom' or 'tradition' and therefore sacrosanct, is in fact the product of a complex and dynamic history of contestation, cooption, reconstruction and invention.[15] The Cornfields case study is a vivid example of this process as it continues to unfold in one particular community in the 1990s. However, 'tradition' is never pure nor static. It is dynamic and, as the women's movement needs to insist, having already been refashioned in relation to the shifting forces of the past, it is perfectly capable of being refashioned again, to better fit contemporary goals of a non-sexist and non-racial society. Here it is the principle of gender equality that needs to be reaffirmed – a modern principle and a product of modern conditions, but, arguably, not in itself incompatible with what Nhlapho has identified as the underlying morality of customary law, that of social responsibility for the wellbeing of all members of society:

> I believe that if enough understanding of these values is acquired . . . it ought to be possible to salvage from them a 'usable residue' of African-ness which enhances rather than diminishes the human rights ideal in family law. In other words, a clear distinction must be drawn between the substance (or function) of the value and the form of its expression.[16]

What I want to emphasise is the gendered nature of the commitment to 'tradition' and 'traditional leadership' in the past. Successive white governments have worked to refashion precolonial society in the interests not only of a white but also of a patriarchal supremacy, in colonial times as a cheap form of administration, later to shore up the migrant labour system and more recently, under apartheid, as part of the legitimation of the bantustans as the true 'homelands' of the various ethnic groups into which the state attempted to divide the African population.[17] In this process, two critical institutions were redesigned – the chieftainship and what is called 'customary law', i.e. indigenous African law as interpreted and/or codified by white jurists and administrators.

Under successive white governments, the institution of the chieftainship was stripped of its independent authority as well as its accountability to the local community, and redefined in the service of the central government. Those chiefs who were perceived as disloyal to the white state were deposed and replaced by more compliant individuals. The chief became a lowly state functionary, whose title, authority and income depended on the approval of the centre, supplemented by his powers of patronage and skill in manipulating local resources. Here his power to allocate land was of critical importance: a power that served the interests of apartheid planners but will enormously complicate the rural reconstruction programme of the new government. What was not diluted – if anything, was strengthened – was the patriarchal nature of this institution, and this too will frustrate and complicate the implementation of a future reconstruction programme. With one or two exceptions which do not challenge the patriarchal essence of the institution, chiefs are male.[18] More significantly, the culture and ethos of the institution and the 'tradition' that it claims to protect is deeply masculinist, while most of the holders of this office are strongly committed to upholding patriarchal norms and practices.

As Chapter 2 in this volume by Gerhard Mare points out, the gendered content to tribal 'tradition' has been particularly strongly exemplified in the case of KwaZulu. Gatsha Buthelezi has spoken of chiefs as having a 'depth of commitment . . . to each other as Zulu brothers born out of Zulu warrior stock . . .'.[19] In the masculine and hierarchically-ordered view of 'Zuluness', what is now cast as customary law is not only sexually discriminatory but also a construct of the past 100 years of white colonial rule.[20] In his discussion of this in the 1960s Jack Simons singled out the Natal Code of Law adopted by the colonial government in 1891 as particularly oppressive since it stereotyped a 'concept of feminine inferiority unknown to the traditional society'.[21] The Code was reformed in KwaZulu in 1981, though this was largely in respect of unmarried women. African women married under customary law, in KwaZulu/Natal as elsewhere, continue to be deemed minors, under the guardianship of their husbands. The stereotype moreover continues to be reinforced by the dominant discourse on 'proper' gender relations and gender roles in the institutions that impact most significantly on rural society, i.e. local and regional government, magistrates' and tribal courts, schools, hospitals, clinics, churches and the popular media.

CONSTITUTIONAL GENDER EQUALITY

While patriarchal norms and practices have been institutionalised in rural society, the interim Constitution represents a dramatic break with the legislative and judicial structures of the past. After years of feeling themselves politically marginalised, feminists in South Africa are entitled to a sense of vindication and achievement. The ANC-led government now officially recognises the patriarchal nature of South African society and the political legitimacy of the movement to challenge this. Women's rights are unequivocally on the agenda in developing the broad policy commitments of the Government of National Unity.

The commitment to eradicate gender discrimination is most authoritatively spelled out in the Chapter on Fundamental Rights within the interim Constitution, where clause 8(2) states:

No person shall be unfairly discriminated against, directly or indirectly, . . . on one or more of the following grounds in particular: race, gender, sex, ethnic or social origin, colour, sexual preference, age disability, religion, conscience, belief, culture or language.

In the accompanying 'Constitutional Principles' clause III gives greater prominence to the concept of gender equality:

The Constitution shall prohibit racial, gender and all other forms of discrimination and shall promote racial and gender equality and national unity.

The Constitution also provides for a Commission on Gender Equality 'to promote gender equality and to advise and to make recommendations to Parliament or any other legislature with regard to any laws or proposed legislation which affects gender equality and the status of women' (section 119(3)).

These clauses represent significant victories for women. The ANC's thinking on gender relations has been considerably sharpened in the past four years, since the pathbreaking acknowledgment of the National Executive Committee in May 1990 that 'the emancipation of women is not a by-product of a struggle for democracy, national liberation or socialism' but 'has to be addressed in its own right'.[22] The gains have not been easily won. Driving the process has been an increasingly vociferous and actively mobilised women's lobby within the ANC (the Commission for the Emancipation of Women and the ANCWL), as well as the National Women's Coalition and activists in some of the other political parties.[23]

The extent of the gains becomes apparent upon a re-examination of the ANC's original 'Constitutional Guidelines', published in 1991. At the time a close reading of them by Dorothy Driver concluded that while gains had been made, many questions remained about the understanding of gender and the implicit role assigned to women within the family. Speaking specifically about the way in which an unproblematised 'family' was positioned in these Guidelines as in need of protection, she noted the lack of clarity about the relationship between this clause and a proposed charter of gender rights. Driver also pointed to the 'fundamental ambivalence' within the ANC on the position of women, which she described as a 'jostling' of the radical moment with the conservative one.[24]

By 1994 this particular interplay of radical and conservative moments in ANC thinking has been recast, as a result of a far clearer commitment to women's rights as individual rights, separate from and overriding any concern with protecting or restoring family integrity. Gender equality is treated as one of the fundamental injustices to redress, on a par, in terms of its formal positioning in important texts, with the eradication of racial discrimination, racism and white privilege. Significantly, the discussion of the family has been dropped from the interim Constitution's chapter on Fundamental Rights, apart from one small but troubling reference to it in the clause guaranteeing freedom of religious expression; here, provision is made for legal recognition for 'a system of personal and family law adhered to by persons professing a particular religion' (section 14(3)(a)).

As noted above, the adoption of the gender equality clause did not pass without challenge from the representatives of the traditional leaders at the World Trade Centre, nor, when pitted directly against the claims of the traditional leaders, did this clause have the unequivocal support of the major political parties. At least one legal expert is of the opinion that the women's lobby gained what may be seen as a 'pyrrhic victory':[25] as a result of a separate compromise on the applicability of the chapter on Fundamental Rights, the negotiating Council decided to make this chapter binding on the legislature and executive branches of government only, and exclude reference to the judiciary. In the opinion of Professor Mureinik of the University of the Witwatersrand, this means that 'indigenous law is only reviewable under the Bill of Rights when it has been translated into legislation or is being applied by government':

> This means that where the unwritten customary law is being applied by a court to a dispute between private individuals, the Bill of Rights seems to put it beyond challenge for a violation of a right guaranteed in the Bill.[26]

Customary law has been given some degree of recognition within the interim Constitution. The significant point of tension in the new Constitution is now no longer between the principle of gender equality and the protection of 'the family', but between gender equality and respect for 'tradition', cultural rights and 'indigenous law'. This emerged as a point of contention early on in the drafting of the document and the Constitutional Principles, but although the women's lobby won a significant victory in relation to the chapter on Fundamental Rights, this was not a complete rout.

The Constitution as a whole recognises both the institution of the chieftainship and customary law, and makes some attempt to incorporate traditional leaders into government at an advisory and ex officio level. The chapter on Fundamental Rights limits the protection of custom to two general clauses enshrining freedom of thought and religion and respect for cultural diversity. Clause 14 recognises 'the right to freedom of conscience, religion, thought, belief and opinion', and provides also for legal protection of 'religious' (undefined) 'personal and family law', while Clause 31 confers on everyone 'the right to use the language and to participate in the cultural life of his or her choice'. These principles are carried through into the Constitutional Principles, which are binding on the drafters of the final Constitution. Here it states that 'the diversity of language and culture' is to be 'acknowledged and protected, and conditions for their promotion shall be encouraged' and it is here that 'traditional leadership' is specifically recognised:

> The institution, status and role of traditional leadership, according to indigenous law, shall be recognised and protected in the Constitution. (Principle XIII)

It is not, however, an unconditional recognition. The clause continues:

> Indigenous law, like common law, shall be recognised and applied by the courts, subject to the fundamental rights contained in the Constitution and to legislation dealing specifically therewith.

The Constitution also provides for the establishment of a National Council of Traditional Leaders and provincial Houses of Chiefs in most of the provinces, with the authority to advise and make proposals to their respective levels of government, but not to initiate or veto any act. Significantly, indigenous law and traditional authorities are both designated as falling within the legislative competence of the provinces, rather than the central government, and the Constitutional Principles specifically state that 'provision in a provincial constitution relating to the institution, role, authority and status of a traditional monarch shall be recognised and protected in the Constitution' (Principle XIII).

How is one to interpret this clear yet limited endorsement in the Constitution of what I have identified as the major elements of 'official' rural patriarchy, and what are the implications for women? According to one member of the technical committee that drafted the Constitution, there are sufficient ambiguities in the document to allow for challenges both to defend or promote gender equality and to assert the authority of customary law and traditional leaders[27] – including, therefore, the domain of land allocation and land rights. In all probability the Constitutional Court will adopt a liberal rather than a conservative interpretation with regard to women's rights, partly because of the undoubted importance the Constitution accords gender equality and the fundamental status the equality clause enjoys in general, but also because of the political leverage of the women's lobby within Parliament, the Constitutional Assembly and the ANC itself. Here one is beginning to move into the terrain of political mobilisation – and, as is discussed more fully below, the ANC is certainly not indifferent to the traditionalist lobby. The protection offered to the ultimately very diffuse constructs of 'culture' and 'indigenous law' in the interim Constitution will, clearly, be used to strengthen the claims of the traditionalists in these political struggles.

Despite the concerns about both judicial loopholes and political will, the constitutional provisions on gender equality undoubtedly represent a major victory for women. The constitutional principle of gender equality has been formally adopted as a primary point of departure and a judicial mechanism for institutionalising that principle in society has now been established. Both represent significant achievements and signal potential new opportunities for the women's movement.

CONCEPTUALISING 'WOMEN' AND 'GENDER' IN RECONSTRUCTION AND DEVELOPMENT

The mobilisation of women sympathetic to the national liberation movement, combined with exposure to international debates on the empowerment of women has propelled the ANC towards greater gender sensitivity in its own structures and policy documents. Nowadays no politically correct speech maker will miss the opportunity to stress his (or her) commitment not only to a non-racial but also to a non-sexist democracy. Whereas a few years ago feminists might have been justified in viewing this as largely rhetorical, today such easy cynicism needs to be reviewed. The degree of concrete detail on women and gender that informs ANC policy documents is impressive, notably in the RDP.

Nevertheless, echoes of the dissonance that Driver detected in the ANC's original Constitutional Guidelines can still be heard. There remains a significant gap between the formal statements and political practice, as the IDASA report on the struggle over the status of indigenous law suggests:

> ... women are feeling angry at the fact that they received very little support or assistance from the various party leaderships. In the final analysis, a handful of women were pitted against an unyielding block of traditional leaders. ... One suspects that political considerations (the chiefs wield considerable influence in the rural areas) may have outweighed a commitment to basic human rights principles.[28]

The male monopoly on real power is still very evident – in the cabinet, where only three women are full ministers; in the trade unions, civic organisations and the various negotiating forums cited by the RDP as key agents of reconstruction; and in the very drafting of the RDP and MERG report. The authors of the RDP, judging by the photographs on the back cover, were all men, while somewhat under 15 per cent of the academics involved in MERG were women, and feminist economists and social scientists struggled to obtain an acknowledgment that gender should be treated as a key variable in the research and modelling process. The women's ANC parliamentary caucus is determined to make its presence felt and South Africa now boasts one of the highest levels of female representation in central government, by international standards; yet, at under a third of the total of 400 members in the national Parliament, South Africa's women parliamentarians are very much a minority.

The way in which women's advancement and gender are conceptualised in ANC thinking, as exemplified in both the RDP (1994) and the MERG Report (1993), remains flawed.[29] The RDP is in many ways an extremely impressive document, with its vision of a democratic, caring society and its commitment to a policy of reconstruction linked to development. Its attention to the position of women is also striking and in many important ways the RDP is an enormous advance on previous ANC documents in terms of its endorsement of gender equality at the policy level. Thus both the RDP and the MERG report single out women as specific targets of state intervention to redress poverty and develop a people-centred economy:

> The role of women within the RDP requires particular emphasis. Women are the majority of the poor in South Africa. Mechanisms to address the disempowerment of women and boost their role within the development process and economy must be implemented. The RDP must recognise and address existing gender inequalities as they affect access to jobs, land, housing etc.[30]

The aim of the MERG framework is to secure a rapid improvement in the quality of life of the poorest, most oppressed and disadvantaged people in South Africa. The policy recommendations stress projects to initiate job creation and training programmes for the unemployed; to improve the status of the poorest women in rural areas; to improve the availability and quality of education, health, housing and electrification; to raise the minimum level of wages of low-income earners; and to improve the skills of employed workers.[31]

Overall the RDP is commendably conscientious in drawing attention to the disabilities of women in key areas of the economic, social and political life of the nation. In relation to land reform specifically, the RDP is also quite explicit that women are envisaged as key beneficiaries:

> Women face specific disabilities in obtaining land. The land redistribution programme must therefore target women. Institutions, practices and laws that discriminate against women's access to land must be reviewed and brought in line with national policy. In particular, tenure and matrimonial laws must be revised appropriately.[32]

There are also some useful proposals for specific reforms scattered through the document, such as the requirement that a legal aid fund be established specifically for women 'to test their rights in court',[33] and the acceptance of the need to introduce tax reform and end tax discrimination against women.

A close reading of the RDP reveals a problematic unevenness in the way in which the category 'women' and the concept 'gender' are used. Women are singled out for attention only in certain, apparently randomly selected sections, with no indication why they merit specific mention in the discussion on some sectors of the economy but can be ignored in others. Why, for instance, is attention to gender and women specified in the discussion on the corporate sector (briefly), micro, small and medium businesses (in greater detail), science and technology policy, the financial sector, and agriculture, but neither 'women' nor 'gender' feature as reference points in the discussions on tourism, forestry and fisheries, mining, commerce and distribution? This demarcation hardly reflects the existing distribution of women in the economy and such a justification would in any case be in conflict with the RDP's stated commitment to address women's disempowerment and 'boost their role' within the economy.

Rather than reflecting economic realities or the state of gender relations in the society, this unevenness is more indicative of uncritical thinking on the part of those who put the document together. The writers of some sections were clearly more gender-sensitive or politically conscientious than others. However, because 'gender' is not well-integrated within the overall policy framework and conceptual universe of the ANC, the anomalies this unevenness creates were not apparent to those responsible for the integration of the final document and the overall conceptualisation of the RDP.

This careless, add-on approach leads to some unfortunate discrepancies. For instance, the section on labour and worker rights specifies the need to 'provide job security for pregnant women and promote the provision of child care ... to further women's equality in employment' (p. 115) and also refers to steps to eradicate sexual harassment at work. The immediately preceding section on workplace empowerment on the other hand is entirely gender-neutral, talking merely of the need for legislation that will 'facilitate worker participation and decision-making in the world of work' (p. 114). Surely 'ensuring a full and equal role for women' in every aspect of the economy demands careful thought about how to tackle the barriers preventing women workers participating in decision-making, on the shop floor and in worker organisations? The problems facing women workers do not only revolve around maternity leave, child care and sexual harassment, important as these are, and highlighting only these issues allows others to drop off the agenda: for instance, gender bias in recruitment and training as well as within organisational cultures.

Furthermore, major weaknesses remain in the understanding of gender that informs the policy formulation, with worrying implications for policy implementation. Firstly, there is no clear indication from the ANC how it understands 'gender equality', nor what guidelines the Constitutional Court is likely to adopt in adjudicating on this. The debate on what a non-sexist society might look like has only just begun in South Africa.[34] It is relatively simple to isolate examples of gender discrimination. But how does one define gender equality? Should this be taken to mean that everybody should be treated exactly the same, or are men and women to be recognised as significantly different in some respects, requiring differentiated treatment by the law? It is a debate that has sharply divided feminists in other parts of the world. In an article reviewing a fierce controversy in California concerning the most progressive treatment of pregnancy in the workplace, Vogel sets out the parameters of the debate as follows:

> As feminists, is our objective simply the dismantling of barriers to equal participation in social life? Do we want to push beyond assimilation, which effectively leaves male norms in place, toward a balanced androgyny in a social structure transformed to symmetrically meet women's and men's needs? Or should we frankly recognise women's special and different nature through the development of woman-centred analysis and a rich women's culture? Is it reasonable to focus just on sexual specificity in a world torn apart by class, race, national, and other differences? What if a person's identity is not fixed but, rather, fluctuates – drawing variously on multiple sources, only one of which is gender?[35]

The Women's Charter of the National Women's Coalition takes the line that 'true and effective equality will sometimes require distinctions to be made',[36] adopting the view that there are differences between men and women, who cannot be treated as exactly the same as a result. But this thinking has not been refined and no clear position on how 'gender equality' is to be interpreted (and hence measured) informs the RDP: although there is, as suggested below, a presumption of 'maleness' in the definition of the norm.

Perhaps even more crucial is the way in which 'women' and 'gender' continue to be conflated in the presentation of the issues, so that attention to gender is seen as synonymous with talking about women, and women are themselves stripped of the full range of social identities that informs (differently) their consciousness and their experience. This has become a standard complaint in feminist critiques of political and academic debates, but the shunting of gender relations, gender ideology and gender identity into a lean-to marked 'women' continues apparently unabated in mainstream 'progressive' thinking.

In the RDP any discussion of 'gender' invariably means paying attention to and rectifying disadvantages suffered by women. It does not signal attention to male privilege or advantage or problems, nor spell out steps to deal with these. Women's problems are presented routinely in the passive rather than the active voice – they are 'excluded from decision-making structures'[37] but by whom or what is not spelled out. Gender as a relationship and gender as informing male politics (cultural weapons come to mind), male employment patterns and male identities are not issues. Gender relations, it appears, are to be restructured without addressing masculinity and women empowered without disrupting men's lives.

Implicit within the discussion lurks the presumption that the remedy for women's problems lies in their being treated according to male norms. 'Worker', 'citizen', 'farmer', 'youth' remain fundamentally although surreptitiously gendered – male – in the official South African political lexicon.[38] This implicit ordering of social categories becomes occasionally, embarrassingly, explicit in the RDP, as in the section on 'Building the Economy'. Here what is addressed is the need to 'democratise the economy and empower the oppressed, particularly the workers and women and their organisations . . .'.[39] The subliminal if not the intentional message is that there are workers (who are not women) and there are women (who are not workers). Similarly, in the discussion on the corporate sector in the same chapter one reads that there are black people and there are women:

> The domination of business activities by white business and the exclusion of black people and women from the mainstream of economic activity are causes for great concern. . . . (p. 93)

The suspicions these distinctions arouse are confirmed when one immediately goes on to read, following the previous quotation, that 'a central objective' is to 'deracialise business ownership and control completely' and that the aim is 'to make it easier for black people to gain access to capital'. Suddenly 'women' have vanished from the discussion. Were they ever really present?

Other, more subtle examples of the problem can be found in the discussion on education and training. In relation to rural development, the RDP identifies a need for developing and training Community Development Officers whose training, it is stated, 'must include sensitivity to gender issues' (p. 85). What is meant by 'gender issues' is not spelled out, but in the context of the RDP it is clear that they refer to women's problems (always problems), specifically, in the rural context, female poverty, the responsibility women carry for 'all aspects of their families' lives' (p. 84), and their exclusion from decision-making structures. In the section on 'Education and training', appropriate training for women and girls is also specified, so as to encourage them to pursue 'non-traditional' subjects and choices (p. 62) but nowhere is there a mention of the training of boys and men, nor the 'non-traditional' directions their education could, or should, take.

The discussion on democratising the state and society is also revealing. The primary focus is clearly on eradicating minority rule and racial discrimination:

> We will not be able to unleash the resources, neglected skills and stunted potential of our country and its people while minority domination of state and civil institutions persists. Without thorough-going democratisation, the whole effort to reconstruct and develop will lose momentum. (pp. 119–20)

Democratisation is elaborated upon – enfranchisement, equal citizenship, accountable institutions, modernised structures of government, civilian control of a restructured military and police force, a strong civil society, including recognition of community organisations and non-governmental ones, democratisation of information. Finally:

> Ensuring gender equity is another central component in the overall democratisation of our society. The RDP envisages special attention being paid to the empowerment of women in general, and of black, rural women in particular. There must be representation of women in all institutions, councils and commissions, and gender issues must be included in the terms of reference of these bodies. (pp. 121–2)

Here again, ensuring gender equity clearly translates into directing attention at women – in isolation from men and men's roles in institutions, councils etc. And the way to achieve this equity is through 'representation' of women in otherwise unreformed structures. There are many problems with this understanding of representation, not the least the lack of a guarantee that the 'representatives' will be committed to the issue of gender equality and the presumption that any woman is able to represent other women simply by virtue of a shared sex. In relation to rural development in particular, Michelle Friedman has argued that putting women on committees when they are not comfortable with being in a position of authority may actually be counter-productive for any longer-term strategy of empowerment.[40] The limits of the ANC's understanding of 'representation' have, in any case, already been pointed out in relation to both government and party structures, where a conscious or unconscious quota mentality keeps the number of women holding positions of authority in a small minority.

THE POLITICS OF TRADITIONALISM

This may seem an unduly stringent reading of the RDP and the ANC's understanding of gender equality, but it is important to draw attention to these deficiencies. They signal the deeper problem of a superficial and ultimately incoherent approach to women's disabilities and the restructuring of gender relations. There are many daunting constraints on the successful implementation of the RDP, including global economic forces beyond the control of local policy-makers. But also significant as far as women are concerned is the deeply gendered – in this case, masculinist – understanding of the major players and their failure to engage seriously with the need for a fundamental reorganisation of familiar social practices and gender hierarchies.

One major consequence of this add-on approach to gender equality is that it allows the ANC to ignore the contradiction between its commitment to gender equality and its handling of the claims of the traditionalists – precisely because the understanding of gender is not integrated into ANC thinking about society at large or its strategising overall, but is dealt with as a separate (and relatively minor) topic labelled 'women'. This is a more serious problem in the murky politics of traditionalism that the ANC has embarked upon than in the Constitution itself, although even here, as already noted, there are potentially important points of tension and ambiguity.

At this point it becomes necessary to address the far less transparent politics within which the debate on 'tradition' is inserted where considerations of gender equality have been conspicuously absent. The limited constitutional protection afforded the institution of the chief and traditional authorities is perhaps less significant than the way in which, by seeking to coopt certain traditional rulers and undercut the appeal of the IFP, the ANC has strengthened the hand of male traditionalists within its own and other ranks. In the pre-election period this was most evident in the manoeuvrings around the Zulu king and the concessions made in the direction of guaranteeing his position as a constitutional monarch in a considerably enlarged 'Zulu kingdom' in what is now termed KwaZulu-Natal.

In the post-election period the Zulu monarchy has continued to be a focal point of bitter ANC/IFP contestation in KwaZulu-Natal, while the clamour from other traditional leaders around the country for recognition and all the perks that go with government office has grown louder. As 1994 drew to a close, the focus of organisation shifted to the structure and status of the national and provincial 'houses' for traditional leaders that are provided for in the Constitution, as well as the role of chiefs in rural local government. In the IFP-dominated province of KwaZulu-Natal, the House of Traditional Leaders Bill, passed in October 1994, establishes a body with the power to advise and make recommendations to the Provincial Parliament 'on any draft Bill or proposed executive action in respect of matters relating to traditional authorities and indigenous and customary law'. That this includes issues of critical importance for the implementation of the RDP is spelled out very clearly – the brief of the traditional leaders includes 'indigenous land tenure systems and all related matters' and 'Zulu traditional and customary law on inheritance, family and marriage'.[41]

In this struggle, the ANC has played an ambiguous role, choosing on many occasions to position itself as a more fitting champion of 'tradition' than the IFP and sympathetic to the claims of traditional leaders – at least of those aligned to it. As the rift between the Zulu king and former Chief Minister Buthelezi has widened, the ANC has emphasised its support for the monarchy – to the extent that one journalist has described King Zwelethini as the ANC's 'newly acquired asset'.[42] What is not being acknowledged, however, is that the Zulu king is a representative and symbol not simply of a Zulu ethnic identity but of a patriarchal social order, which he himself actively upholds and promotes.[43] His gains have not only emboldened other traditional monarchs seeking a similar degree of recognition – 'In KwaZulu Natal they have one king but here we actually have six' a spokesman for the Eastern Cape department of local government has claimed.[44] They have also cemented the official rural patriarchy that is centred on the lesser chiefs in the former bantustans.

One example of how these different elements are playing themselves out is provided by the uproar surrounding the Ingonyama Trust land deal that former President de Klerk signed into law as one of his last acts as State President in 1994, just before the 27 April elections. By means of this Act, 93 per cent of the total land area of the former KwaZulu bantustan was transferred to a trust, in which the sole trustee is the Ingonyama or Zulu king, who is authorised to deal with the land 'in accordance with Zulu indigenous law or any other applicable law'.[45] Initially ANC spokespersons came out strongly against what one described as 'a brake on development stability', while an IFP spokesperson defended the move as 'the continuation of an indigenous political system where power to allocate land was vested in the chiefs under the trusteeship of the king'.[46]

Subsequently, the ANC dampened down its outrage, adopting a somewhat similar stance to the IFP but in a different frame, that of national unity. In one interview an ANC spokesperson talked about the need to preserve the integrity of traditional communities, tradition and existing tribal tenure.[47] In this context there was not a word about the gender implications of preserving 'tradition and existing tribal tenure'.

An unpublished Cabinet Committee Report provides further insight into the political concerns informing the ANC's response to the Act and the irrelevance of gender equality in its calculations. The report acknowledges that the Act poses a threat to transforming gender relations in KwaZulu-Natal, in the section dealing with 'Implications of the Act for Land Reform and Development'. The introduction of the Act, the report notes, 'would probably insulate the areas under control of the Ingonyama Trust from future gender equality initiatives, in contrast to the rest of the country'.[48] There is no follow-through on this observation in the conclusion, where gender equality is not identified as one of the important principles the Cabinet should uphold in seeking a solution to the complex legal and political challenges posed by the Act. Instead, one of the 'underlying principles of such a solution' is that 'there is an important continuing role for the Ingonyama and other traditional authorities in the holding and management of tribally occupied land'.[49] The effective betrayal of the principle of gender equality has not occasioned comment – I would argue because of the conceptual weaknesses in ANC thinking on gender and because the women's lobby was not mobilised or as politically important on this issue as the range of forces clustered around 'tradition'.

The ANC leadership wanted to diffuse an embarrassing situation without having to confront its partners in the Government of National Unity, especially the National Party and Deputy President de Klerk, or alienate King Zwelethini whom it is, with some success, trying to woo away from IFP president Buthelezi. In adopting this strategy, it is neglecting the implications for its longer-term goal of development and its commitment to the principle of gender equality – or 'democracy' itself, for that matter. Respect for 'tradition' not 'democracy' is how the national and provincial debate is now framed.

IMPLICATIONS FOR THE RDP AND SPECIFICALLY THE LAND REFORM PROGRAMME

These politics have particular relevance for the rural reconstruction programme outlined in the RDP. As already noted, the RDP singles out women as key beneficiaries of its agrarian reform programme and spells out customary tenure systems and matrimonial laws as the chief blocks to women's access to land. These have already been identified by *inter alia* the Rural Women's Movement and the CLC conference in February 1994.

Given the issues outlined above it is difficult to see how the ANC proposes to dismantle these blocks and how far it will be prepared to go in restructuring the very real authority and power of the traditional leaders on the ground in allocating land and running local government. Because of its 'add-on' approach to 'gender' (equals women), the ANC has strengthened the hands of the patriarchal traditionalists despite its own undoubted support for the idea of gender equality as an abstract policy goal. It has treated the two issues in isolation. 'Women' and 'chiefs' have been seen as distinct and separate constituencies that the ANC, in its quest for both power and national reconciliation, has attempted to accommodate in its broad-church movement.

But it is not possible to be everything to everyone. While one must appreciate the political imperatives of stemming the political violence that seems endemic in certain rural areas as well as neutralising or coopting anti-democratic forces as prerequisites for reconstruction, nevertheless the strategy with regard to traditional leaders is a highly risky one. If not reformulated, it is likely to negate the ANC's commitment to gender equality and undermine its own reconstruction programme in the rural areas. In order for the latter to work along the lines envisaged by the RDP, patriarchal structures need to be reformed, not entrenched, and 'tradition' reconceptualised in the manner suggested by Nhlapho.

If the ANC is serious about gender equality, it faces a mammoth task in the rural areas. It has to dismantle the existing patriarchal structures, while managing the assertive traditionalism of the IFP and CONTRALESA and engaging seriously with rural people's own gendered understandings of and commitments to 'tradition', 'custom' and the chieftaincy. It also has to incorporate the principle of gender equality into its strategic planning, and not address it simply at the level of macro policy statements. Such a programme requires the democratisation of the institution of the chieftainship as a matter of priority, as well as legislation empowering all women, regardless of their marital status, to enjoy secure access to land in their own right. Enforcing this will also require a Constitutional Court that is sensitive to gender equality – not just in the narrow sense of 'women's problems' but in the broader sense outlined above.

The ANC also has to take a much harder look at what the principle of gender equality means for women on the ground. The education and empowerment of rural women – capacity building – has to be accompanied by programmes aimed at men as well. There is also a place for much more focused research aimed at plotting and understanding the complex and varied responses of rural women and men to 'tradition' and to the choices being offered them through the rural reconstruction programme. One of the goals of such research should be to build up a clearer picture of the differences and the extent of stratification among rural women, so that they are not all lumped together misleadingly as the equally deserving poor. Another would be to probe women's own assessment of their needs, their priorities and the choices they would make if there were wider employment, mobility and status opportunities open to them.

There is also a major need for encouraging a much wider debate on what is meant by gender equality and how one might measure it. The new government and many of the organs of civil society are themselves in need of education in these matters: this, clearly, is a major task facing the broad but disorganised coalition of organisations making up the women's movement which has not responded clearly to the challenges posed by the mobilisation of traditional leaders in defence of their power and authority in rural local government.

Gender equality is set out as a basic principle in the Constitution and this opens up new political possibilities for women and the proponents of gender equality. But unless the Government of National Unity is made to engage seriously with the strategic and tactical implications of this in policy terms – in the RDP, in rural development, in land reform – its practical application is likely to be severely compromised by countervailing political and ideological forces mobilised around the politics of 'tradition'.

NOTES

1. Earlier versions of the arguments in this chapter have appeared under the title 'Women, "Tradition" and Reconstruction' in *Review of African Political Economy*, 21, 6 (1994) and *South Asia Bulletin* (forthcoming).
2. The definition of 'rural' is complicated by the historical division of the South African countryside into white-owned, predominantly commercial farming land (87 per cent of the total) and the 13 per cent set aside in the African 'reserves' where communal tenure under the jurisdiction of tribal chiefs and authorities has been largely preserved. The reserves formed the basis for the ten separate 'homelands' under apartheid. The 'rural society' examined in this article is essentially that found in the former bantustans and on African-owned land and does not cover the full spectrum of the

South African countryside. It is estimated that currently about 9 million people live in the rural areas of the bantustans.

3. Institute for a Democratic Alternative for South Africa (IDASA), *Negotiation News*, 15 (1993), 5.

4. *Sunday Times*, 19 June 1994.

5. Transvaal African Action Committee, *The Rural Women's Movement: Holding the Knife on the Sharp Edge* (Johannesburg, TRAC, 1994).

6. Association for Rural Advancement (AFRA), 'Report on a Community Meeting at Cornfields' (unpublished).

7. 'Community Land Conference. 1 Land Charter', *Afra News*, 26 (1994), 13.

8. 'Women and Land', *Agenda* (1994), 123.

9. *Afra News*, 26 (1994), 15.

10. Cherryl Walker, 'Report on Cornfields: Gender and Land Research Project', unpub. report, AFRA, Pietermaritzburg and National Land Committee, Johannesburg, 1994, p. 31.

11. *Ibid.*

12. *Ibid.*, p. 16.

13. *Kgotla* is the local term used to describe the traditional council of male elders.

14. Quoted in Transvaal Rural Action Committee, *op. cit.*, p. 8.

15. See, *inter alia*, Jeff Guy, 'Gender Oppression in Southern African Precapitalist Societies' in Cherryl Walker (ed.), *Women and Gender in Southern Africa to 1945* (Cape Town: David Philip and London: James Currey, 1990), Ann McClintock, 'Maidens, Maps and Mines: King Solomon's Mines and the Reinvention of Patriarchy in South Africa' in *ibid.*, Cherryl Walker, 'Gender and the Development of the Migrant Labour System, c. 1850–1930' in *ibid.*

16. Thandabuntu Nhlapo, 'Women's Rights and the Family in Traditional Customary Law' in Susan Bazilli (ed.), *Putting Women on the Agenda* (Johannesburg: Ravan Press, 1991), p. 116.

17. Linzi Manicom, 'Ruling Relations: Rethinking State and Gender in South African History', paper presented at Conference on Women and Gender in Southern Africa, University of Natal, Durban (1991).

18. Wendy Annecke, 'Sibongele Zungu: Chief of the Madlebe', *Agenda*, 13 (1992).

19. Quoted in Gerhard Mare, *Brothers Born of Warrior Blood: Politics and Ethnicity in South Africa* (Johannesburg: Ravan Press, 1992), p. 68.

20. H.J. Simons, *African Women: Their Legal Status in South Africa* (London: Hurst, 1968).

21. *Ibid.*, p. 26.

22. African National Congress, *Statement of the National Executive Committee of the African National Congress on the Emancipation of Women in South Africa* (Johannesburg: ANC, 1990).

23. In the past five years a series of important workshops and conferences have initiated discussion on what it means to 'put women on the agenda', including an in-house ANC seminar in Lusaka in 1989, the ANC and Mass Democratic Movement's 'Malibongwe' conference in Amsterdam in January 1990, the Lawyers for Human Rights conference in Johannesburg in November 1990 and the 'Women and Gender in Southern Africa' conference at the University of Natal in Durban in early 1991. The mobilisation of women was first

demonstrated in the constitutional negotiations at CODESA, when a Gender Advisory Committee was established, followed by the agreement at the Multi-Party Talks in 1993 that every party should have a woman delegate. This was accompanied by the launch of the Women's National Coalition in 1992, with the ambitious goal of formulating a Women's Charter, which was finally presented to Parliament on the newly proclaimed National Women's Day, on 9 August 1994. The Rural Women's Movement has also become increasingly visible, its leaders playing a key role in swinging the debate in favour of the principle of gender equality above that of the status of indigenous law at the World Trade Centre. Smaller research projects and lobby groups have also played an important part.

24. Dorothy Driver, 'The ANC Constitutional Guidelines in Process' in Bazilli, *op. cit.*, p. 89.
25. Quoted in George Devenish, 'Fundamental Rights', draft MS, University of Natal, Durban (1994).
26. *Ibid.*, p. 5.
27. Professor Devenish, personal communication. I am grateful to Professor Devenish of the Faculty of Law at the University of Natal in Durban for pointing this opinion out to me and for taking the time to discuss the complicated legal technicalities involved. Professor Devenish also pointed out that Professor Mureinik's opinion, however well-founded, is only an opinion and that the question of applicability and intent will, ultimately, be a matter for the Constitutional Court to decide.
28. *Negotiation News*, 15 (December 1993), p. 2.
29. As already noted, the original RDP document was followed in September 1994 by the release of a Government White Paper which 'establishes a policy-making methodology and outlines government implementation strategies' within the framework provided by the original document, described in the White Paper as the Base Document. Unless otherwise indicated, this discussion focuses on the original 'Base Document' since this is the more fully developed exposition of the assumptions and principles informing the policy.
30. *Reconstruction and Development Programme*, p. 17.
31. Macroeconomic Research Group (MERG), *Making Democracy Work. A Framework for Macroeconomic Policy in South Africa* (Cape Town: Centre for Development Studies, University of the Western Cape, 1993), p. 2.
32. African National Congress, *The Reconstruction and Development Programme: A Policy Framework* (Johannesburg: Umanyano Publications, 1994), p. 21.
33. *Ibid.*, p. 124.
34. For a useful discussion of the issues from a legal point of view, see Christina Murray and Catherine O'Regan, 'Putting Women into the Constitution' in Bazilli, *op. cit.*
35. Lise Vogel, 'Debating Difference: Feminism, Pregnancy and the Workplace', *Feminist Studies*, 16, 1 (1990), 10.
36. *Reconstruction and Development Programme*, p. 1.
37. *Ibid.*, p. 84.
38. Manicom, *op. cit.*, p. 1991.
39. *Reconstruction and Development Programme*, p. 79.
40. Michelle Friedman, 'Is a Feminist Development Strategy Appropriate in

South Africa?', paper presented at the Conference on Women and Gender in Southern Africa, University of Natal, Durban (1991).

41. Province of KwaZulu-Natal, *House of Traditional Leaders Bill* (Ministry of Traditional and Environmental Affairs, 1994), section 4.

42. *Weekly Mail*, 2–8 December 1994.

43. For the historical background to this see Shula Marks, 'Patriotism, Patriarchy and Purity: Natal and the Politics of Zulu Ethnic Consciousness' in Leroy Vail (ed.), *The Creation of Tribalism in Southern Africa* (London: James Currey, 1989), pp. 215–40.

44. *Sunday Times* (Johannesburg), 20 November 1994.

45. Peter Rutsch, 'The Ingonyama Trust and its implications for the Region' in KwaZulu-Natal Economic Forum, *Proceedings of the Land Reform Workshop: Rural Land Reform in KwaZulu Natal* (Mayville, Durban: KwaZulu Natal Regional Economic Forum, 1994), p. 6.

46. *Weekly Mail*, 27 May–2 June 1994.

47. South African Broadcasting Corporation, *Radio Today*, 16 June 1994.

48. Cabinet Committee, *KwaZulu Ingonyama Trust Act: Report of the Cabinet Committee* (unpublished MS, 1994), p. 27.

49. *Reconstruction and Development Programme*, p. 37.

8 The Restructuring of South African Education and Training in Comparative Context

Linda Chisholm

South Africa's first democratic election was a watershed in the country's educational history. In the first instance, it signalled a move away from the determination of policy by a white minority state for a black majority; in the second, official state education policy, historically geared towards building a united white nation, was now re-oriented to redressing inequalities and 'nation-building' between white and black; in the third, instead of being predicated on exclusion and denial of rights, social, political and educational policy became based on the principles of inclusion, social justice and equity. Finally, the economic argument for the reform of education was based on the need not for unskilled, but for skilled labour and professional and managerial expertise.

These changes are a consequence of the wider transition to democracy, have found expression in specific policies, and will find their way into legislation. They are also the consequence of monumental and sustained struggles in and over education since at least 1976. The South African transition has however been a negotiated one resulting in a Government of National Unity (GNU) for a five-year period, a market-led economy and a federal constitution. These specific features of the transition define the parameters within which short- to medium-term educational change will take place, and deserve closer scrutiny. In order to understand adequately any set of educational reforms, one has to place them in both a national historical and a world economic context. Placed in this context, education policies for a new South Africa show remarkable congruence with international trends. Here the commitment is to equity, redress, cost-recovery, cost-sharing and decentralisation of government.

Emerging education policy for transcending the apartheid legacy and overcoming inequalities are rooted in the history of opposition to apartheid education but draw on conceptual frameworks and policies dominant in the 1970s and then in the 1980s amongst particularly UNESCO and the

170

World Bank.[1] Two major approaches to poverty and development emerged in UNESCO and the World Bank under the presidency of McNamara (1968–80): the 'redistribution with growth' and 'basic needs' approaches. These were policy competitors in the sense that 'the "basic human needs" approach cast a far wider social and economic net, and was considerably more profound in its insistence on structural economic change.'[2] Despite the differences, the 'basic needs' approach suffered from inadequate analysis of the political, institutional and administrative framework required to remove obstacles to fulfilling basic human needs. In addition, even as there was a 'dramatic liberalisation of lending criteria' these were still 'intended for *universal* application, and the broad rationale for Bank involvement in education remained intact: the production of trained manpower capable of raising productivity'. UNESCO, which was used far less by the Bank after its reorganisation in 1972, remained an important advocate of integration between formal and non-formal education. Debt and recession in the 1980s produced changes which determined the context in which education systems functioned. Structural adjustment loans became heavily dependent on public sector restructuring; there was a sharp move away from the welfarist concerns of the McNamara period to direct intervention in education policies of developing countries and promotion of policies which shifted financial responsibility from public to private sources, and an emphasis on cost-recovery and cost-sharing.[3]

There are significant overlaps in these and recent discourses in South African education policy, although in South Africa itself the provenance of human capital theory in education has also been linked to expressions by both Anglophone and newly risen Afrikaner industrial capitalists in the 1960s of the need for educational reform.[4] It is too simple to argue that adoption of these approaches exemplifies either a conspiracy on the part of international agencies or the poverty of options and weakness of the left in South Africa.

An explanation for these themes, and contradictions between them, may be found on the one hand in the universalising tendency of the globalising force of modernity and on the other in the new class alliance found in the Government of National Unity. Modernity is understood here not so much as a Hegelian spirit finding expression in all things, but as a consequence of the 'restless transformative activity of capital accumulation and speculative change'.[5] 'Generally perceived as positivistic, technocentric, and rationalistic, universal modernism has been identified with the belief in linear progress, absolute truths, the rational planning of social orders, and the standardisation of knowledge and production.'[6] It is sometimes suggested that a relationship can be found between Fordism and modernism and between flexible accumulation and post-modernism. Harvey argues convincingly that 'the degree of Fordism and modernism, or of flexibility and post-modernism is bound to vary from time to time and from place to place, depending on which configuration is profitable and which is not'.[7] In South Africa, the degree of dominance or interpenetration of the two must be related to the country's dependent position in the world economy. This should help to provide some of the explanation for the powerful modernist and modernising thrust in contemporary South Africa.

The effect of the unbanning of political organisations in 1990 was as much to end South Africa's isolation as to provide the conditions for a fuller incorporation than has hitherto been the case into an increasingly globalised market economy. These conditions also produced the context and homogenising framework within which intellectual and policy work occurred. Not only were new policies produced, but the way in which spheres such as education were thought about underwent fundamental changes. The traditional divide between conservatives, liberals and radicals that had dominated educational discourse throughout the 1970s and 1980s became irrelevant; education was reconceptualised in such a way that it could anticipate the development and growth path that was in the process of being created while destroying the orthodoxies of the past.[8]

In the 1950s and 1960s the primary educational discourse was one of racial supremacy; modernisation and human capital theory provided the frame of reference and oppositional discourse of liberalism. In the 1970s and 1980s, critical and Marxist theories of education emerged; the critique of human capital theory, however, had little impact. The latter surfaced powerfully in the state's de Lange Report on education in 1981 and continued to provide the rationale for both capital and the reforming wing in the state to change the education system. In the 1990s, with the collapse of the Soviet bloc and the successful revival of modernisation and human capital theory under the auspices of donor agencies in the continent as a whole, education policy as developed by the ANC deployed a complex range of discourses which included strands and elements from both older and more recent approaches to education. The specificity seemed to lie in the linkage of redistributive strategies with policies designed for a context of financial stringency. The policy that emerged was congruent with that of the liberal democratic state that was being created, and consistent with the perceived complementarity of states and markets.[9]

Clearly there has been and will continue to be a process of active selection, conflict, contradiction and struggle in policy determination. The role of old and emergent social classes in supporting and advancing particular approaches is also critical in explaining new tendencies and contradictions:

accommodation by new social forces in the Government of National Unity to aspects of the old order in the adoption of neo-liberal economic approaches, federalism and constitutional guarantees for incumbents of the old civil service; adaptation of the old to the new conversely manifested in a commitment to the achievement of racial equality.

The object of this chapter is to examine the restructuring of South African education and training in the light of these considerations. Clearly, the sweep will have to be fairly broad, and the risk of over-simplification will have to be run. The main documents in which new policies have to date been elaborated are the 13 reports of the NECC's National Education Policy Investigation,[10] the ANC Education Department's *Policy Framework for Education and Training* (January 1994), its *Implementation Plan for Education and Training* (April 1994), the new Education Department's *Draft White Paper* (September 1994), and the *Reconstruction and Development Programme.*

This chapter is written in three sections. The first explores a number of themes current in both the national and international context about the link between education, economic growth and international competitiveness, as these have occurred in relation to the shift from Fordism to flexible accumulation in the developed world and from modernisation theory to structural adjustment in the developing world. In South Africa, however, post-Fordist conditions are not yet dominant in the economy, and the development of human resources will be constrained by a sluggish economy. In the second and third sections, the specific themes of flexibility and integration, cost-recovery, and public sector restructuring are examined. It is argued that themes of integration and flexibility share something with and owe something to UNESCO of the early 1970s, new regimes of accumulation, and radical conceptions of ending divisions between mental and manual labour advanced by sections of the organised working class. Cost-recovery and cost-sharing strategies, on the other hand, owe more to contemporary neo-liberal policies in both the developed and developing worlds to shift the relationship between public and private provision, states and markets. These have not been challenged by the new state; indeed, they characterise its approach. Whereas the emphasis on flexibility and integration promises access and equity, cost-recovery and cost-sharing mechanisms may also have the contrary effect of supporting new forms of inequality.

In the fourth section, the tension between 'internationalism and nationalism, between globalism and parochial ethnocentrism, between universalism and class privileges'[11] is captured in the tensions and changing political relationships between centre and region and between old and new loci of power. This section argues that decentralising tendencies contained in the constitutional devolution of power to the provinces are strongly constrained by historically constituted centralising tendencies in the old bureaucracy. Devolution of financial and governing powers to de-racialising white schools in 1991 is a trend that predated this period, and that will be difficult to reverse in the context of constitutional conditions outlined.

WORLD AND NATIONAL ECONOMIC CONTEXT

A fundamental impetus to the reform of education has come from the perceived link between education, economic growth and international competitiveness. This is also the mainspring of educational restructuring in the UK, Australia, New Zealand and the USA amongst others. *Learning to Succeed*, the title of a Report of the National Commission on Education in the UK (1993), most effectively captures the connection. Both the National Education Crisis Committee's (NECC's) *National Education Policy Investigation* (1992) and the ANC's *Policy Framework for Education and Training* (1994) emphasise the importance of education on the one hand to democratic participation and, on the other, to international competitiveness. 'Higher economic development', the NEPI *Framework Report* argues, 'will only be achieved and sustained if the economy is competitive in world commodity and manufacturing markets' and will mean 'that the education system must be geared to produce sufficiently highly skilled citizens'.[12] The high-skill development path advocated is considered to require 'a strong state which has a flexible bureaucracy and is open to civil society'. For the ANC Education Department, the legacy to be addressed includes the 'lack of skilled and trained labour and the adverse effects of this on productivity and the international competitiveness of the economy'.[13] Linked to this argument is the view expressed in the *Reconstruction and Development Programme* (1984) that economic growth is the principal mechanism for financing socio-economic and poverty alleviation programmes.

The main problems of South Africa's low economic performance are, in this view, the low levels of productivity and lack of skills on the shop floor: 'a sustained increase in the growth rate can only come from investments in human capital and technology that raise the productivity of other factors of production'; such investment is particularly critical at the secondary school level and in vocational training, but it needs to be combined with an improvement in the 'quality and relevance of education' and vocational training.[14] The NEPI *Education Planning, Systems and Structure Final Report* is a little more cautious, but concurs that 'it is possible that weaknesses in labour productivity associated with general deficiencies in education have contributed to the slowdown of employment growth'.[15] Education and training should, in this view, produce multi-skilled, flexible and problem-solving workers capable of spearheading South Africa's entry into new markets.

Underlying these emphases are major changes in the world and regional economies. Increasing integration of the world economy, the transition in regimes of accumulation and modes of social and political regulation, the growth in services relative to other sectors of the economy, the explosion and impact of information technologies, economic recession, debt, high levels of unemployment and the increasing power of transnational agencies such as the IMF and World Bank, have all combined to ensure that those economies that are able to compete successfully in the world market do so on the basis of trade in value-added manufactured goods. Effective trade in manufactured goods in turn rests on the skill and know-how of the working population. Those economies, such as many African countries, which rely on primary commodities and have poorly skilled and educated populations, are marginalised. Simultaneous with this development, and related to it, has been the enhanced role of market-oriented policies, and the 'emergence of a shared belief on the part of both investors and developing country governments that market-oriented reforms will lead to much improved economic performance.'[16]

At the heart of the move from Fordist to post-Fordist production methods is the replacement of the core principles of mass production, a clear division of labour and a hierarchy of authority with an emphasis and concentration on more flexible and smaller production units, product innovation and quality. Under accumulation regimes of flexible production, labour is no longer a cost of production which has to be minimised, but a key resource which has to be maximised. Success in the use of new technologies can be achieved only on the basis of educated and skilled labour, improved management systems and a better infrastructure of transport and services.[17] In South Africa, the adoption of post-Fordist work processes has been limited; where there has been a turn to flexible specialisation, such as in the clothing, textiles, jewellery and motor vehicle assembly, 'new Japanese organisational forms have been *indigenised* and adapted to the largely semi- and unskilled, and low-waged South African workforce'.[18] The pattern of growth developed in South Africa over the last four decades, and described as 'racial Fordism' is, with minor exceptions and despite support amongst sections of capital, labour and the ANC for flexible specialisation, still substantially in place.[19]

Part of the attempt to transcend the legacy of apartheid and pioneer a new growth path which overcomes the obstacles of the old has involved a renewed emphasis on human resource development. This emphasis on the need for human resource development as being at the root of economic growth echoes those elements of modernisation and human capital theory which were dominant in African education in the post-independence period. Modernisation theory, with its certainty and naivety about economic 'take-off' in Africa following the same route indicated by Western democracies, had its educational counterpart in human capital theory, or the view that education was the key to economic growth. Liberal historiography, modernisation theory and human capital theory were everywhere in the ascendant in the middle 1960s, favouring an ordered decolonisation, through agreement rather than armed struggle.[20] The failure of the model led in the 1970s to critiques which questioned, amongst others, the relationship between these theoretical approaches and legitimation of the role of new elites, and the capacity of either Western development models or education on its own to generate the changes anticipated. In the African context, the critique of modernisation theory by dependency theory, and of the latter by Marxism in the 1970s, however, had little impact on policy making and educational practice. Indeed, some have argued that the critique of dependency theory by Marxists convinced of the pioneering role of capitalism opened the way for neo-liberals to 'sing the praises of capitalism, the free market forces and the brilliant industrial prospects of the whole of the third world'.[21]

The crisis of the 1980s saw the revival of human capital theory which was now modified to incorporate the extension of the logic of the marketplace into the public service. Applied to education in the developed world, this involved policies for the abandonment by government of its role in education, an emphasis on policies in the financing, management and organisation of education which included cuts to education, privatisation of education services, and devolution of control and responsibility to local levels.[22] In the African context, educational expansion of the 1960s, followed by debt, paved the way for structural adjustment loans. Educational development has become increasingly donor-driven; the structural adjustment package has typically included cuts to public expenditure, removal of state subsidies, restraints on wages and public sector employment, limits on credit expansion and currency devaluation. The high human costs and declining quality of education suffered as a result of the 'culture of cuts' and crisis management were masked by the use of concepts such as cost-recovery, efficiency and revitalisation.[23] Policies intended to limit the sphere of the state and promote privatisation were increasingly cast in terms of notions such as 'partnership funding.' Thus, however, human capital theory, predicated on expanding budgets to education, paradoxically became linked to arguments for cuts in social spending.

The assumptions and language used in the current African context to define the problems and solutions 'underlines the continuity of theoretical assumptions which were dominant in the first two decades of African independence' and contributes to the 'theoretical crisis which surrounds the study, analysis and formulation of solutions to existing problems'.[24] The assumption underlying all the variations was a universalising developmental model which, in its assumption that African development should and could occur in the image of Western industrialised countries, denied the diversity and difference of African countries. This same model appears to be dominant in South Africa today.

In South Africa, human capital theory, as elsewhere, has provided support to proposals for the reform, expansion and development of education rather than its curtailment. In the 1960s and 1970s it was the chief rationale used by business to improve African education in order to meet needs for skilled labour. Significant sections of contemporary South African education policy have also been cast in the universalising language of modernisation and human capital theory. The theory has drawn on approaches taken by the World Bank and UNESCO in the 1970s to poverty alleviation through meeting 'basic needs' and integrating formal and non-formal education. Whereas one of the problems with this approach may be that universalising approaches occlude specific and substantive issues of race and gender, this approach has also committed South Africa to expansionist and redistributive policies within a framework of capitalist development. Thus the first budget of the Government of National Unity (GNU) increased educational spending by providing for an 11.5 per cent increase on the corresponding amount for 1993/4. This means that South Africa now spends R29.2 billion on education, or about 8 per cent of GDP, a substantially higher sum than other semi-industrialised countries.

The short-term economic prospects are bleak, however, and underpin cost-cutting austerity strategies which co-exist with human resource development policies. The resuscitation of modernisation and human capital theory has gone hand in hand with the revival of neo-liberal economic and educational policies.[25] South Africa has had a declining real rate of growth since the 1960s, with a low real GDP growth rate of 0.9 per cent per annum being recorded over the two full business cycles between 1982/3 and 1993/4. The impact of the two recessions between 1982/3 and 1984/5 and then again between 1989/90 and 1992/3 has been severe, resulting on the one hand in a level of government borrowing to service its debt which even the Department of Finance considers unsustainable, and on the other in falling wages and high levels of unemployment. By 1993, the recession had begun to bottom out: real GDP increased by approximately

1 per cent; inflation slowed, amounting to 9 per cent by the beginning of 1993; the capital account of the balance of payments had improved markedly as a result of return-flow of short-term funds. The effective exchange rate had depreciated significantly, however; given South Africa's dependence on imports, this did not signify well. Overall, despite the achievement of political stability, the slightly improved performance of the economy and a projected growth rate of $2^1/_2$ per cent for 1994, South Africa remained vulnerable in a changing world economy because of its continued structural dependence on primary commodities, for which prices remained low; on expensive imports, combined with falling gross domestic savings and its mounting debt burden.[26]

New approaches in South African education embody a plethora of themes eclectically drawn from a variety of older and newer sources. The significance attached to multi-skilling, integration, and flexibility has emerged in the context (in the developed world) of the shift from Fordist to post-Fordist methods of production; education cuts and privatisation policies have accompanied economic recession and high unemployment. The revival of modernisation and human capital theory has arisen (in the African context) of the poor overall performance of national economies and donor-driven educational development. Flexible specialisation, modernisation and the language and disciplines of austerity have been central to the educational vision developed for the 'new' South Africa. The image of multi-skilled, flexible workers to ensure South Africa's international competitiveness has been created as part of a vision for modernisation of the society and education system through human capital and resource development. Even as the need for modernisation and human resource development has provided the rationale for greater educational investment, fiscal constraint, partnership funding, and cost-recovery strategies have all become integrated into the discourse and politics of redistributive educational change conceived as part of a techno-bureaucratic, rational planning exercise. A key issue is that even though South Africa's Government of National Unity has chosen a market-led approach to recovery, some of the themes in education (and in particular modernisation and human capital theory) are consistent with both state and market-led educational development.

THE EDUCATION AND TRAINING POLICY FRAMEWORK

Apartheid bequeathed an enormous legacy of educational inequality. At the same time, resistance to apartheid spawned a rich history of ideas and approaches to the transformation of education.[27] After 1990, a new phase under new historical and international conditions was entered and new emphases were linked to older ones.

Flexibility and Integration

Flexibility and integration are central to the ANC's *Policy Framework* and *Reconstruction and Development Programme*. Whereas the emphasis on flexibility corresponds to envisaged changes in the production process, the commitment to integration of both black and white education as well as education and training derives from both older and newer themes in educational change. The integration of formal and non-formal education by bringing schooling and adult education into one system was a hallmark of UNESCO's approach in the 1970s, and was counterposed to the narrower World Bank policy of isolating particular aspects of the system for change. The concept of 'lifelong learning' has similar historical roots.[28]

ANC positions and priorities have gone beyond expansionist policies, and incorporate a vision of 'lifelong learning', the provision of 'quality' education, and the integration of education and training. This vision, pioneered from within COSATU, draws on both new international trends attempting to harness educational reform to changing global economic conditions, new forms of flexible specialisation and on radical traditions which have historically challenged the division between mental and manual labour, academic and vocational education and training, and between conception and execution as underlining wider social, political and economic divisions.

The ANC *Policy Framework*, for example, argues that:

> The separation of education and training has contributed significantly to the situation where most of our people are under-educated, under-skilled, and under-prepared for full participation in social, economic and civic life.[29]

The policy device to ensure integration is a national standards and qualification structure, the South African Qualifications Authority (SAQA). Through a credit-based qualifications framework, the system will seek to link currently divided technical and academic qualifications and skills; 'link one level of learning to another and enable learners to progress to higher levels from any starting point in the education and training system'; recognise prior learning and experience and ensure the development of a national curriculum based on the integration of academic and vocational skills. Education and training will accordingly not be separated into academic and technical tracks or routes, but into a General Education and Training Council, a Further Education and Training Council and a Higher Education Council which will be responsible for ensuring equivalence between qualifications achieved in different settings. Modularised competency-based training is critical to this conception. The novelty of the approach is such that, despite widespread acceptance of these proposals by labour and business, constitutional provision that training will be a national and education a provincial competency may yet be its undoing. The Draft White Paper on Education and Training released by the national Ministry of Education also carried a much attenuated version of this approach, the probable result of compromise on the part of the ANC drafters working with National Party educationists not so committed to the concept.

In addition to the integrated qualifications framework, and in order to address the situation of out-of-school youth and high levels of illiteracy amongst the general adult population, the ANC Education Department, Draft White Paper and RDP have proposed ten years' compulsory general education; the expansion of pre-school, adult basic education and training and special education; programmes for an improvement in the quantity and quality of teachers at all levels, restructuring of the further and higher education systems through national commissions and provision of early childhood development and school meals. These are all considered to be 'basic needs'.

Curriculum reform is at the heart of enhancing access and breaking down historical divisions between academic and vocational. Here, the concept of a unified and flexible, modularised curriculum has informed ANC/COSATU policy. The Draft White Paper also emphasises the encouragement of 'independent and critical thought' in the development of new curricula.[30] Both In-Service Education and Training (INSET) and Pre-Service Education of Teachers (PRESET) of teachers and trainers working in early childhood, schools, adult basic education and workplace education and training and colleges are prioritised.

Immediately after the election, the National Education and Training Forum (NETF), established in August 1993 to halt unilateral restructuring by the government, drove the process of syllabus revision in schools. Field and Phase committees (covering the different fields of curricula and phases of schooling) were officially appointed to cleanse syllabi of offensive, racist and sexist content. Their work has been completed, and these syllabi will be implemented in 1995. Longer-term curriculum revision and resourcing of curricula are likely to become the task of newly constituted National and Provincial Institutes for Curriculum Development. In addition, it has been proposed that certification and assessment cease to play its gate-keeping function and be connected to the new qualifications structure. Much more work remains to be done on teacher education syllabi which are dominated by 'Fundamental Pedagogics'. Language and medium of instruction policy in schools is linked to constitutional provisions which recognise the right of every person to 'instruction in the language of his or her choice where this is reasonably practicable.'[31] The Draft White Papers on Education and Training released by the national Ministry of Education endorsed this approach.

While there are similarities with the significance attached to 'basic education' at the Conference on Education for All held at Jomtien in 1990 by UNESCO, UNICEF and the World Bank, it is important to note that the provision of ten years' free and compulsory education has long been a goal of the ANC. In addition, its concept of 'basic education' as an integrated system including ten years of compulsory schooling goes beyond the conception of Universal Primary Education (UPE) as a policy goal. The education and training framework of the ANC thus borrows from and has similarities with those policies considered appropriate for the developing world by international agencies; the definition and content given to those goals and policies is however defined historically.

The vision for a unified and flexible curriculum advanced by the ANC and COSATU is clearly linked to the flexible specialisation thesis. Important constraints on transforming this vision into reality include the constitutional provision that made schools and colleges a provincial function and universities, technikons and training a national one. Interest in the bureaucracy and sections of the education sector which are not committed to the integration of education and training, and the laggardly nature of educational change in the classroom are linked to the enormous basic problems that continue to plague the system.[32]

Cost-recovery and Cost-sharing

The ANC and GNU are generally reluctant to prioritise any one area as more deserving than the other, although the exercise of power and pressures from above and below will generally force a set of priorities to be established. It is in the financing that the shape of the future system and incorporation of new themes and their application to racial inequality becomes clearer.

Internationally, cost-recovery, 'user pays' and cost-sharing schemes have been a vital dimension not only of making resources beyond those of the state available to education, but also of changing the relationship between public and private provision of education in such a way that the burden of educational provision is carried by 'parents' or 'communities'. Likewise public sector restructuring and wage cuts of public servants have characterised structural adjustment policies. All these dimensions have found an echo in South Africa; firstly, in the conceptualisation of the financing of black education through semi-privatisation of white schools; secondly, through fees envisaged at different levels of education, and thirdly, by approaches to the restructuring of teachers' salaries. These will be considered briefly in the context of proposals put forward for the financing of education in a number of recent policy documents.

Debates on how education should be financed have been rich and varied, and only a skeleton of the different approaches can be provided here. The main point to be made is that strategies for redistribution have gone hand in hand with strategies for a differentially fee-based and therefore inequitable system. Debates around redistribution have largely revolved around the education budget. Some proponents have argued that the total education budget is already high, and that reallocation within and reorganisation of aspects of it should be sufficient. Greater educational expenditure should be financed, in the long term, by economic growth; in the short term, there should be reduction of government funding to white schools, which should be expanded and desegregated; increased state support for congested township and rural schools and decentralisation of suburban schools to release financial and administration funds and bursary and loan schemes for higher education. Thus funds should be redistributed from white to black, but the quality of white schools now serving an expanded multi-racial clientele should be retained by making up the shortfall in the state subsidy through fees.[33] The Draft White Paper on Education and Training (September 1994) proposed both a means-related and market-related system of fees, but made it clear that no one would be denied education for failure to pay fees. There have been proposals based on the same principle that the rich should pay for their privilege in order to reallocate expenditure from tertiary education to schooling.[34] Others have maintained, though, that reorganisation of the education budget alone will not be enough, and that parity in education will have to be supported by intervention in the total environment of education, including jobs, housing, transport and nutrition.[35] Within these broad perspectives, teacher salaries, which constitute the highest item of expenditure at 78 per cent of the total budget, have been considered necessary for revision.

Within the framework that the education budget should not be expanded, a specific approach to how teacher salaries should be restructured has been developed which has sought to delink qualifications from remuneration.[36] The argument here is that the need to expand provision of teachers and upgrade un- and under-qualified teachers will force spending upwards and thus place unsustainable strains on the budget. In addition, the linkage of qualifications to pay scales has led to a 'paper chase' which has not been reflected in improved classroom performance by either teachers or pupils. In order to address this situation, two options are proposed. The first is to compress the salary scales to improve the position of poorly paid teachers at the bottom of the scale. The second is to delink remuneration from academic and professional qualifications, and base payment instead on evidence of classroom competence and the level of responsibility held by the incumbent. Performance appraisal of teachers should, in this view, provide the link between classroom performance and remuneration. Realistic minimum qualification levels and alternative career paths to reward and keep excellent teachers in the classroom are important adjuncts of this strategy. One-off cash grants would form the reward for further study. The South African Democratic Teachers' Union (SADTU) is not opposed to the compression of scales in order to raise the position of un- and under-qualified teachers, but is not convinced about the delinking of pay from qualifications. There is substantial international evidence to suggest that the latter policy is unworkable and extremely controversial.[37]

The Draft White Paper on Education and Training (September 1994) included the most important of these proposals: an expanded, three-tiered, fee-differentiated system of private, state-aided and state schools and the restructuring of teacher salaries. The approach of the Government of National Unity to financing in education has thus been shaped and influenced by both a redistributive and a cost-cutting imperative which may very well undermine its redistributive efforts. Overall, the emphasis is on working within existing constraints and parameters and on effecting educational reform gradually, incrementally, and on the basis of rational planning.

The RDP programme confirms that programmes should be financed in ways that do not cause undue inflation or balance of payments difficulties, and that the overall debt burden should not increase. The policy imperatives of the Government of National Unity suggest an accommodation to a 'user pays' approach (particularly at the level of secondary schooling and tertiary education) which is in effect a policy of partial privatisation of suburban or ex-tricameral schools, state support for African schools, and delimitation of access to higher education through a new fee structure. Whatever the emerging structure, new values and principles designed to transcend the legacy of apartheid, desegregation, expanded access, greater equity in financing, guiding the reconstruction of the education system are vital elements of the new system.

How this will translate into practice will be the crucial issue for the medium term. Change may at once be slower than anticipated and fuelled by conflicts and issues which re-shape the educational terrain in very different ways.[38]

THE CONSTITUTIONAL FRAMEWORK: CENTRALISING AND DECENTRALISING TENDENCIES

The modernist tendency in education, represented in policy documents such as the National Education Policy Investigation (NEPI), and the ANC *Policy Framework for Education and Training*, has represented the legacy of apartheid in terms of a fragmentation and chaos which it was the task of the process of restructuring to master and overcome. Order can be imposed on the inchoate apartheid past by the construction of a new regulating framework of governance for South African education and training. The Grand Design image of apartheid was refashioned in terms of a Chaos and Fragmentation picture which required to be given a new coherence. In practice, the realities of change continued to be chaotic and fragmented, if not by race alone, then by new and older configurations of power.

South Africa's Interim Constitution, drawn up at the end of 1993 on the basis of negotiation and compromise, has ensured the reorganisation, unification and decentralisation of education, one of the major features of recent trends in the control of education.[39] In reality, as argued by the NEPI *Governance and Administration Final Report*, this dichotomy is not particularly helpful, because most systems are a mixture of both. The key issue is the power relations at work at the different levels, the redistributive powers and strategies adopted and the nature of democracy.[40] The historical character and overlays of different periods are also significant. The governance and administration of South African education 'is one of extraordinary complexity', a '"system of systems" differentiated on the basis of the racial, ethnic and regional divisions of South African society'.[41] Before 1948, white education was provided by the state on a provincial basis, and black education largely by missionary societies. After 1948, African, coloured and Indian education was brought under state control in 1953, 1963 and 1965. After 1968, the ten bantustans had the right to develop their own education systems and policies, although the central South African state continued to control funding and a common examination system. Even as education became more centralised after 1948, there were powerful decentralising tendencies manifested in the putative authority granted to the bantustans and continued provincial authority over white education.[42]

Between 1984 and 1994, South African education was governed in terms of the 1983 Constitution and the 1984 General Education Affairs Act which provided for the administration of education outside the bantustans in terms of 'own' and 'general' affairs. By 1994, then, there was a multiplicity of education departments (19 in all), a situation frequently described in terms of its byzantine, fragmented and chaotic character. All policy development before 1994 was concerned with unification of the system, rational planning and coordination and monitoring. Both NECC and ANC education policy anticipated a national, unitary state and education policy. In the event, in order to accommodate the interests of KwaZulu, a federal system was negotiated. Education accordingly became a provincial competence, but 'subject to a national policy framework'.[43] Complex provisions govern law-making: provinces may legislate on all matters relating to education except universities and technikons. Where a national and provincial law are in conflict, the provincial law will prevail, except in specific areas designated as falling under national norms and standards. Conflict between the national parliament and a provincial government will be referred to the Constitutional Court.

Centralising and decentralising forces were very much at odds in the new political economy of education. In terms of the Interim Constitution, new education policy is to be implemented not in a unitary state, but in nine provinces, each with differing conditions, and in a context where the balance of power is still unevenly weighted in favour of the old state, and the power of the old bureaucracy remains substantial. In addition to the problems of integrating the old bureaucracy and creating a new civil service in education, the new constitution effectively created four new power centres. These four power centres included the national ministry, nine provincial ministries, the office of the Minister without Portfolio which was responsible for the RDP, and the parliamentarians who began to whittle away powers of Cabinet and ensure more effective power of the standing committees. The Office of the Minister without Portfolio, responsible for the Reconstruction and Development Programme, defined its mission as both exercising leverage over the old bureaucracy by ensuring through performance audits that RDP priorities and targets were being met, and ensuring that 'value for money' was being achieved. Without effective power in or over the bureaucracy, both sections of the Parliamentarians and the RDP Office saw its role in terms of changing it from the outside. This was not the consequence of it having been foisted on South Africans, but was an outcome of conflict between fissiparous social forces. Integrating, centralising forces and modernising forces are constantly at odds with the social realities of fragmentation and social division, finely imbricated in power relations. Two areas are of significance: the devolution of powers from the centre to the nine provinces in terms of the new Constitution, and the devolution of powers to historically white schools.

The Constitution has created a powerful dynamic for the provincialisation of education, an issue sternly opposed in education before 1994 as being antagonistic to unification and national coordination. In the immediate aftermath of the elections, jurisdiction over all legislation reverted to the national level. Provincial legislatures expected almost immediate delegation of powers to the provinces; in the absence of this, as well as of budgetary power, something of a power vacuum developed, whereby the ANC was in office, but not in power in the provinces. New provincial ministries, as well as national, became appendages to existing departments, with little power over or within them, yet required to intervene in and account for educational (dis)order. This created a dynamic whereby the provincial legislatures began to *demand* powers, thus giving the constitution a reality and creating the conditions for entrenching decentralised governance.

The position was exacerbated by the lack of budgetary power. Allocations in the 1994/5 budget were made to the 17 education departments of old but, within individual departments, ministers have the ability to shift expenditure. No allocations would be made to the new provincial government departments, but should an education minister decide to divert funds from one department to another, s/he would be able to do so.[44] The Draft White Paper on Education and Training released in September 1994 suggested that the movement to full provincial budgetary control would be slow and fully effected only in the 1996/7 financial year. The lack of powers meant that the position of civil servants from the pre-1994 period was strengthened, and the process of integration delayed. One of the major tasks in this period, the integration and rationalisation of racially-divided departments, was the responsibility 'primarily but not exclusively' of the national government which must exercise its responsibility in co-operation with the provincial governments and the Commission on Provincial Government and with 'due regard to the advice of the Public Service Commission'. The power of the Public Service Commission was such that the movement towards integration sought by new bureaucracies, which would assist in consolidating their power, was significantly blocked, at least in the short term.

A major attempt by the National Party prior to the 1994 April election to maintain control over education occurred through its introduction of the Model C school system. In terms of this model, as in the Local Management of Schools in the UK, powers were devolved to school governing bodies; the state would pay for teachers' salaries within a given pupil/teacher ratio; any additional funds would need to be raised by the school.

Governing bodies were given the right to determine admissions policy, and to ensure that 51 per cent of enrolments remained white. The immediate consequence was admission tests testing for language and numeracy, and the imposition in most cases of high fees. Where black students have gained entry to Model C schools, an assimilationist policy has been pursued whereby the object is not to question the norms and values of the school, but to ensure that black students are assimilated into them. This has also been the case in desegregating Indian and 'coloured' schools. Fees, however, have been the main exclusionary and/or discriminating device, such that schools are effectively able to transform themselves into institutions for the reproduction of class no longer determined by colour alone.

The Interim Constitution has provided conditions that would make it difficult to reverse this situation and return schools to the state. In the first instance, schools are allowed to decide on their language of instruction, and, in the second, changing the status of Model C schools requires negotiation with every governing body, a near-impossibility which will require complex legal manoeuvring. Pronouncements by the national Minister of Education towards the end of 1994 suggested that policy regarding these schools would focus on their de-racialisation. Many of these schools have accommodated to the need for desegregation, but also argue for continued state-aided status. Finally, the argument for devolution, namely that the rich should pay for their schooling in order to finance upgrading township and rural schools, has developed into an apparent consensus.[45]

In other contexts, it has made little real difference whether control over education is centralised or decentralised; national systems have varied widely. What does make the difference is the power configuration and its expression through these structures. There is no simple equation between the *strength* and the *location* of educational control.[46] A centralised system can for example have powerful local bodies which use the system to their own ends, as in France; decision-making can still be centrally determined, even if the system is a strongly decentralised one, such as in the UK. In South Africa, a system is in the process of developing where the centre is relatively weak and the demand for regional and local control is strong.

CONCLUSION

South Africa's negotiated transition to a Government of National Unity (GNU) has occurred at a unique historical juncture. In many parts of the world, older post-war 'settlements' have been dismantled, and new educational orders predicated on bringing the market into education have been created. New forms and methods of production have led to demands for a restructuring of education systems. In the developing world, educational systems are being subordinated to the imperatives of structural adjustment. Economic crisis and financial stringency underlie both contexts and the emergence, on the one hand, of privatisation strategies and the resuscitation of modernisation and human capital theories on the other. South Africa has not escaped these developments; indeed, national liberation has allowed for its fuller participation in them.

In South Africa, a consensus and settlement has been built around educational change which shares features of both the older, dismantled 'settlements', of new international trends and the specificities of the South African transition. The most important features of the new educational order are on the one hand, the contradictory marrying of human resource development and fiscal constraint discourses on the one hand, and of expansion, redistribution and structural adjustment discourses on the other. On the other, there is the contradiction between the national, centralising and provincial, decentralising imperatives. In the long run, the education system is bound to take its shape not only from these new policies, but also from its deeply divided and inequitable legacy, the role of the new state as manifested in national and provincial government, and the emergence of new classes. Education shapes as much as it is shaped by the power and influence of different social classes.

NOTES

1. Philip W. Jones, *World Bank Financing of Education: Lending, Learning and Development* (London and New York: Routledge, 1992) provides a useful historical account of changing emphases in and conflicts between education policies of the World Bank and UNESCO. Its introduction is an epiphany of the centrality of schooling to the modernist impulse: 'Education – and mass schooling in particular – is a phenomenon that unites the world, in the sense that it is a key aspect of that steady process whereby a global technological civilisation is being forged. All around the world, the variety and the dynamics of local culture have collided with the steady transformation of societies along the lines implied by modernisation', p. xiii.

2. *Ibid.*, p. 117.

3. *Ibid.*, p. 102.

4. See, for example, *Education and the South African Economy: The 1961 Education Panel in South Africa*, vol. 11 (Cape Town: Juta, 1966); Jonathan Hyslop, 'School Student Movements and State Education Policy: 1972–1987'

in William Cobbett and Robin Cohen (eds), *Popular Struggles in South Africa* (London: James Currey, 1988), p. 184.

5. David Harvey, *The Condition of Post-modernity: An Enquiry into the Origins of Cultural Change* (Oxford: Basil Blackwell, 1989), p. 344.

6. *Ibid.*, p. 9

7. *Ibid.*, p. 344.

8. David Harvey, *op. cit.*, writes about the 'creative-destructive' force of modernity in Chapter 1.

9. Macroeconomic Research Group, *Making Democracy Work*; and M. Lipton and C. Simkins (eds), *State and Market in Post-Apartheid South Africa* (Johannesburg: Witwatersrand University Press, 1993).

10. Cape Town: Oxford University Press, 1992.

11. Harvey, *op. cit.*, p. 25.

12. NEPI, *Framework Report* (Cape Town: Oxford University Press, 1992), p. 24; see also the *Education Planning, Systems and Structure Final Report* and the *Human Resources Development Final Report*.

13. ANC Education Department, *Policy Framework for Education and Training: Draft Discussion Document* (Johannesburg, 1994), p. 2.

14. S. Lall, 'What will Make South Africa Internationally Competitive?' and A. Joffe et al., 'Meeting the Global Challenge: A Framework for Industrial Revival in South Africa' in P.H. Baker, A. Boraine and W. Krafchick (eds), *South Africa and the World Economy in the 1990s* (Cape Town: David Philip, 1993), pp. 54 and 214.

15. National Education Policy Investigation (NEPI), *Education Planning, Systems and Structure Final Report* (Cape Town: Oxford University Press, 1992), p. 3.

16. P. Krugman, 'Changes in Capital Markets for Developing Countries' in Baker, Boraine and Krafchick, *op. cit.*, p. 40.

17. C.M. Rogerson, 'Flexible Production in the Developing World: The Case of South Africa' in *Geoforum*, 25, 1 (1994), 1–17.

18. *Ibid.*

19. Stephen Gelb, *South Africa's Economic Crisis* (Cape Town: David Philip, 1991); see also Andre Kraak, 'Human Resources Development and Organised Labour' in G. Moss and I. Obery (eds), *South African Review 6* (Johannesburg: Ravan Press, 1992).

20. Alessandro Triulzi, 'Decolonising African History' in R. Samuel (ed.), *People's History and Socialist Theory* (London: Routledge & Kegan Paul, 1981), p. 290.

21. Jorge Larrain, *Theories of Development: Capitalism, Colonialism and Dependency* (Cambridge: Polity Press, 1989); Martin Bienefeld, 'Dependency Theory and the Political Economy of Africa's Crisis', in *Review of African Political Economy*, 43 (1988).

22. See, for example, B. Lingard, J. Knight and P. Porter (eds), *Schooling Reform in Hard Times* (London: Falmer Press, 1993).

23. Sarah Graham-Brown, *Education in the Developing World: Conflict and Crisis* (London: Longman, 1991); see also Joel Samoff, 'The Intellectual/Financial Complex of Foreign Aid', *Review of African Political Economy*, 53 (1992), 70, and Judith Marshall, 'Structural Adjustment and Social Policy in Mozambique', *Review of African Political Economy*, 47 (1990).

24.   Kairu Kinyanjui, 'African Education: Dilemmas, Challenges and Opportunities' in U. Himmelstrand, K. Kinyanjui and E. Mburugu, *African Perspectives on Development* (London: James Currey, 1994), p. 285.
25.   Joel Samoff, *op. cit.*; Judith Marshall, *op. cit.*
26.   The information for this paragraph is drawn from the Department of Finance, *Budget Review* (Pretoria, 22 June 1994).
27.   For recent periodisation and analysis see Jonathan Hyslop, 'School Student Movements and State Education Policy: 1972–1987'; Shaun Johnson, ' "The Soldiers of Luthuli": Youth in the Politics of Resistance in South Africa' in Shaun Johnson (ed.), *South Africa: No Turning Back* (Basingstoke: Macmillan, 1988); P. Kallaway (ed.), *Apartheid Education* (Johannesburg: Ravan Press, 1984); J. Muller, 'Peoples' Education and the National Education Crisis Committee' in G. Moss and I. Obery (eds), *South African Review 4* (Johannesburg: Ravan Press, 1987); M. Nkomo (ed.), *Pedagogy of Domination: Toward a Democratic Education in South Africa* (Johannesburg: Africa World Press, 1993).
28.   See Philip W. Jones, *World Bank Financing of Education: Lending, Learning and Development* (London: Routledge, 1992).
29.   *Policy Framework for Education and Training.*
30.   *Draft White Paper*, p. 12.
31.   *Ibid.*, p. 24.
32.   For a critique, in relation to education, see for example, G. Jeppie, 'Second Chances in Formal Education: Towards a New Adult Curriculum' (London: University of London, Institute of Education, MA, 1994).
33.   A. Donaldson, 'Financing Education' in A. and R. McGregor (eds), *McGregor's Education Alternatives* (Cape Town: Juta, 1992), pp. 304–10; 'Basic Needs and Social Policy: The Role of the State in Education, Health and Welfare' in M. Lipton and C. Simkins (eds), *State and Market in Post-Apartheid South Africa* (Johannesburg: Witwatersrand University Press, 1993), pp. 271–321.
34.   P. Pillay, 'Reassessing Strategies for Financing Education in South Africa', *Social Dynamics*, 15, 2 (December 1989), 25–39; P. Pillay, 'Financing Educational Transformation in South Africa' in E. Unterhalter et al. (eds), *Education in a Future South Africa: Policy Issues for Transformation* (London: Heinemann, 1991).
35.   Macroeconomic Research Group, *Making Democracy Work: A Framework for MacroEconomic Policy in South Africa* (Centre for Development Studies, University of the Western Cape, 1993).
36.   J. Hofmeyr, C. Simkins, H. Perry and R. Jaff, 'Restructuring Teacher Supply, Utilisation and Development (TSUD): Report for IPET Task Teams' (Johannesburg: EDUPOL, Urban Foundation, 1994).
37.   *Ibid.*
38.   L. Chisholm and B. Fine, 'Context and Contest in South African Education Policy: Comment on Curtin', *African Affairs*, 93, 371 (April 1994), 233–48.
39.   J. Lauglo and M. McLean, *The Control of Education: International Perspectives on the Centralisation-Decentralisation Debate* (London: Heinemann, 1991) and Robert F. Arnove, Philip G. Altbach and Gail Kelly (eds), *Emerging Issues in Education: Comparative Perspectives* (New York: SUNY, 1992).

40. *Ibid.*, p. 3.

41. National Education Policy Investigation, *Governance and Administration Final Report* (Cape Town: Oxford University Press, 1992), pp. 6–7.

42. For fuller discussion, see P. Buckland and J. Hofmeyr, 'Governance Working Paper' (Johannesburg: Urban Foundation, 1992) and E.G. Malherbe, *Education in South Africa*, vol. 2 (Cape Town: Juta, 1968).

43. *Draft White Paper*, p. 26.

44. *Business Day*, 8 June 1994.

45. For the argument, see A. Donaldson, 'Financing Education' in R. and A. McGregor (eds), *McGregor's Education Alternatives* (Cape Town: Juta, 1992), p. 311. See also P. Pillay, 'Reassessing Strategies for Financing Education in South Africa', *Social Dynamics*, 15, 2 (December 1989), 25.

46. Patricia Broadfoot, 'Towards Conformity: Educational Control and the Growth of Corporate Management in England and France' in Lauglo and Mclean, *op. cit.*, p. 105.

9 Transkei on the Verge of Emancipation

Jeff Peires

> Despite the bright prospects looming on the horizon for South Africa, there were many people in the ranks of the oppressed who harboured intense fears about the future, General Holomisa said. It was an irony that people who were on the verge of emancipation from the ruthless tentacles of racial domination and oppression should be sad and depressed.[1]

General Bantu Holomisa was so eager to get shot of Transkei independence that he ordered the homeland's flag lowered for the last time on 14 April 1994, two weeks before its official reincorporation into South Africa. And yet, as he indicated in his address, the majority of Transkeians present at the ceremony were filled not with euphoria but with sadness and depression. The irony of the situation was not, however, contingent or accidental. It was inherent in the essential contradiction at the heart of the apartheid homeland concept.

Despite the fact that the homeland strategy impoverished and uprooted literally millions of black South Africans, it empowered and enriched a small minority, the so-called 'beneficiaries of Transkeian independence'. It is this elite group who belatedly mourn the death of the Bantustan system which they did not lift a finger to save. Though many of them have temporarily abandoned their posts to steal what remains from the passengers, one may anticipate that they will soon be back to resume their grip on the helm and to attempt to steer the same leaky ship back to more familiar waters. The question is: will they succeed?

The same question might be asked of any of the ten 'independent' or 'non-independent' homelands, but it has a special piquancy in Transkei. For Transkei is the largest and longest established of the homelands, and the one most closely aligned with the African National Congress. Unlike the other homelands, there is no white in any position of authority anywhere in the Transkei government or the Transkei security forces. Nobody in Transkei, except its disgraced ex-President Kaiser Matanzima, has questioned the necessity of Transkei's reincorporation into the new South Africa; indeed military ruler Bantu Holomisa has done everything in his power to expedite the process. And yet the future of Transkei, if not sad and depressed, is certainly murky and unclear.

This chapter begins with a brief overview of Transkei's recent history, and its place in the political economy of South Africa. It then considers the several sectors of Transkeian society, such as the salaried bureaucracy, the middle classes, the urban working class and the vast mass of rural dwellers. After that, the chapter continues with an analysis of the political forces at work in the territory: the Transkei government, the ANC and its allies, SANCO, the PAC and, finally, some spontaneous rural movements. It concludes with a brief summary of the current state of play in Transkei, and in the new Eastern Cape Province of which Transkei now forms part.

A LITTLE HISTORY

The Transkei homeland was born in 1963 and given 'independence' in 1976. For the first 23 years of its existence, it was ruled with an iron hand by Kaiser Matanzima, who was a genuine convert to the ideology of Dr Verwoerd. But when Kaiser retired in 1986, his younger brother George was incapable of maintaining the same level of control. Two military coups in 1987, initiated by Kaiser with the connivance of the South African authorities, installed General Bantu Holomisa in power as Chairman of the new Military Council. Holomisa was nobody's puppet, however, and he soon broke with Kaiser and drew closer to the African National Congress. The first public sign of this realignment came in October 1989 at the reburial of the exiled Paramount Chief, Sabata Dalindyebo, when Holomisa suggested that Transkei's 'independence' might be overturned in a referendum. Shortly thereafter, he announced his intention to unban the ANC and the PAC, more than three months ahead of F.W. De Klerk's famous speech of 2 February 1990.

Despite the new South Africa, relationships between the De Klerk and Transkei governments deteriorated rapidly. In November 1990 Colonel Craig Duli, a former associate of Holomisa, attempted an armed coup with the assistance of South African Military Intelligence. The coup failed, and the incident was marked by an enormous outpouring of popular support for the General. Ever since that time, despite various attempts by Pretoria to destabilise Transkei financially, Holomisa's military government has ruled unchallenged. His reputation as a hard line opponent of the De Klerk regime has been further enhanced by his sensational disclosures concerning South African covert operations in the Eastern Cape and by his unabashed protection of APLA cadres wanted in the Republic for crimes against white civilians. When the General was placed 13th on the ANC National election list, nobody was at all surprised, except maybe the General himself.

It is all too easy to write off Holomisa's Transkei as an ANC stronghold ruled over by an ANC strong man. The reality, however, is far more
complex. The Transkei Bantustan was after all forged by Kaiser Matanzima
as a small component of a far greater apartheid machine. The mere advent
of General Holomisa could not in itself wipe away more than 20 years of
Matanzimas. And now that the General has exited local politics to become
a Deputy Minister in the national government, it becomes more pertinent than ever to elucidate the social structure of the Transkei region, in
order to arrive at some tentative conclusions concerning what is likely to
happen next.

A LITTLE POLITICAL ECONOMY

It has long been generally accepted that one of the main reasons for the
initial establishment of black homelands such as Transkei was the provision of cheap labour for South Africa's mining industry. This was
confirmed by the Chamber of Mines itself in its testimony before the
1943 Witwatersrand Native Mine Wage Commission.[2] It is clearly to the
advantage of the mines that native labourers should be encouraged to
return to their homes after the completion of the ordinary period of service.
The maintenance of the system under which the mines are able to obtain
unskilled labour at a rate less than ordinarily paid in industry depends
on this.

By the 1950s, however, the situation in South Africa had fundamentally
changed. First, the agricultural deterioration of the homelands had proceeded to such an extent that they were no longer able to provide adequate
subsistence to the migrant and his family. And, second, the major problem
facing South Africa's white rulers was no longer the procurement of cheap
labour but the exercise of political control over hundreds of thousands of
black Africans who were resident in the 'white' areas but who were surplus to the labour needs of the white population.

That this surplus, under the leadership of the ANC, was seriously challenging white domination certainly influenced the National Party to come
up with a solution that was political as well as economic. This solution,
as everybody knows, was the creation of 'independent' homelands such as
Transkei, where blacks would theoretically enjoy all the rights which they
were denied in 'white' South Africa. Political control rather than cheap
labour was the South African government's primary objective, and it was
quite prepared to finance the creation of a black auxiliary ruling class to
take care of the problem.

Whole populations were uprooted from their homes and dumped in such homelands as Ciskei and Bophutatswana. Transkei, thankfully, was spared actual resettlement camps, but it too absorbed its quota of destitute people through the less dramatic but equally malignant operations of the South African pass laws. As Fred Hendricks has shown in his neglected study of Transkei 'betterment' schemes, the conservation aspects of these schemes, together with the recommendations of the government's own Tomlinson Report, were jettisoned in order to facilitate the relocation of the maximum number of discarded Africans within the 'tribal' framework of the homelands.[3] The total number of Africans living in homelands more than doubled between 1960 and 1980, resulting in the percentage of the total African population living in homelands increasing from 39.45 per cent in 1960 to 54 per cent in 1980.[4] The population of Transkei tripled in 30 years, from 1 546 522 in 1960 to 4 509 824 in 1991. 52.6 per cent of this population was female, and nearly 42 per cent was under 15 years of age.[5]

The utter financial dependence of the entire population of Transkei – from bureaucrats to migrant workers – on South African sources of income constituted the economic context in which the Matanzima brothers practiced the politics of clientelism.[6] The Matanzimas have long since gone, but more than six years of the Holomisa government have not mitigated the grim statistics of the Transkei region's abject economic helplessness.

No less than 62 per cent of all Transkei government revenue in the 1991/2 financial year came in the form of transfers from Pretoria, with only 38 per cent generated within Transkei itself.[7] Even so, the government is unable to balance its budget, and only survives through an overdraft facility of 1 243 billion Rand, guaranteed by South Africa.[8] Agriculture within Transkei has all but collapsed, and local studies show that rural households get only about one-third of their subsistence requirements from their agricultural plots. The demand for labour within Transkei itself amounts to only 15.6 per cent of the potential labour force, leaving 84.4 per cent to seek work in the peripheral and migrant sectors. On average, every working person in Transkei supports 10–14 other people.[9] 42.2 per cent of Transkeian household income is provided by the 70 per cent of the economically employed Transkeian population which is working in South Africa.[10]

This extreme dependence, bad enough in 1985 when the foregoing figures were compiled, has lately got much worse. The Chamber of Mines requires less and less mine labour and has shut down several recruiting centres. The total number of Transkeians working on the mines has declined from 125 900 in 1980 to 104 328 in 1990. The phasing out of industrial decentralisation incentives will be catastrophic for Transkei's struggling manufacturing industry, which has already declined from a peak of 19 200 in 1988 to 15 500 in 1992.[11] It is difficult indeed not to characterise Transkei as an economic basket case, kept alive only by constant and increasingly exorbitant infusions of central government funds.

THE STAKEHOLDERS

In my previous article on Transkei, I failed to be theoretically explicit, and my incautious use of terms such as 'the middle classes' has only led to greater conceptual confusion, as we will see below.[12] It is not, however, possible to embark on a thoroughgoing class analysis of the people of Transkei in these pages, especially inasmuch as Transkei does not constitute an autonomous social formation. The people of Transkei form part of South Africa, and the majority of the people of Transkei form part of the dominated working class of South Africa ('displaced proletarians', in Hendricks's terminology). The dominant class to which this majority is subordinated is not located in Transkei at all, but in the metropolitan districts of South Africa.

The Transkeian elite, who might appear to the unwary observer as a dominant class within Transkei, constitute nothing more than a mixture of members of secondary classes when viewed in the broader South African context. Because of its underdeveloped and subordinated position within South Africa as a whole, Transkei lacks an indigenous capitalist class and therefore – except in a few peripheral cases such as shopkeepers and their employees – there is no direct exploitative contradiction between members of different classes resident in Transkei. Despite all the internal tensions, there is little possibility of class polarisation, let alone class struggle, within Transkei itself.

It is nevertheless true that Transkei has existed as an autonomous political entity for more than 20 years, and everybody and everything within it has acquired a recognisably Transkeian flavour. It is equally true that there are evident social distinctions and tensions which generate 'pertinent effects' in political terms. For the sake of progress, and in accordance with the latest negotiation-speak as perfected at the World Trade Centre, let us refer to these distinct elements as 'stakeholders'.

Stakeholders I: The Elite

There is a general consensus in the literature that relatively wealthy African elites, such as the one which exists in Transkei, cannot be called classes because they cannot be defined in terms of their relationship to the mode of production.[13] All agree that, whereas a true bourgeoisie uses its wealth to gain power in the state, African elites use their power in the state to gain wealth. Nicos Poulantzas called such a social group a 'state bourgeoisie'; Roger Southall, in a more specific context, called them 'the beneficiaries of Transkeian independence'.[14]

It matters less what we call the group than how we define it. Southall, who pioneered the class analysis of the homelands, lumped Transkei's chiefs, politicians, bureaucrats, businessmen and teachers all together as fractions of 'a dependent African petty bourgeoisie' whose interests were tied to the white regime in South Africa. I think I showed, however, that the homeland bourgeoisie did not control the homeland state, and that one needed to make a clear distinction between the Transkeian state apparatus, who were an integral part of the apartheid structure, and the Transkeian middle classes, who were not.[15]

Apart from insisting that the chiefs were state functionaries like magistrates and policemen, I did not attempt to define who belonged to the 'middle classes' and who belonged to the state apparatus. Southall is therefore quite right to point out the similarities between the chiefs and the remainder of the bureaucracy, who both depend financially on the state.[16] But Southall's own solution is equally fraught with difficulties. He suggests that we distinguish between *state managers* ('directly in control of the bantustan apparatus and . . . benefits directly from the bantustan programme') and the *civil service bourgeoisie*, 'which shares many of the conditions of the working class in its relationship with state and bantustan authorities.' This distinction has a certain appeal inasmuch as it seems to coincide in Transkei with the distinction between TRAPSA (Transkei Public Servants Association) and DUCS (Democratic Union of Civil Servants, now combined with NEHAWU).[17] It is not easy, however, to distinguish any essential difference between higher and lower paid employees as far as their relationship to the state is concerned. The magistrate's clerk who bullies an illiterate in a rural district is just as much of a state functionary as his Director-General in Umtata.

It is evident that the whole debate has become rather messy, and rather than muddy the waters still further, I would like to start again right at the very beginning. Let us agree to start with the fact that there exists in Umtata a social category called an elite. Some members of the elite actually use this English term to describe themselves. Similar connotations are captured in the Xhosa word *amanene* ('gentlemen') and related expressions. This elite includes businessmen, professionals and most civil servants above the rank of clerk. It is differentiated from other social categories not only by the level of its income and the style of its dress, but by the degree of its education and its capacity to converse in English. Rural Transkeians have no better way of expressing the difference between the elite and themselves than the terms *abafundile* ('the educated') and *abangafundanga* ('the uneducated'). Conventional education is, in fact, the most important social marker within Transkei society. Given that 87 per cent of pupils drop out before finishing school and only 2.26 per cent obtain university entrance qualifications, this is hardly surprising.[18]

This elite is not, however, homogeneous. One major distinction is between those who are directly employed by the state, such as the civil servants, and those who are not, such as professionals and businessmen. Although Southall is quite correct to refer to the close financial and personal links which initially bound the state and the business elites, it is worth noting that these links have loosened considerably in recent years and are set to loosen some more.[19] One reason for this is that the stock of former white businesses and properties with which the Matanzimas used to reward their clients has long since run out. Another reason is that, apart from landlordism, business activity is far too strenuous for the average civil servant. Transkei is no longer as protected as it was against competition from white South Africa, and many moonlighters have sold their businesses to others more capable than themselves. Emboland Hotels, a consortium through which many Eastern Transkei chiefs owned hotels, is a case in point. Licences have become more freely available, and it is quite possible for aspirant black businessmen to set themselves up without reference to the state. A survey in Baziya locality, Umtata District, showed, for instance, that of 34 shopkeepers in the area, only four had loans from the Transkei Development Corporation, and only three were members of the Transkei Chamber of Commerce. Eighteen out of the 34 never purchased on credit.[20] It remains true that the interests of many black businessmen are tied to those of the Transkei state, which is able to extend credit and contracts to favoured individuals as well as providing businessmen with cash-flush consumers in the shape of over-abundant and over-paid civil servants.

The civil servants on the state payroll can be divided into three categories: the administrative bureaucracy, the law enforcement agencies including the chiefs, and social service personnel such as teachers, nurses and agricultural extension officers. Of these categories, only the first and the commissioned ranks of the second are inextricably linked to the fortunes of the Bantustan state. The police are something of a special case. During the Matanzima era, they selectively enforced repressive legislation and entered into cosy alliances with local power cliques such as stock thieves. They have much to lose, and therefore constitute an extremely conservative element. But the rank and file of the army and the prison service, together with the social service personnel generally, relate to the state as employees to employers. They play little part in the shaping of state policy. We may therefore confirm and amplify Southall's distinction between 'core elements . . . whose occupational role is premised upon the very existence of the bantustan state' and 'more peripheral' elements who doubt the state's ability 'to provide for their long-term class interests'. In other words, only bureaucrats and senior law enforcement officers including chiefs constitute the Bantustan core. Teachers, health workers, soldiers and, increasingly, businessmen belong on the periphery.[21]

We are now in a position to reconsider the comments I made about the behaviour of the elite in my 1992 article on the 'implosion' of Transkei. My major point was that the Matanzima brothers did not in fact represent the Transkei elite. There was a disjuncture between the homeland leadership and the homeland bourgeoisie and the homeland elite was not necessarily committed to the continued existence of the Bantustan state and its alliance with the Pretoria regime. I also depicted the homeland elite as a link in a clientelist chain starting in Pretoria, and I further indicated that the elite did not much care where the patronage originated provided that it continued to maintain the flow of goodies. But in my eagerness to demonstrate that the aforesaid disjuncture was contingent rather than inevitable, I probably went too far. My comment that the elite was 'well placed' to capture the homeland state was rightly criticised by Southall and Bank.[22] In any case, the passage of time and change of circumstance has subsequently shed additional light on the political orientation and the likely future role of the Transkei elite. It is to this critical issue that we now turn.

When the elite cheered Holomisa's victory over Craig Duli in November 1990, the reincorporation of Transkei was a pleasing but immensely distant prospect. But the closer the prospect came, the less attractive it appeared. Far from looking forward to better (and more challenging) positions in Pretoria, the elite started to betray anxiety about the security of their jobs back home.[23] They suffered a severe setback in November 1993 when the ANC idea of a Greater Eastern Cape Province (including Port Elizabeth) was adopted in place of the Transkei government sponsored plan of a smaller Border/Kei region, which Transkei could easily dominate. ANC local government head, Thozamile Botha, explained on television that 'we do not want a Bantustan by another name'. But that is exactly what the Transkei elite did want. Products of a Bantustan environment, they began to dread its imminent demise. They became even more apprehensive when the Eastern Cape ANC (including its somewhat reluctant Transkei ANC component) proposed that Bisho (in the former Ciskei) rather than Umtata should be the capital of the new province. And this despite the many ingenious arguments put forward by Transkei's business community, such as the fact that Umtata dam was the sixth largest in South Africa! The proposal was roundly condemned by top civil servants, from the General to the Postmaster-General, but their objections were over-ridden and Bisho is now firmly established as the capital of the new province.

Belatedly, the elite and, more especially, the bureaucracy, discovered that they had few friends in positions of influence within the Transkei ANC. This was partly due to the fact that, when the ANC and the PAC were unbanned in Transkei, the government issued a circular forbidding civil servants to take a party political stand. The few civil servants who openly disobeyed were warned off in personal letters. But it also had a lot to do with the fact that the top ranks of both business and the bureaucracy, even in 1994, were the proteges of the Matanzimas and hence the enemies of the ANC. After the fall of the Matanzimas, almost the whole of their faction went into the PAC en bloc, and it is possible to name at least three cabinet ministers and numerous ranking civil servants who were and are, more or less openly, PAC. By contrast, it is possible to name only three senior civil servants who were unequivocally ANC, although these were prominent in the leadership of the Transkei Public Servants' Association.

As it became increasingly clear that the ANC was unstoppable, quite a number of senior bureaucrats tried to jump on the bandwagon, but their efforts cut no ice with the local ANC. In the end, only two additional representatives of the elite (St Ella Sigcawu, the former Prime Minister, and Zam Titus, the government law adviser) made it through to the ANC's inner circle. Ultimately, the overwhelming majority of the elite were neither ANC nor PAC, but were happiest on the fence prepared to sell their allegiance to any future government which was willing to indulge them. Lacking a specific political vehicle to articulate their aspirations, the Transkei elite nevertheless assumed that they would be provided for in the new dispensation. The rude awakening which they experienced in the aftermath of the 1994 elections left them severely disaffected towards the new ANC regime, as the concluding section will show.

Stakeholders II: The Rural Masses

94.06 per cent of the Transkei population, 4 282 241 people altogether, lived in the Transkei rural areas in 1991, compared to the mere 5.9 per cent who lived in the towns.[24] This great mass of the rural population, like the peasants of nineteenth-century France, 'is formed by the simple addition of isomorphous magnitudes, much as potatoes in a sack form a sack of potatoes'.[25] The isomorphous magnitudes of Transkei consist of 1 016 Administrative Areas, often described as 'locations' in colloquial English. Of these 1 016 locations, 566 have been subjected to rehabilitation or 'betterment' schemes, while 450 have not.[26] Of the 28 districts, 21 have been more or less continuously ruled by chiefs since precolonial times, whereas the other seven were more or less held by independent free holders up to the introduction of Bantu Authorities in 1951. There are perceptible local variations in the physical and economic geography of the region but, in spite of these, the underlying similarities created by the under development of Transkei as a labour reservoir and dumping ground justify us in analysing the entire rural area as if it were a single undifferentiated unit.

Even though some 94 per cent of Transkeians live on the land, economists estimate that only 10 per cent of the region's income is produced by subsistence agriculture. Transkei, a predominantly rural region, imports about 70 per cent of its total food needs.[27] Viewed from the angle of the average rural household, this translates into a scenario of nightmare poverty. Numbers of detailed local surveys were undertaken in the 1980s and, despite some variations in quality and focus, a depressingly uniform picture emerges. Over 60 per cent of households cannot provide for their own food needs. In Baziya, for example, only 33.3 per cent of households are self-sufficient in maize and only 47 per cent have maize for more than nine months of the year. In Bizana, a more fertile district, the figure (33 per cent) is exactly the same, and 94 per cent of all households earn less than the estimated Primary Rural Subsistence level. 98 per cent of landholders live on unviable plots.[28] The total number of cattle in Transkei is actually declining and, due to the rapid increase in population (much of it due to forced removals), per capita possession of cattle has dropped quite precipitously – from 1.17 in 1946 to 0.46 in 1985. Between 40 per cent and 54 per cent of all households have no cattle at all. This has not only affected the supply of milk, but it severely constrains the ability of Transkeians to plough their land. Only 27 per cent of households in Bizana had access to a ploughing team, and a mere 2.8 per cent of households had a ploughing team of their own.[29]

Despite the abject poverty and widespread landlessness, which in Bizana district for instance runs at 7.7 per cent with some locations more than 20 per cent, and despite vocal demands by the PAC for the return of *Izwe Lethu!* (Our Land!) from white farmers, there are huge tracts of underutilised land throughout Transkei. In Shixini, Willowvale District, 27 per cent of arable fields were completely unused and another 10 per cent were seldom used. In Baziya, 28 per cent of those owning fields did not work them, and another 17.2 per cent cultivated half or less of their allotments. From Libode, Hendricks reports that only 21 per cent of field holders cultivated their fields despite the fact that 46 per cent of the households in his sample had no access to arable land at all.[30]

The main reason for this vast underutilisation of resources in Transkei has yet to be fully studied, but I would suggest that the main problem is the high cost of inputs relative to the meagre anticipated profits. A prominent lawyer, the son of a Qumbu chief, explained the paradox as follows: 'Let's say you have a thousand Rand. You can take the thousand Rand and put it into your land, and if it rains and all goes well, you can get enough maize to eat for a year. Alternatively you can take your thousand Rand to the shop and, with no risk and no hard work, you can buy enough maize to eat for two years.' This disparity between costs and outputs also featured in the Bizana survey, which showed that high yields of up to 33 bags of maize per hectare were possible, but that the necessary inputs were so costly that capital-intensive farming remained unprofitable. However, part-time farmers cultivating only 3–5 hectares and producing only 2.6 bags per hectare could still make profits of 300–500 per cent due to lower cost inputs.[31] The ambitious TRACOR maize schemes of the early 1980s failed for similar reasons. They produced high yields of maize per hectare, but they did not succeed in covering their costs. Marketing is another huge barrier to commercial agriculture in Transkei. At the moment, there is only one functioning maize silo in the whole region. And a dairy project in Qumbu failed because the milk market in Qumbu town was too small to absorb all the milk; the remainder had to be sold in Umtata at a loss.

There remains a small percentage of rural households, between 6 per cent and 8 per cent, that are distinctly better off than the others. They usually own more than ten cattle, and they regularly produce sufficient to provide a small surplus for sale. This group has awakened the interest of commentators such as Innes and O'Meara, who have seriously suggested that they might form the nucleus of a stable, rich peasantry.[32] William Beinart has pointed out that although this class is quite small in percentage terms, it nevertheless constitutes about 60 000 households altogether, which is a sizable number of potential commercial farmers.[33] Most important, this view is shared by TRACOR, the agricultural parastatal, which differentiates between 'productive farmers', 'marginal farmers' and 'token farmers', who merely scratch at the land to retain their land rights.[34] One of the main thrusts in TRACOR's policy, therefore, is to introduce freehold title in the hope that productive land will pass from the useless token farmers into the hands of productive farmers who will utilise it more effectively. Another suggestion, backed also by McAllister, is that freehold villages should be built in select rural areas so as to absorb rural dwellers whose primary interest in land is social security rather than agriculture.[35]

As Southall and McAllister have both pointed out, the notion of separating potential commercial farmers from the mass of rural incompetents is a goal which has been fruitlessly pursued ever since the time of the Glen Grey Act (1894) and the Tomlinson Commission (1951).[36] Part of the problem is that, in the recent past, substantial farms were allocated to corrupt individuals posing as commercial farmers, including the Matanzimas themselves. These either neglected the farms or leased them back to their former white owners. Another problem is that many of the so-called commercial farmers made more money out of loans and subsidies than out of farming. At this very moment, the secretary of the Consolidated Transkei Farmers' Union is not a professional farmer, but an ex-headmaster employed full-time in the Transkei Archives.

Blatant corruption and misallocation could perhaps be rectified by an honest and efficient government. But there are also important structural reasons which militate against the transformation of the small minority of serious peasants into fully-fledged capitalist farmers. The first is that many of the top 10 per cent seem to be chiefs and headmen, and chiefs and headmen are the last people to interfere with the existing land tenure system. Of the others, many have succeeded because they enjoy access to cash inputs through migrant remittances.[37] Migrant labour is thus more of a sugar daddy than a wicked uncle as far as homeland agriculture is concerned. But as the Bizana survey, which confirms the importance of migrant remittances, goes on to say, less than 10 per cent of migrant remittances goes on agricultural inputs and there is a tendency for this percentage to fall as migrant income rises. There is thus a social ceiling on agricultural investment which is almost certainly due to the fact that migrant workers view their rural dwellings as a social rather than an economic resource.

A great deal more could be written about the various attempts to develop Transkeian agriculture, ranging from giant schemes like the Ncorha irrigation scheme and the Magwa tea plantations to retrenched miners' co-operatives and other NGO projects. The whole of Transkei is littered with the remnants of such schemes, some of which have not actually failed but none of which have totally succeeded.[38] It should be said that parastatals like TRACOR have, to some extent, learned from their mistakes and that, here and there, commercial farming is beginning to make an appearance. Since this is a paper on the political dynamics of Transkei rather than its development problems, it is not necessary to probe more deeply. But enough has been said to indicate that the problem is a complex one, and that the initial draft of the ANC's *Reconstruction and Development Programme* tragically underestimated the scale of the difficulties by reducing them to the (completely incorrect) proposition that 'agriculture in the homelands is starved of resources'.[39] Equally important is that these complexities help to explain why the 94 per cent of the population who live in the rural areas are unlikely to take the political lead, or to play a significant political role.

Not even the chiefs, whom Southall thinks I underestimate.[40] The power of chiefs in Transkei has never remotely approximated that of the Zulu king. Moreover, whereas every chief in KwaZulu is subject to the same Zulu king, there are five different Paramount Chiefs in Transkei, more or less equal in status, together with at least ten other chiefs, lesser in rank but totally independent of any of the Paramount Chiefs. The power which the Transkeian chiefs exercised during the Matanzima period was due not to their traditional status as chiefs, but to the power which they acquired as Matanzima's hangers-on. The chiefs had no legal right to allocate land, for example, but they did so with impunity during Kaiser's time, just as several of them arbitrarily seized the property of their subjects without compensation.

The unbanning of the liberation movements first manifested itself in the rural areas through challenges by the youth to the arbitrary powers of the chiefs. The chiefs reacted by forming the TTLA (Transkei Traditional Leaders Association) which pointedly distanced itself from CONTRALESA, the ANC-aligned chiefs' organisation. The leading light in TTLA was Julius Matutu, a minor chief and former Cabinet Minister, also a leading businessman and mayor of Mqanduli. Matutu had the will and the ability to rally the conservative interest in Transkei, but after his (as yet unsolved) murder in 1992, the chiefs lost their sense of purpose. Their capacity to resist change was further undermined by government circular number 4 of 24 September 1992, which ordered them to allow political organisations to operate freely in their areas of jurisdiction.

The two major chiefly families, the Dalindyebos of Thembuland and the Sigcawus of Eastern Mpondoland, have joined the ANC and appear on the ANC election lists. As far as the other chiefs are concerned, it is *sauve qui peut*. Chief Gwadiso, a close associate of the late Matutu, has organised most of the chiefs of Ngqeleni to join the PAC. Chief Victor Mditshwa, on the other hand, has joined with a radical faction of the ANC in Tsolo district, and headed a march to the local police station to accuse the police of collaboration with stock thieves. Chief Lehana of Mount Fletcher has formed his own vigilante group, the Lekgotla leNtaba (Regiment of the Mountains) to fight stock thieves and preserve the traditional version of Sotho circumcision. Chief Msingapantsi of Umzimkulu joined Inkatha, and was murdered by the youth after he had engineered the assassination of one of their leaders.

In Flagstaff, Comrade Nomazele Bala has challenged the authority of his cousin, Chief Mwelo Nonkonyana, and told the people that they should allocate land and cut wood just as they please. Elsewhere, particularly in Lusikisiki and Willowvale Districts, the right of chiefs to allocate land has also been challenged, and rural civics are in the process of taking over the meetings of the Tribal Authorities. Anti-stock theft movements provide another vehicle for genuine popular sentiment. But, for the most part, as one female development worker in Mount Frere remarked to me, 'People in the rural areas are preoccupied with survival. They have little time for anything else.' And, for the foreseeable future, they will probably continue to take their cue from the 6 per cent of the population who live in the towns.

Stakeholders III: The Urban Workforce

The most important point to make about the urban workforce is that it is extremely small compared to the rural sector. Excluding the departments of education, health and agriculture, the Transkei government employed about 16 000 people in 1990. Another 26 000 were employed in manufacturing industries.[41] There were then about 3 600 industries in Transkei, of which only 75 could be called large industries. The majority (15 000) of these workers were employed in industries set up by the Transkei Development Corporation with the help of generous concessions in respect of credit, transport and tax relief. Another attraction for industrialists was the fact that trade unions were, de facto, banned from Transkei under the provisions of the Labour Relations Act of 1977. Wages were consequently very low – 34c an hour was the minimum wage at the beginning of 1988 – and workers in Transkei earned very much less than relatives doing the same job for the same company in East London.

The shock waves out of South Africa hit Transkei's workers in 1988, spearheaded by the mine workers dismissed in the Gencor strike of 1987.[42] Strikes soon spread to the public sector, notably the Post Office and the notoriously problematic Road Transport Corporation (TRTC). The drive for worker rights gathered pace after King Sabata's reburial in October 1989, culminating in a massive general strike in the main industrial centre of Butterworth. Holomisa's government appointed Professor Nic Wiehahn to make recommendations on a new labour dispensation. These recommendations were embodied in the Labour Relations Decree of 1990 which brought Transkei labour legislation into line with South Africa.

The high point of worker power in Transkei was the mass action of April 1990, during which striking workers, organised by the Workers' Co-ordinating Committee, brought the whole of Umtata to a standstill. But it was a Pyrrhic victory, and one which demonstrated the latent contradiction between Transkeian workers and Transkeian businessmen. For the strikers, in quest of solidarity, had gone from shop to shop 'persuading' workers to join the strike. This was more than TRACOC could bear, inasmuch as the capitalist exploiters in question were not the bloated white plutocrats of Johannesburg but their own gallant selves. Similar conflicts between black shopkeepers and their miserably paid employees also erupted in the district towns, notably Idutywa and Lusikisiki.

General Holomisa did not like it either. He was already secretly committed to the liberation struggle, and this was a blow to black unity. Moreover he, together with many other well-informed persons, was deeply suspicious of worker leader Oupa Khumalo whom he regarded as an agent provocateur. COSATU leaders from Johannesburg visited Holomisa, and shortly thereafter Khumalo departed on permanent 'study leave'. COSATU unions replaced the Workers' Co-ordinating Committee. This incident is worth pondering, and not only because it was significant at the time. The workers' leadership in Transkei has been notably reluctant to shatter black unity by attacking exploiters who happen to be black. I remember attending two ANC workshops where this issue was raised, one in Engcobo and one in Idutywa. Comrades debated the meaning of the term *ngxowenkhulu* ('big-bag', i.e. a capitalist). The consensus in both towns was that the term should only be used to describe very rich people such as Harry Oppenheimer. Homegrown businessmen were part of the people, and needed to be educated rather than destroyed.

No such restraint, however, was evident in the confrontations between the public sector unions and the state sector. Bitter strikes broke out at schools, hospitals, the TRTC, the Transkei Broadcasting Corporation, the Transkei Agricultural Corporation and the Transkei Alternative Technology Unit. In TRACOR, for example, the workers were led by TRACOR accountant, FAWU office bearer and sometime ANC executive member Noni Maqhutyana. The Managing Director of TRACOR and some of the other top managers were forced to leave. But the bureaucrats were not without the will to fight back. In December 1992, Noni Maqhutyana was gunned down while leaving a social occasion. Nor is this a unique event. The security guards at TRTC carry automatic weapons which they have not been reluctant to use on over-zealous officials. Other employees of the agriculture department have also perished in mysterious circumstances. Commissions of enquiries into parastatals are curiously prolonged. The enquiry into the Transkei Development Corporation, for instance, which was set up in 1992 has still not generated any substantive actions.

Another brake on worker militancy is the shrinking industrial base. Employers openly admitted to Professor Wiehahn that they had been attracted to Transkei by cheap labour, no trade unions and generous concessions. Having lost the first two by the events already described, the industrialists stood to lose the third as well due to the 1991 decision of the Government to phase out the Regional Industrial Development Programme over a period of seven years.[43] Manufacturing employment in Butterworth has declined from 6 849 in 1985 to 5 076 at present, which might seem insignificant unless one realises that this represents about 10 per cent of the economically active population of the district.[44] Meanwhile, living conditions in Butterworth continue to deteriorate as a result of mass unemployment leading to anti-social behaviour such as the destruction of the town's sewage plant in a civic-related mass action of 1993.

The Achilles heel of Transkei manufacturing has always been that it was artificially attracted to Transkei, and that it developed few linkages within Transkei itself. It is difficult to see how this situation is going to change, and even with massive assistance from an ANC government, it is likely to get worse before it gets better.

THE PARITY CRISIS AND THE ARMY MUTINY OF SEPTEMBER 1992: A CAUTIONARY TALE

We have looked at the various components of Transkei society, but we have not yet considered any specific incident which might illustrate how the tensions inherent in such an internally differentiated society might translate into political action. Fortunately, an example is at hand in the shape of the parity crisis and the army mutiny of September 1992, certainly the biggest crisis faced by the Holomisa government since the Duli coup of November 1990, and one which reveals the most vulnerable aspects of the homeland structures as they reluctantly advanced towards reincorporation.[45]

The trouble began in August 1992 when the Transkei government distributed a circular giving precise details of the new salary scales which would become applicable in the name of 'parity'. 'Parity' between South African and Transkeian salaries had been agreed on by the joint Transkei–South African working committee on 'structural adjustment'. This was a broader programme. It was designed to harmonise South African and Transkeian salary and tax structures prior to reincorporation. The essence of parity was theoretically very simple. Transkeians who were earning less than their South African counterparts would get their salaries increased to the equivalent level. But Transkeians who were already earning the same as South Africans would get nothing at all.

The problem arose because top-ranking Transkeians got enormous increases whereas lower-ranking Transkeians got nothing or very little. To make matters worse, the Transkei government did not circulate the original South African document, which was incredibly bulky, but thoughtfully provided a shorter summary. This aroused suspicions that the top officials had adjusted the salary scales for their own benefit. The military government, including General Holomisa himself, totally underestimated the seriousness of the situation. They had understood extremely well that parity did not necessarily imply an increase for everybody. They had made provision for civil servants to appeal against their salary adjustments if they could prove that they were earning less than South Africans. But the Transkei government had reckoned without the almost irrational passion which the prospect of increased salaries had generated among state employees.

Pay parity discontent among the lower ranks of the Transkei Defence Force (TDF) was augmented by suspicion of their commanding officers. Several of these officers, notably Military Intelligence head Colonel W. Ndzwayiba, had been in close contact with the late Colonel Duli but had bailed out of his ill-fated coup. The same officers were extremely hostile to the ANC's mass action campaign of July/August 1992. This was a national campaign, but in Transkei it had included the closure of shops, the barricading of streets and, in Qumbu, the burning of the Transkei flag.[46] Some of the officers had been stopped at the barricades and disrespectfully treated. They confronted Holomisa about this and, according to some rumours, even demanded his resignation. Other rumours alleged that they had hatched a plot to assassinate him when he visited Butterworth. To make matters worse, some of these self-same officers had awarded themselves extra pay during the 1989 salary adjustments.

On 1 September 1992, rank and file soldiers of the TDF surrounded the big government building in Umtata town and arrested a number of officers found inside. They took them to Ncise military base and held them captive until they had collected every one of the 27 officers of the rank of colonel and above. Eventually, the Transkei government was forced to bow to the mutineers' demands and restructure the high command of the TDF. Brigadier T.T. Matanzima, the Acting Commander, was sent on study leave abroad, and three of the most unpopular officers were transferred to civilian posts – as Cabinet Ministers! The soldiers were quietly given a pay increase, and, when the police complained, they got a salary increase as well. Such promotions help us understand the fact that when the TDF was finally integrated into the South African National Defence Force, it contained more than 3 000 officers but not a single private.[47]

The 'parity' dispute rumbled on and on. Despite the fact that the Transkei government spent R489 million on parity, rather than the R178 million actually allocated by South Africa,[48] the Departments of Health, Justice and Education were never accommodated. The teachers, organised under the banner of SADTU (South African Democratic Teachers Union), continued to strike, however. They alleged that a sum of R22 million, given by South Africa for parity, had disappeared. They further objected to the PAC-leaning Minister of Education, S.P. Kakudi. Kakudi's persistence in office came to symbolise the lack of consultation and transparency in the Transkei government, and, ultimately Kakudi's removal became the focal point of the teachers' mass action. The teachers struck for most of 1993, and they sat in the Education Department building until they were forcibly ejected with tear gas and gratuitous brutality by the Transkei police (June 1993). Teachers did not have the same political clout in Transkei as soldiers, policemen or civil servants, and they returned unhappily to work in 1994.

The pay parity and army mutiny crises show that the biggest threat to the homeland state came not from any element of civil society but from within the state itself. Although the civil service was absurdly small as a percentage of the total population, it possessed the capacity to bring the state almost to its knees. The fall of Bophuthatswana and the chaos in Lebowa also shed light on the vulnerability of the homeland state to a mobilised civil service, especially one whose rapacity is inflamed by the imminent prospect of more money.

The Players I: The Transkei Military Government

The Military Government governed Transkei for more than six years, during which time it demolished much of Matanzimaism but left a lot still standing. At no time did it make any attempt to perpetuate itself, or to create a surrogate party which might represent or defend its interests. The problems which the new Eastern Cape Provincial Government has encountered in Transkei are its inheritance from the Military Government, and it is therefore essential to understand the nature of that inheritance.

In the first place it is essential to note that, despite widespread external perceptions, the Military Government was not an ANC government. Apart from one man, General Holomisa, it was not even a progressive government. It was Holomisa's head on Matanzima's body. The overwhelming majority of the Cabinet and the Directors-General were Matanzima appointees, who filled vacancies in their ranks through personal contacts within the narrow social boundaries of the elite. It would not be going too far too assert that they constituted a self-perpetuating bureaucratic oligarchy, accountable to nobody but themselves. As an oligarchy, they were hostile not so much to the ANC as a national political organisation but to the social forces represented by the Transkei ANC: the youth, the civics, the teachers' organisations. Hostility between this oligarchy and the Transkei ANC was mostly latent, though occasionally it did flare up in such cases as the mass action campaign of August 1992. The oligarchy stood firmly by its prerogatives, and it passively resisted ANC initiatives – with regard to the allocation of sites to squatters, for example – in the name of bureaucratic normality.

General Holomisa did not, for the most part, interfere with the operations of the Cabinet and Directors-General. Although admirably equipped as a mediator, in terms of both his personal ability and his political prestige, he tended to refer domestic problems back to the standing bureaucracy rather than to try and solve them himself. He was very careful, domestically, to avoid taking sides with either the ANC or the PAC. He appeared impartially at the rallies of both, but never gave any salute, and he even declined to take public part in the singing of the anthem, *Nkosi Sikelel' iAfrika*. He had close personal links with Nelson Mandela and Chris Hani, but these links did not extend to the Transkei ANC as such. In his external policy, his deep suspicion of South African securocrats and his scepticism of the negotiations process led him to take something of a PAC line, for example his refusal to recognise the National Peace Accord and his hard line on APLA bases in Transkei. His upbringing as a chief and a military man, together with his own decisive personality, led him to a certain impatience with the ANC's tedious processes of consultation and accountability.

On the other hand, it is impossible to over-estimate Holomisa's contribution towards the political liberation of Transkei, even excluding discussion of his achievements at the national level. He effectively unbanned the ANC and the PAC before they were unbanned in South Africa. He authorised them to operate in every corner of the homeland, whether the chiefs wanted them there or not. He refrained from starting his own party, or any party representing the local elite which might have tended to parochialise Transkeian politics. More broadly, he ended the flagrant abuse of state power for personal profit which was so prevalent during the Matanzima era, and he brought labour legislation into line with national legislation so that the Transkeian worker is no longer the most exploited in the whole country.

Unfortunately, this extension of freedom was not without its negative consequences. The Transkei state became infinitely weaker than it had been in Matanzima's time, and this led to a decline in the level of security of persons and property. As ex-Minister K. remarked at the 1991 funeral of ex-Minister Matutu, shot dead in his own backyard: 'They say we stole money. Well, maybe we did. But at least people could sleep peacefully at night.' Many people in Transkei, especially General Holomisa, point to South African destabilisation to help explain the spate of car hi-jackings and outright murders which have given Transkei a very bad name in South Africa generally. There may be something in this, and it is also true that the violence on the Rand and Natal has spilled over into Transkei. But it is also true that the Transkei police are severely demoralised. Not only are they ineffective, but they are themselves occasional participants in criminal activities.[49] Up and down Transkei, in towns like Qumbu, Flagstaff, Tabankulu and Mqanduli, competing local power cliques of businessmen, civics, stock thieves, police, teachers and others battle it out for local domination. Long before the upheavals which followed the 1994 election, the forces of 'civil society' had the Transkei state on the run. It remains to be seen whether the new Eastern Cape government will fare any better.

The Players II: The African National Congress

The Transkei Region of the African National Congress is a vast organisation consisting of more than 350 branches and over 100 000 paid-up members. It has branches in every district of Transkei, though some districts are weaker than others. Many branches are dead, and others are only sporadically alive. The election campaign gave the branches a shot in the arm, but since the election they have been going down again.

The demands of modern politics, and the tedious delays and technicalities associated with the negotiations process drained most of the spontaneity and enthusiasm out of the local ANC branches at a relatively early stage. Pressure from the National Office to support Holomisa and the Transkei government, and to lay off the chiefs and other local oppressors, severely restricted the Transkei ANC's scope to wage meaningful local campaigns. These constraints seriously undermined any potential rural militancy, and delivered the local branches into the hands of literate people who could speak English, keep minutes of meetings, issue membership cards and drive to Umtata to attend workshops and regional conferences. The Transkei ANC is not a populist organisation.

ANC office-bearers in Transkei tend to be teachers, lawyers and shopkeepers, petty and fringe-bourgeois rather than elite insiders or grass-root peasants. An analysis of the occupations of the 1994 ANC Transkei Regional Executive yields the following results: political veterans 7; education 6; commercial 3; professionals 3; chiefs 1; unknown 2. The Transkei ANC is thus distinct from, and critical of, the ruling elite. Moreover, many of the political veterans are either former Umkhonto we Sizwe cadres or else former workers retired to their rural homes. These do constitute a link between the organisation and the grass-roots, although it has to be admitted that the grass-roots operate at one remove from the decision-making process.

The SACP and COSATU are also active in Transkei. The SACP is small but remains influential on account of the high calibre of its members, many of whom are political veterans or trade union officials. SACP opinions are openly put forward at meetings of the Tripartite Alliance; there is no question of a secret Party infiltration of the ANC. COSATU is inevitably weak in Transkei because of Transkei's scanty industrial base. There are active COSATU locals in Butterworth, Umtata and Kokstad, but there is no COSATU structure which is Transkei-wide as such.

The Players III: SANCO

SANCO (the South African Civic Organisation) took root in Transkei much later than any of the Tripartite Alliance structures, but its growth has been spectacularly rapid. This is due to two factors. First, SANCO addressed concrete and comprehensible local issues such as low-income housing, allocation of sites and the corruption and incompetence of the established town councils. Second, SANCO has succeeded in attracting genuine mass popular participation through an uninhibited programme of direct action. The youth has also played an active role in the seizure and allocation of land.[50] SANCO strikes and sit-ins spread like wildfire in the wake of the August 1992 mass action. Mount Ayliff, Tabankulu, Ngqeleni, Cala, Lusikisiki, Mount Frere, Ezibeleni, Mqanduli, Port St Johns, Qumbu and, especially, Butterworth were all affected, and in the end the Transkei government had to threaten overt military action to get the protestors to vacate the various municipal offices.[51] In November 1993, SANCO again embarked on a rolling mass action to force the government to meet its demands. Among its successes was the resignation of the Mayor of Idutywa, after SANCO had dumped dead dogs and piles of rubbish in his yard.[52] 1994 was relatively quiet due to the national elections and the formation of Transitional Local Councils, but the advent of local government elections scheduled for October 1995 will inevitably lead to an increase in tensions.

The Butterworth case is the most instructive. Butterworth is Transkei's second largest town, and it is here that the civic struggle has been longest and most bitter. SANCO was launched in Butterworth in 1991 by a group that had been ousted from the local ANC branches. It organised a gigantic disruption at the time of the August 1992 mass action, barricading the national road with wrecked cars and burning tyres. Its list of demands included the removal of the existing undemocratic municipality, and fixed rents and services at low rates. The municipal councillors were forced to resign, and a senior civil servant was sent from Umtata to run the town until an alternative structure could be installed. By June 1993, after more than nine months of a rent and services boycott, agreement seemed to be at hand. Rents would be cut by 50 per cent, arrears would be written off, and new councillors would be nominated by concerned structures.[53] But SANCO dragged its feet over participation, and put forward fresh demands. Mass action was stepped up, and it was back to the old cycle of rent boycotts, water cut-offs, burning barricades and sewerage sabotage.[54] The advent of the Local Government Consultative Forum seemed to improve relationships for a while, but, in April 1994, conflict flared again after the Town Clerk bought himself and several councillors new motor vehicles out of funds earmarked for urban development.

The Players IV: The Pan-African Congress

The PAC is the only other political party in Transkei besides the ANC. Its members are a motley crew, consisting of three disparate elements. First, there are its traditional supporters who joined the organisation in 1960. They are thickest on the ground in southern Transkei, where the migrant labourers go to Cape Town rather than the Rand or Natal. Second, there is the old Matanzima faction among the chiefs and the civil service. They feel that the PAC is the party of the *amanene* (gentlemen) while the ANC is the party of the rural illiterates and the disrespectful youth. Third, there are radical and intellectual elements, attracted by the PAC's Africanist ideology and slogans like 'one settler, one bullet' and 'APLA sticks to guns'.

I am not in possession of reliable information concerning the internal organisation of the PAC. They have fewer members than the ANC, and maintain fewer branches and organisational structures. But they make up for their limitations by the superior commitment of their members and by their capacity to activate their membership for decisive and headline-grabbing action. For example, when they decided they were not getting sufficient favourable coverage in the local newspaper, the *Daily Dispatch*, they occupied the newspaper's offices, hi-jacked its delivery vans, terrified its distribution network, and ultimately forced the newspaper to come to an agreement. Similar campaigns were waged against Radio Transkei and the *Sunday Times*.[55] Another campaign took place around the SADTU strike of 1993. PATO (the Pan African Teachers Organisation) opposed the strike, and its Butterworth branch occupied the Butterworth campus of the University of Transkei, claiming that SADTU teachers were neglecting African pupils and devoting their time to improving their own qualifications. Since the PAC suspended its armed struggle in January 1994, much to the disgust of many of its Transkei supporters, it has been in some disarray.[56]

Little publicised fighting occurred between the PAC and the ANC at Cofimvaba, Cala, Kentani and Ngqeleni. The PAC in Mqanduli (basically, the old Matutu faction) accused the ANC of co-operating in the SADF Umtata raid, in which five PAC youth were killed. The most serious incidents occurred in Port St Johns where a PAC principal, opposed to the SADTU strike, was killed (October 1993). G. Mposelwa, a local PAC activist, built up a force of self-styled APLA from all over the region and beyond. This force was involved in a series of retaliatory raids on local ANC supporters and, surprisingly, fired on Transkei security forces more than once. Mposelwa was eventually killed at a TDF roadblock in March 1994. Another PAC unit, which had previously attacked white civilians in Transkei, attacked Willowvale police station at about the same time. It is not yet possible to clarify the exact causes of these incidents, but they seem to derive from the wish of certain PAC members to continue the 'armed struggle' against any available target.[57]

While all of these activities demonstrated that the PAC had an active presence in Transkei, they did not amount to a programme of action, much less a programme of government. Towards the end of the election campaign, the PAC took advantage of the ANC's support for a Greater Eastern Cape Region, with a capital tentatively in King William's Town, to suggest a smaller Border/Kei Region with its capital in Umtata.[58] This option was undoubtedly more popular with the Transkei elite. They also nominated Mr T.T. Letlaka, formerly a Matanzima Cabinet Minister but latterly very quiescent, as their Premier-designate for the Eastern Cape.

These opportunistic moves did not help the PAC even in the short run, and they lost members left and right. Hard liners were suspended for opposing the national leadership, after which supporters of the national leadership quit politics for fear of the hard liners. Predictably, the April election was a disaster for the PAC in Transkei as well as everywhere else. Nowhere did they get as much as 10 per cent of the vote, not even in their supposed stronghold of Cala. The ANC, on the other hand, ran up percentages of 95 per cent or so in almost every district, crowned by a towering 99 per cent in Bizana, home of the 1960 Mpondo revolt. The result for Nqamakwe district may be taken as typical: out of 30 701 valid votes cast, the ANC received 29 007 (96.7 per cent), the PAC 776, the National Party 80, the Democratic Party 32, while Inkatha on 6 votes trailed both the Kiss and the Soccer parties. Although the PAC remains the only party in Transkei capable of challenging the ANC, it clearly lacks the capability to take advantage of this.

CONCLUSION

The twilight days of 'independent' Transkei were marked by a crescendo of salary demands and wildcat strikes. Top of the range bureaucrats awarded themselves salary increases of 18–20 per cent, while parastatal managers acquired state assets under the cloak of 'black economic empowerment', and armchair farmers applied for legal title to state-owned farms. Secret memoranda poured in to the Military Council, which showed every disposition to grant final favours to old buddies.[59] As late as 29 April, after the election, the Public Service Commission pushed through a 'new promotion policy' although it admitted quite openly that 'the expenditure involved could not be computed'.[60]

Honest officials who tried to stand out against the tide were simply washed away. The Acting Commissioner of Police refused to ratify illegal promotions, and was brought at gunpoint to General Holomisa who ordered him to acquiesce. The Chief Director of the Treasury similarly refused to approve the new promotions policy. He was attacked at home and beaten up so badly that, while he was still hospitalised, his demoralised colleagues caved in. Government cars were misappropriated on a massive scale, and government services virtually broke down as civil servants sat idly in their offices, declining to work and referring even the most routine task to the new government in Bisho. Attempts by Eastern Cape Premier Raymond Mhlaba to impose discipline were met by public jeers and passive resistance.[61] Senior civil servants were in the forefront of a 'Mhlaba must go' campaign, which attempted to paint the veteran leader as old and out of touch. Mhlaba's real crime was not his ineptitude, but his willingness to stand up to Transkei's rampant bureaucracy.

Transkei, on the eve of emancipation, was a deeply divided society, and nobody should be surprised that its reintegration into South Africa was attended by seriously negative manifestations. General Holomisa showed himself to be quite aware of the contradictions in a frank valedictory interview, published on the day of the flag-lowering ceremony.

> We helped the people in trying to bring the two worlds together: that of the privileged and [that of] the people who suffered all the time. We brought together the activists . . . and the beneficiaries of independence to share the facilities [of Transkei] . . . We gave back to Transkei recognition and respect . . . I am proud Transkei has played a meaningful role in the march towards a united, democratic, non-racial and non-sexist South Africa.[62]

Nobody should begrudge the General a single word of this modest self-assessment. His achievement was indeed an extraordinary one, especially inasmuch as he operated almost entirely alone during the darkest days of P.W. Botha's National Security Management System. But as this is a chapter which is primarily concerned with the deeper structures of Transkeian society, it is legitimate to ask whether Holomisa did indeed succeed in harmonising the two worlds of the privileged and the sufferers. He himself offers us a clue in another remark during the same interview:

> You cannot blame the Military Council for the anxiety among civil servants. We cannot promise them anything as a Military Government because we will not be there after April 27. This is not a merger of governments and I don't know in what way we could have secured their future. The Military Government, in other words, was nothing more than a temporary expedient whose time eventually expired. Problems were not solved, but merely bequeathed to the new Eastern Cape government. Is there any possibility that the Eastern Cape will succeed where the Transkei Military Government failed?

Premier Mhlaba's government was assaulted almost in its very cradle by the three leading servants of the Bantustan state: the civil servants, the police and the chiefs. The battle still rages, but at the time of writing the infant, though still sickly, looks set to survive. The problem of the civil servants became subsumed in the wider problem of the integration of the three former administrations of Transkei, Ciskei and Cape Provincial. Programmes were drawn up, posts were advertised, appointments were made, and a single, clear chain of command has been established.[63] By September 1994, new financial controls had been set in place including, *inter alia*, the removal to Bisho of all government chequebooks and associated equipment.[64] Parity has taken on a new meaning, as inflated Transkei salaries are cut to normal South African levels, and inflated service benefits such as housing subsidies are due to be cut in April 1995. TRAPSA, the civil servants association, fought back as best it could, through court interdicts, newspaper advertisements and appeals to the National Minister. But they have failed. No longer in charge, they are the prisoners of the very purse-strings which they once controlled. All they have to look forward to is the recently-appointed Browde Commission of Enquiry into the misdemeanours of April/May 1994.

The Transkei Police were disaffected even during the regime of the Military Council. It will be recalled that they seized the opportunity of the government breakdown of April/May 1994 to promote themselves and to increase their pay. Two hundred and fifty-five of these 'promotions' were subsequently declared invalid, but the police continued to insist. A police strike, accompanied by violence, erupted in June 1994 and was only called off after the intervention of National Minister Mafumadi.[65] He appointed a task team to look at police grievances, but while it did its work, the balance of forces slowly turned against the Transkei Police. A Provincial Commission of Enquiry exposed many malpractices, including collusion with stock thieves and motor hi-jackers. Units of the South African Internal Stability Division were deployed in Umtata and Butterworth, protecting government property and conducting sensitive operations such as the recovery of stolen minibuses. As the investigation proceeded the Deputy Chief Commissioner of the Transkei Police, General W. Mbulawa, was gunned down in an Umtata street, presumably by his fellow-policemen.[66] Finally, in February 1995, the Transkei Police blockaded all roads leading into Umtata. They promised 'civil war' if the Internal Stability Unit was called in, but they crumbled very quickly as soon as they were attacked by the South African National Defence Force.[67] A similar army mutiny, on a much smaller scale, was put down in June 1994.

The chiefs' resistance to the new order, though relatively low profile, has been long sustained. TTLA, the more conservative of the two chiefs' organisations, eventually joined forces with CONTRALESA, thus allowing the chiefs to present a united front. The chiefs fear that their powers, already threatened by SANCO, will evaporate after the local government elections. These fears are enhanced by the fact that they do not trust Max Mamase, a former SANCO leader who is now the Eastern Cape MEC for Local Government. The chiefs are therefore opposing all measures of the Eastern Cape government which directly concern them. They boycotted the Provincial Government's public hearings on a House of Traditional Leaders for the Eastern Cape Legislature.[68] They are attempting to block registration for the local government elections, and Chief K.D. Matanzima, still active in his home district of Cofimvaba, has warned his followers that the elections will mean the end of headmanship. The chiefs' trump card is their direct access to President Mandela, himself a Transkei chief.[69] But the chiefs are unlikely to succeed in the long run. The local government elections will go ahead without them, just as the Provincial House of Traditional Leaders went ahead, and they will have to abide by the results.

That the Eastern Cape government is weak, nobody can deny. But at least it deserves credit for a clear and consistent line of policy with regard to dismantling not only the formal structures of the Bantustans, but their informal social and political support systems as well. Plans are afoot to divide the new Province into sub-regions. Already, the local government elections in Butterworth will be run from East London, and the local government elections in Engcobo will be run from Queenstown. The Transkei Region of the ANC has been divided into five autonomous regions which will report not to Umtata, but to King William's Town. Everything points to the eventual break-up of the old Transkei and the end of a distinctly Transkeian political consciousness.

It remains to be seen whether the poison of Bantustan practices will eventually infect the new Provincial government. For the time being, the tension between the old and the new is keeping the Eastern Cape government firmly on the track of financially disciplined and clean administration. Even if the Eastern Cape fails in the long run, the mere fact that it is currently confronting the forces of reaction is a clear sign that it is something more than a Bantustan by another name.

NOTES

1. *Daily Dispatch*, 15 April 1994.
2. Harold Wolpe, 'Capitalism and Cheap Labour Power in South Africa: From Segregation to Apartheid', reprinted in H. Wolpe (ed.), *The Articulation of Modes of Production* (London: Routledge & Kegan Paul, 1980), p. 298.
3. F.T. Hendricks, *The Pillars of Apartheid: Land Tenure, Rural Planning and the Chieftaincy* (Uppsala: Acta Universitatis Upsaliensis, 1990), Chapter 6.
4. *Ibid.*, p. 145.
5. S.A. Mpambani, 'Transkei Regional Profile', *Project for Statistics on Living Standards and Development* (Cape Town: SALDRU, 1993), pp. 19, 22.
6. J.B. Peires, 'The Implosion of Transkei and Ciskei', *African Affairs*, 91 (1992), pp. 383–7.
7. Mpambani, *op. cit.*, pp. 29, 54. A. Donaldson, 'Dependent Transkei: the Economics of a Labour Reserve and a Caretaker Regime', *JCAS*, XI (1992), gives an even higher figure of 78.5 per cent of Transkei's revenue coming from South Africa.

8. Donaldson, *op. cit.*, p. 137; *Daily Dispatch*, 7 October 1993.

9. Personal communication from L. Holbrook, Director of the Transkei Chamber of Industries, 25 March 1994; E. Nel and J. Temple, 'Industrial Development and Decentralisation in Transkei and the Border Region', *JCAS*, X1 (1992), 165.

10. Donaldson, *op. cit.*, pp. 130–1.

11. Holbrook, *op. cit.*

12. Peires, *op. cit.*

13. See for example J. Forrest, 'The Contemporary African State: A "Ruling Class"?' *Review of African Political Economy*, 38 (1987).

14. N. Poulantzas, *Political Power and Social Classes* (London: New Left Books, 1973), pp. 84, 334; Roger Southall, 'The Beneficiaries of Transkei "Independence"', *Journal of Modern African Studies*, XV (1977).

15. Peires, *op. cit.*

16. Southall, *op. cit.*

17. TRAPSA was set up by the Transkei government to look after the interests of civil servants. It is theoretically non-partisan. DUCS was set up by COSATU activists, and consequently concentrated on clerks and unskilled workers. There was some overlap of membership between TRAPSA and DUCS. DUCS joined up with NEHAWU in 1993.

18. S.M. Matoti, 'The State of Education in Transkei – 1990', paper presented to the University of Transkei Senate (21 August 1992).

19. Roger Southall, 'Introduction: Rethinking Transkei Politics', *Journal of Contemporary African Studies*, XI (1992), 11.

20. VARA, *Baziya Survey*, vol. 1 (Umtata: 1988), pp. 11–12.

21. Southall, 'The Beneficiaries of Transkei Independence', p. 185. D. Innes and D. O'Meara, 'Class Formation and Ideology: The Transkei Region', *Review of African Political Economy*, VII (1976), 78–80 also differentiate between the 'collaborationist' bourgeoisie and other elements of the petty bourgeoisie who cannot be accommodated in the Bantustan state. But they see this primarily as a problem of numbers; Transkei's productive forces are too underdeveloped to finance the whole of the Petty bourgeoisie.

22. Southall, 'Introduction: Rethinking Transkei Politics'; L. Bank, 'Squatting and the Politics of Urban Restructuring: the Case of Cala', *Journal of Contemporary African Studies*, XI (1992).

23. *Daily Dispatch*, 18 December 1993.

24. Mpambani, *op. cit.*, pp. 20–2.

25. A. Marx, *Lessons of Struggle: South African Internal Opposition, 1960–1990* (New York: OUP, 1992), p. 239.

26. P. McAllister, 'Rural Production, Land Use and Development Planning in Transkei: a Critique of Transkei Agricultural Development Study', *Journal of Contemporary African Studies*, XI (1992), 217–18.

27. Donaldson, *op. cit.*, 131; William Beinart, 'Transkei Smallholders and Agrarian Reform', *Journal of Contemporary African Studies*, XI (1992), 187.

28. Southall, 'Introduction: Rethinking Transkei Politics', p. 221; VARA, *Baziya Survey*, vol. II (1988), p. 29: Baseline Survey No. 1 of Isikelo/Ntshamate/Esikhumbeni Administrative Areas of Bizana District . . . for the Farmer Support Programme of the Transkei Agricultural Corporation' (Umtata:

BDRT Research Report No. 5, October 1987), pp. 13, 37, 67 (hereafter known as 'Bizana').

29. Beinart, *op. cit.*, 180–1; Bizana, *op. cit.*, p. 45.
30. Bizana, *op. cit.*, p. 37; P. McAllister, 'Proposal for a Development Plan for Shixini Administratve Area, Willowvale District', unpublished paper, Rhodes University (1989), p. 24; VARA, *op. cit.*, vol. II, pp. 23 ff; Hendricks, *op. cit.*, p. 86.
31. Bizana, *op. cit.*, pp. 13, 23; D. Cooper, 'Agriculture in the Bantustans: Towards Development Policies' in M. De Klerk (ed.), *A Harvest of Discontent: the Land Question in South Africa* (Cape Town: IDASA, 1991), p. 250.
32. Innes and O'Meara, *op. cit.*, 76–8.
33. Beinart *op. cit.*, 188–94.
34. TRACOR (Transkei Corporation), *Report*, 1990 pp. 104–7.
35. McAllister, 'Proposal for a Development Plan'.
36. R. Southall, *South Africa's Transkei: the Political Economy of an Independent Bantustan* (London: Heineman, 1982), pp. 223–5; McAllister, 'Rural Production, Land Use and Development Planning in Transkei'.
37. Beinart, *op. cit.*, 184.
38. Cooper, *op. cit.*
39. African National Congress, *Reconstruction and Development Programme* (6th draft) (Johannesburg: ANC, 1994).
40. Southall, 'Introduction: Rethinking Transkei Politics', p. 16.
41. Republic of Transkei, *Statistical Bulletin* (Umtata: Central Statistical Office, 1992), p. 15; N. Wiehahn, *Report of the Commission of Inquiry into Labour Matters in Transkei* (Umtata: 1990), Chapter I; Southall, *South Africa's Transkei*, pp. 230–40.
42. R. Roux, 'Workers Rock the Transkei', *South African Labour Bulletin*, XIV (1990).
43. E. Nel and J. Temple, 'Industrial Development and Decentralisation in Transkei and the Border Region', *Journal of Contemporary African Studies*, XI (1992), 169–70.
44. Holbrook, *op. cit.*
45. The events discussed below were covered in the *Daily Dispatch*, especially the issues of 22, 26 August, 2, 3 September, 16, 22, 31 October, as well as the *Weekly Mail* and the alternative press generally. My own version, which is based on discussions with many of the participants, differs in important respects.
46. *Daily Dispatch*, 23 July and 6 August 1992.
47. *The Argus*, 3 September 1994.
48. *Second Interim Report on Investigation of Bank Overdraft*, Transkei, 24 August 1994.
49. J.B. Peires, 'Unsocial Bandits: the Stock Thieves of Qumbu and Their Enemies', History Workshop Paper, University of the Witwatesrand, 1994.
50. L. Bank, 'Squatting and the Politics of Urban Reconstruction in Transkei: The Case of Cala', *Journal of Contemporary African Studies*, XI (1992).
51. *Daily Dispatch*, 7 and 8 October 1992.
52. *Daily Dispatch*, 3 and 12 November 1993.
53. *Daily Dispatch*, 7 and 27 August 1992; 11 June 1993.
54. *Daily Dispatch*, 23 July, 6 August, 3 and 12 November 1993.

55. *Daily Dispatch*, 29 January, 2 February and 30 March 1993.
56. *Daily Dispatch*, 22 and 29 January 1994.
57. *Daily Dispatch*, 29 and 30 March 1994.
58. *Daily Dispatch*, 9 March 1994.
59. *Daily Dispatch*, 31 March, 8 April 1994; secret memo in author's possession, 11 February 1994.
60. *Interim Report Concerning Cashflow Problems obtaining to Transkei Administration*, 16 August 1994.
61. *Daily Dispatch*, 19 May 1994.
62. *Daily Dispatch*, 14 April 1994.
63. *Daily Dispatch*, 21 February 1995.
64. *Kei Mercury*, 24 November 1994.
65. *Daily Dispatch*, 10 June and 8 July 1994.
66. *Daily Dispatch*, 18 January 1995.
67. *Daily Dispatch*, 25 and 27 February 1995.
68. *Daily Dispatch*, 20 January 1995.
69. *Daily Dispatch*, 8 February 1995.

10 South Africa's Foreign Policy: Current Realities, Future Options

Jack Spence

Under the apartheid regime South African foreign policy was severely constrained by the well nigh universal hostility which the country's racial policies generated abroad. Unable to play a role in major international organisations ranging from the Olympic Committee to the Organisation of African Unity, the government for much of the post-war period was forced into a defensive mode seeking allies where it could. This had varying degrees of success even when it tried to make itself indispensable to the West in economic and strategic terms.

The domestic roots of South Africa's foreign policy in the first 30 years of National Party rule have been examined in depth elsewhere, but it is worth remarking that it was in the 1980s that the burden of external pressure (by the 'creeping' sanctions imposed by a variety of governments and international organisations) combined with a growing internal opposition became too great to bear. The result was a dawning recognition that the price of external rehabilitation – especially with respect to a profoundly depressed economy – was major political reform at home. Paradoxically, F.W. De Klerk's decision to initiate change (the substance of his speech on 2 February 1990) was helped by the fortuitous coincidence of a more favourable external climate and in particular the collapse of the Soviet Union. Henceforth, the latter could no longer be regarded as a significant threat to the Republic; the traditional prescription of a 'total strategy' to counter a 'total onslaught' from Moscow was patently absurd. De Klerk gave a hint of what was to come with his virtual abolition of the National Security Management System in November 1990 and the downgrading of the State Security Council. His task was also eased by the absence of hostile public reaction to South Africa's withdrawal from Namibia and the achievement of that country's independence in 1990. Hitherto, fears of a white right wing backlash had served as a powerful constraint against efforts to meet Western demands for conciliation on the Namibian issue.

Moreover, it was clear by the time of De Klerk's election to the state

222

presidency in September 1989 that the domestic struggle was in stalemate: the National Party government, despite an ever increasing commitment of resources, could not defeat its black opponents represented by the United Democratic Front and the Congress of South African Trade Unions, while the latter (and their ANC allies abroad) were unable to mount a successful revolutionary campaign designed to capture state power. Then again, the NP government recognised that time and demography were against them: in 1990 South Africa's population was 38.1 million; by 2 000 the figure would be 47.5 million. A white minority regime with a declining economy could hardly deliver the 3–4 per cent growth rate required to sustain numbers on that scale. True, violent revolution – in the absence of change – might not be the outcome, but the spectre of slow, haphazard social disintegration was presumably more than enough to convince De Klerk – a pragmatic realist – that the time had come to negotiate from a position of relative strength in terms of bargaining power. In these circumstances (and they included the political demise of President P.W. Botha whose failure to 'cross the Rubicon' of meaningful reform in the mid-1980s was to prolong the struggle for four more years), De Klerk and his colleagues concluded that the risks involved in negotiation with imprisoned and exiled enemies far outweighed the costs of continued attempts at repression.

During the three and a half years of constitutional negotiations, the major actors understandably concentrated their efforts on devising a new political structure to give expression to black political aspirations and at the same time incorporate a variety of power sharing devices into the interim constitution. The new state's foreign policy was a matter of some debate and argument, but the energies of the principal actors – De Klerk and Mandela – were absorbed in trying to maintain their partnership through the vicissitudes of negotiation, although both made effective use of overseas visits to extol their particular interpretations of what the future new South Africa had to offer its peoples and a range of external constituencies with an economic and political interest in the final outcome.

The international community maintained, indeed intensified its interest in events in the Republic. The period 1990–4 has been well described by Deon Geldenhuys as 'a new era of international engagement in South African politics'.[1] A variety of external bodies including the United Nations High Commission for Refugees, the Commonwealth, the Organisation of African Unity and the International Commission of Jurists offered good offices 'to the major players, . . . [performing] . . . various fact-finding, monitoring and facilitating roles'.[2] Both leaders, in effect, were using the external arena as a vehicle for their domestic competition: Mandela sought 'aid packages, to seek to control the timing mechanism for the lifting of sanctions and to build a supportive international consensus for the ANC's policy of a non-racial majoritarian unitary state as the basis for the new South Africa'.[3]

De Klerk, by contrast, argued the case for a constitution based on the principle of power sharing guaranteeing the rights of minorities via the mechanism of a federal structure. There is also the promise given by F.W. De Klerk and Nelson Mandela to Chief Buthelezi (as the price of his participation in the election) to accept international mediation on the issue of greater provision for the federal principal when the new constitution is revised by the Constituent Assembly. Indeed, that promise has come to haunt the Government of National Unity (GNU) given Buthelezi's refusal in 1995 to participate in the work of the Assembly unless and until mediation is accepted.

INTEREST AND REPUTATION

The 'new' South Africa's readmission into respectable international society symbolised by the extraordinary celebrations at the Union Buildings in Pretoria on 10 May 1994 confounded the cynics and the pessimists and moved even the most hardboiled political observer to a fleeting tear.[4] A massive world-wide television audience watched the great and the good of some 159 foreign states celebrate the inauguration of State President Nelson Mandela's new government – the one event in an otherwise dismal year which seemed to hold out the prospect of regeneration and reconciliation in a country which for over 50 years had defied the customary norms of law and morality exemplified by the United Nations Charter and a host of international conventions and prescriptions of best practice. Indeed, there were those who saw in South Africa's successful four-year transition a role model for conflict resolution to democratic government elsewhere, in Ulster and the Middle East, for example.

These reflections might strike the reader as sentimental in tone, but their substance does have a bearing on the theme of this paper if only because of the impact that the transition made on the external world and the well nigh constant reference made to South Africa's success in speeches, leading articles and media coverage in general in the months that followed the election of the GNU.[5] It is almost as if the outside world – whether in government statement or reflected in international media coverage – is willing the South African experiment to succeed!

In one important sense, following the demise of apartheid South Africa has become 'just another country' having to make hard-headed calculations of national interest, but in quite another sense its government has acquired a 'reputation' and part of its foreign policy thrust will involve trying to live up to that reputation in its dealings with the outside world. All this, of course, assumes a prior condition: that the GNU can and will transform South Africa and make good the promises of its leadership to the electorate. Failure to do so would be a source of acute disappointment for all those who over so many decades opposed apartheid and all its works. Thus the need to achieve success at home – not simply for its own sake and those of the deprived in South Africa but also to satisfy sympathisers abroad (and they are many) – becomes part of the burden of new-found reputation and hence a new dimension of foreign policy.

In other words, international society – and Africa in particular – entertains expectations about the sort of role South Africa can and should play in international affairs. It could be two roles – one based on calculation of narrow national interests or else one based on what its people (and the external world) expect of it in the years ahead. Here there is a certain irony: in the past the Republic's foreign relations were saddled with the burden of apartheid; room for manoeuvre was limited, the mode of action was defensive, profoundly rooted in the need to preserve a privileged way of life for a minority of South African's from external interference. Foreign policy thus began at home with a vengeance and was circumscribed accordingly, whether defending the homelands policy as a peculiar version of Western decolonisation or declaiming the significance of South Africa's mineral resources to the needs of Western security in the Cold War.

Despite these efforts, as Graham Evans has argued, '. . . opposition to apartheid in South Africa . . . [became] . . . the only moral absolute in world politics on which all the dominant ideologies, North, South, East and West, [could] agree'.[6] Now, precisely because the transition from apartheid to non-racial democracy was so dramatic and unexpected, the burden of apartheid and all the constraints it imposed on the conduct of South Africa's external relations has been replaced by its opposite – an exaggerated expectation of what the new state can achieve by force of domestic example and a saviour-style diplomacy abroad.

These expectations are bound to be disappointed: the model of negotiation so successful in the South African case may well inspire leaders and oppressed groups elsewhere with a vision of what can be done given the emergence of leaders willing to compromise and take risks after years of protracted conflict. This is certainly not to be despised, but it would be foolish to assume that transitions elsewhere can and will duplicate what happened in South Africa. To do so is to ignore the unique antecedents attending the demise of apartheid and the very different historical and cultural experiences of those involved in conflict elsewhere. The force of good example may, then, count for something, but in the last analysis politicians locked in stalemate will only come to the conference table when they mutually recognise that the costs of continuing a conflict outweigh the benefits of compromise. That calculation will inevitably be based on a local perception of gains and losses, and appreciation of a specific 'correlation of forces' and their probable resolution.

Similarly, however much may be expected of the new government in the realm of foreign policy, progress is bound to be slow and undramatic. This will be so for a number of reasons:

- The task of transforming the ethos and the personnel of the Department of Foreign Affairs is handicapped by the need to train and place a more fully representative cadre of new recruits and at the same time ease out by early retirement, etc., a substantial number of those who represented the old regime. Several new ambassadors and high commissioners have been appointed[7] and – to its credit – the GNU has sensibly avoided the temptation of packing the diplomatic bureaucracy, thereby adding to the burden of public expenditure.

- The GNU is subject to the constraints operating upon any new government entering office for the first time and attempting to redefine the means and ends of foreign policy. This applies with particular force to the GNU emerging into an international society where the constraints on sovereignty are much greater than was the case in the heyday of the apartheid regime. The impersonal and remorseless impact of the global economy driven by a communications technology makes excessive demands on the diplomatic skills of all states, testing their mettle in a fiercely competitive global marketplace. Hence the need to draw – unlike apartheid South Africa – on the widest range of talent available, and train it quickly enough to cope with pressures of this kind. Paradoxically, the ANC has inherited the levers of state power at precisely the moment when their successful manipulation in the external realm has become correspondingly more difficult.

- In the arena of domestic policy, the government can stake its reputation and legitimacy on a successful implementation of the Reconstruction and Development Programme. This provides a dramatic benchmark with success or failure, but no such equivalent exists in the field of foreign policy which does not easily or sensibly lend itself to ringing declarations of intent about what can and will be achieved. And the force of this argument will be amply demonstrated in later examination of particular foreign policy interests and how best they can be asserted and defended both in the southern African region and the wider world beyond.

THE INTERNATIONAL CONTEXT

The external milieu in which South Africa now has its foreign policy objectives has changed profoundly. In the past South Africa was a beneficiary of the precarious order established by the Cold War. That order has now disappeared to be replaced by a new world 'disorder' and the new government will have to make its way in a profoundly different international order from the one in which its predecessor had to cope. It might be helpful, therefore, to set out a rough and ready scenario for the next five years. Thus we might assume that:

- Western Europe will be preoccupied with the debate over widening and deepening; the European Community will enlarge itself by the addition of new states from Eastern Europe and elsewhere and make halting progress towards closer political and economic union. The Community – as a result – may become inward looking, absorbed in solving the problems arising from the process of closer union. In this context South Africa may seem distant and less important than was the case when apartheid ruled. As 'reputation' fades, South Africa might well become 'just another country' having to compete with counterparts for great power attention.
- The Commonwealth of Independent States (CIS) will be preoccupied with a) trying to hold the enterprise together and b) modernising its inefficient economic system. Ethnic conflict within the republics and border disputes will remain a persistent threat to Commonwealth integrity and its capacity to play a constructive role in international politics.
- The wars in Yugoslavia will end via either Serbian conquest or mutual exhaustion of all the parties, but instability will remain a major threat. This will present Western governments with complex problems, not least of which will be pressure from immigrants desperately seeking sanctuary from their war-torn societies. Western perceptions and pressure on politicians to act will to a great extent be media driven and this will limit the amount of interest and commitment available for distant regions like Southern Africa.
- Powerful regional trading blocs may well emerge. They will be self-contained and determined to keep out immigrants from whatever source. What has happened to the Hong Kong Chinese and the Vietnamese boat people is a potent signpost to the future.
- There will be a progressive demoralisation of parts of the Third World and their ultimate marginalisation to the very edge of the international agenda.

International order will not be achieved in the short to medium term. The 'time of troubles' is with us for a long time to come. How will this affect South Africa and the region?

- Southern Africa will struggle to keep a modest place on the international agenda.
- If things go well domestically and do not fall apart then Western governments and multi-national companies will be concerned to protect and enhance their interests in the region but their calculation will be based on the hard reality of economic and political self-interest and the strength of competing claims elsewhere.
- If the region experiences its own 'time of troubles' then interest may turn to indifference. Once again competing claims on time, energy and resources may reinforce that trend. In these circumstances the double standard alluded to by Dr Boutros-Ghali, the UN Secretary General, will operate – witness the fate of Somalia and Liberia.
- From South Africa's point of view there is much to be said for working out a profitable relationship with the European Community and precisely what form this should take is discussed later.
- These observations suggest that regional integration must be pursued with vigour. Hanging together may just be preferable to hanging separately!

THE DOMESTIC POLITICAL CONTEXT OF FOREIGN POLICY

A note of caution is required here. The past, it could be argued, is never entirely wiped clean whatever the expectations and aspirations a people may have as their society undergoes transformation of the kind effected in South Africa. This applies to the prospects for the emergence of a democratic tradition of politics in South Africa as much as it does with respect to the formulation and conduct of foreign policy. With respect to the latter, success or failure in policy making will depend not only on the stability of the polity but also on the extent to which South Africa succeeds in its efforts to establish a democratic tradition of political behaviour. Hence this digression into speculation about the future structure and process of South African politics.

The term 'tradition' implies that the structure and process of a country's politics is the evolving product of a peculiar history and culture. This explains why no political system is identical to another; it also explains why the wholesale transplantation of Western political values and institutions failed to take root in Third World societies such an Angola, Mozambique and Zaire. In these cases, there was simply no tradition, however latent, of democratic participation on which to build the new state. Portuguese and Belgian autocracy was an inadequate basis, irrelevant and ultimately harmful to the long-term political development of former colonies. In India, though, the British had prepared the ground decades before independence by incorporating local elite groups into colonial structures. Hence the relative success of Indian democracy.

The new South Africa paradoxically has advantages inherited from the past, however traumatic:

- An institutional framework incorporating a tradition of parliamentary government (admittedly exclusive) and a judicial system which has survived the battering of apartheid. The notion of the rule of law is not, after all, a new and exotic foreign import into South African political culture; it has roots in the country's legal history and has also been vigorously defended when attacked and undermined, as it has been during the past 46 years. Moreover, there is a commercial legal framework for regulating market transactions – sorely lacking in, say, Eastern Europe and the former Soviet Union;
- An economic infrastructure (telephones work and aircraft fly on time), human and material resources and elite political groups that have learnt to accommodate one another through the transition process whilst at the same time trying to satisfy diverse constituencies with different expectations;
- A tradition of strong statehood. This is largely a legacy from the past, rooted in the gross abuse of state power and its instruments by the apartheid regime. On the other hand, it is because South African statehood is not fragile that negotiators were encouraged to seek the transformation of the state and society within existing boundaries in the hope of avoiding the ethnic fragmentation that has occurred elsewhere.

The new government starts, therefore with the advantage that it does not have to engage in the business of state and nation-building simultaneously, as was the case elsewhere. The task in much of post-independence Africa of nation-building will be formidable enough, but the basis for doing so is there, not least in the existence of a vibrant civic culture – in part the product of the United Democratic Front in the 1980s and the subsequent proliferation of non-governmental organisations in the present decade.

The hope remains that, by a combination of debate, constitutional revision and learning from experience, a peculiarly South African version of democratic government may well emerge. It will certainly be difficult, it will not necessarily reflect in detail the theory and practice of democracy elsewhere, but it will, with luck and judgement, be home grown – that is, autochthonous.

By the same token it could be argued that a country's foreign policy is – to a degree – shaped by past preoccupations but these are not immutable. As Bruce Miller once put the matter in a perceptive analysis:

> National interests cannot be separated from the minds of the men who formulate them. . . . Ideas of national interest have a grounding in the facts of geography and economics, but these facts are subject to change . . . Ultimately, ideas of national interest depend upon the ideas which men have of the place which they would like their country to occupy in the world; and these ideas change in time, apart from never being unanimous within a country at a given time.[8]

Thus it could be argued that while Pretoria's new policy makers have inherited a set of national interests defined by their predecessors and constrained by the 'facts of geography and economics', nonetheless those self-same policy makers will put their own particular interpretation on those 'facts' and seek to maximise advantage for their country. For example, the new government aspires to play a critical role in the Southern African region; likewise did the apartheid regime (indeed, one can trace this particular tradition of foreign policy behaviour all the way back to Smuts) but with this difference, that apartheid made it impossible for South Africa to play a constructive role, enhancing its political and diplomatic status as a reflection of its dominant economic position. Indeed, in the 1980s the Republic was actively engaged in destabilising the region by military means. The point to stress in this context is that while the 'new' South Africa is constrained to give high priority to a regional role, its government has options available to it which were unthinkable for its predecessors.

Similarly, South Africa in the past laid great stress on its traditional economic links with Western states, but their development was – especially during the sanctions phase – hampered by extraneous political obstacles arising from the National Party's refusal to abandon apartheid. The new government has more leeway in this respect, although the competition for investment from abroad is far more acute today than was the case in the 1960s when South Africa appeared to be a very attractive prospect.

The arguments outlined above may seem self-evident, but it is worth emphasising nonetheless that the new government has an opportunity to examine the legacy of past interest, to redefine it where this is possible, but to do so in the knowledge that the options available are not unlimited and that policy will be constrained by geographical position, resource limitations, and the general capability of a state of South Africa's size and standing in international society.

DOMESTIC ECONOMIC FACTORS AND FOREIGN POLICY

How the economy responds to the policies of President Mandela's government will affect the state's capacity to pursue a foreign policy both in Africa and abroad. This applies particularly to those aspects of policy driven by economic imperatives and the need to scramble for markets and new foreign investment. Similarly, external perceptions will be influenced by the performance of the economy, and the following observations – it is hoped – will be helpful in placing foreign policy incentives and constraints in a domestic and economic context.

The new government inherits an economy emerging out of long recession; inflation has fallen to single figures, while exports of commodities increased by 25 per cent in the first three months of 1994; agricultural production has improved, and debt relief has been secured to help South Africa gain the benefit of international capital markets.

Business leaders and industrialists welcomed the electoral outcome, and in particular the appointment of Derek Keys as Finance Minister. In effect, Keys (and Christo Liebenberg, his successor) have exercised bargaining power on behalf of the business community: this commitment to free market principles is well known, and were the latter forced to resign because of disagreement with ANC strategy the impact on business confidence at home and abroad in South Africa's future would be devastating. In the past there has been concern that the first green shoots of growth (likely to be 3 per cent in 1995–6) may wither if the GNU follows a policy of high taxation, decreased public expenditure to finance the RDP and artificial job creation in the public sector. Debates in the National Economic Forum (with representatives from COSATU, the business community and the ANC) have been instrumental in reaching a consensus on measures required to liberalise the economy. Certainly the traditional ANC emphasis on large-scale nationalisation has been substantially modified, although the ANC – and COSATU in particular – still see a significant role for the state in regulating the economy. Nonetheless, business leaders were reassured by Nelson Mandela's address to the National Assembly on 25 May 1994, in which he endorsed the virtues of fiscal orthodoxy and free market solutions for South Africa's problems. Equally the budgets of 1994 and 1995 were well received both at home and abroad.

Moreover, it is significant that deregulation and privatisation – both strongly supported by business groups – are entering the realm of political discussion on the agenda of the GNU, and large corporations such as Anglo American and Gencor have begun to 'unbundle' their corporate assets in the interests of encouraging overseas investors to establish corporate ventures. As for the mining industry, there is agreement that taxation should not be increased, but according to Roger Riddell of the Overseas Development Institute it is not clear how far the government will 'take reserves into state ownership and precisely how it would encourage the industry to increase the degree of priority to export'. What is likely, argues Riddell, is that a mining forum (consisting of representatives of the government, the (non-foreign) mining companies and unions) will be established to devise a new mining policy.[9]

All the major actors in politics and the business community accept that a growth rate of 5 per cent is essential to sustain a major programme of social and economic reconstruction over the next five years and meet the needs of an expanding population. Overseas investment is vital if this target is to be met, but the decisions of investors (at home and abroad) will be governed by hard-headed calculations of economic and political interest. And these will only be positive if the economic environment is shaped by market principles, free of excessive government regulation. It is this constraint – according to the business community – which must govern the new administration's economic and social decision-making, but success in this context will depend on the final outcome of a debate in the GNU about the ultimate role of the state in the economy. This debate will intensify and strain consensus, as hard decisions have to be made by a government torn between devising short-term expensive palliatives to relieve poverty and the harsher strategies required to foster long-term growth. With respect to relations with the European Union (EU), the precise form of the relationship between Pretoria and Brussels has yet to be worked out. According to Martin Holland, the options are as follows:

1. The standard 'Most Favoured Nation' (MFN) status within GATT framework.
2. The generalised System of Preference (GSP).
3. The full Lomé status.
4. 'Associate' Lomé status.
5. A non-reciprocal association agreement.
6. A reciprocal association agreement.

In a detailed analysis he contends that the most likely outcome is a 'bilateral agreement that offers reciprocal terms'. This would mean the negotiation of a 'free trade agreement geared specifically to South Africa's needs' but in time this would require South Africa abandoning certain protectionist measures in exchange for access to the EU market. Assuming such an agreement would be forthcoming (and it will be a time-consuming process), EU policy would stress 'promoting economic cooperation, industrial cooperation and trade and investment promotion.'[10]

It is worth noting, however, that in late April 1995 South Africa rejected the European Union offer of a free trade agreement, stressing its preference for membership of the Lomé Convention. It is still too early to predict what the final outcome will be.

SOUTH AFRICA AND THE SOUTHERN AFRICAN REGION

South Africa's dominant position in the region arises from:

1. The size, experience and operational capability of its security forces. Following the absorption of recruits from the private armies of the liberation movements, the size of the South African National Defence Force (SANDF) is expected to rise from 87 000 to 120 000. Coupled with the size and self-sufficiency of South Africa's arms industry and the absence of any obvious military threats from abroad, this is a source of concern for neighbouring governments. Regional security arrangements may diminish these fears, but discussions on this theme have still to begin. Even when they start, they will be prolonged.

2. Economic superiority. South Africa's GDP is four times that of its neighbours to the north. A quarter of the region's total trade is with South Africa, with an overwhelming balance (5.5 to 1) in South Africa's favour. Botswana is particularly dependent, relying on South Africa for 90 per cent of its transportation requirements, 40 per cent of its electricity and all of its oil. Some 40 per cent of Malawi's imports emanate from South Africa while two-thirds of Zairean imports and one-third of its exports are routed through South Africa. The persistence of civil war in Angola and Mozambique and the disruption to east–west communication systems have only enhanced the region's reliance on South Africa's network of road and rail communications for shipment of foreign trade.

In 1981, the Southern African Development and Coordination Conference (SADCC), which was renamed the Southern African Development Community (SADC) in 1992, was established to reduce this dependence and promote regional integration. But the poor performance of the regional economies, exacerbated by war and drought and administrative inefficiency, has made this objective difficult to achieve. It is widely acknowledged that the economic future of the region will hinge on South Africa's economic performance. If it prospers there will be spillover effects in terms of increased trade and investment throughout the region. Debate on whether South Africa can perform a credible regional role has thus focused on three differing assumptions:

- that given a stable polity and economic revival, South Africa could become an 'engine for growth' for the region, co-ordinating investment and technical assistance, with ready and increased trade benefiting all;
- that the new government in Pretoria would be so absorbed by social and economic reconstruction that it would have little left to spare for its poorer neighbours; and
- that, regardless of whether South Africa prospers or not, Pretoria would be sensitive and restrained in its dealings with its neighbours and would avoid pursuing its own interests at the expense of others.

The outcome will be determined by the policies adopted by South Africa following its accession to power. All member states of the SADC, including South Africa, acknowledge that trading blocs are becoming a more important part of the world trading system. Hence, regional integration of southern Africa, building on the foundations of the SADC, is deemed to be essential to avoid marginalisation. However, formidable obstacles may impede achievement of this goal:

- A successful strategy of regional integration requires the creation of competent and legitimate governments in both Angola and Mozambique following the conclusion of civil war.
- The sheer size of South Africa as a regional power and its ability to attract foreign investment and trade threaten to widen the economic gulf between Pretoria and its neighbours.
- South Africa has obvious advantages in terms of infrastructure, with which weaker neighbours will have to compete. Mozambique, for example, is concerned that the harbour at Richards Bay in Natal will take business from Beira and Maputo.
- The issue of refugees from neighbouring countries will become a point of conflict if South Africa tries forcibly to repatriate them. There are some 50 000 refugees from Mozambique in South Africa and their return would put huge strains on the former's debilitated economy, both unskilled and professional.
- The movement of workers to South Africa in search of better wages and conditions will be another irritant. The Pretoria government is committed to job creation for its own unemployed – some 47 per cent

in the formal economy – and will therefore resist an influx of workers from abroad. At the same time, other regional governments will resent the emigration of scarce skilled professionals to South Africa.

- There may be a conflict of interest between competing trade agreements. Reconciliation will be needed between the objectives of the Preferential Trade Area in southern and eastern Africa, from which South Africa is currently excluded, and the South African Customs Union (SACU) which provides for free trade between South Africa, Lesotho, Botswana, Swaziland and Namibia.

The creation of a southern African common market (SACM) will remain as a long-term objective, but it will be unacceptable to South Africa if it means free movement of labour across the boundaries of member states. There is, however, scope for a degree of political integration with respect to policy coordination in areas such as transport, water and power resources, but progress will be slow unless and until structures are created that cater for the diverse interests of all the parties concerned.

SOUTH AFRICA AND AFRICA SOUTH OF THE SAHARA

During the period of the transition to democratic government, there was debate about the role South Africa might play in the international politics of the African continent as a whole. One strongly held view was that South Africa might use its dominant role in the region as a 'gateway' to the rest of the continent. This is an understandable aspiration given the ideological and practical support that African governments both unilaterally and via the mechanism of the Organisation of African Unity gave the ANC during the years of exile and the struggle for liberation. This, too, is reflected in the aspiration of some in the ANC hierarchy to establish diplomatic relations with the great majority of African states regardless of whether there is a commensurate economic and political advantage to be gained from doing so. I remain sceptical about the utility of this obligation on the grounds that too great a dispersion of scarce diplomatic resources will be counterproductive. What is to be gained, for example, from diplomatic missions in Equatorial Guinea, Chad, or Niger? A more selective strategy would seem to be essentially concentrating on states, for example Nigeria, Kenya and Egypt, with clearly defined regional importance and which in turn serve as conduits to poorer, weaker neighbours. This is not to deny the importance of trade with Africa: according to the South African foreign trade organisation 'African countries have become the main export destination of South African goods such as food products, chemicals, railway components, and mining, engineering pharmaceuticals, and agricultural equipment.' Total exports to South Africa grew to £1.24 billion in value in 1993 compared with £1.1 billion in 1992.

South Africa, though, has a legitimate aspiration to become a leading power on the continent with its voice heard at the OAU and in other continental-wide organisations on issues that affect Africa's standing, interests and influence in the world at large. Indeed, the new government will have a direct and important interest in the outcome of attempts to reach negotiated settlements in Angola and Mozambique, although it is unlikely in the short to medium term to become directly involved. President Mandela has indicated as much on the grounds that his government's first priority is to concentrate on his country's domestic problems. Hence his refusal – to date – to mediate in Angola and Rwanda.

What this brief analysis does suggest is that:

- South African diplomacy in Africa will in the main be driven by economic imperatives. Trade missions on a selective basis will become increasingly important, but this should not necessarily require the plastering of the continent with full-scale embassies and high commissions. Indeed, the new government has been cautious in this regard, acknowledging the expense involved and recognising the case for multiple accreditation on a regional basis.

- The temptation to be a major player in each and every one of the continent's conflicts will probably be resisted, although President Mandela will come under pressure, by virtue of his high standing, to provide 'good offices' from time to time. But there is a limit to what he can do – even at a symbolic level – and this has been implicitly acknowledged in the period since his inauguration. Yet we should note the success with which President Mandela, together with his Zimbabwean and Botswana counterparts Robert Mugabe and Quett Masire, managed the Lesotho crisis in August 1994. Failure here would have been a crucial set-back for South Africa's aspiration to play a creative and helpful role in the region.

- There will be attempts to involve a newly-constituted South African National Defence Force (SANDF) in peacekeeping operations. How the new government will respond is difficult to say at this stage. Yet however tempting the prospect may be, South Africa will face precisely the same constraints against intervention – especially with respect to questions of peace enforcement in areas racked by civil war – that have been characteristic of states elsewhere. Its armed forces will, in any case, also require training in contemporary peacekeeping doctrine.

SOUTH AFRICA AND THE WEST

South Africa will strive to enhance its economic links with its traditional trading partners in the West and Japan. These remain as important as ever as witnessed by the spate of conferences in Western Europe addressed by prominent ANC leaders concerned to persuade would-be investors and traders that South Africa remains a profitable and secure market for foreign investment. In 1990 the EC accounted for 27.3 per cent of South African exports while the USA (4 per cent), Japan (6.4 per cent) and Africa (6.7 per cent) were the next most important customers. Similarly, the EC (44.7 per cent), the USA (11.4 per cent), Japan (9.8 per cent) and Africa (1.6 per cent) supplied the bulk of South Africa's imports.[11]

But South Africa's economic attraction depends in large part on external perceptions of the new government's economic policies and its commitment to ensuring free market theory and practice, and on how far it can project itself as a stable polity in which the level of violence has been significantly reduced.

Both these conditions for success in attracting a greater share of world trade are rooted in the investment complexities of South Africa's domestic politics: the possibility of stressful competition, for example, between ministers like Christo Liebenberg (the Minister of Finance) committed to fiscal rectitude and the demands of high spending 'social service' ministers equally committed to implementing the *Reconstruction and Development Plan* (RDP) as a means of eradicating the poverty and deprivation endured by the black majority. Moreover there is a widespread assumption that success in this context will do much to lower the incidence of violence over the long term. Thus the new government has to keep the state together during a period of high expectations and contradictory pressures from external funders – whether public or private – insisting that long-term rewards depend on deferred satisfaction in the short term. And the support of external funders is vital if the economy is to prosper and deliver the growth required for ultimate redistribution of resources to redress massive inequality in the socio-economic sphere.

SOUTH AFRICA AND INTERNATIONAL ORGANISATIONS[12]

It has been fashionable to dismiss organisations such as the UN and the Commonwealth as mere 'talking shops', lacking the will and the means to give political effect to the high moral principles inscribed in their charters. Yet the fact remains that the apartheid regime was continually forced onto the defensive in international forums, e.g., the UN (to which it did belong – however uncomfortably – until 1974); or, alternatively, denied the benefits of membership which in many respects were significant.

South Africa paid a high price for the wasted years of apartheid. A state denied membership of the formal structures of international society is, in effect, denied participation in the endless task of realising in practice the notion of an international community; of fashioning the substance of international co-operation from the motley collection of disparate, conflicting national interests of over 150 states. To some, no doubt, this ideal is based on pure illusion about the true nature of international society; for them the latter is closer to anarchy than to community as states and trading blocs scramble for economic and political advantage or dissolve into violent ethnic fragmentation.

In this context international organisations arguably reflect the world as it is and rarely – if ever – do international organisations rise above the competing interests of their members. Yet there are moments – increasing in number since the end of the Cold War and the era of superpower rivalry – when international organisations are more than just the sum of their national parts; when genuine attempts are made at co-operation, whether to liberalise trade, e.g. the work of the newly established World Trade Organisation (WTO); provide peacekeeping forces to cope with the phenomenon of state collapse in Bosnia, Liberia or Somalia; or supervise via externally monitored elections the birth pains of a 'second independence' of African peoples determined to reform corrupt one-party states.

We do not propose to debate these contrasting perceptions of the role of organisations in the international political system. Both interpretations – nascent community or perpetual anarchy – are extreme theoretical positions; in practice one may be a more accurate perception than the other depending on time and circumstance. What is relevant to the theme of this paper is a recognition that for a 'new' state like South Africa membership of international organisations is essential whether one takes an optimistic or a pessimistic view about their role and significance in international politics.

The Commonwealth of Nations

South Africa's formal re-entry into the Commonwealth of Nations occurred at a moving ceremony at Westminster Abbey on 20 July 1994 and was dramatically reaffirmed with the visit of Her Majesty The Queen – the head of the association – to the country in March 1995.

What can South Africa expect from membership?

- A sense of solidarity with its Third World neighbours in Africa and further afield as their governments struggle to come to terms with the pressures of globalisation on fragile sovereignties and growing Western indifference to the prospects of marginalisation for the very poor and deprived in an international society fragmenting into powerful trading blocs.
- More positively, the prospect of providing a degree of leadership and enthusiasm for rejuvenating the Commonwealth ideal, given South Africa's competitive advantages in terms of resources, skill and political energy. South Africa is peculiarly placed in the association as a bridge between the rich and the poor members and can, therefore, be expected to maximise its role via a skilful and articulate diplomacy. Indeed, the fact that eight SADC members belong to the Commonwealth provides a useful continuing linkage which might well be collectively exploited on the larger stage of the Commonwealth. Thus overlapping membership offers the opportunity to establish common positions on issues of mutual interest which can thus be defended and asserted in the wider forum.
- The benefits to be derived from Commonwealth programmes of technical assistance and economic and social co-operation. These are not to be despised, despite the low-key manner of their implementation via the Secretariat. South Africa as the latest recruit to the association can be expected to reap considerable benefits in the short run. One obvious and by no means trivial example is the Commonwealth Scholarship and Fellowship Programme; another is the Secretariat's arranging of meetings between professionals (lawyers, doctors, journalists, etc.) which contrive to pass on the benefits of best practice in a variety of fields.
- Above all, South African politicians (and their constituents) can only gain from exposure to the attitudes and policies of their fellow members, the denial of which in the past made for a stultifying insularity.

The Organisation of African Unity

South Africa took its seat at the OAU on 13 June 1994. This was – like Commonwealth re-entry – a moment of high symbolic importance for 'it signalled a return to the African family and ... tangible evidence of a genuinely new "outward movement" in foreign policy'.[13]

Yet South Africa's role will be circumscribed by the weaknesses of the organisation and its evident failure over the years to grapple effectively with the immense problems facing the continent: the spectre of the collapsing state in, for example, Somalia, Zaire, Liberia, and Rwanda; the OAU's inability to mediate profitably in states such as Nigeria where the democratic process has been subverted by an obdurate military machine; the failure to voice Africa's global aspirations in a world which appears increasingly to view the continent as beyond political and economic redemption. Moreover, the demise of apartheid has removed the one unifying issue on which all member states could agree – if only at a rhetorical level.

Of course, the OAU is not unique in this respect. The UN has fared no better when faced with state disintegration in the former Yugoslavia; indeed, international organisations faced with the awesome nature of the problems that confront them in a post-Cold War environment can only be as effective in finding a solution as their members will allow. In these circumstances, the whole is rarely greater than the sum of its parts. Thus South Africa – despite its reservoir of political and diplomatic resources – will be wary of a too hasty involvement in crises far from its borders, given the intractability of the problems that confront the OAU. There is, as remarked earlier, the force of example in conflict resolution, but only when a window of opportunity arises for effective assistance, and that depends on a combination of propitious local circumstances rather than the wishes and strategies of outside powers, however well intentioned. On the other hand – as with the Commonwealth connection – the new government and especially the State President, Nelson Mandela, will, no doubt, attempt to exploit South Africa's new-found status to speak for Africa and, by implication, the OAU in distant and more influential forums, thus ensuring that 'African peoples are not forgotten or ignored by mankind'.[14]

As for peacekeeping, South Africa may well be crucially involved in attempts by the OAU to formulate a doctrine and establish a standing capability appropriate for Africa's needs. Here genuine efforts are under way; witness a series of conferences of senior officers from 50 countries held in the course of 1994–5 in Accra, Cairo, and Harare. However, South Africa's role is likely to be defined in regional rather than continental terms if only because of pressures on military and financial resources and the recognition of the primacy of local and regional interest in deciding what can be done to alleviate conflict both within and between states.

The Non-Aligned Movement

South Africa joined this organisation on 31 May 1994. Nelson Mandela pledged that South Africa would play an 'active role' and seek 'to share with developing countries its technology, economic expertise and experience in overcoming divisions of wealth and race'.[15]

With the end of the Cold War, however, the Movement finally lost its raison d'etre, namely, to act as a 'Third Force' in the competition between superpower blocs – a trend which was already visible in earlier decades as particular states succumbed to superpower blandishments in the form of weapons and economic assistance designed to help regimes maintain power against revolutionary movements. In 1992 the thrust of the Movement's posture changed as the leadership attempted to act as 'the lobbyist for the underdeveloped "South" on issues such as debt relief, the unpopular GATT global trade agreement and greater access for Third World goods to northern markets'.[16]

But the Movement's sheer size (some 102 countries) by 1989, its ideological diversity and differing levels of state development, has drastically reduced its effectiveness and bargaining role. South Africa is, therefore, unlikely to place high priority on its membership of the NAM given the more central position that organisations such as the Southern African Development Community and the Commonwealth will occupy in the formulation and conduct of its foreign policy.

Indeed, given South Africa's dependence on Western markets for investment and trade – essential for domestic economic revival – the GNU will recoil from adopting a radical isolationist anti-Western stance. There is little to be gained from leading a crusade on behalf of the poorest of the poor at a time when some of the original founders of the Movement (India in particular) have the potential to become great economic powers in their own right and when Western models of 'good governance' and liberal economic development are urged upon Third World states as the only route to survival if not salvation. In other words the 'unthinkable has happened: terms are now dictated to NAM members by a triumphal and hegemonic West'.[17] At best all the Movement can hope for is that South Africa will support the claim for 'a better economic deal'[18] knowing well that the rhetoric may well fall on deaf ears in the absence of any real bargaining power for the Movement as a whole. Like so many states in the NAM, South Africa will put its own interests first, competing, as it must, for Western technology, investment and trade with a host of rival claimants.

The United Nations

South Africa returned to the General Assembly of the United Nations in 1994 after an absence of 20 years. More than any other international organisation the UN proved to be the most potent mobiliser of hostile reaction to apartheid. Year after year South Africa's policies were debated at the UN, and as the Third World increased its membership of the General Assembly large majorities were found to back a multitude of resolutions directed at forcing change on the National Party government. Anti-colonialism was the dominant ideology of the Third World coalition at the UN; indeed the organisation, in effect, legitimised anti-colonialism both as ideology and strategy, and, in doing so elevated racial equality and national self-determination to the status of norms by which the action of states in both domestic and foreign policy would be judged. South Africa was deemed to be a special case of colonialism and provided a major source of Third World unity for much of the post-war period.

Thus the UN – and the General Assembly in particular – provided a vehicle for orchestrating the international community's concern with apartheid and one to which exiled liberation movements such as the ANC could appeal for support and justification of their cause. In other words, the UN provided the means for de-legitimising the South African government and the result was a slow but nonetheless effective erosion of its standing in international society. In this respect South Africa was unique, and few would argue with the proposition that the UN and the publicity and hostility it generated against apartheid helped bring about the latter's eventual collapse. UN debates on apartheid, in effect, provided symbolic recognition of South Africa's isolation in the international community – a burden which ultimately proved too heavy to bear for the white minority regime as symbolism was replaced by sanctions and a host of other pressures, both internal and external.

South Africa re-enters an organisation which is much changed since the heady days of globalised anti-apartheid rhetoric. Following the successful conclusion of the Gulf War, and President Bush's definition of a New World Order in which a US-led UN coalition would enforce the peace whenever and wherever it was threatened, the Security Council came into its own as the five permanent members – forswearing the veto – tried hard to cope with internal conflicts raging from the former Yugoslavia to Somalia. The doctrine of humanitarian intervention and the attempt to redefine the UN's role as peacekeeper inevitably gave the Security Council a decisive role in the organisation, overshadowing the General Assembly which to all intents and purposes appears to have lost its raison d'etre as the forum representing and articulating the interests of the small and medium sized states. Given the disarray of the Third World since the end of the Cold War, the profound loss of influence of the Non-Aligned Movement over the policies of the superpowers, and the demise of apartheid as a mobilising issue, this is hardly surprising.

In these circumstances South Africa will, no doubt, attempt to add its voice to those states clamouring for debt relief and an easing of structural adjustment programmes, but it will inevitably be constrained by the need to pursue its own economic interests and in particular to make itself as attractive an investment prospect and trading partner as possible to the West and the newly industrialising countries in the Asia–Pacific region. Nevertheless, South Africa will remain keenly interested in one area of UN decision-making: the possible reform of the Security Council to include new permanent representatives. In this context South Africa can be expected to be a strong competitor disputing, for example, Nigeria's claim on the seat. But there is the possibility of a clash of interest here: the African states will seek to appoint a representative capable of defining and asserting the continent's aspirations in an indifferent world. A South Africa linked too closely to the Western economic terms and desperately trying to escape from perceived Third World status may well not seem the most obvious candidate to represent a marginalised African continent.

CONCLUSION

Much of this chapter has inevitably been speculative. The foreign policy of the new South Africa is still in its formative stages. What I have tried to do is outline the role of tradition in shaping that policy – especially as it applies to the facts of 'geography and arithmetic' as well as the scope for innovation. Much will depend on the shape of a reformed Department of Foreign Affairs; a sizeable group of able embryonic diplomats have been trained abroad during the last four years and their input into decision-making will generate debate about means and ends, interests and objectives, the outcome of which is far from clear at this early stage.

What will be especially interesting to observe is the interaction of the Ministry of Defence and the Department of Foreign Affairs; the former has begun to flex its muscles under the leadership of Jo Modise who has the backing of the white general staff for a larger army and the technological hardware to go with it. In the past the MOD and the DFA were often at loggerheads over the substance and process of South African foreign policy – especially with respect to the destabilisation strategy of the 1980s. There is also the question of South Africa's arms production for use at home and sale abroad. A debate is currently in progress on the morality and utility of ARMSCOR activity, with many in the ANC arguing for accountability and transparency in the manufacture and sale of weapons. How far the new dispensation will provide for a meeting of minds on the most appropriate and cost-effective relationship between both defence and foreign policy makers will be a matter of considerable interest to scholars and practitioners over the next five years.

NOTES

1. Deon Geldenhuys, 'The Changing Nature of Foreign Involvement in South Africa', *South Africa International* (April 1993), 147–55.
2. Graham Evans, 'The International Community and the Transition to a New South Africa', *Round Table*, 330 (April 1994), 179.
3. *Ibid.*, 179.
4. For an entertaining and instructive account of the inauguration see Peter Henshaw, 'Land of Hope and Glory: Mandela's New South Africa', *Queens Quarterly*, 101/2 (Summer 1991), 439–50.
5. See for example Douglas Hurd's eulogistic reference to South Africa in his address to the 'Britain and the World' conference organised by the Royal Institute of International Afairs in London, 29 March 1995.
6. Evans, *op. cit.*, 178.
7. On 7 April 1995 for example the Minister of Foreign Affairs, Alfred Nzo, announced the appointment of 14 new diplomatic representatives following earlier changes at senior level in London, Paris, New York and the Hague. South Africa is now represented in 140 states.
8. Bruce Miller, *The Commonwealth and the World* (London: Duckworth, 1958).
9. Roger Riddell, 'Prospects for a New South Africa', Overseas Development Institute, special paper (1994).
10. M. Holland, 'From Pariah to Partner: Relations with the EU' in Greg Mills, *From Pariah to Participant: South Africa's Evolving Foreign Relations, 1990–1994* (Johannesburg: South African Institute of International Affairs, 1994), pp. 133–55.
11. Sheila Page and Christopher Stevens, *Trading with South Africa: The Policy Options for the EC*, Overseas Development Institute, special report (1992).
12. For a more detailed examination of this topic see James Hamill and J.E. Spence, 'South Africa's Role in International Organisations' in *South African Year Book of International Law* (forthcoming).
13. *Ibid.*
14. Statement by ANC Working Group on Foreign Policy in a New Democratic South Africa, quoted in Greg Mills, *op. cit.*, p. 223.
15. *The Times*, 1 June 1994.
16. Hamill and Spence, *op. cit.*
17. *Ibid.*
18. *Ibid.*

11 Federal Aspects of the New South African Constitution: Prospects for Regional Integration

Klaas Woldring

INTRODUCTION

Federalism has traditionally divided scholars as a method of government. Harold Laski in his days at the London School of Economics believed that 'federalism was dead' and William Livingston argued in 1956 that federalism was only meaningful if the various diversities in a society, such as ethnic, cultural and language differences, could be 'territorially grouped'.[1] William Riker on the other hand turned against federalism in the 1960s – having been formerly a champion of it – since he believed it blocked the civil rights movement and equal opportunity in the US.[2] Now that totalitarian socialism is dead federalism may be workable and enduring for many plural societies based on diverse cultural and ethnic groups.

Ethnic identity can be become a conspicuous motivator for action when politicised, manipulated or suppressed. It can also be the motivation behind beneficial, positive action. The awareness of ethnic identity is not always strong but may be awakened unexpectedly by changes in circumstances such as travelling or settling abroad.[3] The rejection of ethnicity in constitution-making in South Africa is a remarkable break-through but, while logical and understandable in view of the apartheid experience, it is not necessarily realistic to continue to ignore ethnic differences. Prior to the first non-racial, democratic general election in South Africa in April 1994, the break-through was qualified by the refusal of the Freedom Alliance to participate in the Transitional Executive Council and in the first non-racial general elections. Last-minute negotiations and concessions resolved the objections by the 'rejectionists' at least for the purpose of participating in the elections.

The Interim Constitution is *potentially* a de facto federal arrangement, a fact that has surprised many commentators. Thinking about federalism, especially in some ANC and PAC quarters, was conditioned and clouded by the apartheid experience and was often viewed as simply a new phase in its workings. A more realistic assessment of its potential for reorganising South Africa emerged from October 1992 onwards.

The need for economic development to satisfy the rising expectations is now the overriding imperative. In the post-election period South Africa's *Reconstruction and Development Plan (RDP)*, which provides blueprints for housing and services, water and sanitation, electricity and electrification, education, health care and land reform programmes, is unquestionably of paramount concern. These massive tasks require not just the right policies, funding and staffing but also an appropriate governmental framework for implementation. The new provincial legislatures and administrations, some of which are quite influential, e.g. in Gauteng, KwaZulu/Natal and the Cape, could well play significant roles in the implementation of the RDP. This is to be expected particularly because the ANC as a political party and majority partner in the Government still has a long way to go before it has the capacity to perform as the core of a strong central government.[4]

This chapter will examine federalism's relevance to the new situation in South Africa in five major respects: i) why federalism failed in the past in Southern Africa; ii) the convergence of NP and ANC constitutional proposals; iii) key provisions of the Interim Constitution; iv) whether the new constitution is a de facto federation; and v) economic reconstruction or civil war?

WHY FEDERALISM FAILED IN THE PAST IN SOUTHERN AFRICA

If we go back to the second half of the nineteenth century the history of federalism is one of failures all the way. A first attempt was made by Sir George Grey in 1858 during what is referred to as 'the first Basuto war' to establish a strong federal government in South Africa that could maintain the peace for Britain. The overriding question though was 'the native problem' and, as the historian Eric Walker noted 'if federation was the goal and the need for a common native policy the main incentive to attain it, the divergent native policies of the various colonies and still more of the republics were the principal obstacles.'[5]

Grey overstepped his instruction from London however and did not get the necessary backing for the federal plan, which fell through. A second federation scheme was engineered some years later in 1874 by the Colonial

Secretary Lord Carnarvon, who had assisted in federating the British colonies in North America into the Dominion of Canada in 1867. This time the plan met with opposition from the Cape which had been granted 'responsible government' a few years earlier. Its government, led by John Molteno, felt bypassed and opposed the proposal, as did the Free State. A later attempt by Carnarvon, in 1877, this time by intervention in the affairs of Transvaal, was equally unsuccessful.

Cecil Rhodes made further efforts in the 1890s but his ambitious federal plans were wrecked by the ill-fated Jameson Raid in 1896. Finally, the federation issue was again activated during the years immediately preceding Union in 1910, when it was presented as an alternative to a unitary form of state. The desire for some form of amalgamation was prompted by the need for a strongly centralised 'native policy' and difficulties connected with differences between the colonial railway administrations as well as conflicting tariff policies. The alternative of federal government proper was rejected for a number of reasons. Firstly, the President of the National Convention (Sir Henry de Villiers) which discussed the issue in Durban in 1908 'had learnt much of the weaknesses of even close federation in the course of a recent visit to Canada' and, furthermore, 'neither of the outstanding champions of federalism attended the Convention (Schreiner and Hofmeyer) . . . the five by no means outstanding Natal delegates were thus left to fight alone for federalism. They interpreted it so obviously to mean "Natal" that the issue went by default'. Apart from 'native policy' delegates argued against federation believing it to be more expensive than a unitary system.

The efforts at the end of the nineteenth century can be compared with similar movements in Australia and Canada and would probably have resulted in a federal construct but for the ethnic and colonial complexities peculiar to South Africa. In retrospect the unification of South Africa in 1910, which represented a political victory for the Afrikaner people over the imperial government, laid the ground work for subsequent institutionalised racial domination, typical of the former Boer Republics, and found its first expression in the 1913 Land Act.

The wholesale abandonment of racial discrimination in the new Interim Constitution of South Africa and the proposed measures to introduce compensation to dispossessed landowners opens up the prospect of a re-examination of the distribution of governmental powers and functions in a new political climate. To a large extent that is what has been done in the period leading up to the agreement reached in November 1993. The convergence between the two major players in that process is truly remarkable in the light of the history of South Africa.

THE CONVERGENCE OF THE NP'S AND ANC'S CONSTITUTIONAL PROPOSALS

The ANC's position towards the new Constitution was developed in four principal documents: the *Freedom Charter of 1955*, the *Draft Bill of Rights*, the *Discussion Document on Structures and Principles of a Constitution for a Democratic South Africa*, and the *Strategic Perspective* paper. The National Party's proposals were outlined in a document entitled *Constitutional Rule in a Participatory Democracy*.

The national constitutional proposals by the ANC and NP were not put forward as blueprints. They were significant statements of intent subject to refinement, negotiation and adjustment. There were wide areas of agreement, at least on paper. Both sets of proposals favoured a devolved and decentralised unitary state with strong regional and local government authorities, the NP increasingly leaning towards a federal structure. Both favoured PR as the electoral system at all levels with a preference for the list system. The need for a non-racial, democratic constitution and the protection of individual rights was stressed and detailed. At the national level a bi-cameral parliament was desired. The extension of the franchise, that meant to 84 per cent of the population, was no longer disputed by the NP. Private property rights were also enshrined in both sets of proposals.

The ANC's Proposals

The ANC's proposals aimed for a modern highly liberal democratic constitution. Some important matters were raised only briefly and left for further discussion. Such an issue was whether the ANC should continue with the Westminister system whereby MPs must be 'in and of the Parliament' or adopt an extra-Parliamentary executive. There was a recommendation for the amendment procedure for the constitution (two-thirds of the National Assembly or two-thirds of the electorate – similar to the NP's proposals) but who should initiate popular referendums and who decides which method is to be used? Surprisingly, there was no specific section dealing with the role of the state to direct economic recovery, state enterprise or financial support for disadvantaged regions (of which there are several). There was no mention either of the role of unions or the encouragement for enterprise democracy in the workplace. The ANC did foreshadow an important role for the state in economic recovery in other statements, e.g. in the *Harare Declaration*, but soon after his release Mr Mandela played down the earlier emphasis on the command economy.

The adoption of PR, apart from it being a desirable democratic device generally, would certainly suit the ANC. According to opinion polls in 1991/2, nationally it would gain around 55 per cent of the vote (later polls suggested over 60 per cent). This raised the prospect that all other parties could be permanently in opposition. Although there was widespread agreement on the introduction of PR, other parties, e.g. ultra conservative white parties, Inkatha and the PAC, could be expected to seek to strengthen their minority status in some way.

The NP's Proposals

The NP government's position shifted considerably in recent years. Statements made early in 1991 by the then Minister for Constitutional Affairs, Dr Gerrit Viljoen, made the 1985 dismantling of the provincial legislatures look premature. Clearly the later package of proposals was the result of pressures building up following the unbanning of the ANC, PAC and SACP. By and large the NP had adopted the federal constitutional platform of the Democratic Party, its long-time Parliamentary Opposition. For example, Dr Viljoen said that he envisaged

> a series of checks and balances. For example, the parliamentary lower house could be elected on a simple majority basis and the upper house along the lines of the United States and Australian Senates. The courts could play a balancing role similar to that of the US Supreme Court. I contemplate a form of federation in which regional governments would have considerable autonomy. We accept that nothing can be done without the majority, but not to the total exclusion of the minority. The majority must rule, but not alone and exclusively.[6]

In the latter half of the 1980s the NP government was attracted to the idea of a minority (group) veto. This idea was borrowed from the concept of 'consociational democracy' developed by Lijphardt on the basis of of studies of mostly European systems of government.[7] That plan was formally discarded in the 1991 proposals, though these still retained devices to strengthen the position of minorities in the way the Senate was to be elected and in its powers which would require 'weighted majorities' for minority and regional interests. If these had been adopted, a popularly elected National Assembly would possibly have found itself frustrated.

The second contentious aspect was the collegiate-style Presidency. John Dugard, for instance, claimed in an interview that this 'belongs to the realm of fantasy. It didn't work in Yugoslavia and it doesn't seem realistic for a New South Africa.' Decisive aspects of the proposals were the emphasis on a high degree of devolution of power and on constitutional sovereignty.

Understandably the desire for devolution of power and decentralisation of decision-making stemmed from the fear of concentration of black power. The NP made a 180° about-face. From a highly centralised, authoritarian system of government they moved to a preference for dispersal of power and insistence on a Charter of Fundamental Rights. This they now perceived to be their best plan for the protection of minority interests.[8]

Differences

When all is considered the differences between these proposals, on paper at least, were relatively minor and it became possible therefore, especially after November, 1992, to bridge them quite quickly. There remained three potential areas of contention:

- The question of the collegiate Presidency and the Cabinet. The ANC was likely to agree to discarding the Westminster system but the nature and composition of the extra-parliamentary (political) executive remained a grey area.
- The election, composition and powers of the Senate. The prospect of a minority veto through the backdoor would not be acceptable to the ANC.
- The question of entrenched clauses. This was raised but not spelt out. The protection of the Afrikaans language was an unresolved issue. The ANC didn't favour entrenched clauses, wanted all languages to have equal status but indicated elsewhere that it preferred English as the common language.

Marina Ottaway, in a recent analysis of the developing situation, has argued that both major parties have a state-centred view of politics historically intent on using central state power for the achievement of political, social and economic policy. What actually emerged as a common framework, admittedly from quite different starting positions, is a liberal democratic constitution characterised by a combination of decentralised unitary and federal constitutional aspects. Ottaway argues that that 'the 1991 constitutional guidelines revealed not a change in the basic goals of the government but a definite slippage in what it thought was attainable'.[9] This is what happened in the ANC camp as well by November, 1992. The *Strategic Perspective* document basically completed the political bargain which made progress possible. The lack of progress at that stage seemed to have been caused more by other factors than the actual constitutional proposals. The Democratic Party (the former Progressive Federal Party) played quite an important role in bringing the parties together at a time when the constitutional proposals of Inkatha's strident ethnic nationalism were causing considerable tension in CODESA and the subsequent multi-party negotiations, and in some quarters even raised the prospect of civil war and secession. Buthelezi endeavoured to portray the ANC as basically a Xhosa organisation and tried to promote King Goodwill Zwelithini as the guardian of the Zulu nation, though this was later to backfire against him as Goodwill has moved increasingly towards the ANC-led government in the wake of the April 1994 elections.[10]

Both Ottaway and Gerhard Mare refer extensively to the manipulation of ethnic nationalism by Buthelezi for political ends. His endeavours to get a new constitution for Natal off the ground, begun in 1986 with the KwaZulu/Natal (Indaba) power-sharing proposal, which had a good deal of white support, tested the Government's power-sharing philosophy but found it wanting. At the national level, Buthelezi's frequent references to Zulu nationalism have not created much of a following *nationally*. In Natal many Zulus sympathise with the ANC as several mass rallies held in Durban in 1993 demonstrated. Before and during the election campaign in March/April 1994 the ANC staged rallies in Natal to bolster its support which somewhat erratic opinion polls suggested was growing steadily to national levels – until Inkatha finally decided to enter the race anyway.

KEY PROVISIONS OF THE INTERIM CONSTITUTION

The new Republic of South Africa is a constitutional state, with the Constitution of the Transitional Period being the supreme law of the land. It reflects quite closely the packages of the two major negotiating partners. The constitutional bill endorsed *by an ordinary majority* of delegates assembled at the Multi-party Negotiating Forum on 18 November 1993 at the World Trade Centre in Kempton Park also provides for the repeal of South African legislation which established the 'independence' of Transkei, Boputhatswana, Venda and Ciskei (TBVC states). The bill was subsequently approved by South Africa's tri-cameral Parliament which was then dissolved.

The Constitution provides for a Government of National Unity, three tiers of democratic government and an extensive chapter on fundamental rights. A Schedule in the bill sets out 32 binding and justiciable Constitutional Principles to which a final constitution must adhere. Elections will be held on the basis of a system of proportional representation, detailed in the Constitution.

South Africa is now divided into nine provinces for election and constitutional purposes. Both the Cape Province and Transvaal were split up into three parts each. The new PWV area (now re-named Gauteng), Natal and Eastern Cape are the most populous provinces, providing between them more than half of the regional list seats in the National Assembly. North West is a new province bordering on Botswana, and with an ethnic affiliation to that country.

The National Parliament comprises a 400-person National Assembly and a 90-person Senate. The National Assembly is made up of 200 persons from the national lists and 200 persons from the regional lists of the various political parties, elected on the basis of proportional representation. The Senate is made up of ten persons indirectly elected by each of the nine provincial legislatures. Ordinary laws must be passed by a simple majority in each house and if one house rejects a bill, it must be passed by a majority of the total number of members of both houses. Finance bills, such as the budget and taxations laws, can only be introduced by the National Assembly. Should the Senate reject such a bill, it will have to be reconsidered by the National Assembly.

The Head of State is an Executive President. The first President (Nelson Mandela) was elected by the National Assembly at its first sitting. Provision was made for Executive Deputy Presidents from parties that obtain 80 or more seats in the National Assembly. Should no party or only one party hold 80 or more seats in the National Assembly, the party holding the largest number of seats and the party holding the second largest number of seats are entitled to designate one Executive Deputy President each.

The multi-party Cabinet is composed, according to proportional representation, of those parties that obtain 5 per cent or more of the vote in the election. There will be a maximum of 27 Ministers. The various portfolios are to be designated by the President. Decisions are to be taken by consensus, in a manner which gives consideration to the spirit underlying the concept of a Government of National Unity as well as the need for effective government.

Provinces

Each of the nine provinces has been provided with a Provincial Legislature, elected by proportional representation from the regional party lists of the various political parties. The number of seats in a Provincial Legislature is determined by dividing the total number of votes cast in a province by 50 000. Provincial Legislatures should, however, not have fewer than 30 or more than 100 seats (e.g. Gauteng 86, Natal 80 and Eastern

Cape 52). The Legislatures have extensive powers concurrent with the national government to make laws on issues set out in a Schedule of the Constitution, such as local government, agriculture, police, environment, provincial language policy, housing, public transport, health and welfare, education at primary and secondary level, public transport, roads, traffic control, trade and industry, casinos and public media within the province.

Each province is entitled to an equitable share of revenue collected nationally. A Financial and Fiscal Commission is to be appointed by the President. This Commission will apprise itself of all financial and fiscal information relevant to national, provincial and local government, administration and development, will render advice and make recommendation to the relevant legislative authorities. A provincial government is entitled to raise other taxes, surcharges or levies provided that they are authorised to do so by an Act of Parliament, taking into account the recommendations of the Financial and Fiscal Commission.

Each province shall have a Provincial Executive Council consisting of a Premier and ten executive members to administer provincial departments and determine policy. A party must obtain at least 10 per cent of the seats in the legislature to qualify for an executive portfolio. The Executive Council will take decisions by consensus. After the first general election each Provincial Legislature is entitled to adopt a constitution for the province, as long as it is consistent with the Constitutional Principles. The Interim Constitution also makes provision for an autonomous third tier of government. There are provisions for restitution of land.

A Constitutional Court was established in October 1994 with controversial appointments. This has the final jurisdiction on matters relating to the interpretation, protection and enforcement of the Constitution at all levels of government. Its role is to certify amendments to the Constitution and to protect the fundamental rights and freedoms contained in the Constitution.

The Constitutional Assembly, i.e. the National Assembly and Senate sitting in joint session, has been given the task to draft a final constitution for South Africa within two years of its election. This requires a two-thirds majority of MPs or, in the case of deadlock, referral to a special Constitutional Panel of five, or a 60 per cent majority in a referendum. The multiparty Cabinet and Government of National Unity will continue to function for five years unless it loses the confidence of Parliament in which case a new election will be held earlier.

Although the new Interim Constitution provides a wide range of issues on which provincial governments have jurisdiction, it does not cede exclusive power to the provinces on these matters. The Constitution also provides various broadly defined conditions under which the central government's will prevails over provincial law, e.g. maintenance of minimum stand-ards nationally, promotion of inter-provincial commerce, and protection of national interest. Some commentators have argued therefore that the transitional constitution 'has the appearance but not the substance of a federal system with entrenched provincial power'. Given the history of the so-called 'original powers' of the former South African provinces they ex-pect that any such powers as could be exercised in the new situation could also be whittled away. Nevertheless following the election result, two of the provinces are not governed by the ANC: Western Cape was won by the National Party – on the strength of the Coloured vote – and KwaZulu/Natal was won by Inkatha. The Premiers of these provinces (Hernus Kriel and Frank Mdlalose) can be expected to protect and promote regional autonomy.[11]

The issue is whether or not the Premiers of these provinces will take in-dependent positions or become mere administrators as previously happened in the apartheid Republic. Much will depend on the strength of the ANC as an organised, cohesive senior party in government and on that party's capacity and inclination to operate a fully fledged command economy. As capacity is dubious at present and inclination has been tempered many times already, the potential for provincial autonomy seems considerable.

A DE FACTO FEDERATION?

The NP Government's proposal for a devolved and decentralised unitary state was not far removed from the model of a de facto classical federa-tion. Even the ANC's proposals could be so regarded. The emphasis on strong regions and regional governments suggested a realisation that (a) both ethnic and territorial aspirations needed to be accommodated and (b) regional development had to be taken seriously. In the aftermath of the bargain struck in November 1993 the insistence of regional autonomy and ethnic nationalism has grown stronger. The 'rejectionists' of the Freedom Alliance first objected to the single ballot paper which would favour the ANC and reduce the chances of majority control by other parties over provincial governments.

Nelson Mandela's offer to the Freedom Alliance on 17 February 1993 seemed to go a long way to meet the rejectionists' objections:

- Separate ballot papers for provincial and national legislatures rather than a single ballot – providing a better chance for smaller parties at the provincial level

- A constitutional provision on the principle of 'self determination' for the AVP
- A greater say for provinces over their finances, legislative and executive structures
- A commitment that regional powers would not be 'diminished substantially' in a future constitution draft by elected legislators after the April poll
- The dropping of an ANC demand that the Alliance make an advance commitment to participate in the election and the TEC
- A change in the name Natal to KwaZulu/Natal.[12]

The package did *not* promise the extended concurrent and exclusive regional powers demanded by Inkatha. A further statement would be made on King Goodwill Zwelithini's demand for a separate Zulu Kingdom outside the present Interim Constitution, Mandela promised. Although the package was rejected by Buthelezi as 'cheap politicking' the door remained open for a change in the electoral law and the registration of political parties at the 11th hour.

The growing prospect of Inkatha losing in the provincial election, as opinion polls suggested, became a major factor in Buthelezi's strategy. During March the Freedom Alliance began to crumble following the forcible removal of Chief Lucas Mangope in Boputhatswana by the TEC, the resignation of Brigadier Oupa Gqozo of Ciskei and the resignation of Freedom Front Leader General Constand Viljoen from the Freedom Alliance.

It was not until 19 April, after a brief, futile mediation exercise by Henry Kissinger and Lord Carrington, that a bargain was struck between the main political contenders. Increasingly flexible deadlines had made it possible for Inkatha to hold out until the last moment, an exercise of considerable brinkmanship. Amendments were made to the Interim Constitution to accommodate sovereignty demands by King Goodwill Zwelithini and an undertaking was given by the ANC to provide a framework for post-election mediation on constitutional matters pertaining to regional autonomy, conceivably under international supervision.[13] The ANC was anxious not to see a repetition of the violence that had preceded the elections while Inkatha was desperate to prevent the transfer of its power base to the new provincial government. The major factions were thus keen to avoid any further deterioration of the situation. This joint decision resulted in a remarkable drop in the level of violence and tension during the election period.

Federalism as institutionalised bargaining

In South Africa's apartheid past, liberal whites such as Leo Marquard and Alan Paton advocated federal proposals to establish a constitutional framework in which apartheid could be peacefully and rationally dismantled.[14] They were instances of liberal meliorism which took inadequate account of the realities of power relationships in South African politics and presumed that a federation could come about through the force of reasoned argument. A rather more satisfactory thesis to explain why federal government is agreed on invokes bargaining theory. It is based in part on the thesis of Riker regarding *the origin of and the making of a federal bargain*. This explanation is also quite different from the experiences with the (former) colonial federations where the departing colonial power was first instrumental in the making of the bargain and then withdrew, frequently with adverse results. Riker studied federations which were the result of *largely* domestic/regional power adjustments. This presupposes a climate suitable for negotiations and coalition formation.

Applying his thesis to South(ern) Africa the following possible scenario presents itself.[15] Federal Government for South Africa is the likely outcome of conflicting black and white political, economic and social forces as well as external pressures and would be agreed upon because:

1. The cost of escalating ethnic and class conflict would be considered too high by (a) black leadership; (b) white leadership (political and business interests); (c) external interests; (d) the people.
2. It would offer the opportunity for black leadership to exercise substantial power at the central level which would otherwise not be attainable or attainable only after many years of violence and chaos.

The Machiavellian/Hobbesian analysis of federal government, as presented by Riker, fits the emerging situation in Southern Africa reasonably well. He distinguished between the politicians of the 'core' and the 'periphery' and postulated a two-pronged hypothesis about the origin of federations, i.e. the making of the federal bargain:

1. The politicians of the core who offer the bargain desire to expand their territorial control, usually either to meet an external military or diplomatic threat or to 'prepare for military or diplomatic aggression or aggrandisement.
2. The politicians of the periphery who accept the bargain, giving up some independence for the sake of union, are willing to do so because of some external military–diplomatic threat *or* opportunity (emphasis added).

Riker's analysis is perhaps one-sided and concentrates heavily on the military–diplomatic aspect of the matter. Furthermore, the situation is much more complex in Southern Africa now than merely a conflict over territory. Domestic and external capitalist interests are at stake even though the ideological heat has been extinguished. The Labor Movement (ANC, SACP, COSATU, UDF, PAC, AZAPO) has become organised and is claiming its stake. The bargain is multi-faceted, and involves various international actors (not discussed here) but this is nevertheless what is happening in that a bargaining process has occurred between a variety of stakeholders. Further new dimensions now are the impact of Zulu ethnic nationalism, insistence on a white 'homeland' by the AVP (although this has now considerably faded since the election) and the implied threat of secession by at least one peripheral area: KwaZulu/Natal.

It was the armed struggle waged by the Liberation Movement which set the scene for bargains to be struck. They do entail, at least formally, the question of control over the sovereign state of South Africa. The more complex issues, such as who are now representatives of 'the periphery' and the strife between the ANC and IFP, suggest a negotiated political and constitutional reorganisation of both South Africa and, very likely, the entire Southern African region. Neighbouring countries such as Lesotho, Botswana, Swaziland, Mozambique, Angola and Zambia all have economies which are historically and infrastructurally closely interwoven with that of South Africa. They are all affected by the outcomes in South Africa itself and may, at least informally, become involved in the process themselves in the post-election period. Intensive economic cooperation between these states, the core and the periphery, would now seem to be an absolute requirement to sustain economic recovery.

Some observers, though, such as Roger Southall, are sceptical about the prospects of regional constitutional integration, even as far as tiny land-locked Lesotho is concerned. Southall has argued for instance that 'South Africa is a unitary state, a historical fact which the future is unlikely to undo', and 'modern federations which have arisen not from a union of previously separate states but from a unitary past, have been imposed from outside'. The issue of neighbouring states forming a constitutional union with South Africa is 'way down the track', according to Southall, and may not be desired by those states at all because they have international status and aid which they would not wish to forego.[16] One may ask what would happen if this aid dries up in the aftermath of apartheid as has been signalled by some donors?

Growing economic imperatives in Southern Africa have already transformed the former *Southern African Development Coordination Conference*

(SADCC) into the *Southern African Development Community* (August 1992), now including the former enemy South Africa itself. This was the economic arm of the Front Line States, an African regional anti-apartheid device to lessen economic dependence on the Republic in the 1980s. In terms of size of GDP, SADCC combined was less than 30 per cent of South Africa's while the majority of South Africa's trade and other external links are not directed towards the SADCC region. Although the experience gained through SADCC has no doubt been valuable for the countries concerned, the shift in emphasis regarding the economic development of the region has introduced new scenarios and priorities. In late 1994, for instance, President Mandela moved to stem the growing flow of unemployed, illegal migrants from Mozambique. Clearly, the problems of the periphery are now of a different order for South Africa from that under apartheid but the expectation of assistance from the new South African government is much greater as is the desire for closer cooperation and integration. There may in the longer term be some potential for a region-wide federalism and it seems reasonable to expect that this will eventually affect the future political alliances within the Republic.

Kader Asmal (AAM leader, now a Cabinet Minister in Mandela's government) rejected federalism for a new South Africa by referring to the findings of a British Royal Commission report of 1969–1973 on the issue in the case of the UK.[17] This Commission argued that federalism was only really appropriate for states coming together to form a single unit as opposed to states breaking up into smaller fragments. This theory of federalism has though been somewhat disproved in the case of Belgium, and does not apply to the (West) German Basic Law of 1949. It also sits uneasily with the revamping of the former USSR into the CIS. In Italy and Spain, moreover, regions were created after long periods of dictatorship with considerable autonomy in the case of Spain. Asmal's rejection of federalism on those grounds is, therefore, not wholly convincing. Questions like 'How many regions (provinces)?' and 'Where would the boundaries be?' and those concerning fiscal and other financial transfers emerged as the practical ones to be sorted out in South Africa during 1993/4. In any case what model is there for a new South Africa, given the totally unique circumstances which have given birth to it? The large disparities in size and economic strength of regional states are a potential problem that could make federal government difficult to operate, but firm transfer formulas and redistribution agencies can be built into a federal constitutions (as in Australia). Still, any future South African government will have to deal with the massive existing inequalities between some regions. An assessment of regional development policy would thus be appropriate.

Regionalism and Regional Development in Southern Africa

In the 1980s the debate on regionalism has occupied, amongst others, the government, the Urban Foundation (UF), the Private Sector Council (PSC), the Human Sciences Research Council (HSRC) and the Development Bank of South Africa (DBSA) as well as several academics.[18] In a report by the Urban Foundation entitled *Regional Development Reconsidered* (produced with the PSC), the result of five years research and 40 major research papers, the NP Government's Regional Industrial Development Policy (RIDP) was thoroughly discredited.[19] 'In SA current regional policy is built around the growth-centre strategy', the Report stated. 'In essence a range of incentives are used to attract industry: 1) to remote places far from the cities (decentralisation); 2) to places separate from and on the outer edges of the metropolitan areas (deconcentration).' In both cases the policy was coupled with 'homeland' development as almost all growth centres are in or next to 'homeland' borders.

The debate on regions (now again named 'provinces'), their functions, development, boundaries and autonomy, is clearly part of the continuing constitutional debate. Several South African scholars, mostly Afrikaners such as Albert Venter, Fanie Cloete and Louw van Wyk, unpacked the regional concept in detail before the constitutional debate commenced.[20] The latter actually suggested that the (then) nine economic development regions could become the basis for 'a' federal structure although he argued, in a somewhat contradictory fashion, that a federal state would not be a viable option for Southern Africa 'because there are too many requirements that could not be fulfilled'. Here again, the federal state was not seen as the outcome of a bargaining process but as a desirable structure to meet predetermined criteria! Van Wyk added that it would make sense to subdivide at least three of these regions into smaller ones: A (Western Cape), D (Eastern Cape) and E (Natal), which would have yielded 12 in all. What has happened is not far removed from these ideas. The importance of the debate on (internal) regions is that they must be 'empowered' to assist regional development where it more or less naturally occurs, within their boundaries, on the basis of local, comparative advantages. This still leaves the need for equalisation schemes for regions which have considerably fewer comparative advantages than others. This dimension of the debate on regions has not figured prominently in the reports by private sector organisations, though the report of the DBSA recommended that 'the overall support from the central government level for development in the less developed regions should not be reduced, but that it should be channelled through a financial system that allows more flexibility for the various authorities to apply such funds in support of their chosen development strategies'. Such a recommendation can be seen as compatible with a federal structure of government, though the issue of 'constitutional development' was outside the panel's ambit of investigations.[21]

ECONOMIC RECONSTRUCTION OR CIVIL WAR?

Many, perhaps most Afrikaners regard the idea of a separate *Volkstaat* as both unworkable and unnecessary for achieving recognition of ethnic identity. Members of the Freedom Front are said to have committed themselves now to the long road now – by peaceful means.[22] The first Deputy President, Thabo Mbeki, has also proved to be very conciliatory to the desires of the more moderate Volkstaat proponents like Viljoen. He said the ANC 'would like to pay sincere tribute to them because they saved the country from a conflict that would have been very destructive'.[23] A 20-member Volkstaat Council was established by Parliament in May 1994 with a brief to report on the concept and its possible implementation.[24]

The political aspirations of the Zulu leadership and the potential strength of KwaZulu/Natal require serious consideration on account of its appeal, territorial concentration, population numbers, economic strength and control over the major port of Durban. The insistence by the Zulu King that he represents the entire Zulu nation and that the nation is entitled to a large degree of independence, on historical grounds, goes beyond Inkatha as a political movement and Buthelezi's personal ambitions. The inclusion of Inkatha in the elections and the quite favourable, although disputed, result for that organisation has defused the prospect of major ethnic conflict, at least in the interim. Although tensions exist between the King and Buthelezi, with the King increasingly asserting his independence, this may not affect the overall strength of Zulu nationalism; on the contrary. It may however take on a less overt political character. In May 1994 the IFP indicated its preparedness to serve in the Cabinet and portfolios were allocated to make it part of the broad governing alliance.

The prospect of civil war, fuelled by ethnic tensions, has therefore receded but, as the experience has shown in many new nations, non-delivery of anticipated economic improvements after independence is productive of civil war and even secession. The latter scenario can be the result of a long military conflict, as in the case of Eritrea or, as in the case of Singapore, more peaceful withdrawal. The bottom-line question thus remains: will the New South Africa be characterised by a de facto federal government allowing the provinces to exercise their considerable potential for a semiautonomous existence? Or is the ANC to go it alone, at least for a while, and attempt to introduce a new order which may be resented by significant sections of the population? It seems unlikely. The wider regional issue has become an integral part of the overall solution. To argue that the periphery is a separate issue which should be dealt with at some future time when South Africa itself is well on the way to implementing its RDP seems both unrealistic and, almost certainly, counterproductive.

NOTES

1. W. Livingston, *Federalism and Constitutional Change* (London: Oxford University Press, 1956), p. 4.
2. W.H. Riker, *Federalism, Origin, Operation, Significance* (Boston: Little, Brown, 1964), Chapter 6 passim.
3. 'The South African Wave', *Australian Financial Review (Week-end Review)*, 10 (December 1993), 11–12.
4. These continuing problems of the ANC were aired frankly by Party Secretary Cyril Ramaphosa in his report to the 49th Congress of the ANC held in Bloemfontein in December 1994.
5. E.A. Walker, *A History of Southern Africa* (London: Longmans Green, 1962).
6. *The Australian*, 27 October 1990.
7. A. Lyphardt, *Patterns of Majoritarian and Consensus Government in Twenty One Countries* (New Haven: Yale University Press, 1984).
8. Albie Sachs, in *Sechaba*, May and July 1990, made a strong plea for a Bill of Rights; see also John Dugard, 'Do we need a Bill of Rights – The South African Experience', *Amnesty International* (Australian Newsletter), 10, 3 (April 1992).
9. Marina Ottaway, *South Africa – The Struggle for a New Order* (Washington: The Brookings Institution, 1993).
10. For further details of Buthelezi's use of Zulu ethnicity see Chapter 2.
11. Patrick Laurence, 'Provinces Face Test of Autonomy', *Sydney Morning Herald*, 11–18 May 1994.
12. *Sydney Morning Herald*, 17 February 1993.
13. *Business Day*, 20 April 1994.
14. Leo Marquard, *A Federation of Southern Africa* (Oxford: OUP, 1971); Alan Paton, *From Utopia to Uitenhage* (Johannesburg: SAIRR, 1985).
15. This section draws on Klaas Woldring, 'The Desirability and Feasibility of Federalisation in South Africa', unpublished MA thesis, University of Sydney (1969); 'The Prospect of Federalisation in Southern Africa', *The African Review*, 3, 3 (1973), 453–78.
16. Roger Southall, 'Lesotho and the Reintegration of South Africa', occasional paper, Department of Political Studies, Rhodes University (1991).

17.   Kader Asmal, 'Constitutional Issues for a Free South Africa: Decentralisation of a Unitary State', *Transformation*, 13 (1990), 81–95.

18.   Development Bank of South Africa, *Report of the Panel of Experts of the Regional Industrial Development Programme as an Element of the Regional Development Policy in Southern Africa* (Halfway House, DBSA, 1989); HSRC, 'Regionalism as Approach to Constitutional Change' in RSA, *2 000: Dialogue with the Future – Constitutional Development in South Africa* (Pretoria: HSRC, 1988).

19.   Urban Foundation, *Policies for a New Urban Future Series: Regional Development Revisited* (1990).

20.   Fanie Cloete, 'Regionalism in South Africa – Constraints and Possibilities', paper presented to the HSRC conference on regionalism (February 1991); Louw Van Wyk, 'The Economic Development Regions as a basis for federalism in South Africa', conference paper read at University of Bonn (1990); Albert Venter, 'South Africa: (Con) Federal Structures', *Plural Societies*, XIX, 1 (1990).

21.   *Report of the Panel of Experts of the Regional Industrial Development Programme*, p. xxviii.

22.   *The Star International Weekly*, 19–25 May 1994, 3.

23.   *The Sydney Morning Herald*, 19 June 1994.

24.   *The Star International Weekly*, 26 May–1 June 1994.

12 Ethnic Fragmentation: Why South Africa Probably Won't Follow the Yugoslav or Soviet Route
Norman Etherington

INTRODUCTION

The break-up of the Soviet Union and Yugoslavia sparked off a general intellectual panic about nationalism, a subject already under review for various reasons. When intellectuals panic, the academies rain paper.[1] There have been special issues on nationalism from a score of journals, frequent reprintings of modern classics on the subject and too many articles to read in one lifetime.

In addition to the stimulus from Eastern Europe, the following causes probably contributed something to the current interest:

- Worries about European Union (EU) after the initial Danish rejection of the Maastricht Treaty. Nationalism perpetually threatens to derail the process of European integration.
- Worries about American economic nationalism focussed on Japan. For the first time in several decades, protectionist sentiment affected the course of electoral politics in the United States presidential contest (1992).
- Worries in Western Europe over the rise of right-wing xenophobic movements hostile to immigration from Eastern Europe, Africa and the Middle East.
- Worries that militant nationalism may raise the ghosts of anti-Semitism and fascism.[2] This fear has been especially focussed on the states which have emerged from the wreck of the Soviet Union.
- Feminist suspicions of the nationalist record on women's rights sparking new research into the gendered experience of nationalist movements.[3]
- A general post-modern sense that resurgent nationalism is a hallmark

of our time. This is not universally deplored. Renewed scholarly interest in cultural difference has led some to postulate the importance of
multi-culturalism as a counter to oppressive 'hegemonic discourses'.

The virulence of political violence in the lead-up to the South African
election, right-wing demands for a white homeland and Buthelezi's flirtation
with secession – combined with the spectacle of balkanization in the Soviet
Union and, of course, the Balkans – generated in many quarters expectations that South Africa too might fragment. This knee-jerk reaction was all
the easier because it could so easily be wedded to old conventional wisdoms
about 'complex South Africa', tribalism being the curse of the continent,
and conservative beliefs that authoritarian white rule 'kept the lid on'
violent ethnic conflict. This chapter argues that the panic over nationalism
has been overdone. The situation of contemporary South Africa bears no
profound resemblance to the ex-Soviet Union or Yugoslavia, and powerful
obstacles stand in the way of nationalist movements of any sort breaking
up the country.

Much of the general panic about nationalism is based on shallow thinking and dubious metaphors. Branka Magas rightly complains about the
'obscurantist litany' underlying much loose thinking about nationalism:

> Ethnic cleansing is dreadful, but they all do it you know; once the lid
> came off . . . old ethnic passions . . . goes back to World War II. . . . goes
> back centuries . . . warring factions . . . competing nationalisms.[4]

This banter commonly substitutes metaphor for analysis. Here is a clutch
from a recent article on Macedonia:

> Until the advent of Communist dictatorships in the Balkans, the region
> known as Macedonia was Europe's Lebanon. Today *the lid is coming
> off* once again, offering a timely reminder of the destructive power of
> ethnic passions. Macedonia . . . is a historical and geographical *reactor
> furnace*. Here the ethnic hatreds released by decline of the Ottoman
> Empire first exploded, hatreds that would permeate Europe and the
> Middle East. . . . Czar Alexander II's war to liberate Bulgaria . . . *lit the
> fuse of the Balkan powder keg*. Macedonia would become the *well-spring*
> not only of modern world war but also of modern political terrorism and
> clerical fanaticism. By the turn of the century Macedonia was a *cauldron*
> of ethnic and sectarian violence. . . . on August 2, 1903, Macedonia
> *exploded*. The Second World War provided another sickening *replay*. At
> that point Communist totalitarianism settled over the Balkans and stopped
> history there until now.[5]

Other popular metaphors flee to the opposite end of the temperature scale.

> ... the Soviet Union put the ethno-national question in the fridge, forgetting to add ice. The door is now wide open. ...'[6]

Still others flee to classical sources – 'opening Pandora's Box', trying to put 'the genie back in the bottle'.[7]

After the metaphors come the wild generalisations.

> ... ethnic conflict; once it begins, it seems to take on a life of its own, reaching ever higher degrees of irrationality and violence, and, at the same time, increasingly eluding attempts to resolve it. One has only to glance at Northern Ireland, Lebanon, the Philippines, the Punjab, Israel, South Africa, Sri Lanka, and the Soviet Union to realize the truth of this formulation.[8]

> Everywhere in the region, nationalism – exclusivist, atavistic, irrationalist, contemptuous of democracy, often openly racist and at least potentially violent – is on the rise. ... the new xenophobes of eastern Europe are increasingly reviving an old and hideous language. ... both liberalism and social democracy are identified and attacked as Jewish.[9]

With this last observation we are on the slippery slope sliding towards what Tom Nairn has wryly termed 'the Ethnic Abyss'.[10]

> ... in the present uncertainty, worst-case scenarios spring easily to mind.[11]

> [there are] not just Bosnian Serbs nor Palestinians and Kurds, but, according to one recent survey, at least 250 other minorities currently at risk. To give statehood to all such minorities would more than double the number of states in the world. Furthermore, we should remember that there are perhaps eight thousand languages in the world, most of which could be used to put forward nationalist claims.[12]

There is literally no end to what Aviel Roshwald has called *matrioshka* nationalism (after the famous Russian dolls-within-dolls), for, 'as soon as the one ethnic minority achieves independence, a minority within the new state promptly commences its own struggle for liberation.'[13]

What, it may be asked, is the evidence supporting such dire predictions? Contrary to what is implied in much current literature, the disintegration of states due to ethnic nationalism is far from being a general phenomenon. No country in North or South America has broken up. Only Quebec stands out a future candidate for nationhood in the western hemisphere. Sub-state nationalism has not succeeded in winning even a partial victory in any part of Western Europe. Africa, where ethnically-based fragmentations

have been longest and most confidently expected by merchants of pess-
imism, has preserved post-colonial boundaries with remarkable success.
Eritrea has scored the only secessionist victory, for reasons outlined below.
To expect *matrioshka* nationalism to flourish in Eastern Europe, when it
has not flourished in the West (or in Africa or Southeast Asia), is pure
Orientalism.

Turning from metaphor to history, it is useful to briefly review the causes
which, in a general sense, scholars recognise as promoting nationalist particularism. Some are grounded in the special experience of European states
where the trajectory of nationalism has been succinctly summarised by
Miroslav Hroch:[14]

- territorially bounded ethnicity, especially language
- folkloric, historic and linguistic work by intellectuals
- rise of nationalist agitation, backed first by intelligentsia, then spread-
  ing to the masses

Others stress economic and sociological factors

- economic and industrial conditions favouring the creation of an undifferentiated national base for the state (Ernest Gellner)[15]
- creation of colonial states (Benedict Anderson[16] and others)
- blocked mobility for specific groups which would not be blocked if
  those nations had their own states (Liah Greenfeld)[17]
- a conflict situation exacerbated by cognitive dissonance (Karl Deutsch)[18]

Although all of these factors were present in the former Soviet Union
and Yugoslavia, they were long overlooked by Western scholars obsessed
by nineteenth-century Marxist theory and the totalitarian model of the communist state. A vast literature developed among communism watchers
emphasising

- pure theory, embodied in Marx's slogan that the worker has no country
- the supposed suppression of nationalism by communist states and individual leaders such as Stalin and Tito.

The proposition that twentieth-century communism was dominated by a
theoretical insistence that the worker has no country is simply mistaken.
During the first two decades of this century when Bolshevik doctrine
matured, frank recognition of problems with nationalism was general. True,
Lenin agreed with Rosa Luxemburg that Karl Kautsky's SPD betrayed
the world revolution when it voted for war credits in August 1914. But
the Bolshevik leadership was profoundly influenced by the Austro-Marxist

debates on how to deal with nationalism: debates with far more relevance to the future Soviet Union than the German situation.

Otto Bauer and Karl Renner confronted precisely the question that would face Lenin after the Russian revolution: how to deal with the multi-national colonial empire built by the old regime.[19] The victorious Bosheviks were aware that their relationship to Central Asian territories was an imperial one. As one put it, 'the dictatorship of the proletariat took on a typically colonialist aspect'.[20] Although the Bolsheviks found flaws in the Austro-Marxist solutions, they agreed that nationalities must be accorded recognition.[21] This was not a pragmatic, opportunistic strategy seized on at the time of the Brest-Litovsk Treaty. Stalin recognised in 1913 that a 'nation is an historically evolved stable community of language, territory, economic life and psychological make-up manifested in a community of culture.'[22] From the beginning, the new Soviet state was grounded on a recognition of territorially based ethnic groupings.[23]

The legend of the communists as nationality crushers relies principally on the forced removals of Georgians, Germans, Crimean Tatars, Kalmyks, Karachaevs, Chechens and Ingushes accused of complicity with the Nazi invaders during World War II.[24] These were the exception, rather than the rule, and even most of these were later reconstituted. Contrary to its foreign reputation, the USSR was an unrivalled promoter of territorially-based ethnic units. By the Gorbachev era it consisted of 15 Union republics (SSRs), 20 other so-called autonomous republics (ASSRs, each within one of the SSRs), eight autonomous provinces (Autonomous Oblasts) and ten autonomous districts (Autonomous Okrugs).[25] Here was truly *matrioshka* government. Under these circumstances, local intellectuals were not needed to celebrate local language, folklore and history; where they did not exist, the Soviet state invented them. Once created, they could and did turn against their creators.[26]

While some of the subdivisions of Soviet territory were created virtually from scratch through the diligent discovery of ethnic difference, the majority were an inheritance from the nineteenth-century Russian empire. For all the talk there has been of the Bolsheviks carrying on the work of the Tsars in an 'evil empire', widespread assent to the totalitarian model prevented most scholars from making analogies with Western colonial empires such as the British and the French.[27] Comparative study has not been done, but would surely help a great deal in explaining the post-1989 situation. In some ways the Soviet state related to its peripheral republics in the way that the British related to colonies variously ruled as settler dominions and through indirect rule. In other ways it resembled the French Empire which maintained (maintains?) that eventually national differences would disappear and there would be '200 million Frenchmen' scattered round the globe. However, with its local peculiarities (such as theoretical rights of succession and representation of all nationalities in assemblies at Moscow) the Soviet state represented 'colonialism of a special type'.

As a colonial empire, it could be expected to be as much a maker as a crusher of nationalisms. Benedict Anderson, following in the footsteps of the Africanist Thomas Hodgkin,[28] has shown how economic development in a colonial situation brings together a local elite who discover in their common situation both a bond of brotherhood and a shared sense of exclusion from the far-off centres of real power. Colonial states themselves are powerful structures, with a tendency to outlive the empires that created them. As Anderson observes:

> ... successful revolutionaries also inherit the wiring of the old state: sometimes functionaries and informers, but always files, dossiers, archives, laws, financial records, censuses, maps, treaties, correspondence, memoranda, and so on. Like the complex electrical system in any large mansion when the owner has fled, the state awaits the new owner's hand at the switch to be very much its old brilliant self again.[29]

Every particular listed by scholars of nationalism as preconditions for the rise of nation-states was to be found in the old Soviet Union. The fact that official centralism after about 1934 put a permanent brake on nationalist aspirations for autonomy simply added to the 'blockage' of upward mobility that so often fuels nationalist sentiment.[30] When economic problems brought the Soviet system to the point of collapse, 'winds of change' blew through its national units which quickly claimed independence, much as the African colonies of Britain and France claimed independence in the period 1957–68.[31] In many ways, 1989 was the Soviet Union's 1960. There is no more reason to expect its successor states to fragment further, than there was then to expect postcolonial Africa to fracture further into 800 ethno-linguistic states.

While post-World War II Yugoslavia was a very different kind of state from the Soviet Union, it too proved to be a great promoter of internal nationalisms. Rather than standing as successor to a previous imperial state, it was built from fragments of two different defunct empires. The parts known as Croatia and Slovenia formerly belonged to the Austrian Habsburgs; Serbia, Macedonia, Montenegro and Bosnia-Herzegovina, to the Ottoman Turks. This historical division overlaid an older religious demarcation between Roman Catholicism and Eastern Orthodoxy. A lesser but an important group are descended from converts to Islam. Aside from these historical factors, the entire area encompassed by ex-Yugoslavia is ethno-linguistically one.[32] It was this very unity of language and custom that first inspired the idea of a south Slav nation in the wake of the invading French Revolutionary armies who called the area Illyria (after the ancient Roman province).[33]

However, nineteenth-century political development pushed the component parts in disparate directions. With the withdrawal of the Ottomans, Serbia emerged as an independent monarchy with the full panoply of statehood: army, bureaucracy and economic infrastructure. Militarisation was more or less forced upon it by the aspirations of the Habsburg 'drive to the east' and its neighbours, Bulgaria, Albania and Greece, who emerged about the same time from the wreckage of the Ottoman Empire. It lived in relative harmony only with the small states of Montenegro and Bosnia-Herzegovina until the latter was annexed by the Habsburgs in 1908.

Croatia was different. A province of the Austrian empire for centuries, its independence existed only in the minds of intellectual nationalists looking back to a medieval kingdom whose sole living remnants were a weak, arrogant nobility. The task of Croatian nationalists was therefore a typically colonial one: to win independence from Vienna. Hatred between Croat and Serb was no more an ancient historic fact than hatred between Zulu and Xhosa. It had to be fostered, mainly by Croat romantic revolutionaries whose dream of a reconstituted Croatian kingdom could only be built at the expense of the Serbian state.

When World War I finished off the Austro-Hungarian empire, a Yugoslav state was built with the connivance of the victorious allies, especially Britain, France and the United States. It was not, however, imposed in any direct way by the Great Powers. Without widespread support for an ethno-linguistic south Slav state it could not have come into being at all. Within a few years, however, a sharp antagonism developed among Croat nationalists angered by the way the key institutions of the state clustered around the pre-existing structures of the Serbian kingdom.

The newly formed Communist Party of Yugoslavia seized upon these tensions to promote its own fortunes. At no time did it promulgate the doctrine that the worker knows no country.[34] (Arising as it had from the Austro-Marxism of the Viennese socialists, it would have been extremely odd if it had.) Instead it opposed Serbian hegemony with support for independence of a number of Balkan republics. Thus, when King Aleksandar proclaimed a dictatorship in 1931, the communists responded:

Down with the military-fascist dictatorship! Down with the bloody Serbian monarchy! Down with the great-Serbian policy of national oppression! Long live the union of workers, peasants, and oppressed nations!

Long live independent Croatia, Macedonia, Montenegro, Slovenia, Bosnia, Vojvodina, and Serbia! Long live the worker-peasant government! Long live the federation of worker-peasant republics of the Balkans.[35]

It was Aleksandar, not the communists, who attempted to abolish history with brute force. In the 1931 constitution, all pre-war territorial distinctions were obliterated. In their place were created nine *banovine*, with borders in deliberate contempt for the aspirations of Serb and Croat nationalists.[36]

Within a decade these too were swept away by the onset of the Second World War and fascist invaders. As is well known, the communists under the Croat Tito dominated the partisan internal resistance while nationalist politicians in exile bickered over their respective attitudes to the genocidal terror directed against Serbs by the Croat Ustasha organisation. With the prestige born of wartime struggle, the Communist Party needed no assistance from the Russian Red Army to take control of the country. Although by this time the Party had retreated from its early support for breaking the country into autonomous nations, the Constitution of 1946 was genuinely federal, recognising six constituent republics based on historic principles: Bosnia and Herzegovina, Croatia, Macedonia, Montenegro, Serbia, and Slovenia. As Sabrina Ramet reminds us, 'the Yugoslav Communists promoted the interests of their respective national groups a good deal more than is usually imagined'.[37] The republics were proclaimed to be equal in all aspects of their rights and duties.[38] Each had its own party organisation and responsibility for a wide range of local government functions. Moreover, each was proclaimed the 'sovereign homeland' of a sovereign nation. This, despite the evident fact that their borders did not correspond with ethnic or religion divisions. Especially in Bosnia, Croats, Serbs and Muslims were highly intermixed.

Thus the Communist Government of Yugoslavia helped in a myriad of ways to foster local particularism. As with the Soviet Union, when the economy collapsed, the Republics were there to provide alternative conceptions of the state.[39] Once the prospect of autonomy loomed they speedily created legends of ethnic suppression under Tito.[40] In the case of Bosnia-Herzegovina, and in the eastern parts of Croatia nationality was contested. It is no surprise that these are the war zones of 1992–5.

Turning now to South Africa, can we find conditions similar to those of Eastern Europe? Vladimir Tikhomirov has drawn attention to many parallels that can be drawn between the Soviet Union and South Africa in the post-1945 era.[41] It is equally important to notice differences, especially as they bear upon the question of ethnic nationalism.

Afrikaner nationalism itself can readily be assimilated to European models,[42] its sole peculiarity being the aspiration of a fraction of a white minority to rule as a sovereign nation. The building of the apartheid state, however, was conducted in a totally different manner from the construction of the Soviet Union or the Yugoslavian federation. Although the flag remained an inelegant collage of the ensigns of the old republics and colonies, National Party governments pursued a ruthless centralisation of power which ended in the abolition of all provincial assemblies.

The homelands designated for Africans did not derive from any precolonial political entities. Nor were they fashioned with respect for ethnolinguistic boundaries. The great Nguni/Sotho-Tswana language divide was not a consideration. Mostly the bantustans replicated the borders of native reserves drawn by British colonial administrations. None bore the least resemblance to the stuff of any black nationalist's dreams.

Nor did any of the homelands contain a city worthy of the name with taverns or coffee houses where nationalist intellectuals might foment separatist dreams. No Tashkent, no Tiblisi, no Kiev, Zagreb or Belgrade.[43] Their borders were not frontiers to be defended against attack. More than anything, they resembled the Berlin Wall, a device to hold prisoners in. Escapees were returned to them by armed escorts. Other suppressed minorities lacked even the shadow of a homeland, Coloureds and Indians being confined to suburban ghettoes.

In the constituent republics of Yugoslavia and the Soviet Union, ethnically relevant agricultural regions surrounded the cities; in South Africa an ethnic wasteland of white commercial agriculture built on the backs of captive farm workers separated the 'homelands' from the urban centres. The Group Areas Act efficiently accomplished the separation of racial and ethnic entities achieved by less formal mechanisms in America or Ulster. But none of the townships looks remotely like a focus for nationalist sentiment. And, in any event, multi-cultural urban environments have not fuelled the fires of any truly nationalist conflagration.

Nationalist movements aimed at breaking up other African states have been notable failures, even where ethnic rivalries run deep and ancient. Nigeria and Zaïre remain unified within their original colonial frontiers. So do Ghana, Chad, Uganda and Angola. The only places where secessionist movements have ever come close to succeeding are where they aim to *restore* colonial divisions. Eritrea fought to regain boundaries laid down by Italian colonialism. Conflict in the Sudan perpetuates the peculiar administrative divisions of the old Anglo-Egyptian condominium. Somalia constantly threatens to fragment along the old colonial faultlines, despite unity of religion and ethnicity. There are no comparable lines of fracture running through the contemporary South African state.

Another vital factor of nationalist movements is missing in South Africa. At the core of every such movement is an aspiration to self-determination and self-sufficiency. Believers need a credible heaven. A designated Zion of a White Homeland which cannot hold out the promise of a reasonable material standard of life will not move even die-hard AWB members to cross the Jordan. The same goes for most conceivable ethno-linguistic black countries of the imagination. An African paradise of self-determination that looks no better than Lesotho or Swaziland is unlikely to attract nationalist pilgrims.

This thought brings another consideration to mind. Amidst all the loose talk currently circulating about resurgent nationalisms, there is little recognition of how much the world economy has done to undermine the possibility of economic autarchy of any sort. The game of party politics played in multi-party systems is grounded on an agreed suspension of disbelief. All the players connive at pretending that prosperity can be produced by good government and depression by mismanagement. The reality is that all governments are at the mercy of external forces beyond their control. It is widely acknowledged that Irish nationalism is a spent force except among the cadres of the Provisional IRA.[44] Why? Because it could not deliver sustained economic growth nor stem the eternal tide of emigration. Among all the ex-homelands of apartheid only Transkei and KwaZulu stand out as conceivable independent states. In the unlikely event that either were to secede, even if KwaZulu included old Natal, they would be very poor states, dependent as ever on South Africa.

For all these reasons, it would be unreasonable to predict that South Africa might follow the Yugoslav or Soviet route to ethnic fragmentation. That does not, of course, mean that the reconstructed state does not confront many perils and dangers. Democracy is not part of the South African way of life. Racial thinking will be hard to eradicate. The destructive potential of the military and security apparatus will present temptations as it has elsewhere on the continent. Above all, the gulf separating rich and poor will perpetuate the public squalor and personal insecurity that are already endemic. But fragmentation along ethno-nationalist lines seems highly unlikely.

Reflecting on the deeper causes of nationalist fractures raises warning signals against unthinkingly adopting the proposition that nationalist and cultural fissures are likely to dominate the twenty-first century in Africa or any other part of the globe. The relationship of nationalism to modernity and post modernity is a contentious issue. For some, nationalisms are atavars – primordial entities predating modernism and fundamentally at war with the Enlightenment. For others, like Robert Licht, nationalism is the quintessential 'political pathology of modernism'.[45] For still others, nationalism is the post-modern riposte to totalising ideologies such as Marxism and liberalism. It is therefore doubtful that nationalism can readily be accommodated to the modern/post-modern divide. A curious intellectual paradox of our times is that the vigorous reassertion of cultural difference comes precisely at the time that cultural boundaries seem most fragile and permeable. As Benjamin Barber remarks, 'the world is falling apart and coming together at the same time'.[46] It may well be that the juggernaut of globalisation is operating to bring cultures and nationalities into sharp relief just prior to obliterating them forever.

NOTES

1. For examples of intellectual panic at the highest level, see articles in the special edition of *Daedalus* (Summer 1993).
2. See, for example, Marla Stone, 'Nationalism and Identity in (Former) East Germany', *Tikkun*, 7 (1992), 41–6.
3. See especially the special number of *Gender and History* (Summer 1993) and *Feminist Review*, No. 44 (Summer 1993); feminist objections to nationalism in an African-American context are explored in E. Frances White, 'Africa on my Mind: Gender, Counter Discourse and African-American Nationalism', *Journal of Women's History*, 2 (1990), 73–97.
4. Branka Magas, 'The Destruction of Bosnia-Herzegovina', *New Left Review*, No. 196, (November/December 1992), 103.
5. Robert D. Kaplan, 'History's Cauldron', *The Atlantic Monthly* (June 1991), 93–104; my italics.
6. Daniel-Louis Seiler, 'Inter-Ethnic Relations in East Central Europe: The Quest for a Pattern of Accommodation', *Communist and Post-Communist Studies*, 26 (December 1993), 366.
7. Murray Austin, 'Geographical Perspectives of Nationalism', *History of European Ideas*, 15 (1992), 625.
8. George M. Scott, Jr., 'A Resynthesis of the Primordial and Circumstantial Approaches to Ethnic Group Solidarity: Towards an Explanatory Model', *Ethnic and Racial Studies*, No. 2, 13 (April 1990), 164.
9. Stephen Howe, 'The New Xenophobes', *The Atlantic Monthly* (June 1991), 14.
10. Tom Nairn, 'Internationalism and the Second Coming', *Daedalus* (Summer 1993), 155.
11. J.F. Brown [senior staff member, RAND Corporation], 'The Resurgence of Nationalism', *Report on Eastern Europe* (14 June 1991), 37.
12. John A. Hall, 'Nationalisms: Classified and Explained', *Daedalus* (Summer 1993), 22.
13. Aviel Roshwald, 'Untangling the Knotted Cord: Studies of Nationalism', *Journal of Interdisciplinary History*, 24 (Autumn 1993), 303.

14. Miroslav Hroch, 'From National Movement to Fully Formed Nation', *New Left Review*, 198 (1993), 6–7.

15. E. Gellner, *Nations and Nationalism* (Oxford: Blackwell, 1983).

16. Benedict Anderson, *Imagined Communities: Reflections on the Origin and Spread of Nationalism*, rev. ed. (London: Verso, 1991).

17. L. Greenfeld, *Nationalism, Five Roads to Modernity* (Cambridge MA and London: Harvard University Press, 1992). Though Greenfeld's scholarship is dense and elaborate, at the root of all the emerging nationalisms she examines is a single factor, the *ressentiment* felt by social classes blocked in their aspirations or threatened in some way.

18. K. Deutsch, *Nationalism and Social Communication: an Inquiry into the Foundations of Nationality*, 2nd ed. (Cambridge MA: M.I.T. Press, 1966).

19. Shlomo Avineri, 'Marxism and Nationalism', *Journal of Contemporary History*, 26 (1991), 652.

20. N. Etherington, *Theories of Imperialism: War Conquest and Capital* (London and New York: Croom Helm and Barnes & Noble, 1984), pp. 193, 197–8.

21. P.F. Dostal and Hans Knippenberg, 'Russification of Soviet Nationalities: The Importance of Territorial Autonomy', *History of European Ideas*, 15 (1992), 631.

22. *Ibid.*, 653.

23. Pragmatism and opportunism in Lenin's nationality policies are emphasised in B. Williams, 'Lenin and the Problem of Nationalities', *History of European Ideas*, 15 (1992), 611–17.

24. To a lesser extent, it is grounded also on periodic flirtations with Soviet versions of Russian nationalism. See: D.G. Rowley, 'Russian Nationalism and the Cold War', *American Historical Review*, 99 (1994), 155–71; F.S. Zuckerman, 'To Justify a Nation: Inter-war Soviet Nationalism', *History of European Ideas*, 15 (1992), 383–90; G. Liber, '*Korenizatsiia*: Restructuring Soviet Nationality Policy in the 1920s', *Ethnic and Racial Studies*, 14 (1991), 15–23.

25. Lee Schwartz, 'Regional Population Redistribution and National Homelands in the USSR', in Henry R. Huttenbach (ed.), *Soviet Nationality Policies: Ruling Groups in the USSR* (London and New York: Mansell, 1990), pp. 121–61; see also Dostal and Knippenberg, *op. cit.*, pp. 631–8.

26. Eli Weinerman shows how Central Asian historians over several decades used vigorous criticism of Czarist colonialism as a surrogate for direct attacks on the nationalities policies of the Soviet Union; 'The Polemics between Moscow and Central Asians on the Decline of Central Asia and Tsarist Russia's Role in the History of the Region', *Slavonic and East European Review*, 71 (1993), 428–81.

27. A notable scholarly project which did draw inspiration from analogies between the ending of empires in Europe and Africa was the long collaboration between Lewis Gann and Peter Duignan. Gann has recently emphasised that in the 1960s they 'likened post-colonial Africa to the Balkans, where economic backwardness and national minority problems had posed insoluble problems to the successor states of the Austro-Hungarian monarchy'; 'Ex-Africa: an Africanist's Intellectual Autobiography', *Journal of Modern African Studies*, 31 (1993), 487.

28. T. Hodgkin, *Nationalism in Colonial Africa* (London: Muller, 1956).

29. Anderson, *Imagined Communities*, p. 160.

30. Greenfeld, *Nationalism*, pp. 487–8.

31. In the Gorbachev era, competing versions of Soviet nationalism and multi-national pluralism vied for supremacy among policy makers. See G.W. Lapidus, 'Gorbachev's Nationalities Problem', *Foreign Affairs*, 68 (Fall 1989), 92–108.

32. For a summary of linguistic, religious and other ethnic markers, see Ivo Banac, *The National Question in Yugoslavia* (Ithaca and London: Cornell University Press, 1984), pp. 47–58.

33. Aleksa Djilas, *The Contested Country, Yugoslav Unity and Communist Revolution, 1919–1953* (Cambridge MA: Harvard University Press, 1991), p. 24.

34. Though the opposite is often asserted. For the view that Tito ran a standard-issue Marxist-Leninist dictatorship, see A.N. Dragnich, *Serbs and Croats, The Struggle in Yugoslavia* (New York: Harcourt Brace, 1992). A similar, though more nuanced view is put forward by J. Seroka, 'The Political Future of Yugoslavia: Nationalism and the Critical Years, 1989–1991', *Canadian Review of Studies in Nationalism*, 19 (1992), 151–9. He argues that the Soviet 'attempt to isolate and destroy the Yugoslav regime forced Tito and his compatriots to emphasize the pan-Yugoslav character of the regime and to sacrifice pluralism or tolerance of interethnic diversity for national unity and discipline'.

35. Djilas, *The Contested Country*, p. 88.

36. *Ibid.*, p. 80.

37. S. Ramet, *Balkan Babel, Politics, Culture and Religion in Yugoslavia* (Boulder: Westview Press, 1992), p. xi. See also D. Sekulic, G. Massey and R. Hodson, 'Who were the Yugoslavs? Failed Sources of a Common Identity in the Former Yugoslavia', *American Sociological Review*, 59 (1994), 83, who assert that 'the identification of people with their nationality was accepted [by the Communist Party] to the neglect of an identity associated with the state as a whole'.

38. See Serge Flere, 'Explaining Ethnic Antagonism in Yugoslavia', *European Sociological Review*, 7 (1991), 183–93.

39. Robin Blackburn, 'The Break-up of Yugoslavia and the Fate of Bosnia', *New Left Review*, 199 (1993), 102–3.

40. The most powerful of which was that Tito had been guided by the maxim 'Weak Serbia, strong Yugoslavia'. See 'Albanians and Serbs – the Conflict Continues', *Geographical Magazine* (May 1989), 21–2.

41. Vladimir Tikhomirov, *States in Transition: Russia and South Africa* (Bryanston, South Africa: International Freedom Foundation, 1992).

42. As, for example, was done by F. Van Jaarsveld, *The Awakening of Afrikaner Nationalism* (Cape Town: Human and Rousseau, 1961).

43. The urban factor in the manufacture of nationalism is examined by Alexander B. Murphy in 'Urbanism and the Diffusion of Substate Nationalist Ideas in Western Europe', *History of European Ideas*, 15 (1992), 639–49.

44. Jim Smyth, 'Nationalist Nightmares and Postmodernist Utopias: Irish Society in Transition', *History of European Ideas*, 16 (1993), 157–63.

45. Robert A. Licht, 'Israel among the Nationalisms', *First Things, A Monthly Journal*, 12 (1991), 30.

46. Benjamin Barber, 'Jihad Vs McWorld', *Atlantic Monthly* (March 1992).

Index